Institutional Economics:
Theory, Method, Policy

Recent Economic Thought Series

Warren G. Samuels, Editor
Michigan State University
East Lansing, Michigan, U.S.A.

Previously published books in the series:

Asimakopulos, A., Theories of Income Distribution
Earl, P., Psychological Economics: Development, Tensions, Prospects
Peterson, W., Market Power and the Economy
DeGregori, T., Development Economics
Nowotny, K., Public Utility Regulation
Horowitz, I., Organization and Decision Theory
Hennings, K. and Samuels, W., Neoclassical Economic Theory, 1870 to 1930
Samuels, W., Economics as Discourse
Lutz, M., Social Economics
Weimer, D., Policy Analysis and Economics
Bromley, D. and Segerson, K., The Social Response to Environmental Risk
Roberts, B. and Feiner, S., Radical Economics
Mercuro, N., Taking Property and Just Compensation
de Marchi, N., Post-Popperian Methodology of Economics
Gapinski, J., The Economics of Saving
Darity, W., Labor Economics: Problems in Analyzing Labor Markets
Caldwell, B. and Boehm, S., Austrian Economics: Tensions and Directions

This series is devoted to works that present divergent views on the development, prospects, and tensions within some important research areas of international economic thought. Among the fields covered are macromonetary policy, public finance, labor and political economy. The emphasis of the series is on providing a critical, constructive view of each of these fields, as well as a forum through which leading scholars of international reputation may voice their perspectives on important related issues. Each volume in the series will be self-contained; together these volumes will provide dramatic evidence of the variety of economic thought within the scholarly community.

Institutional Economics: Theory, Method, Policy

edited by
Marc R. Tool
Professor Emeritus of Economics
California State University, Sacramento

Kluwer Academic Publishers
Boston/Dordrecht/London

Distributors for North America:
Kluwer Academic Publishers
101 Philip Drive
Assinippi Park
Norwell, Massachusetts 02061 USA

Distributors for all other countries:
Kluwer Academic Publishers Group
Distribution Centre
Post Office Box 322
3300 AH Dordrecht, THE NETHERLANDS

Library of Congress Cataloging-in-Publication Data

Institutional economics : theory, method, policy / edited by Marc R. Tool.
p. cm. — (Recent economic thought series)
Includes bibliographical references and index.
ISBN 0-7923-9346-5
1. Institutional economics. I. Tool, Marc R. II. Series.
HB99.5.I58 1993
330—dc20 93-10050
CIP

Printed on acid-free paper.

Printed in the United States of America

Contents

Contributing Authors

John Adams
Chairman, Department of Economics
Northeastern University
301 Lake Hall
Boston, MA 02115

Frank Borgers
c/o Professor S.L. Mangum
Department of Management
and Human Resources
Ohio State University
Columbus, OH 43221

Paul D. Bush
Department of Economics
California State University
Fresno, CA 93740–0020

James L. Dietz
Department of Economics
California State University
Fullerton, CA 92634

F. Gregory Hayden
Department of Economics
University of Nebraska
Lincoln, NE 68588–0479

Geoffrey M. Hodgson
Lecturer in Economics
Judge Institute of Management Studies
University of Cambridge
Mill Lane, Cambridge CB2 1RX
UNITED KINGDOM

Philip A. Klein
Department of Economics
Pennsylvania State University
University Park, PA 16802

Milton D. Lower
4103 Yupon
Houston, TX 77006

Stephen L. Mangum
Department of Management
and Human Resources
Ohio State University
Columbus, OH 43221

Edythe S. Miller
580 Front Range Road
Littleton, CO 80120

Yngve Ramstad
Department of Economics
University of Rhode Island
Kingston, RI 02881

Linda R. Robertson
Department of English
Hobart & William Smith Colleges
Geneva, NY 14456

Marc R. Tool
Professor Emeritus of Economics
California State University, Sacramento
5708 McAdoo Avenue
Sacramento, CA 95819

William T. Waller
Department of Economics
Hobart & William Smith Colleges
Geneva, NY 14456

1 INTRODUCTION

Marc R. Tool

This book of especially solicited contributions is intended to appraise, refine, and extend the institutionalists' evolutionary theory of political economy in six different areas of inquiry. These areas are the institutionalist challenge to move beyond dissent, methodology of institutional economics, theory of instrumental value, institutionalist theory of labor markets, institutionalist theory of economic development, and institutionalist policymaking.

This collection appears at an especially opportune time. There is widespread and accumulating analytical dissatisfaction with received economic doctrine (West and East) and its often abortive application to policy. The traditional neoclassical and Marxist views of how to order and operate a political economy are now heavily discounted, especially by those who must bear the brunt of flawed or ineffectual policies derived from these views. Appeals are increasingly made for more populist and pragmatic, less doctrinaire and dogmatic, approaches to problem solving. Institutionalists are responding to this concern by contributing policy-relevant analysis.

A concerned and perceptive viewer of economic change will readily acknowledge that the decade of the 1980s was one of conservative resurgence in the United Kingdom and the United States in which a return to "first principles" of traditional orthodox economics and its ideological appendages was attempted. Both the Thatcher government and the Reagan administration sought to shrink government, deregulate the economy, privatize enterprise, and "return" to free market controls. In consequence, by design or inadvertence, a large number of fundamental economic and social problems were left insufficiently addressed and unresolved, including protracted unemployment, increasing inequality of income, increasing poverty, neglect of children and their needs, corrupted and deferred environmental management, underfunded infrastructure, deficient support for education, destabilized financial structure, and the like.

Similarly, a concerned and perceptive viewer of economic change in the 1990s must be astounded at the extent and rapidity of the political fragmentation of the former Soviet Bloc, including the decomposition of the Soviet Union itself, and at the accompanying compulsive and convulsive abandonment of Marxist–Leninist doctrine and its tenets of "democratic centralism" and comprehensive planning. Production and distribution inefficiencies, simplistic and authoritarian directives, impediments of self-serving Party bureaucrats, constriction or suppression of intellectual pursuits, retardation of nonstrategic technological developments, and environmental indifference are among the outcomes of this flawed approach to the creation and maintenance of a viable and efficient provisioning process. The reconstitution and redirection of self-separated Soviet republics as productive and coordinated mixed economies will require the mustering and application of their best brains and talent for at least the next generation. The direction that is forward will be dislocative and difficult.

Given the increasing political "fallout" from these deteriorating economic and social conditions West and East, it is perhaps probable that the remainder of the 1990s and the early years of the new century will be a period in which both the analysis of problems and the nature of proposed solutions will be less ideological in character and less insensitive in impact. More pertinent, responsive, and compassionate approaches to problem solving are desperately needed.

The purpose of this book is to build on a century of growth in research and publication on *institutional economics* and signficantly to contribute relevant *theory*, facilitative *methodology*, and instructive *policy* analysis for such an approach. The continuing priority of institutionalist inquiry is to provide a more instructive and pertinent body of theory and policy to inform and guide economic change in an efficient and humane direction. In the last quarter-century in particular, the institutionalist literature in political economy has expanded enormously. Recent examples: *the Journal of Economic Issues*, in its 27th year of publication, provides the primary journal outlet in the United States for scholarly papers of institutionalist authors; the two-volume *Evolutionary Economics* (edited by Tool, 1988) provides major comprehensive articles on the basic ideas of institutional thought; the three-volume work *Institutional Economics* (edited by Samuels, 1988) republishes both historically significant and contemporary essays on institutional topics; the two-volume *The Elgar Companion to Institutional and Evolutionary Economics* (edited by Samuels, Hodgson, and Tool; forthcoming) provides a sophisticated introduction to nearly 200 major topics and scholars in institutional and evolutionary economics.

More directly, the purposes to be served by this book, *Institutional Economics: Theory, Method, Policy*, are:

1. To refine and extend institutionalist inquiry in several major subject areas, all of which address core constructs of the institutionalist perspective. Although this collection of six chapters and commentaries cannot presume to be comprehensive in presenting the institutionalist approach, it does offer a fresh reconsideration of significant elements of the heartland of that theoretical contribution.

2. To generate insights and analytical tools that will permit economists more knowledgeably and effectually to contribute to the public dialogue on pressing policy issues and problems in political economy.

3. To present elements of the institutionalist approach in sufficient depth and extent to help foster the development of a viable and applicable alternative perspective to that of hegemonic neoclassicism in general and its orthodox and conservative policy proposals in particular.

The Chapters and Commentaries comprising this book all reflect a compulsive commitment to address the economic and social world as it is, actually and demonstrably. Authors pose questions and pursue theoretical and evidential inquiry "straight" without recourse to "chasers of fancy" (Muller). Contributors are experiential and intellectual realists. They are dedicated to the proposition that inquiry matters, that problems can be resolved, and that economic and social life can be enhanced thereby. They are not fatalists, apologists, or relativists; neither are they absolutists, number-crunchers, or power-trippers. They do not defer to alleged rigor over relevance.

All the chapters in some measure involve an assessment, in their respective areas of interest, of the present status of the development of the institutionalist alternative. Where is it on target? On what issues do its proponents disagree? Where does it need strengthening? Contributors are constructively critical of prior institutionalist formulations, even as they remain pervasive critics of neoclassical orthodoxy. The main quest is to enhance the explanatory capacity and policy relevance of institutional analysis. Accordingly, assessments of neoclassical orthodoxy are incidental to, not primary in, the chapters this book.

Finally, all contributions reflect an encompassing scope. All deal with institutionalism in general but with differing foci of inquiry and exposition. Each author brings a somewhat different mind-set and concern to his or her respective topic and selects, for exploration, particular aspects of this coherent and substantial alternative perspective in political economy. The part is pursued with the whole in mind.

One of the many attractive features of this set of essays, as readers will soon observe, is that the differing mind-sets and concerns converge on the general character and importance of institutional thought, but may diverge significantly at times on particular constructs and their use. Thus, on exhibition will be the evolving instrumental inquiry process itself, reflecting inquirers' corrective judgments concerning focus, substance, evidence, outcomes, and assessments, in all their complexity. No homogeniety of position is imposed; neither should it be expected. The processual concepts and analytical tools of institutionalism reflect and guide change, including change in the inquiry mode itself. Institutionalists offer no terminal arrivals—places which when you get there, you never have to leave; they offer provisional "way stations" enroute to further tentative conclusions. Inquiry outcomes or conclusions pose questions for further inquiry reflecting the inherent continuity of institutionalist methodology.

A brief introduction to each of the chapters follows.

The lead chapter, "The Institutionalist Challenge: Beyond Dissent," is by Philip A. Klein. In it he demonstrates that institutionalists from the beginning accepted the challenge to move beyond dissent from neoclassical orthodoxy. Among the founders, only Veblen was particularly hostile. It is not antipathy to neoclassical price theory that historically or currently unites institutionalist scholars. It is rather the conviction that a different kind of perspective in economics is required if problems are to be resolved. Their approach has reflected a processual view of inquiry, an emphasis on realism, a recognition that theory creation is a necessary tool for policy formation, and an insistence that interventionism is one viable option. Among the characteristics of the institutionalist tradition, Klein emphasizes its status as a normative science; its continuing inclusion of the public sector in analysis; its quest for a "higher efficiency" of equity, freedom, security, and compassion beyond orthodox allocative efficiency; and its concern with power and performance. Of the latter, he observes that "concentrated power affects all resource allocation"; institutionalists provide an "explicit focus on actual deployment of power." After reviewing some recent contributions to the broadening and deeping of the institutionalist contribution, to theory extension and policy application, Klein concludes with a most instructive paradigmatic summary. In a dozen and more basic conceptual categories, he offers comparisons among mainstream economics, institutionalism, and political science. Clearly evident are not only the fundamental differences between institutionalism and mainstream economics (and political science) but, more importantly for this book, the persuasive demonstration of the compehensiveness and coherence of the institutionalist perspective itself. Institutionalists move beyond dissent indeed, and with vigor and commitment. For Klein the institutionalist perspective becomes a viable option in its own right.

The Commentary of Edythe S. Miller on the Klein article reinforces Klein's view of the extent and substantive development of institutional thought that historically and currently goes far beyond dissent from orthodoxy. But she is uneasy with Klein's statement that "Institutionalist economists consistently have adopted and adapted, applied and extended, a common, unified and unifying core of institutionalist analysis in their work." She suggests it does not sufficiently acknowledge wide disagreements among institutionalists on matters of fundamental theoretical substance. She also invokes an evaluative consideration concerning Klein's special formulations of value constructs, including "the collective ought," "the value floor," and "the higher efficiency." She senses some ambivalence in his treatment of "emergent valuation." Is it other than "codified conventional wisdom"? On this and other topics, she participates constructively in the continuing dialogue on social value issues raised by Klein.

The second article, "The Methodology of Institutional Economics: A Pragmatic Instrumentalist Perspective" by Paul D. Bush, probes the philosophical underpinnings of the institutionalist approach to inquiry. "[T]he dominant themes in the methodological literature of American institutionalist thought can be best understood," he argues, "as an application of pragmatic instrumentalist philosophy to the study of economics" derived in the main from the work of John Dewey. Understanding the essence of this philosophy and demonstrating its relevance to institutionalist methodology, then, is the task of this chapter.

Bush uses three characterizations of pragmatism developed by Richard Rorty as organizing constructs: 1) "pragmatism is . . . simply anti-essentialism applied to notions like 'truth,' 'knowledge,' 'language,' 'morality' "; 2) "there is no epistemological difference between truth about what ought to be and truth about what is"; 3) "there are no constraints on inquiry save conversational ones." In development of the first characterization, Bush explains the pragmatic instrumentalist rejection of, for example, the foundationist orientations of Kant and others, the quest for certainty in inquiry, and the spectator theory of knowledge generation. Instead, knowledge derives from a cognative construction in a relevant inquiry context of problem solving perceived, in Dewey's term as "warranted assertions." In consideration of the second characterization, Bush observes that "Dewey's rejection of the Cartesian knowing–doing dualism logically entails his rejection of the value knowledge dualism in all of its forms." Valuation is an inherent part of the quest for warranted knowledge generally: it is an integral part of the process of inquiry. Accordingly the objective–subjective dualism is abandoned and methodological individualism is undercut. In consideration of the third characterization, Bush identifies the pragmatic instrumentalist approach as a paradigmatic selection in a context of exploring Kuhnian and hermeneutical abandonments of metaphysical grounds for theory selection. Competing theories, Bush argues, "must be evaluated for their capacity to constribute to the problem-solving processes of real, living communities."

The Commentary of Geoffrey Hodgson on the Bush article extends deliberations on philosophical and methodological matters in two significant areas: Bush's linkage of American pragmatism, rooted in Dewey, with elements of European philosophical realism, and Rorty's claims of epistemological identity between fact and value propositions. Regarding the former, Hodgson joins Bush in rejecting Cartesian dualisms and urges the further recombination of pragmatism and realism through the joining of the ontological insights of Charles Sanders Peirce and the organicism of Alfred North Whitehead. Regarding the fact–value distinction, and unlike Bush, Hodgson takes exception to Rorty's contention that "there is no epistemological difference between truth about what ought to be and truth about what is." At issue, for Hodgson, is whether an "ought" can be derived from an "is." Responding negatively, he offers propositions for a more tenable position and explains their significance.

The third chapter, "The Theory of Instrumental Value," is my contribution to the dialogue of this book and is intended to review, refine, and extend previous institutionalist scholarship in the area of criteria of social value and economic choice. The essay opens with a restatement of the instrumental value principle for those unfamiliar with it. The fundamental tenets of continuity of human life, recreation of community, pursuit of noninvidious change, and the instrumental use of knowledge are reintroduced as elements of the instrumental value principle. The principle is then characterized as grounded in human experience and in the ability to reason about that experience continuum; as free of nonevidential or unreasoned sources of knowledge or insight; as uncluttered by normative–positive dichotomies in all forms; as neither ethically relative (in the utilitarian sense) or ethically absolute; as an instrument of institutional choice not of the advocacy of a utopian institutional recipe; as addressed to real problems facing real people; and as an approach that serves no special interest groups or power systems.

The second part seeks to demonstrate that the process of instrumental valuation provides the primary judgmental standards for modern inquiry. The instrumental principle is profoundly embedded in the inquiry process itself as criteria of judgments are continuously required and used, for example, in the choice of inquiry topics, evidences to seek, hypotheses to form and appraise, and outcomes to assess.

The third part canvasses the contributions of Paul D. Bush to value theory over the last decade or so. Bush, in exploring the analytical implications of instrumental value theory, derives a "deductively formulated model" from pattern theories of the institutionalist paradigm. It is an axiomatic formulation of the logical relationships involved. In so doing, he refines and extends the theory of ceremonial encapsulation and provides a cogent formulation of the distinction between progressive and regressive social change.

In the fourth and final part of my chapter I attempt to clarify certain aspects of the instrumental value principle in response to contentions by Wendell Gordon that the principle has the status of an eternal verity to which he objects, and in response to concerns of Anne Mayhew that the development and use of the principle constitutes an attack on the concept of culture.

The Commentary of William Waller and Linda Robertson on the Tool chapter sets their observations in the context of "the social construction of knowledge and the cultural construction of meaning." They acknowledge the significance of instrumental valuation and suggest that it must be pursued with "dialectial reasoning" (in the debate or dialogue sense) rather than as "demonstrative reasoning" (in the ordinary causal and predictability sense). Instrumental inquiry is purposive, processional, and problem-relevant. Moreover, although they grant the logical coherence and consistency provided by Bush's axiomatic analytical structure, they suggest that I have overlooked an important aspect—that the axiomatic formulation may lead to the "reification of the categories of analysis." The "abstract category" itself should not become the primary object of inquiry rather than "the existent phenomena for which the category was developed." They conclude with an appraisal of the critiques of Gordon and Mayhew.

The fourth chapter, "Institutional Economics and the Dual Labor Market Theory," is by Yngve Ramstad. His concern is to seek valid theories that explain what they purport to explain in the area of labor markets and labor economics. He observes that although several of the founders of institutionalist thought early in this century addressed and wrote about labor market issues, there is at present no discernable community of scholars now pursuing labor market analysis from an institutionalist perspective. Institutionalists have so far failed to develop an "explicitly" institutionalist theory of the labor market. Ramstad's chapter is addressed to that hiatus. His central purpose, developed in three segments, then, is to show in what manner "the dual labor market theory in fact manifests philosophical and theoretical propositions associated with the institutionalist standpoint." Accordingly, he first demonstrates, through an extensive canvas of the recent institutionalist literature, the absence of an explicitly institutionalist theory of labor markets. Second, he presents a probing analysis of the characteristics that a theory of labor markets must reflect if it is to be consistent with mainstream institutionalist thought. He disclaims that there is a *single* institutionalist paradigm or research program; there is, however, a "general standpoint" that encompasses the nature of the economy, the nature of human action, and the manner in which valid knowledge is generated that gives identity and commonality to the approach. Finally, he demonstrates at length that the dual labor market theory, especially as developed by Michael Piore, does indeed reflect the perspective of institutionalists. In this demonstration he reviews the intellectual history of three post-World War II approaches to labor market analysis: neoclassical, neoclassical "plus," and "neorealist." He sees recent developments of institutionalist labor market theory as an outgrowth in large part of the neorealist tradition.

The chapter concludes with an extensive exploration of the corollary elements between Piore's dual labor market theory and and the "institutionalist standpoint." "What has been shown," Ramstad argues, is that "as an overarching conception of labor market segmentation, the dual labor market theory evinces a conception of 'economic' (producing, pricing, exchanging) behavior wholly in harmony with the philosophical preconceptions constituting the 'institutional' standpoint."

The Commentary on the Ramstad chapter contributed by Stephen Mangum and Frank Borgers is written from a viewpoint somewhat more sympathetic to neoclassicism than that of other contributors. These authors find much to commend in Ramstad's characterization of the institutionalist standpoint. They consider his analysis of the institutionalist position on labor markets to be especially instructive and useful. Yet they think his separation from orthodoxy is excessive. They write: "The goals of theory: description, prediction, and prescription . . . are approachable, not by supplementing the neoclassical pattern model with institutionial reality but by gradually replacing its starkness with the rich detail of institutional patterns that develop with exposure to real world institutions. In this view, the neocassical framework is far from useless; rather it is the (often necessary) first cut." They raise questions as well about Ramstad's characterizations of the intellectual antecedents of Piore's defacto institutional view of labor markets. It is a provocative Commentary.

The fifth chapter, "Institutions and Economic Development: structure, Process, and Incentive," is by John Adams. Here his concern is to demonstrate contributions of institutionalists to the emergence of the inquiry and policy field of economic development. In consideration of "structure," Adams demonstrates that "institutions matter." They shape economic comportment in dissimilar social systems; they explain "how societies and economies differ across time and from each other." Adams denies "that economic principles transcend the institutional arrangements that define a particular culture." People "behave in accord with conventional and continuing practices" even as they retain "the capacity to manipulate and transform those arrangements." Development economics must be *institutional* economics. In consideration of "process," Adams sees institutionalists as introducing "time, sequence, and order into the study of economic systems." Different institutional structures foster different processual arrangements. Societies "thus have clearly distinguishable rates of capital accumulation, export growth, consumption, or capacity utilization." In consideration of "incentive," Adams eschews the conventional rational agent of orthodoxy and explores the inherent and changing complexity of motivation induced by all manner of cultural (habitual) and discretionary (innovative) influences. In Adams' view, "the role of individuals is particularly salient in a dynamic context where the balance of reward and restraint tilts in favor of innovation in all its forms: technological, legal, political, and social." The pancultural and pantemporal rationality premise of orthodoxy is abandoned.

The Commentary of James Dietz on the Adams article reaffirms the commitment of institutionalists to the analysis of economic development. After drawing a fresh contrast between neoclassical and institutionalist approaches, Dietz proposes to augment Adams' position. "I would," he suggests, ". . . put more emphasis on the empirical relevance of technology as the primary progressive force for social and economic development and the potentially constraining capacity of those institutions found to be inapproporiate to further progress." In addition, his research indicates that local ownership, local sources of capital, local control over technological processes, and local adaptation of knowledge for productive purposes, together with a visionary and supportive government, will significantly enhance development efforts.

The sixth major article, "Institutionalist Policymaking," is contributed by F. Gregory Hayden. The placement of this chapter at the end of this book is intended to permit readers to bring much of the foregoing institutional analysis and theory building to bear most directly on the real world of issues and problem solving. Having clarified views of institutional contributions in the several areas considered, how can these and similar formulations be employed to enhance the well-being of the community generally? How can enhanced theoretical understanding be used to guide institutional change and adjustments? It is to the "nuts and bolts" of theory creation and policy applications that Hayden's chapter is addressed.

It is Hayden's widely shared opening observation that the developers of institutional thought, Veblen excepted, have always correlated their analyses with a concern for policymaking and have continuously sought significance in its relevance thereto. Accordingly, Hayden seeks "to extend the institutionalist concern for policy more explicitly in the realm of public policymaking." He wants to help fashion a tighter interlock between social and economic research and policymaking. For this interlock to become more effective, institutionalists' insights are needed, and their more extensive involvement in policy analysis and implementation is required. Moreover, "since much of the activity at the national level in the United States in the 1980s has been to dismantle the institutionalist policy legacy from past decades," this is a particularly opportune time to pursue institutionalist policymaking.

The structural character of the Hayden article is provided in a chart that identifies, in an overarching view, the various "Phases and Levels of Institutionalist Policymaking." Ten *phases* of policymaking include: "Institutionalism," "Philosophy," and "Ideology," on the left side; through "Problem Definition," "Context," "Measurement," and "Select Programs, in the middle; to "Advocacy," Program Budgeting," and "Sociotechnical Change" on the right side. They provide policymaking guidance to move researchers, not necessarily in a tightly ordered fashion, from theoretical/analytical underpinings, to problem identification, to policy formation, and to practical implementation. For *each* phase, considerations of "Policy," "Strategy," and "Tactics," buttressed by their respective sciences—policy sciences, strategic sciences, management and adminstrative sciences—are required. Although for Hayden this is not necessarily a model, linear sequence, or complete taxonomy, it does identify and suggest inquiry questions and foci, methodologies, relevant behaviors, communicative requirements, and implementative approaches that more consistently allow ideas to guide experience in new and constructive ways. Special skills and knowledges will be required for the topical analyses at each level of each phase. Understanding the interlocks and interconnections among and between the elements of this tableau is essential. Effectiveness is enhanced when all phases and levels are consistent and integrated, but it is not "a mechanistic lock step operation." Hayden contrasts his institutionalist policymaking/problem-solving approach with three others that are quite inadequate: bureaucratic, pseudostrategic, and scholarly-king. More particularly, Hayden makes clear that most contemporary policymaking is controlled by and in the service of economic power systems pursuing their own agendas, not those constituting the public interest. Hayden's inquiry approach is open ended, analytically cogent, empirically grounded, logically credible, and both problem-relevant and problem-specific.

The Commentary contributed by Milton Lower provides a penetrating supplement to the Hayden article. Drawing on his extensive experience as a research specialist, author, and advisor for several Congressional committees, Lower provides something of an immediate assessment of the cogency and relevancy of the Hayden analytical approach. As he puts it, "Hayden's roadmap to the phases and levels of policymaking—and perhaps especially to the hazards along the way—seems accurate almost to the last pothole, unmarked curve, and dangerous detour." He draws examples from Congressional deliberations over policies concerning auto safety and oversight of energy policy (especially pricing practices). He is particularly familiar with the Hayden-identified nonstarter (smoke and mirrors?) approach of the bureaucrats to policy formation, and of the neoclassical "expert" proponents of cost-benefit analysis. More generally, he joins Hayden in the recognition that, as Hayden puts it, "the aspect of policymaking which is most ignored in the policy science literature and most emphasized in the institutionalist literature is technology. . . . the integration of the two literatures is essential for theoretical advances in policymaking." Finally, in recognizing the extent to which Hayden draws on and contributes to the general theoretical and policy-oriented literature of institutionalists, Lower provides an appropriate summary comment about the character and intended significance of this book.

In conclusion, let me most sincerely extend my thanks to all those who have participated in the preparation of this book: to Warren Samuels for extending the initial invitation as Series Editor and for his encouragement throughout; to the individual chapter authors for their major scholarly accomplishments; to those who wrote Commentaries for their provocative and candid contributions to the continuing dialogue; and to Zachary Rolnik at Kluwer Academic Publishers for his extraordinary patience and support as unforeseen events and circumstances delayed the book's completion.

It is our mutual hope that this book will contribute significantly to the advancement of the institutionalist approach to politico-economic analysis and to its use in problem and policy deliberations.

References

Samuels, Warren J. *Institutional Economics I, II, III*, (Cheltenham: Edward Elgar, 1988).

Samuels, Warren J., Hodgson, Geoffrey M. and Tool, Marc R. eds., *The Elgar Companion to Institutional and Evolutionary Economics, I, II*, (Cheltenham: Edward Elgar, forthcoming).

Tool, Marc R. ed., *Evolutionary Economics I, II*, (Armonk, N.Y.: M.E. Sharpe, Inc., 1988).

2 THE INSTITUTIONALIST CHALLENGE: BEYOND DISSENT

Philip A. Klein

No charge is leveled more consistently at institutionalism (when it is referred to at all) than that it has nothing positive to offer—it is "mere dissent."

We shall examine this charge in the following section from the perspective of the founders of institutionalism and later through a reconsidered characterization of the institutionalist perspective and an assessment of the contributions of some recent institutionalist scholars. It is true that institutionalists customarily dissent from the assumptions, the methodology, and the conclusions of neoclassical economics. But they go on to offer a variety of their own positive contributions.

We present in the pages to follow the institutionalists' paradigm: their approach to economic theory and methodology. Frequent comparison of neoclassicism with institutional analysis will sharpen and clarify both the differences between the two and the extent and character of the institutionalist contribution. There are instutionalist applications to a number of the conventional fields in economics—from development economics (which has in a sense always been ineluctably instutionalist), through business cycles, to industrial organization and public sector economics.[1]

The Roots of Institutional Economics

It has been fashionable for some time to assert that what held the work of the founders of institutionalism together—indeed, what justified calling institutionalism a movement—was that Veblen, Mitchell, and Commons were all hostile to neoclassical theory, particularly micro theory. It is perfectly true that in one way or another all three had reservations about the adequacy of neoclassical micro theory. It is also true that common negative reactions have historically been a profoundly effective bonding device in the creation of political and social movements as well as schools of thought. (One could say that the American Colonies were "mainly hostile" to King George III. It could be argued that early classical economists were "mainly hostile" to mercantilism, that Marxists were "mainly hostile" to capitalism, and so on)

So while institutionalists had significant reservations about the prevailing neoclassical theory of their day, this was in fact never the primary preoccupation of the group that founded institutionalism. The first use of the term appears to have been in a paper entitled "The Institutional Approach to Economic Theory" delivered by Walton H. Hamilton, in December 1918 to the annual meeting of the American Economic Association. Hamilton saw this paper as part of a "reconstruction of economics" which he felt was necessary in order for economics to cope more effectively with the economic challenges of the day. This interpretation of Hamilton's purpose comes from Joseph Dorfman, a close student of the early days of institutionalism.[2] According to Dorfman, Irving Fisher (scarcely an institutionalist), while president of the American Economic Association, appointed a Committee on Cooperation (of Economists) in Economic Research, chaired by Allyn Young. This committee was to increase available information to make economic research more germane to (then current) economic problems. In connection with the formation of this committee, both Veblen and Mitchell were consulted on their views concerning "the prospects of a serious shift by the profession, especially by the American Economic Association." Veblen is reported to have been interested in the idea. (Dorfman reports that Veblen called Hamilton "a disturber of otherwise untroubled water."[3]) Mitchell was also interested in the idea, though he was less optimistic. Both, in short, were aware of the need for a shift in the perspective of their colleagues, but neither made the formation of a new school of economic thought a prime focus, however intransigent they may have considered the American Economic Association to be. Rather, they concentrated on developing their own views, and in the process contributed to a new way of thinking about economic problems.

In this early period Walton Hamilton articulated the essential difference between neoclassical and what he was then calling institutionalist economists. He regarded the difference as stemming from basic postulates: neoclassical economics was "mechanistic," attempting to "encompass industrial activity within a formula, a set of principles, an equilibrium of forces. The attention of the institutionalist is directed to the industrial process: . . . his principal concern is with the fabric of industrial usage which emerges—and with its compulsions over human conduct."[4] Note that even here, in perhaps the first formal statement of the differences between neoclassical and institutionalist economics, what was being "dissented from" receives no more and no less attention than what—in a positive way—was being advanced. As Dorfman's account of these early years suggests, Veblen and Mitchell seemed at least aware of their common dissent from the postulates of neoclassical economics. As with Hamilton, however, their emphasis on process (distinctive in each, but complementary) was quite as crucial as—perhaps more so than—their dissent from mechanistic equilibria. We shall return to this common emphasis.

It is not clear that Veblen himself ever used the term *institutional economics*. It is doubtful, as already noted, that he regarded himself as the founder of any school. Commons, following in the footsteps of Walton Hamilton, did use the term prominently, albeit a good deal later (in the title of his two-volume 1934 book).[5] By the time Mitchell's lecture notes were transcribed (in the 1940s) as *Types of Economic Theory*,[6] he did indeed include a section on institutional economics, with which he associated his own work, but it is not clear, as has been suggested above, that in the formative years of his work he thought of himself as taking part in founding a school.

There have been many efforts by now to state "what institutionalism stands for," what is its paradigm, and so on.[7] These efforts can and should be judged on their merits, but to continue to claim that only antipathy to price theory unites institutionalists is simply not consonant with the facts. All three founders—as noted—had reservations about neoclassical theory, but of the economists under consideration, only Veblen had a reputation based significantly on his hostility toward mainstream economics. (Arguably, he had—and no doubt deserved—a reputation for hostility to the mainstream American society of his time.) Even in Veblen's work the lasting insights were mostly positive, not negative (For example, his celebrated paragraph on hedonstic man as a "homogeneous globule of desires of happiness" is followed on the next page with an anthropological view of man as "a coherent structure of propensities and habits seeking expression."[8] A major thread to Veblen's work was his emphasis on Darwinian evolution. By adding to it the dichotomy between industrial and pecuniary activities (or the technological and institutional aspects of economic life, to employ the terminology that institutionalists in the post-Ayreas era have tended to use), Veblen came to his view of economic process (the "life process' from an economic perspective) which involved what he called "cultural lag."[9] Veblen's emphasis on process and the role he assigned in his view of economic process to business values is, as noted above, very closely related to Mitchell's view. In Mitchell's work on business cycles, he was struggling to express what he regarded as the essential nature of economic process: business cycles were manifestations of economic behavior in an institutional setting, the latter in our society (that is, a market-oriented economy) being permeated with business values. (When Mitchell stresses that business cycles occur in "economies that organize their work mainly in business enterprise,"[10] he is focusing essentially on what Veblen called a pecuniary society.) This is not to say that Mitchell's focus duplicated Veblen's in any precise way, but rather (to underscore a point made earlier) that in their perspective toward economic activity, their stress on process, and their view that economic process could be understood only by paying due attention to the institutional setting, they surely shared a common *weltanschauung* in their approach to the study of economic activity. This is not surprising inasmuch as Mitchell was very much attracted to the views of both Dewey and Veblen, in whose classes he sat at the University of Chicago.[11]

Insofar as Commons is concerned, like Veblen and Mitchell he (via Richard T. Ely, his teacher at Johns Hopkins) was influenced by the German Historical School and felt throughout his life that sound economic analysis had to be grounded in a set of societal values. He asserted, moreover, that hard statistical information was very much required to develop sound economic theory, which for Commons always meant that it had to be useful in developing public policy. In his interest in and emphasis on a sound statistical basis for theorizing, he surely had a common bond with Mitchell. As for Veblen, Dorfman has argued that in his central theory of collective action Commons took from Veblen the key notion of "the transaction" employed by Veblen for relations between going concerns.[12] That Commons broadened it to encompass any economic activity involving conflict simply suggests that in Commons, as with any good social science theorist, existing theory is in an endless process of being changed and adapted to new circumstances and insights.

This sketch is obviously no more than cursory nor is it designed to be. It is meant only to suggest that from the beginning, institutionalism's founders had a common processual view of economic activity, one that analyzed various aspects of how business economies in fact carry out their functions. There was in all three of these founders an emphasis on realism, on dynamic analysis, on theory as a necessary tool in policy formation, and on interventionism as one viable option.

Later generations of institutionalists have continued these emphases and this common perspective. Far from turning their backs on this legacy, the institutionalists of the interwar period built on it and refined it. Clarence Ayres was a major figure in this period. Like his predecessors he was surely critical of conventional economic theory, but his primary emphasis and his chief importance lies in his positive contributions. These consisted partly of synthesizing elements from earlier institutionalists and partly in moving institutionalist analysis forward in ways that were distinctly his own. While his contributions were myriad, none was more significant than his combination of the Veblenian dichotomy (industrial versus pecuniary activity) with John Dewey's instrumental theory of value. This led to his fusion of the technological process with Dewey's means–ends continuum (a "technological theory of value") for economic analysis, and his clear focus on economics as a dynamic problem-oriented discipline struggling always to define for contemporary society the meaning of economic progress.[13]

This approach was consistent with that of his contemporaries—John Gambs' insistence that economics must move "beyond supply and demand,"[14] and Allan Gruchy's "holistic" view of economics and his insistence on focusing on economic process.[15] Gruchy was particularly articulate in echoing the view of others who associated themselves with institutionalism (for example, Rexford Guy Tugwell and Gerhard Colm) by reasserting their belief that even a market economy requires some overall explicit view of—and attention to—where it is going.[16] Gruchy's most recent contributions, of course, have consisted in relating the work of newer institutionalists to the institutional tradition, as he understands it, based on a lifetime of study as well as participation in its development.[17]

Overseas Gunnar Myrdal reminded us that institutionalism had its roots in the Old World and can still with profit be applied in that setting as well. Myrdal's background, which included full appreciation of the Swedish approach in mainstream economics, nonetheless did not prevent his stressing always the importance of grounding economic analysis, including assessment of market performance, in the institutional setting from which it derives. More than most he not only insisted on analyzing domestic economic activity in a societal framework, but he was also acutely aware of the impact of international factors, both technological and institutional, on domestic economic activity.[18] No recent economist since Schumpeter has taken so broad a view of the institutional milieu within which economic analysis must be set if economic theory is to be meaningfully formulated.

Finally we mention two other institutionalists who began their work in the interwar period and are still active. They have become so widely discussed that their institutionalist roots are often overlooked. John Kenneth Galbraith, far from being merely negative about price theory, has developed a view of economic activity that is culturally embedded, richly appreciative of Veblen's insights, and overwhelmingly cognizant of the critical role that power plays in modern economic affairs.[19] As such Galbraith has made many institutional insights clearer to a vast public even if mainstream economists prefer all too often to dismiss him as a nonrigorous theorist who has had influence far beyond his due because, unlike many economists, he is an effective writer and speaker.

The other institutionalist who has had considerable influence on public discussion is Robert Heilbroner who, like Galbraith, has written extensively.[20] The distinctive features of a Heilbroner treatise include his unfailing attention to the bedrock institutionalist perspective. He never forgets that economic activity is always meaningfully observed only in an institutional setting. For him this would encompass assessing current economic activity in light of economic history. Like Veblen, Heilbroner utilizes the detachment of the anthropologist in observing his own economy, and like any good institutionalist he focuses on the actual economy rather than consigning the economy to be studied to what remains "segregated in Marshall's pound," to use Robert Lekachman's telling phrase.[21]

In summary the roots of institutionalism lay in the work of economists who from the beginning were much more than mere dissenters. The prewar and interwar institutionalists who followed in their footsteps (and we have no more than scratched the surface in this brief review, leaving many who worked in this tradition out of the discussion altogether) formed a reasonably coherent whole and took a tolerably consistent set of positions. Their perspective was, to be sure, not consistent with the position taken in mainstream economics, but it was positive rather than "merely negative." We shall argue that this consistency and commonality continues to be displayed in the work of current institutionalists such as Heilbroner, Galbraith, and the other modern institutionalist now writing in the *Journal of Economic Issues* and elsewhere. (It is also true that for reasons institutionalists need to consider, Galbraith and Heilbroner are the principal current institutionalists who have had a significant impact on mainstream consciousness, and then often not even as explicit "institutionalists.") The institutionalist perspective can be disagreed with, and surely institutionalists would welcome debate about the underlying issues with noninstitutionalists, but it cannot accurately be portrayed as "mere hostility to orthodoxy economic theory."

It agreement could be reached on this single point, both fruitful debate about the proper function of economic theory as well as the contribution of institutionalism would have been advanced immeasurably. The remainder of this chapter is devoted to commenting on some of the central aspects of this positive institutionalist contribution. We concentrate on five central areas where there seems to be general agreement among institutionalists.

The Institutionalist Perspective

Is Economics a Positive Science?

Nowhere is the institutionalist perspective clearer than on the fundamental question whether economics is a normative or a positive science. Ever since Lionel Robbins declared in the 1930s, "Economics is the science which studies human behavior as a relationship between ends and scarce means which have alternative uses,"[22] economists have followed in his footsteps by declaring that economics is a "positive science" concerned with "what is" as distinct from a "normative science" concerned with what "ought to be." The pricing process is the stated mechanism for expressing all the allocative decisions about which economists need to bother.

Robbins sought to distinguish economics from "moral philosophy," but he denied that he was advocating "abstention of the economist from all interest or activity outside his own field."[23] By putting it this way, Robbins, we would argue, implicitly undermined his own position. For him, being concerned with values took economists "outside their own field." A bedrock institutionalist position has always been that to be concerned with values—normative economics—is most emphatically "inside economics." This represents a major difference between the approach of institutionalism and that of neoclassical economics. For institutionalists, Friedman's notion—following Robbins's lead and always popular with the mainstream—that economics must be a positive science and thus remain independent of ethical positions is not only wrong but also impossible. To take no position is to accept the status quo. I once tried to make this point by considering how we would react to an economist who commented, "I take no position on the Holocaust, but I would point out that if one wished to exterminate six millions Jews, then gas chambers would be an efficient way to achieve this objective."[24] We would all, I think boot an economist or anyone else who argued this way out of court.

But this is precisely the approach that mainstream economists favor when they tell us that economists "qua economist"—to use their favorite phrase—take no position on any given issue, but instead content themselves with stating. "If you wish to accomplish this end, then this is the most efficient way to achieve it." They fail to note that this positive economics in effect enshrines the status quo. Mainstream economists are devoted to a heavy emphasis on deductive reasoning based on a series of assumptions (the "givens"). Then, having already made the assumptions, they insist the subsequent analysis is positive. This approach in reality places off limits for debate purposes all the factors included in the assumptions. For example, a discussion of market activity in a conventional price theory course (or in its applied field, industrial organization) has historically taken a variety of approaches—workable competition, interproduct rivalry, and more recently "contestable markets" all designed to assume away the significance of the divergence of real markets from text-book competitive markets. All result in positive analysis, and all ignore the critical value problems (embedded in the givens) that the actual deployment of power in the modern economy, for example, poses. Welfare economics, cited below, offers another example. Ceteris paribus assumptions no doubt make analysis much easier (and no doubt used with some moderation even have a legitimate place in scientific research), but as used in orthodox economics they are used at a high cost in relevance. (A doctor who accepted as given that his patient would not survive more than 24 hours might have considerably greater scope for dealing with symptoms, but the usefulness of his treatment to the patient's welfare might be questioned.)

Thus the proposition that to take no position is the essence of positive economics is in fact for value purposes to accept implicitly the status quo. This is a critical institutionalist challenge to the presumed *wertfrei* approach of mainstream economists. Economists, like all other scientists, express value judgments all the time, beginning with their deciding what questions to study—how, if you will, to allocate their time.

In this connection, it is instructive to consider a statement by the Association of Los Alamos Physicists (formed by physicists who worked on the atomic bomb in 1945). Economists should pay attention to physicists; physics is after all the discipline, replete with equilibrium conditions, that is most admired by mainstream economists. The physicists, in setting up their association, said that "... the objective of this organization is to promote the attainment and use of scientific and technological advances in the best interests of humanity. The members of the organization recognize that scientists, by virtue of their special knowledge have, in certain spheres, special political and social responsibilities beyond their obligations as individuals."[25]

This is precisely the point that institutionalists have always made. Economists as economists are part of the economic process, not outside it. It is not a coincidence that the economists who insist most vociferously that economics must be purely a positive science are also the economists who seemingly remain most tranquil in the face of the severe problems—may we call them allocative?—that the modern world faces. Virtually all of these problems—from widespread poverty and starvation to severe inequalities in power, income, and wealth; consumer "bamboozlement" by powerful profit-motivated firms; discrimination, and so on—all are swept under the ceteris paribus rug by mainstream economics. The world—warts and all—is taken as given. "Public choice" economists would simply argue that intervention can't improve on the market's handling (called "market solutions") of any of these difficulties.[26]

Can there really be any doubt about this? Consider welfare economics, the branch of neoclassical economics presumably most sensitive to these matters. It is based firmly on the notion of Pareto optimality that undermines any real notion of greater societal equity by suggesting that insofar as economic analysis is concerned, society has attained an optimal condition when no one can be made better off except by making someone else worse off. Pareto optimality thus always takes income and wealth distribution as given. One presumes all this must mean that a reallocation of resources making several million poor people "better off" is not Pareto optimal if J. Paul Getty or Donald Trump feels "worse off."[27] What else can it mean?

Even more, modern welfare economics never considers that the economy itself has an interactive relationship with society. The choosing process itself can alter values. How can modern welfare economics cope with such issues? Kenneth Arrow, a Nobel Prize winner in this field, once suggested the mainstream approach unambiguously: "We will assume in the present study that individual values are taken as data and are not capable of being altered by the nature of the decision process itself. This is ". . . the standard view in economic theory."[28] He is right. It is the standard view in standard theory. It lies back of Pareto optimality; it is basic to Arrow's approach to welfare; it is embedded in the Bergson "social welfare function."[29] But it is not the view of institutionalists, nor, one dares say, is it the view on Madison Avenue or Fleet Street that has raised to a high art not taking individual values as unalterable data. Isn't it odd that our positive economists can't get beyond thinking of welfare in terms of the sum of individual values—all given—when they also tell us (or they did in the pre-Robert Lucas days) that we need "macro economics" to avoid the fallacy of composition? Is social welfare truly nothing more than the sum of individual values? Could there not be a fallacy of composition here as well? How else can one apply the value process to the public sector? All agree that total resources devoted to national defense cannot be expressed as the sum of individual valuation brought to bear on this part of allocation. But the same thing can be said about many other kinds of public allocation. And debate about allocation in the public sector, which goes on all the time, is the process of rethinking emergent valuation as it pertains to that part of allocation for which individual values do *not* sum simply to societal value. Indeed the process of conversion from allocation via individual valuation to allocation via societal valuation is one of the most complex parts of the continuous and interactive process of emergent societal valuation.

In summary, to take no value position is effectively to embrace current societal values in toto, And no economist sensitive to the value challenges in the modern world can do this unless he or she can rest easy with that world. It is small wonder that it is mainly conservatives, the ones who argue that society as we know it and the economy as we know it are basically ideal and thus worth "conserving," who find this easy to do. But they are virtually the only ones. We find few positive economists in urban ghettos or the Third World.

Institutionalists, in contrast, regard it as an essential obligation of economists as economists to bring their vaunted expertise to bear on economic problems.

Economics: A Science of Price or of Value?

The institutionalist perspective can clearly be contrasted with the neoclassical perspective by noting that for neoclassical economics pricing is the operative mechanism in the market. For institutionalists the operative mechanism is emergent valuation as it is effected in allocative judgments. Clarence Ayres once said, "Whether or not it continues to be a science of price, economics must be a science of value."[30]

What is the value challenge with which institutionalists wrestle? At bottom it is what Veblen called the life process. He once wrote, "There is the life process still awaiting theoretical formulation."[31] Giving the life process theoretical formulation is the challenge to economic theory that institutionalists have always accepted, Continuing the life process is the ultimate value premise. I once called belief in this premise "the value floor"[32] because its acceptance is the basis for all subsequent analysis. Our perspective toward society derives from this premise. Societal values represent the constant reinterpretation of this premise. This is the basis for the institutionalist claim that emergent value is what emanates from the economy. It is the source of the basic perspective of institutionalists: the economy is involved with emergent value—a dynamic process—not just equilibrium market prices—a static state. Economic analysis is the ceaseless effort at restating and reformulating the tasks confronting the economy in the light of changing circumstances, technological and other. The obligation of economists is to advise on how the economy can meet this challenge so as to advance the life process in an optimal manner. An essential aspect of economic performance thus is to channel emergent values, which it is the ultimate task of the economy to advance, into ongoing allocative decisions. This interactive process necessarily involves a constant query (public as well as private) concerning how accurately the economy reflects emergent value, as well as a continuous reassessment of total current societal evaluation in light of changed circumstances. We ask, "How well does the economy succeed in doing what we want it to do?" as well as "How is what we want it do changing?" Economic activity is, therefore, a dynamic and an interactive process because the economy and society are in constant interaction. Institutionalists believe that Veblen's comment about the life process awaiting theoretical formulation was in effect a charge among other things to develop dynamic economic theory. The life process as it unfolds is the fundamental conditioner of value in all fields of human endeavor.

The dynamic interpretation of the value floor is at once crucial and difficult. Consider the field of medicine where belief in the life process translates into working for "health"—making life possible. Here the bedrock value gives rise to the greatest controversies. Debates about abortion and euthanasia are nothing if not debates about what "enhancing life" means. At least in medicine we debate these question. (No doctor would consider that he or she had discharged all professional responsibilities to the patient simply by saying. "If you want to get rid of the baby you are carrying—or end your life or that of a loved one—here is the most efficient way to do so." A doctor would recognize that having expertise carries with it the responsibility to participate in the decision-making process, not by imposing private judgments on others, but by spelling out the full consequences of given decisions to others in light of their own feelings as well as the full panoply of options. This involves helping patients understand themselves, their own evolving views, and their own reactions.) Here and elsewhere, interpreting technological change in light of altered possibilities is a critical part of the process by which societal values change over time.

This is as true for choice in economics as it is for choice in medicine or any other area. In economics, we have seen, however, that for the mainstream professional economist, problems parallel to the medical questions considered here are all too often assumed away. This comes close to simply ignoring them. Little wonder that economics appears often to be irrelevant and economic problems remain unfaced, let alone unsolved.

To institutionalists what happens in markets is often, therefore, to be viewed most accurately as "market mechanics," the mere manipulation of prices. But it is at bottom only a part of the process of societal valuation. The constant provisioning and reallocation of all resources, which is the basic task of an economy, reflects emergent values.[33] Emergent valuation —the total allocational thrust of a society—is the product of the economy. (It represents at any given time the current state of the Veblenian battle between technological possibilities and contemporaneous institutional structures, whether they come to be viewed as "imbecile" to later generations or not.) It is critical never to forget that any economy is embedded in a society and there is constant interaction between the two. Moreover, the economy is itself an interactive entity. In this entity, economists have a role to play in its decision-making process. That role is most particularly larger than making the "If . . . then" statements to which the mainstream economists, who sail so tranquilly through the status quo, insist their "positive economics" must be restricted. Economists need be no more normatively detached than medical doctors or physicists. Economists believe that restricting their work in this way avoids subjectivity. It avoids only overt subjectivity. As we have seen, we may state that any economy exhibits *some* attitude toward all its participants at all times. In this sense there can be no economic analysis that does not involve valuation. We can learn from the physicists that there is in this sense indeed a place for compassion—an unavoidable component of valuation, whether implicit or explicit—in any modern scientist.[34]

The differences between neoclassical and institutionalist economists show up in how they view the economy. To institutionalists, the neoclassical economists view the economy as an ethically neutral vessel in which, via prices, allocative decisions get made. To institutionalists, as we have seen, the economy is not ethically neutral but has at all times some attitude toward its participants (even forcing them all to fend totally for themselves is an attitude). Moreover, the economy itself is part of the interactive process from which societal valuation emerges. This statement means something quite different from saying that any scientist, including the economist, has an obligation to dispassionate analysis through utilizing the scientific method. It is partly to recognize that values color all scientific investigation, beginning as we have already noted with the choice of problems to study. Even more, what we expect of the economy changes as societal values change. If as we have suggested economic analysis is grounded in a "value floor," this claim may be best understood by considering the public sector.

The Public Sector[35]

The evidence is unexceptional; all modern economies include a public sector as well as a private sector. A significant part of total provisioning and allocation is done by the public sector. The staunchest conservative can see this when resources are being allocated to national defense. National defense after all represents allocation deemed societally essential—that is (in the United States), it is given the imprimatur of the Executive and the Congress. To say "We must be strong whatever the cost" is at once to suggest a provisioning and allocational imperative that reaches beyond the confines of the market.

We reach more controversial territory only when we say, "We must be compassionate regardless of cost," although as we have previously noted, no economy can avoid exhibiting "compassion" as a dimension of performance (although it may range from none to a great deal). We shall return to this in the subsequent section on judging economic performance. All societies today, including our own, have a category called "Welfare" to which resources are allocated. But we do have endless debate about how much to allocate.

The debate is obfuscated by an increasing tendency to refer to the public sector as "they." Institutionalists would argue that the public sector, no less than the private sector, is not "they" but "we." A giant firm with monopoly power that negotiates a secret price-fixing agreement is doing "us" in quite as surely as the government bureaucrat who signs a bloated contract.

This is another way of saying that expenditures (which, after all, require the use of resources) can be made wisely or foolishly in either the private sector or the public sector. Neither efficiency nor honesty is the exclusive characteristic of either sector. But if neoclassical economists fixate on the presumed beauties of allocation in the private sector, institutionalists make no such judgment. They would argue that "we" have a right to do whatever "we" want to do. Public sector provisioning and allocation represents what I have called "the collective ought." It encompasses priorities and objectives—values, if you will—that we have concluded cannot be currently attained through private allocation. Like all allocative decisions, public sector activity is constantly under review—a part of the "emergent valuation" which is always part of the dynamic economy. The process of determining the collective ought is no doubt imperfect, but imperfections in the process don't vitiate the validity of our view of ideal dynamic economic decision making. (The parallels with political science discussed below in connection with the institutionalist paradigm are relevant here.)

Judging Economic Performance

We have seen that mainstream economists are willing to grant that an economy as part of society is concerned with security, hence defense. (Even Friedman grants that defense is "the most basic" exception to reliance on individual decision making in markets.) But "humaneness" or compassion cannot be banished to a different part of society. Indeed any economy, as part of the society in which it operates, exhibits a number of characteristics or dimensions of performance in terms of which it can be judged. Efficiency and security are two of them. Other characteristics exhibited by any economy include equity, freedom, and the previously mentioned compassion.[36]

Mainstream economists are fixated on narrow allocative efficiency, carried out in markets via price, output adjustments, or both (and even there they are so confined by oversimplification and reverence for the presumed wonders of what would happen in perfectly competitive markets that they rarely get around to real-world problems). Institutionalists argue that the total allocative thrust of society is revealed by *all* the characteristics mentioned: efficiency, security, equity, freedom, and compassion. Like Moliere's bourgeois gentilhomme, who did not know he had been speaking prose all his life, an economy exhibits all these characteristics, whether it wants to or not, and whether its leaders are aware of it or not. How an economy actually functions will then, for example, produce (to repeat a point made previously) some measure, on a scale from none to a great deal, of compassion. All economies exhibit some kind of compassion willy-nilly. We are accustomed to the ongoing evaluation of security in the public sector, and there is a good deal of talk about efficiency in both sectors (much of it less than objective). But we are not accustomed to this kind of ongoing review of performance in terms of the other characteristics. But they are part and parcel of economic performance. In short, an economy can be judged not only on its narrow market allocation ("efficiency") but also by its handling of security, compassion, equity, and freedom. I have called this broadened measure of economic performance the "higher efficiency." We must interpret this carefully. Although institutionalists would not deny a role for market prices in resource allocation, even in the case of "efficiency" the allocation of markets is subject to societal review. It cannot be assumed that "the market" we find in modern market economies necessarily and invariably achieves even narrow efficiency. "Market imperfections" may well be greater than is commonly granted. In a dynamic world of changing tastes and technology, efficiency over time should not be taken for granted. Resource immobilities or constraints, blockages to input development and training, may all slip through the screening of the modern market. (We return to this problem in the subesequent section.)

Societal review of market allocation (efficiency as it emerges from unregulated imperfect markets before they are subject to any legislative or administrative constraints) requires, therefore, review before the optimal contribution of market allocation to the higher efficiency can be assumed. Mainstream economists have no trouble granting the necessity of such a review in connection with the second criterion, national security. Such review, in fact, is under way more or less constantly.

In summary, a major task of the public sector, to make more explicit a point touched on earlier, is to reflect the emerging values of society with respect to *all* these dimensions of performance (efficiency, security, compassion, equity, and freedom), and to assess critically allocation in the private sector with a view to determining what part of provisioning and allocation should be reserved to the public sector. Presumably the expertise of the professional economist brings with it special responsibilities in helping society to articulate this ongoing reassessment.

Power and Economic Performance

One of the most critical differences between the perspective of neoclassical economics and that of institutionalism concerns the view of economic power.[37]

Mainstream microeconomics tends to take the deployment of power as given. Presumably the status quo has been institutionally sanctioned. In the perfect competition case, so dear to the hearts of neoclassical economists, firms are definitionally all equally powerless in the market (at least they can have no individual useful effect on price through their own efforts), but households can be radically unequal in power. The perspective of "one dollar, one vote" makes it clear that even in a competitive economy the households with the most dollars will have the most influence over resource allocation. Mainstream micro economics has never been very happy with its theory of imperfect competition. In fact, oligopoly theory has always been something of a shambles, and monopolies are presumed to be as rare as perfectly competitive firms.

The point is, wherever you look in mainstream economics, what you see is basically acceptance of the power structure as is. Even the emphasis on antitrust constraint on power in conventional industrial organization theory and practice is being diluted. Judge Robert Bork, for example, wrote a book in the late 1970s called *The Antitrust Paradox* in which he said, "The thesis of this book has been that modern antitrust has so decayed that the policy is no longer intellectually respectable. Some of it is not respectable as law; more of it is not respectable as economics; and now I wish to suggest that, because it pretends to one objective while frequently accomplishing its opposite, and because it too often forwards trends dangerous to our form of government and society, a great deal of antitrust is not even respectable as politics."[38] (Bork does not tell us his definition of "respectable." Respectability often attaches to class or status, in which case one might argue that status-bound respectability and antitrust are more or less antithetical.[39])

The Bork views just quoted appeared in 1978, and since then the deregulation movement has gained much ground. The notion that there is anything dangerous in concentrated economic power is distinctly out of fashion. If Bork does not exactly speak for the mainstream economists, they do increasingly strive to leave all allocation to what it pleases them to call the "free market." But in that market wealth is very unequal; and income, particularly after-tax income, is even more unequal than it was a decade ago. The mainstream seemingly strives to leave large firms and wealthy individuals fee to influence resource allocation (through production and distribution) as they will. Cries to repeal the Sherman Act are heard; never is a voice raised to repeal the Taft–Hartley Act. While no one can deny that power concentrations influence resource allocation, neoclassical economists view the existing distribution of power approximately the way physicists regard the law of gravity. It is part of "what is."

Mainstream economists, we have seen, affect an Olympian detachment—part of their positive economic analysis—which simply swallows the existing power structure whole. (Arguably, orthodox inquiry is served by the power structure.) It is buried in the ceteris paribus assumptions basic to conventional economic analysis—certainly micro economics. Equilibrium has always been imbued with normative overtones. "Clearing the market" is what counts.

Radical economists take a disapproving attitude toward the power system and have their own vision which they articulate of "the ideal power system," presumably some form of a classless society.

Institutional economists take a still different position. They are concerned, we have argued, with how the economy interacts with society. The economy is a valuating mechanism, not merely a price-setting mechanism. As such, institutionalists have always been concerned with how accurately and how effectively the economy transmits the preferences of its participants to those who are charged with "satisfying wants." Institutionalists argue that professional economists engage in the general discussion about how in light of changing societal values the total allocation system operates. (Presumably, their expertise gives them insights that others might not as readily acquire.) From Veblen's concern with the impact of "the vested interests" to Robert A. Brady's 1940s book, *Business as a System of Power*,[40] power has been a focal point for institutionalism. In 1989 Marc Tool and Warren Samuels edited a two-volume collection of essays by institutionalists called *The Economy as A System of Power and State, Society and Corporate Power*.[41] In short, from the beginning of American institutionalism to the present, explicit focus on the actual deployment of power in the economy has been a consistent concern of institutionalists. It is a subject that mainstream economists, in contrast, either ignore, assume away, or defang in some other convenient fashion.

This discussion of the flight from reality by micro economics has revolved around the failure to connect with the realities of concentrated power. Macro economics is similarly engaged in a flight from reality. Whatever John Maynard Keynes's faults and flaws—and we do not lack for economists anxious to point them out—he tried to look at the economy of his time as it actually existed and tried to explain it. His "underemployment equilibrium" had the enormous virtue of suggesting to the profession that equilibrium has no normative implications, a point institutionalists have always tried to make. The failure of the economy to employ its resources fully in the 1930s was not entirely unrelated to the concentration of power and the fixation on "letting free markets clear." (The Temporary National Economic Committee conducted extensive hearings based on the belief that in fact power had been badly misused.[42])

It is not without interest that today's rational expectations adherents pillory Keynesian theory for its failure to explain the stagflation of the 1970s. Their own explanation of the Great Depression—"labor markets failed to clear" from 1929 until 1940—strains credulity. (Alternatively they ask you to believe that the unemployed of the 1930s simply "preferred leisure".[43]) However far-fetched, this view has been rapturously embraced by mainstream economists eager to shed the interventionism that is inherent in Keynesian economics. Rational expectations is a way back to the pre-Keyenesian reliance on free markets. High rates of unemployment, like all other obstacles to reliance on the excessively simple models to which mainstream economics is addicted, have simply been defined away. Keynes worried about high unemployment rates. Now economists call them "natural."[44] Regressive movements in economics are nothing new. I previously termed this one "reinventing the square wheel."[45]

In short, concentrated power affects all resource allocation. Hence neither microeconomics nor macroeconomics can sweep it under the ceteris paribus rug (or the rational expectations rug).

Modern Institutionalists—Beyond Dissent

Our argument has been that institutionalists not only dissent from neoclassical economics but offer a view of their own in many areas. We have presented a distinctive institutionalist view on the question whether economics is a normative or a positive science, the question of whether economics is concerned with value or only price, on the role of the public sector, on judging economic performance, and on the impact of power.

In most of these areas we have made mention of a vast number of institutionalists, past and present. It is important to note that there is scarcely a field in modern economics that has not been considered by institutionalists, and in my judgment they have frequently contributed new insight and broken new ground. The institutionalist perspective has shown itself capable of fruitful application in many areas. This continues to be the case with the generation of institutionalists who have written in the recent past in the pages of the *Journal of Economic Issues* and elsewhere. One hesitates to list recent contributions by institutionalists because any such effort can be no more than illustrative.

A number of recent institutionalists, for example, have attempted to sharpen basic institutionalist concepts developed in earlier times and to redefine them so as to be more easily applied to the current scene. One concept that is crucial is the notion of instrumental value and what has come to be known as "social value theory." The historic institutionalist distinction between price and value has been given greater clarity by Marc Tool's formulation. Building on the work of Veblen, Dewey, Ayres, and Fagg Foster, Tool has integrated their work by defining the social value principle as involving behavior affirming ". . . the continuity of human life and [the] noninvidious re-creation of community through the instrumental use of knowledge."[46] Applying this definition prudently and insightfully,

Tool has analyzed environmental issues, questions of discrimination, the role of women, and a whole host of current issues with institutionalist tools, and, in the process, demonstrated anew their usefulness and analytic power.

Similarly, Jerry Petr made a notable contribution to the ability of institutionalists to clarify for noninstitutionalists the fundamentals of institutionalism. In a brief paper he distilled many of the essential characteristics of institutionalism. He asserted that institutionalist value theory when applied leads thereby to economic policy that is values-driven, process-oriented, instrumental, evolutionary, activist, fact-based, technologically focused, holistic, nondogmatic, and democratic.[47] By carefully characterizing the implications of each of them for economic policy Petr, arguably, was able to facilitate considerably the task confronting all institutionalists of conveying to noninstitutionalists what institutionalism means.

In a similarly insightful passage Edythe Miller recently noted, "Neoclassical economic thought rests upon a series of dualisms. Thus it puts a clear separation, for example, between: essence and existence, reason and experience, theory and practice, thought and action, knowing and doing, means and ends, deduction and induction, and normative and positive. Institutional theory rejects these dichotomizations. This, of course, is part of institutionalism's heritage from John Dewey, to whom it consistently has acknowledged its debt."[48] If one of the major hurdles to greater visibility for institutionalism has been an inability to state the essence of institutionalism with sufficient compactness and clarity, the work of Tool, Petr, and Miller should be of great value. In the same vein my own efforts, alluded to earlier, at distinguishing allocation from valuation, and in identifying what I have called "the value floor," "the collective ought," and "the higher efficiency," have been efforts at clarifying institutionalist value theory and sharpening the emphasis there placed on democratic consensus and the long-run impact of open information channels on such consensus for the development of a meaningful normative science.[49]

A major theme in institutionalism has always revolved around the distinction between institutions and technology. Both have received renewed attention from institutionalists in recent years. Water C. Neale has provided greater specificity to the term *institutions* by reminding us that the fundamental Veblenian contrast (the "dichotomy") was between problem-solving (hence forward-looking) activity (instrumental or technological) and belief systems or attitudes that are essentially backward looking (ceremonial.) He reminds us that certain aspects of institutions can indeed be useful in solving problems and, in the process, he sharpens a fundamental institutionalist tenet.[50]

In a closely related effort, Paul D. Bush has employed the concept of "ceremonial encapsulation" to generate greater precision and specificity in the previous view of the way in which institutions resist incorporating the fruits of technological progress into everyday life. The notion of ceremonial encapsulation goes considerably beyond Ogburn's "cultural lag" or Ayres' "past-binding" behavior to develop a variety of ways in which modern societies attempt to contain the threat to entrenched interests and beliefs represented by new technology.[51]

Finally, Milton D. Lower has examined the other half of the basic dichotomy by reconsidering the importance for institutionalism of technological progress. Drawing on the work of earlier institutionalists he restates what is meant by "the technological life process" and focuses attention once more on economic theory as problem-solving activity directed at developing useful public policy. In this he reminds us, as does Bush, that public policy is in actuality an effort at directing cultural change (the incorporation of new technology into an established social order) and so always involves not just "technological change" but equally important "institutional adjustment."[52]

Institutionalists have not only been concerned in recent years to sharpen basic concepts but they have been exploring the history of institutionalism with a view to increasing both our understanding of what the founders of institutionalism contributed and how that contribution can most meaningfully be applied to current economic analysis. In this connection mention may be made of Anne Mayhew's reexamination of the origins of institutionalism in rejection of "natural law" and the incorporation of Darwinian thought into the methods and perceptions of social processes[53]; and Philip Mirowski's careful review of the philosophical roots of institutionalism in pragmatism and a line of thought found in the works of Pierce through Dewey, as opposed to the Cartesian tradition.[54] Finally we may note Yngve Ramstad's careful reassessment of John R. Commons, arguably the most neglected of the founders of institutionalism. Ramstad finds that interpreting Commons's work in holistic terms, to use Gruchy's term, makes much of the apparent confusion in Commons's work clearer. His conclusion that Commons's central assertion was that collective control of individual transactions is "the general and dominant feature of economic life" is a provocative way of integrating Commons's work into other aspects of the institutionalist approach, thereby enriching the potential application of this approach to current policy challenges.[55]

Application of institutionalist analysis has been made to the various fields of economics. Edythe Miller and Harry Trebing have advanced institutionalist assessment of the question of public utility regulation and the deregulation movement generally. Miller has argued that in public utility regulation, "The theories that guide contemporary public policy are uninformed by any concept of instrumental efficiency. . . ."[56] Trebing has concluded that "market power persists and the control of such power remains a principal task of regulation,"[57] thereby echoing a long-standing institutional concern. Examining the issues in the deregulation debate from an institutionalist perspective, he concluded that in the process of confronting the challenges posed by this debate "a revitalized public interest theory of regulation will emerge. The neo-institutionalists seem uniquely qualified to assume a pivotal role in this effort."[58]

In industrial organization John Munkirs and William Dugger have both made seminal contributions. Munkirs at the empirical level has provided evidence to show that the American economy is dominated by 12 financial institutions and 26 nonfinancial institutions. Together they constitute what he calls Centralized Private Sector Planning (CPSP).[59] Utilizing his empirical observations at the theoretical level, he (along with James Sturgeon) has offered the view that the conventional theory of oligopolistic competition ought in fact to be reversed. CPSP leads to "oligopolistic cooperation" . . . "fewness of sellers, structural intradependence, and personal/psychological interplay between decision makers lead to cooperation."[60] In a similar vein Dugger has analyzed the growth in corporate economic power, relating it to the decline in economic performance,[61] and ultimately has broadened his scope to include the burgeoning impact internationally of large multinational corporations—he calls them "imperial conglomerates."[62]

In the field of agriculture Gregory Hayden demonstrated that while the ever-changing technology of agriculture and the institutional impediments to easy continued integration of the agricultural economy into the rest of society may have changed considerably since Ayres, let alone Veblen, wrote, the institutional approach can be applied with advantage to analysis of the complex and significant difficulties besetting agriculture today. Hayden wrote, ". . . there is probably nothing that more exemplifies the Veblenian dichotomy, which distinguishes between substantive and pecuniary valuation, than the policies applied to agriculture and rural communities."[63]

In many ways the field of development economics has from its outset ineluctably been institutionalist even at the hands of noninstitutionalists. Here it is impossible not to consider "economic" problems in broader societal context. Wendell Gordon, James Street, and Dilmus James have continued to enrich this tradition. Gordon has recently stressed anew the importance of the international transfer of technology to the development process and the barriers to this transfer, concluding that ultimately each country must find its own way of adapting institutionally so as to benefit from imported advanced technology.[64] An implication may well be that proffered suggestions for institutional adaptation from outside, however well intentioned, may be self-defeating. In related work, Street and James have analyzed Latin American development problems at length, most notably perhaps in assessing the relationship between institutionalist and "structuralist" views on obstacles to economic development. The latter reflects the path-breaking work of Raul Prebisch. For our purposes we may note that they find that both these approaches attack conventional neoclassical approaches to economic development and both are essentially holistic.[65]

In macroeconomic analysis Wallace Petersen has contributed major insights both for institutionalists and noninstitutionalists. His analysis of macroproblems is consistently predicated on his assertion of the critical role played by concentrated economic power in the modern economy. In a book-length study he argued that our economy is "overloaded." Our recent crises involving both unemployment and inflation were caused by fundamental structural flaws in the system—the sum of the claims against output by various economic agents are currently greater than the capacity of the system to produce output.[66] More recently he has argued that macroeconomics must explain prices as well as employment and output, and that Keynesian theory in the end offers the means for explaining all three, provided the "New Classical Economics" can be seen for what it is. (Among other things, this will require that we stop regarding unemployment as "natural."[67]) Peterson has argued that a "workable incomes policy" offers the best hope of stabilizing the economy, containing economic power, and restricting the economy's "load" to what it can bear.[68]

Finally we mention the work of two other institutionalists. David Hamilton has reminded us yet again of the technological possibility of confronting one of the initial challenges that led to the view of economics as a "normative science." He has argued that we could raise the standard of living of those who live below the poverty line, if, institutionally, we chose to do so.[69] If thereby Hamilton has brought institutionalism back to one of its original concerns, James Swaney has utilized the institutionalist framework to confront a concern that may yet blunt the innate optimism that suffuses much of institutional thought: the prospect of nuclear annihilation. In a sobering conclusion, Swaney wrote, "If economics is to contribute to resolving . . . grave resource allocation problems, less optimism and more realism are called for. Does technology have a twist that will end it all, or will communication and reason triumph over the pursuit of invidious distribution and power? The technological process holds the long-term solution, but human will must first prevail over imbecile institutions. Otherwise, in the short-run we are all dead."[70]

On this sobering note we end our survey of what some representative institutionalists have been writing recently. As noted at the outset, any such survey must be incomplete. It is included only to suggest that on a wide variety of fronts modern institutionalists are applying the tools of institutionalism to the daunting challenges current economies are producing. In the process, we assert that, far from contenting themselves with "mere dissent," institutionalists are in fact in the forefront of those who believe that the preeminent obligation of economists is to produce better economic policy so as genuinely to enhance the life process.

We have by no means exhausted the examples one could mention of the distinctiveness and the potential usefulness of the institutionalist approach applied to virtually all areas where economic analysis is helpful.

A Paradigmatic Summary

As we noted earlier, the perennial charge to institutionalists has been, "If you don't like the neo-classical paradigm, don't simply criticize it; give us a better one."[71] We have shown that an institutionalist alternative paradigm is available. Figure 2-1 represents an effort I made some time ago to summarize what I believe to be some of the key elements in the institutionalist paradigm and to contrast it both with the mainstream economic paradigm and the prevailing political science paradigm.[72] It summarizes many of the points we have been discussing here. Critically, it most especially focuses on the impact of power on the economy.

To bring the paradigm of institutionalism into sharper focus it is instructive to compare its tenets and characteristics with those of mainstream economists and with political scientists. Mainstream economists and political scientists approach their subject from reverse premises. Political scientists have notions of what is the "ideal" democratic polity, but they devote their effort and attention, we gather, to assessing the operation of the actual polity. While there are notions of "the ideal democratic polity" it is not clear that they are as precise, for normative analysis, as the Smithian competitive model, although the intrusion of modern technology makes the ideal mainstream competitive model more ambiguous than many discussions of it would suggest. In any case, neoclassical economists in contrast customarily make sufficient assumptions to enable them to equate the real world with their ideal world (or at least the world of "stylized facts"), and then devote themselves excessively if not totally to how

	Political Economy: *Mainstream economics*	Political Economy: *Institutionalism*	*Political science*
Basic outlook	1) Invisible Hand (with imperfections) 2) Harmony	1) Cultural conditioning with technological dynamic 2) Conflict	1) Cultural conditioning 2) Conflict
Basic function of system	Allocate scarce resources	Express emergent values of participants through allocative decisions	Allocate values authoritatively
Basic mechanism	Market prices	Interactive value system	Interactive value system
Assumptions:	1) Primarily competitive interaction 2) Automaticity	1) Power distorts value system 2) Values result from interaction of system and participants	1) Power distorts value system 2) Values result from interaction of system and participants
Motivation	Self-interest	Perceived self-interest	Perceived self-interest
Assumed distribution of decision-making authority	One dollar = one vote	Control over constellations of dollar votes, reflecting concentrated wealth and power	Control over constellations of one man, one vote reflecting concentrated wealth and power
Objective of system	The end: market equilibrium (all markets cleared)	End-in-view: progress of economy consonant with emergent community values	End-in-view: progress of polity consonant with emergent community values
"Ideal" system	Pure competition	Decision-making process sensitive to changing views of participants in economic process	Decision-making process sensitive to changing views of participants in the political process
Ultimate arbiter of actual system	Consumer sovereignty plus technological progress	Technological change limited by concentrated power and big producer sovereignty	Concentrated power and big unit sovereignty
Result:	Efficiency and progress through producer acquiescence	Manipulated consumer	Manipulated voters
Basic units in system	Households, firms	Individuals	Individuals
Corollary:	Households and firms express demands (wants) and supplies (costs) through prices with optimal technological productivity	Both households' and firms' decisions are the result of power deployment by individuals	All political units' decisions are the result of power deployment by individuals
Result:	Socially ideal resource allocation	X-inefficiency; x-disutility corrupt results of ideal systems (above)	Actual allocation of values deviates from ideal system (above)
Obstacle:	Imperfect knowledge of households and firms	Power blocs deliberately distort information flows	Power blocs deliberately distort information flows
Solution:	Assume it away	Improve information flows to individuals	Improve information flows to individuals
Welfare assumption	Competitive market equilibria define community welfare (subject to Pareto optimality constraint)	Community welfare as an "end" cannot be defined. The means for moving in the direction of greater community welfare can be discerned in the process	The public interest as an "end" cannot be defined. The means for moving in the direction of greater public interest can be discerned in the process
		There is a means–end continuum that enables the polity or the economy to progress along the continuum despite the absence of a definable absolute end.	

Figure 2-1. Three social science paradigms.

resources are allocated in their highly simplified world. (This is "deductive analysis.")

Institutionalists, on the other hand, try to be realistic: they ask, "How can we enable participants in the economy to be optimally informed?" and "What is required for them to be able to transmit their views optimally through the economy?" They are concerned with mechanisms in the economy that distort the creation and revelation of preferences, as well as with assessing professionally the current status of the preferences. Unlike the radical economists they don't necessarily pronounce for these participants what would be ideal, but they attempt to focus on the implications of extant preferences (emergent value) in all its dimensions—efficiency, security, freedom, compassion, equity, and so on. But as we have been at pains to note, institutionalists are concerned that power concentration leads to withheld information, distorted information, deliberate confusion of participants—in short, to clogged production and distribution channels. All of this means that an economy (even a "free market economy") can manifest a genuine malallocation of resources. Thus the performance of the economy of the real world diverges, as all realize, from the mainstream ideal, but the sources of the divergence are more often than not buried so deeply in the ceteris paribus assumptions as to prevent many critical problems ever being confronted. (Theory as "benchmark theory" becomes an end in itself.)

Freeing the economy through an open interactive process with society to permit the emergence and transmission of societal values in a dynamic context is the objective of the economy as seen by institutionalists. The essential institutionalist expectation, of course, is that in such a world the values ultimately emerging from a democratic learning process will be "instrumental"—that is, noninvidious. Thus the institutionalist's social value principle has a parallel in political science: a representative democracy emerges by improving the ability of the polity to reflect and transmit the enlightened democratic decisions of well-informed participants in the political process. In neither context is the current ideal brought closer instantaneously or without difficulty or error. Concentrated power most particularly is always an obstacle.

In this connection, in an earlier article I noted, "The economy itself and the choices it offers its participants are both affected by power concentrations. Moreover, the total choosing system is partly economic (dollar votes), and partly political (ballot box votes), and *both* operate differently than they would were power and wealth not concentrated. It is as inappropriate to focus on 'free markets' as though markets really were free (making a few ancillary comments about 'imperfections'), as it would be to focus on free elections, making a few ancillary comments about imperfections in the democratic process."[73]

Several other observations concerning the paradigm, suggested by Figure 2-1, are pertinent. Earlier we suggested that there is much in the approach of modern political science theory that with profit could serve as an example to modern economic theorists. (The reverse notion, that the techniques of microeconomic theory could be fruitfully applied to political science, has already been explored in detail. Readers can judge the usefulness of this approach in, for example, Anthony Downs's study, *An Economic Theory of Democracy*.[74]) The major insight of the three paradigms presented is that both institutionalists and political scientists have developed paradigms designed more or less to describe the world in which we live. That would appear to be the appropriate world to look at if we are to develop public policy that is helpful in ameliorating its problems. We have focused at some length on the inadequacies of the assumptions of mainstream micro theory in this respect.

Because the focus is necessarily on allocation the emphasis in Figure 2-1 is more on micro economics than macro economics. But we have already suggested that Keynesian economics, at least, was a major effort to focus on the macro economy as in fact it operates and to consider how its performance can be improved. Modern so-called "new-classical" economics is based on a return to the world of classical economics and is premised on two critical assumptions: rational expectations and "efficient markets"—that is, markets that clear automatically. May we just say that this makes the job of institutionalists easier. Because new classical economics returns macro economics to the cocoon from which Keynes attempted to spring it, the charges institutionalists level at mainstream micro economics are equally applicable to the new macro economics. Institutionalists, therefore, look with jaundiced eye at the efforts of the new classical economists to undo Keynes: while he focused on trying to explain the high levels of unemployment we in fact had in the 1930s, the new classical economists simply tell us the economy suffers from ever more "natural unemployment"[75] and were we to be so foolish as to try and eliminate it we would only bring on accelerating inflation. Another vexing problem has been defined away. (It has never been clear to me why ever more "natural unemployment" is consistent with efficient markets, but *any* rise in the inflation rate is not. An institutionalist might suspect that value judgments are sneaking into the positive science that is mainstream economics!)

The implication of analyzing these three paradigms is clear. The mainstream economic paradigm does not offer a fruitful or relevant solution for economic problems. It has become a critical part of the problem. It offers a way to avoid facing problems. Beyond this overarching conclusion, at least three observations seem appropriate. First, there are clearly many parallels between the assumptions, the perspective, the attitudes, and the results that appear to emerge from the institutionalist paradigm and the political science paradigm. A prime reason for this is our second observation: whatever bows to reality mainstream economics may make, they have never gotten over the theory-as-benchmark perspective which in micro economics continues to result in excessive attention to models of pure and mostly perfect competition. In macro economics it has resulted in the reincarnation of the classical assumption of full employment in our latest and currently faddish escape from reality—rational expectations. In these and other ways economics—both micro and macro—continues to ignore the reality of power in the real world.

The third observation emerging from our comparison of these paradigms is that whatever the limitations of both institutionalism and political science, they do both attempt to confront the deployment of power in both the economy and the polity as in fact it is. We can simplify the world all we want, but if the result is to analyze a world that does not even remotely exist, useful policy is scarcely going to emerge from the theory. As we have been at pains to point out, a peculiarity of mainstream economic theory is its penchant for assuming away the very problems that useful policy would necessarily have to confront, such as unemployment, low productivity, instability, and so on.

Contemplating the Future

Some years ago I commented, "Among the social sciences, economics has long suffered from a superiority complex. The economists's view of his field has been of a discipline that was rigorous and precise, with an advanced and pragmatic methodology leading to a highly developed theoretical structure. All this left far behind the imprecise and murky theoretical strivings of political scientists, sociologists, anthropologists, and historians.

"The promised land which economic analysis made possible was known as equilibrium . . . [economists] embraced mathematics as the true methodological Messiah come at last, . . . measured all visibly quantifiable variables, developed models for all problems, and achieved intellectual orgasm through the contemplation of the possibilities of the electronic computer. [Thus they] enshrined quantification. . . ."[76]

I have not seen any reason to alter this picture of how mainstream economists regard themselves and their discipline. The question that must be asked, however, is whether this superiority complex is in any way justified. It is probably true that conventional economic theory has a degree of abstraction and rigor that most other social sciences cannot claim.[77] But it is achieved by grossly oversimplifying reality through convenient assumptions that severely reduce the applicability of economic theory to problems in the real world. Increasingly graduate students in economics "tell stories." They are drawn to highly esoteric areas: for example, excessively unrealistic game theory, simulation techniques, and endlessly adumbrated econometric modeling of the most abstruse sorts. Today mainstream economists pillory Keynesian theory for failing to explain the inflation or stagflation of the 1970s and without the slightest blush offer us theory or models that rarely pretend to explain *anything* in the real world.

Despite economists' feelings of superiority, the question must be asked, "How good a job is the discipline doing, if success is measured in terms of its ability successfully to confront economic problems?" Arguably economists are doing no better and very possibly a good deal worse than they did 50 years ago in coping with the severe economic challenges posed by modern economies. Unacceptably high long-run levels of unemployment, inflation, and domestic debt; trade imbalance; Third World debt; unacceptably unstable domestic economic performance and exchange rates; and unacceptably low productivity and economic growth—all these are clearly enormous challenges to our most sophisticated efforts to generate economic insight. If an economist wants to argue that all these represent political as well as economic challenges, the argument simply plays into the hands of the institutionalist who argues that political economy must be designed to cope with economic problems that are ineluctably presented to us within a political and social framework. To ignore this is to fail to develop policy which can be pragmatically applied to real-world situations.

I am not very optimistic about the future for economics. Everything that I have seen in the last decade suggests a further retreat from coping with the real world rather than any effort to make economic theory more realistic and more relevant. In micro economics, in addition to the perennial overemphasis on the wonders of pure competition, we have the theory of contestable markets, public choice theory, and other efforts to suggest either that the economy is not so bad or that no matter how bad it may be, efforts at improving it will only make it worse. In macro economics we have probably seen the worst of supply-side economics; certainly the experience of the 1980s did little to give it credence. If one thinks about it, the whole notion that entrepreneurial incentives should be as fragile as the supply-side argument suggests, undercuts the basic rationale of capitalism rather severely. As for monetarism and rational expectations, they try, each in their own way, to suggest that either our macro problems can correct themselves if left alone, or that—as is the case with micro problems—intervention can only make them worse. The notion of a "natural tendency to equilibrium" in a long run that is unspecifiedly long gets a good deal of attention nowdays. It is perhaps logically irrefutable, but practically it becomes a rationalization for accepting the status quo regardless of how unsatisfactory it may be even by mainstream standards prevailing before the arrival of the New Classical Economics.

I have suggested along the way that institutionalists basically believe that we need to improve our techniques for ascertaining what the participants in the economy want to achieve and for enabling them to achieve it. Discerning the implications of technological progress for the life pro cess and freeing the economy to share the fruits of progress widely—this is the work of economic analysis as seen from the perspective of the institutionalist.

Acknowledgments

I would like to thank Barry Clark, Marc Tool, and Warren Samuels for helpful comments on earlier drafts. (To Tool in particular—as is often the case—I own an enormours debt of gratitide for reading and commenting insightfully and generously on several drafts of this chapter.) An earlier version of the article was delivered in the spring of 1988 at a seminar at the University of Wisconsin in Madison and again at the Fachhochschule Rheinland-Pfalz in Worms, Federal Republic of Germany, in the spring of 1989. Parts of the article were also presented at the Universities of Siena, Italy and Osijek, Yugoslavia, in the spring of 1989.

Notes

1. *Cf. Evolutionary Economics: Volume I Foundations of Institutional Thought, Journal of Economic Issues* 21 (September 1987) and *Evolutionary Economics Volume II, Institutional Theory and Policy, Journal of Economic Issues* 21 (December 1978). Both were republished in 1988 by M.E. Sharpe, Inc., Armonk, New York.

2. This is the view of Joseph Dorfman as expressed in his introduction to Walton H. Hamilton, *Industrial Policy and Institutionalism, Selected Essays* (Clifton, NJ: Augustus M. Kelley, 1974), p. 25. For another and interesting (and more recent) account of the origins of institutionalism *cf.* Anne Mayhew, "The Beginnings of Institutionalism," *Journal of Economic Issues* 21 (September 1987): 971–998.

3. Quoted in *ibid.*, p. 27.

4. *Ibid.*, p. 28, footnote 29.

5. John R. Commons, *Institutional Economics: Its Place In Political Economy*, Two volumes published in one. (Madison: University of Wisconsin Press, 1934 and 1959).

6. Wesley Clair Mitchell, *Types of Economic Theory: From Mercantilism to Institutionalism*, Transcriptions of Mitchell's Lectures issued in mimeograph form in 1949. (New York: Augustus M. Kelley, 1967).

7. *Cf.*, for example, P.A. Klein, "Economics: Allocation or Valuation?" *Journal of Economic Issues* 8 (December 1974): 785–811; Marc R. Tool, *The Discretionary Economy* (Santa Monica, CA: Goodyear, 1979); Wendell Gordon, *Institutional Economics, The Changing System* (Austin and London: The University of Texas Press, 1980); Allan Gruchy, *The Reconstruction of Economics* (New York: Greenwood Press, 1987); Jerry Petr, "Fundamentals of an Institutional Perspective," *Journal of Economic Issues* 18 (March 1984): 1–17; Gunnar Myrdal, "Institutional Economics," *Journal of Economic Issues* 12 (December 1978) 771–784; Marc R. Tool, ed., Two volume study published as the September and December 1988 issues of the *Journal of Economic Issues*, republished by M.E. Sharpe; and Wendell Gordon and John Adams, *Economics as a Social Science: An Evolutionary Approach* (Riverdale, MD: Riverdale Press, 1989).

8. Thorstein Veblen, *The Place of Science in Modern Civilization* (New York: Russell and Russell, 1961), pp. 73–74.

9. All these themes are developed extensively. *Cf.*, for example, not only Veblen's most famous book, *The Theory of The Leisure Class*, in which he introduces many of his basic ideas (republished New York: New American Library, 1953) but also *The Theory of Business Enterprise* (New York: Scribner, 1904; Clifton, NJ: Augustus M. Kelley, 1975); *The Instinct of Workmanship and the State of the Industrial Arts* (New York: Macmillan, 1914); *The Vested Interests and the Common Man, The Modern Point of View and the New Order*, 1919 (republished New York: Augustus M. Kelley, 1964); and *Absentree Ownership and Business Enterprise in Recent Times: The Case of America* (New York: Viking, 1923, republished 1945). In addition to these books, these ideas are discussed in several published collections of Veblen's essays, for example, *The Place of Science in Modern Civilization, op. cit.*

10. The view that Mitchell took toward business cycles developed over many years. This particular (and well-known) phrase is from the definition of cycles that occurs in Authur F. Burns and Wesley Clair Mitchell, *Measuring Business Cycles* (New York: National Bureau of Economic Reasearch, 1946), p. 2. For a discussion of the relationship between Mitchell's institutionalism and his work on business cycles *cf.* Philip A. Klein, "The Neglected Institutionalism of Wesley Clair Mitchell: The Theoretical Basis for Business Cycle Indicators," *Journal of Economic Issues* 17 (December 1983): 867–898.

11. *Cf.*, Victor Zarnowitz in an article on Mitchell in *International Encyclopedia of Social Sciences*, 1968, p. 373.

12. Joseph Dorfman in an article on Commons in *International Encyclopedia of Sciences*, 1968, p. 23.

13. *Cf.*, among many other writings principally Clarence E. Ayres, *The Theory of Economic Progress* (Chapel Hill: The University of North Carolina Press, 1944); *The Industrial Economy* (New York: Houghton Mifflin Company, 1952); *Toward A Reasonable Society* (Austin: University of Texas Press, 1961). For Dewey's instrumental theory of value, *cf.* John Dewey, *Theory of Valuation* (Chicago: University of Chicago Press, 1939).

14. John S. Gambs, *Beyond Supply and Demand* (Westport, CT: Greenwood Press, 1976 [1946]).

15. Allan G. Gruchy, *Modern Economic Thought, The American Contribution* (New York: Prentice-Hall, 1947). *Cf.* also Philip A. Klein, "A Reconsideration of Holistic Economics," in

John Adams, ed., *Essays in Honor of Allan Gruchy* (Boston: Martinus Nijhoff, Publisher, 1980), pp. 45–58.

16. Allan G. Gruchy, *Contemporary Economic Thought: The Contribution of Neo-Institutional Economics* (Clifton, NJ: Augustus M. Kelley, 1972).

17. Allan G. Gruchy, *The Reconstruction of Economics: An Analsis of the Fundamentals of Institutional Economics* (New York: Greenwood Press, 1987).

18. *Cf.*, for example, Gunnar Myrdal, *Against the Wind; Critical Essays on Economics* (London: Macmillan, 1974). Much earlier in his career Myrdal, the economist trained in the Swedish school, had demonstrated his breadth as a social science in his classic, *An American Dilemma*, published in 1944. Widely regarded at the time as "a book on sociology written by a trained economist," it might have been described by an institutionalist as a book about economic problems (among others) which paid attention to class and race as well as income and wealth distribution. Consider in contast a treatise that contemplated the welfare and status of the black in the United States in the 1940s but hewed to the constraint of Pareto optimality.

19. John Kenneth Galbraith has published widely. Among his works: *The Affluent Society* (First edition, 1958; second edition, Boston: Houghton Mifflin Company, 1969); *The New Industrial State* (Boston: Houghton Mifflin Company, 1967); *Economics and the Public Purpose* (Boston: Houghton Mifflin Company 1973); *The Anatomy of Power* (Boston: Houghton Mifflin Company, 1983).

20. Robert Heilbroner, too, has written extensively. Among his books are *The Worldly Philosophers* (New York: Simon and Schuster, 1953); *An Inquiry Into the Human Prospect* (New York: W.W. Norton, 1974); *Business Civilization In Decline* (New York: W.W. Norton, 1976); *Beyond Boom and Crash* (New York: W.W. Norton, 1976); *The Nature and Logic of Capitalism* (New York: W.W. Norton, 1985); *Behind the Veil of Economics* (New York: W.W. Norton, 1988).

21. Robert Lekachman in "Comment on P.A. Klein's 'Demand Theory and the Economist's Propensity to Assume," ' *Journal of Economic Issues* 7 (June 1973): 243.

22. Lionel Robbins, *An Essay on the Nature and Significance of Economic Science* (London: Macmillan and Company, Ltd., 1946), p. 16.

23. *Ibid.*, p. viii.

24. This example is from P.A. Klein, "Institutionalist Reflections on the Role of The Public Sector," *Journal of Economic Issues* 18 (March 1984): 58.

25. Quoted in Donald A. Strickland, *Scientists in Politics: The Atomic Scientists Movement, 1945–46* (Layfayette, IN: Purdue University Studies, 1968), p. 38. *Cf.*, also P.A. Klein, "Of Paradigms and Politics," *Journal of Economic Issues* (June 1988: pp. 435–441).

26. *Cf.*, for example, James M. Buchanan and Gordon Tullock, *The Calculus of Consent* (Ann Arbor: The University of Michigan Press, 1962); James M. Buchanan, *Public Finance in the Democratic Process* (Chapel Hill: University of North Carolina Press, 1967); and James M. Buchanan and R.D. Tollison, *Theory of Public Choice* (Ann Arbor: University of Michigan Press, 1972).

27. Some years a suggestion, known as the "Hicks–Kaldor Compensation Principle," was introduced into economic discourse. If the persons who gain gain sufficiently so that they could recompense those who lose to their satisfaction and still have some gain, the change is a Pareto optimum, even if, of course, the suggested transaction remains uncarried out. It is a cosmetic mathematical improvement designed to make Pareto optimality appear more measurable, even though, of course, it is not. (For a recent discussion of this point *cf.* Edythe S. Miller, "Economic Folklore and Social Realities," *Journal of Economic Issues* 23 (June 1989): 339–356.

28. Kenneth Arrow, *Social Choice and Individual Values*, 2nd ed. (New York: John Wiley and Sons, 1963), p. 106. I discussed this point at some length in P.A. Klein, "Economics: Allocation or Valuation?" *Journal of Economic Issues* 7 (December 1974): 797.

29. As I noted in the earlier study, however, "Arrow goes on to note that this standard view has been attacked for its lack of realism by Veblen, Frank Knight, J.M. Clark, and others" (*Ibid.*, footnote 25, p. 807). Arrow made the comment originally in 1963; I commented on his comment in 1974, and to my knowledge no mainstream economist has been perturbed about this matter in the intervening years. The institutionalist objections discussed in the text are, in our view, still valid.

30. Clarence E. Ayres, *The Theory of Economic Progress* (Chapel, Hill: The University of North Carolina Press, 1944), pp. 84–85. (Lionel Robbins once said that he could not make any sense out of this statement. Mainstream economists have been confused about this for many years. As a graduate student I was forced to read John R. Hicks's book, *Value and Capital*. My immediate reaction was that this book was not about value and capital at all, but about price and capital. What mainstream economics often calls value theory is only price theory.)

31. Thorstein Veblen, *The Place of Science in Modern Civilization* (New York: Russell and Russell, 1919, 1961), p. 70. It is quoted by Clarence Ayres on the Frontpiece, *ibid.*

32. *Cf.* "Institutionalist Reflections on the Role of the Public Sector," *op. cit.*, pp. 58–60. Reprinted in M.R. Tool and W.J. Samuels, ed., *The Methodology of Economic Thought*, 2nd ed. (New Brunswick: Transactions Publishers, 1989), pp. 541–564.

33. It is necessary to clarify the terminology. It has become common for institutionalists to follow Allan Gruchy in referring to the economy as both an allocating and a provisioning entity. (Gruchy has written, "A short definition of economics from the institutionalist point of view is that it is the science of social provisioning." [*Cf.* Allan G. Gruchy, *The Reconstruction of Economics*, *op. cit.*, p. 21.) This terminology is designed to convey the fundamental institutionalist insistence on the view that in any realistic market-oriented economy some resources are allocated via market forces and some through decisions made in the public sector. For a good many years I have included both decision-making routes by referring to "the total allocational thrust of the economy" rather than merely to the part of allocation mainstream economics is mostly concerned about (and which they call simply "allocation" for which read "market allocation"). In the institutionalist perspective, as I see it, total allocation has never been carried out solely by the market since the initial public expenditure was made based on social welfare criteria rather than individual firm profit criteria. In conforming to recent usage by referring to both "allocation and provisioning" I mean to encompass precisely what earlier I have included in the notion "total allocation." On occasion, the term "total allocational thrust of society" appears in the text and means "allocation and provisioning" in Gruchy's usage.

34. I discussed this point at some length in *ibid.*, p. 60.

35. This section is based on an earlier article of mine. *Cf.*, footnote 34.

36. *Ibid.*, pp. 63–65.

37. This section is based heavily on P.A. Klein, "Power and Economic Performance: The Institutionalist View," *Journal of Economic Issues* 21 (September 1987): 1341–1377.

38. Robert H. Bork, *The Antitrust Paradox* (New York: Basic Books, Inc., Publishers, 1978), p. 418. *Cf.*, also my discussion of this in "Changing Perspectives on the Factors of Production," *Journal of Economic Issues* 22 (September 1988): 795–809.

39. I am grateful to Marc Tool for pointing this out to me.

40. Robert A. Brady, *Business As A System of Power* (New York: Columbia University Press, 1943).

41. Marc Tool and Warren Samuels, eds., *The Economy As System of Power*, and *State, Society and Corporate Power* (New Brunswick: transaction Books, 1989). These are second revised editions of 1979 publications.

42. For a consideration of the TNEC hearings in this context, *cf.* Marc Tool, *The Discretionary Economy*.

43. Robert E. Lucas, Jr., "Understanding Business Cycles," in *Studies in Business Cycle Theory* (Cambridge, MA: The MIT Press, 1981).

44. The notion is now a key part of the mainstream methodological armor against encroachments by the actual world into the attractive world of economic theory so rudely (if as it turns out only temporarily—for half a century) jolted by Keynes. It was initially introduced in a pair of widely noted articles, one Milton Friedman's Presidential Address to the American Economic Association (*cf.* Milton Friedman, "The Role of Monetary Policy," *American Economic Review* 58 (March 1986): 1–17) and the other by Edmund Phelps (*cf.* Edmund S. Phelps, "Money Wage Dynamics and Labor Market Equilibrium," *Journal of Political Economy* 76 (July/August 1968): 687–711). In connection with the Freidman–Phelps hypothesis it is worth noting that Lucas has asserted that Friedman was still trying in his own—that is, "monetarist"—way to study cycles "along the line initiated by Mitchell," while Phelps' work represented "an attempt to complete the unity promised by the neoclassical synthesis." Despite their different perspectives, Lucas argues that they proved that *any* inflation rate was consistent with *any* unemployment rate (the italics are his) and that subsequent developments have proved "subversive of the main positive and policy presumptions underlying the neoclassical synthesis" (Robert Lucas, *ibid.*, pp. 282–283). Translation: attempting interventionist policy to reduce unemployment below its "natural rate" is futile. I discussed this hypothesis at some length earlier. (*Cf.* "What's Natural About Unemployment?" Paper presented at an American Economic Association–Association for Social Economics meeting, Chicago, December 1987. Published in Philip A. Klein, ed., *Analyzing Modern Business. Cycles, Essays Honoring Geoffrey H. Moore* (Armonk, NY: M.E. Sharpe, 1990).

45. P.A. Klein, "Reinventing the Square Wheel: A Behavioral Assessment of Inflation," in Benjamin Gilad and Stanley Kaish, eds., *Handbook of Behavioral Economics*, Volume B (Greenwich, CT: JAI Press, 1986).

46. Marc Tool, *Essays in Social Value Theory* (Armonk, NY: M.E. Sharpe, 1986), p. 10.

47. Jerry Petr, "Fundamentals of an Institutionalist Perspective," *Journal of Economic Issues* 18 (March 1984): 1–17.

48. Edythe S. Miller, "Economics for What? Economic Folklore and Social Realities," *Journal of Economic Issues* 23 (June 1989): 339–356.

49. P.A. Klein, "Economics: Allocation or Valuation?" *Journal of Economic Issues* 7 (December 1974): 785–811; and "Institutionalist Reflections on the Role of the Public Sector," *Journal of Economic Issues* 18 (March 1984): 43–68.

50. Walter C. Neale, "Institutions," *Journal of Economic Issues* 21 (September 1987): 1177–1206.

51. Paul D. Bush, "Theory of Institutional Change," *Journal of Economic Issues* 21 (September 1987): 1075–1116. The term "cultural lag" was popularized in the 1920s by William F. Ogburn, *Social Change* (New York: The Viking Press, 1950 [1922]), (*Cf.*, also Bush, p. 1113, footnote 46) "Past-binding" is Ayres's term. *Cf. Toward A Reasonable Society*, *op. cit.*, pp. 30, 137, and 233. *Cf.* also Bush, p. 1113, footnote 45.

52. Milton D. Lower, "The Concept of Technology Within the Institutionalist Perspective," *Journal of Economic Issues* 21 (September 1987): 1147–1176.

53. Anne Mayhew, "The Beginnings of Institutionalism," *Journal of Economic Issues* 21 (September 1987): 971–998.

54. Philip Mirowski, "The Philosphical Basis of Institutional Economics," *Journal of Economic Issues* 21 (September 1987): 1001–1038.

55. Yngve Ramstad, "The Scientific Methodology of John R. Commons," *Journal of Economic Issues* 20 (December 1986): 1067–1105.

56. Edythe Miller, Presidential Address, "Economic Folklore and Social Realities," *Journal of Economic Issues* 23 (June 1989): 339–356; Harry Trebing, "Public Utility Regulation: A Case Study in the Debate Over Effectiveness of Economic Regulation," *Journal of Economic Issues* 15 (March 1984): 223–250. *Cf.*, also Harry Trebing, "Apologetics of Deregulation in Energy and Telecommunications: An Institutionalist Assessment," *Journal of Economic Issues* 20 (September 1986): 613–632.

57. Trebing, *op. cit.*, 1984, p. 246.

58. *Ibid.*, p. 247.

59. John R. Munkirs, *The Transformation of American Capitalism: From Competitive Market Structures to Centralized Private Sector Planning* (Armonk, NY: M.E. Sharpe, 1985).

60. John R. Munkirs and James Sturgeon, "Oligopolistic Cooperation: Conceptual and Empirical Evidence of Market Structure Evolution," *Journal of Economic Issues* 19 (December 1985): 899–921.

61. William M. Dugger, *An Alternative to Economic Retrenchment* (Princeton: Petrocelli, 1984).

62. William M. Dugger, "Corporate Power and Economic Performance," in Wallace Peterson, ed. *Market Power and the Economy* (Boston: Kluwer Academic Publishers, 1988), pp. 83–108.

63. F. Gregory Hayden, "A Geobased Agricultural Policy," *Journal of Economic Issues* 18 (March 1984): 181–221.

64. Wendell Gordon, "The Implementation of Economic Development," *Journal of Economic Issues* 18 (March 1984): 295–313.

65. James Street and Dilmus James, "Institutionalism, Structuralism, and Dependency in Latin America," *Journal of Economic Issues* 16 (September 1982): 673–690.

66. Wallace G. Peterson, *Our Overloaded Economy* (Armonk, NY: M.E. Sharpe, 1982).

67. P.A. Klein, "What's Natural About Unemployment?," in Klein, *Essays in Honor of Geoffrey H. Moore*.

68. Wallace Peterson, "Concluding Observations," in Wallace Peterson, ed., *Market Power and the Economy* (Boston: Kluwer Academic Publishers, 1988).

69. David Hamilton, "The Myth is not the Reality: Income Maintenance and Welfare," *Journal of Economic Issues* 17 (March 1984): 143–158.

70. James A. Swaney, "The Future Be Damned: Economists' Optimism and Nuclear Proliferation," *Journal of Economic Issues* 18 (June 1984): 527–536.

71. The term has been widely employed since its use by Thomas S. Kuhn in *The Structure of Scientific Revolutions*, 2nd ed. (Chicago: University of Chicago Press, 1962 and 1970). Kuhn described a paradigm as ". . . a set of recurrent and quasi-standard illustrations of various theories in their conceptual, observational, and instrumental application" (p. 43). He further described a paradigm as "accepted principles and rules . . ." or "shared beliefs" (p. 43). Finally he termed a paradigm ". . . the search for a body of rules competent to constitute a given normal research tradition" and added that this search is "a source of continual and deep frustration" (p. 44). In the case of economics the mainstream does not appear frustrated at all with their paradigm. Their inflexibility is, however, a source of frustration to institutionalists.

72. P.A. Klein, "Confronting Power in Economics: A Pragmatic Evaluation," *Journal of Economic Issues* 14 (December 1980): 882–883.

73. *Ibid.*, p. 890.

74. Anthony Downs, *An Economic Theory of Democracy* (New York: The Free Press, 1973).

75. *Cf.* P.A. Klein, "What's Natural About Unemployment?" *op. cit.*

76. P.A. Klein, "Economics: Allocation or Valuation?" *Journal of Economic Issues* 7 (December 1974): 785–786.

77. For example, Ken Dennis has written on the alleged precision and rigor of economic theory in mathematical terms as is currently so widely practiced by mainstream economists. He has commented, "I have argued in this paper not that mathematical economics is impossible, but that its present claims to logical rigor are dubious, and that the construction of rigorous theories of human behavior is more difficult than has hitherto been acknowledged." *cf.* Ken Dennis, "Scientific Theory and the Problem of Translation," *Journal of Economic Issues* 16(3):691–712; and 16(4):1039–1062 Quotation is from the latter issue, p. 1060.

Commentary by Edythe S. Miller

Mainstream economics persistently has patronized, and even more often ignored, the institutional school of thought. Currently the orthodoxy seems, if anything, intent on defining institutionalism out of existence by cooptation, if my reading of the message of the "new institutional economics" is anywhere close to the mark. Philip A. Klein, in his chapter, attributes the dismissive attitude of the economic orthodoxy to its view that institutionalism is little, if indeed anything, other than dissent; its belief that institutional thought is characterized by neither original theoretical formulation nor unique analysis. It is Klein's contention, a contention to which I subscribe, that while institutional economics consistently has constituted —and appropriately so—a dissent from prevailing orthodoxy, that it also is distinguished by a positive contribution that places it "beyond [mere] dissent."

The task Klein sets himself in this work, then, is the distillation and elaboration of the affirmative paradigm of this heterodox school, a common core that has evolved from the time of its origin to the present. Accordingly, a major part of the work is devoted to a rich and diverse sampling of the institutionalist literature from its early turn-of-the-century beginnings through the efforts of an intermediate generation of students writing during the interwar and immediate post-World War II periods and culminating with the product of contemporary institutionalists publishing currently, most prominently in the *Journal of Economic Issues*. It is Klein's contention that successive generations of institutional economists consistently have adopted and adapted, applied and extended, a common, unified, and unifying core of institutional analysis in their work.

The Common Core of Institutional Thought

What, then, is this common core, this unifying paradigm? From its outset, Klein points out that in the work of such early institutional theorists as Thorstein Veblen, John R. Commons, and Wesley C. Mitchell, the focus of institutionalism was on process. This did not simply differentiate the method of institutionalism from the mechanistic, formulaic, formalistic equilibrium analysis of orthodoxy but also, and importantly, offered a unique world view: a perspective that illuminated the evolutionary nature of societies.

Upon this Darwinian field of vision, then, was superimposed a concept often characterized as the "Veblenian distinction"; that is, the differentiation of ceremonial and instrumental thought and behavior that also was to be central to subsequent institutional analysis. Thereafter, Clarence E. Ayres adopted from John Dewey and joined to these insights the complementary and compatible concept of instrumental value theory. A focus on the means–end continuum postured economics both as a dynamic and as a problem-solving discipline. These perceptions, at the heart of institutional economics from its very inception, have been used as the foundation, and extended and applied, by institutional economists ever since. Klein observes that institutional economists have left their mark on just about every subfield in the discipline, and he capsulizes some of their contributions.

Klein identifies five areas that he posits both as central to the institutional position and as commanding a high order of agreement among institutionalists. Thus, he maintains, the institutional paradigm apprehends economics as a normative, and not a positive, science; perceives it as a science of value, rather than price; accepts public sector provisioning for what it is, an example of the "collective ought"; evaluates economic performance by measures broader than those simply of narrow market allocative efficiency; and appreciates the effects of concentrated power on economic performance.

Classification and categorization are useful for purposes of exposition. Klein's format is both reasonable and well reasoned. It permits identification both of the fundamental institutionalist perspective and its basic approach to analysis. If Klein, however, is, as he seems to be, asserting a unanimity of view among institutionalists on these points, it seems to me that he is overreaching. While I myself am in substantial agreement with most of his conclusions, although I would put a different "spin" on some of them, it is more than probable that some of the positions taken will prove controversial among contemporary institutional economists. The normative–positive question, for example, is far from a settled one within institutionalist ranks.

Indeed, disagreements within institutionalism tend to be rather papered over in this treatment. Moreover, and possibly following from this, in his discussion of the work of contemporary institutionalists, Klein is more than magnanimous, he is uncritically accepting. This is surely Phil Klein in his mellow period.

In a recent article Klein maintains, very reasonably it seems to me, that the existence of a school of thought neither requires nor implies unanimity. He goes on to describe specific differences in the beliefs and conclusions of scholars in a number of well-accepted schools of thought. These differences, he correctly points out, have not resulted either in their dismemberment or their declassification as schools. He concludes that in like manner, and despite differences among institutionalists, there is sufficient agreement upon "core principles" to warrant the acceptance of this group of economists as a school of thought.[1] This essay appears to be in the nature of a follow-on, an attempt to identify those core principles. It is, on the whole, a worthy effort.

It may also be that Klein is attempting to filter out from the institutionalist literature what he sees as the "noise"; that is, to filter out disagreement on nonessentials to get to an agreed-upon fundamental nub of thought. If so, I applaud the purpose. It is important and worthwhile to endeavor to establish relationships and affinities, lines of thought that flow from and fit within a system of belief.

But it also should be recognized that institutionalists, if by no reason other than that of training, are a disputatious lot, unaccepting of authority, questioning, contentious. In fact, some intrainstitutional differences *are* about essentials. Institutional economists do not always agree, even upon what is fundamental. And how could it be otherwise? The content of institutional economics, unlike that of the mainstream, is not the stuff of copybook maxim and virtue that lends itself to an inevitable and invariant conclusion. Differences in perception and application are bound to occur. And that, in and of itself, has certain advantages. Disagreement may encourage the sharpening, the clarification and refinement of position, as well as the correction of misperception and mistake. The dominant school has no need to engage in this type of soul-searching and self-questioning. When the answer to all questions is previously given, and always the same, a comfortable professional rectitude is simple to achieve. Institutionalists do not have an all-purpose response to inquiry, such as that provided orthodoxy by the free market and the prescription of laissez-faire.

I previously have noted that the five categories that Klein has selected through which to present his topic are well suited to the task. It also should be remarked that different classificatory schemes could have and indeed, as noted by Klein, have been used to similar purpose and effect. The dilemma with which the adoption of almost any organizational framework presents us, however, is that the categorization itself subtly may influence the weight and significance afforded various factors in analysis. Moreover, to the extent that it does so, it may thereby influence not only sequence or configuration but also substance. That is, certain facets of a theory that one manner of classification of material will bring to the fore will, even in the absence of disagreement about what is fundamental, be treated almost in passing or not at all in another, simply by reason of the adoption of the alternative classificatory scheme.

Thus, there appear to me to be certain defining features of institutionalism that here receive no more than interstitial treatment. When I speak of defining features, I use the term in both a positive and negative sense. That is, I believe that these features provide at the same time a unique and original perspective and foundation that permeates every aspect of institutional thought and serve also to differentiate it from orthodoxy. I want to make it clear that what is presented in the section that follows is presented not as detraction from or alternative to Klein's systematization, but more for purposes of filling in or rounding out the pattern he weaves.

Some Epistemological and Methodological Considerations

Underlying institutional thought are theories of human learning and human nature, and of the individual-cultural relationship, that inform its every aspect including, and perhaps even most especially, its approach to problem solving. From at least the time of the celebrated European *methodenstreit* of the 19th century, a battle for supremacy between advocates of induction and deduction has been waged in economics. Needless to say, it has been a proper academic battle, the weapons of which are not bombs or bullets but scholarly books and papers. Its results, however, were to be profound. They were to be determinative of the methodology and epistemology of normal economic science from that time forward. And as abstruse and removed from the human life process as these categories may seem, they have had important effects on the public policy proposals of mainstream economics and the economic programs of nations.

The deductive method was the accepted method of classical and neoclassical economics, and remains the method of orthodoxy to this date. To the questions of "How do we learn? How do we know?" it answers: "We learn through the uncovering of a few simple truths, a small number of uniformities and regularities in nature that are amenable to a priori discovery. Once established, the logical inferences of these natural laws can be worked out and applied." This view of knowledge sees it, then, as the discovery of a normal order of things underlying real-world experience that directs the process and toward which things tend, or rather toward which they would tend if not impeded. The condition that results from the unimpeded operation of such natural laws is envisioned as an ideal system. In mainstream economics the "natural laws," it need hardly be remarked, include such "laws" of nature as those of supply and demand, the invisible hand, and laissez-faire, all inclining the system toward the economic equivalent of nirvana: that is, equilibrium. The "natural rate of unemployment" to which Klein makes reference is a further extension of the principle of normality, as are such "as if" formulations as rational expectations, efficient markets, and contestability theory.

The orthodox theory of human nature follows the same pattern. Individuals are rationally motivated by innate (for which, read "natural") preferences. The whole is the strict summation of the parts, with economic performance at any time being the strict summation of the acts of individual agents. Thus, the connection between individuals and society is interpreted as a one-way flow. In their roles as consumers and producers, humans are viewed as rational maximizers or at least as acting, whatever the perceived reality, "as if" they were rational maximizers. No recognition is given to the ways in which a culture affects individuals as in, for example, Commons's cognizance of the restraint, liberation, and expansion provided individual action by collective action,[2] or Klein's designation of a "collective ought" underlying the public response to social ills. These principles of normality dominate every branch of contemporary mainstream economic theory.

Contrast the institutional epistemology and theory of human nature. Following Dewey, institutionalism apprehends that we learn by doing—that is, experientially and experimentally—and that thought and action are essentially intertwined. Individual motivation and behavior are viewed as diverse: combining elements of the rational and irrational, the instrumental and ceremonial, the creative and destructive. There is no normal order toward which things tend. Reality is fashioned by humans, and humans are responsible for its unfolding progress—or retrogress, as the case may be. Reality is always in flux and is, at all times, the culmination of the interactions of individuals acting within the setting of an inherited and continuously evolving social and economic landscape. Individual action most frequently is effectuated by and through the groups with which individuals are affiliated: for example, the business firm, the trade association, the labor union, the church, the family. There is an ineluctable two-way flow between individuals and their culture. The literature of institutionalism, from the work of Thorstein Veblen to that of John Kenneth Galbraith, is replete with sensibility of cultural conditioning. Individuals are seen as creatures every bit as much as creators of the social whole. Each acts on and is acted on by the other; each changes and is changed by the other. Experimentation, trial and error, and not formulaic response, is perceived by institutionalism as required for meaningful confrontation of social problem.

Keynesian analysis was sympathetically received by most institutionalists partly because, as Klein notes, he focused on the real world and not some idealized system. The sympathetic response, however, is also attributable to his appreciation of the cultural whole as consisting of something more than the strict summation of its parts, as well as to the experimental nature of the solutions he proposed, and their clear orientation toward changing the economic and social status quo.

I include, in the category of formulaic response, orthodox analyses based on the actions of individuals who act as if they were rationally motivated, despite recognition of the fact that they frequently are not. I also include analyses of markets that behave as if they were efficient despite the existence of known imperfections,[3] as in theories, referenced by Klein, of contestability and interproduct rivalry. Also included are approaches that posit the voluntaristic, contractual, individual bargain as the social norm.[4] The institutional approach is not formulaic, but pragmatic. The emphasis is on experimentation—"what works"—recognizing that this is not always readily and precisely determinable and that it will change with changing circumstances.

Value Theory

To this point, I have been in general and often enthusiastic agreement with Klein's overall thesis, and have concentrated more or less on attempts to make more explicit what was included only by implication, or to emphasize points that appeared to me to have received insufficient attention. I now turn to a topic of greater ambivalence and perhaps even ambiguity. It has to do with Klein's treatment of value theory, ever a thorny and difficult question—and perhaps even a stumbling block—for institutional economists.

As previously noted, I agree with Klein's conclusions on the first two of the five questions posed; and they are, of course, questions as well as means of classification. That is, I agree that economics is both a normative science and a science of value and feel, moreover, that these are logically consistent positions. Klein's explanation and elaboration of these topics over and above his bare response, however, do not seem to me to be well reconciled within his general scheme of things.

Klein quite correctly points out that economics cannot divorce itself from ethics, that to take no position is to embrace the status quo, including the extant power structure. He also observes that institutional economists take as the "ultimate value premise" the continuity of the life process, his "value floor" and believe that ". . . the pre-eminent obligation of economists is to produce better economic policy so as genuinely to enhance the life process". Economic performance, he contends, should be judged in terms of its fulfillment of a "higher efficiency" which includes not only narrow market allocational efficiency but also security, equity, freedom, and compassion. To this point in the discussion I am in general agreement, with the relatively minor reservation that I would define the security component of any "higher efficiency" more broadly than he seems to: for example, to include security of expectations—say, job security—rather than narrowly confining it, as he seems to, to the national defense.

But this, I suspect, is the point at which we part company. I qualify the comment because it seems to me that Klein himself evidences some ambiguity on the topic. Klein claims that institutional economists should base policy proposals on the "emergent valuations" of the members of society. It is his contention, that is, that the task of the institutional economist is the transmission of "the preferences of [the] participants" in the economic process to policy makers, thus reflecting the "emerging values of society". This translates, in his view, into the belief on the part of institutional economists that, basically, what is required is an improvement in "techniques for ascertaining what the participants in the economy wish to achieve and for enabling them to achieve it". This appears to me to be very close to an orthodox methodological individualism based on "revealed preference."

Of even greater importance, however, is that Klein's view of the task of institutional economics as reflecting "emergent valuation" does not seem to me to square with his "value floor," to say nothing of his perceptive and important conceptions of the higher efficiency and the collective ought. It seems likely to me that these conceptualizations, that is, value as the reflection and transmission of the emergent valuations of individuals and of value as ensuring the continuity of the life process, will often be at odds.

If we take the emergent valuation position at face value, the reasoning appears also to be circular. If participants' values are shaped by the social ethic, as Klein well appreciates, what is emergent valuation other than the codified conventional wisdom, that is, a reflection of the status quo including the existing power structure? Institutional economists should not be attempting to put into effect policies that reflect the conventional wisdom. Instead, they should be trying to change the conventional wisdom—a skill at which mainstream economists have demonstrated a marked proclivity in recent decades—and proposing the adoption of polices that reflect institutional principles. At bottom, they should be making the case for the adoption of policies that enhance the life process.

Admittedly, this is no easy task, at least for institutionalists. It is a simple enough one for orthodox economists precisely because they have a single key to the solution of all problems, a key given by a natural law outside the system. Orthodoxy, regularly and insistently, from behind its gossamer veil of positivism, calls out for reliance upon a singular, seamless solution set: the private market, deregulation, anti-antitrust, voluntarism, contractarianism, choice, efficiency, and so on. And judging from the policy record of the past several decades, they have met with substantial success in shaping both popular values and the national—even the international—legislative and judicial agenda. Institutionalists have no such gossamer veil and no such solution set. The task is more difficult; the answers, less obvious and precise.

Clearly, problem solving will involve crafting policies that make an economy "work for" its members, and will not be tied exclusively and under all circumstances to a particular market form. As a guide, institutionalists have relied upon the Veblenian distinction. But this carries with it its own set of ambiguities.

Much of the difficulty is terminological. The Veblenian dichotomy, it is maintained, distinguishes between institutions and technology. The phrasing is unfortunate. It invites structural conceptualization; that is, it lends itself to the interpretation that institutions (for example, the church, family, business enterprise) are informed and directed only by considerations of rank and status, and that answers to all problems at any given time are to be found in technology conceived as a stockpile. It is an incorrect interpretation, and one that is not at all the message of institutional economics. It also has, it seems to me, led to a facile and incorrect acceptance of such concepts as that of "cultural lag."

The terms *institutional* and *technological* refer to processes, to patterns of thought and action. Human thought and behavior, life itself, is an admixture of the institutional and the technological (how much better if we consistently had substituted ceremonial-instrumental, pecuniary-industrial, exploitative-creative, or some such pairing) at all times. At any given time, the family, the educational establishment, the business enterprise perform both invidious and instrumental functions. Nurturing occurs in the family, learning in the school, on the job training and production in the business enterprise even while participants are taught the niceties of "socially appropriate" behavior and respect for authority, for example. The automobiles we drive, the homes we inhabit, the food we eat—all have important noninvidious functions to perform, even while they "make a statement" about "who" we are. Institutions do not "lag" behind technology. Instrumental and ceremonial behavior is of a piece, two sides of a coin. They are separately identifiable; but the human experience seamlessly webs together both the ceremonial and the instrumental. Moreover, it is not technology per se but an application of the technological or instrumental process that permits identification of the appropriate means to address problems.

I do not suggest that Klein is caught in this terminological trap. When I read, however, of his hope and expectation that in a world in which we have succeeded in removing from the grasp of concentrated power, and in unclogging informational, production, and distribution channels, that "in such a world the values ultimately emerging from a democratic learning process will be 'instrumental'—that is, noninvidious," I have the uneasy feeling that he is treading dangerously close. Such thinking is Utopian; it is, in the luminous phrase of Samuel Johnson, "the triumph of hope over experience." Such a world will never be.

But if perfection, that is, an ideal system, is not within our grasp, the amelioration of particular circumstance is quite another matter. The task of institutionalism is to identify problems, to make the case that these are problems that require attention, and the connection between proposed policy and social result. There will not be full agreement, even among institutional economists, either on the existence of a problem or upon an appropriate solution. Some problems—for example, poverty, homelessness—will be more easily identifiable as problems than will be others. Some proposed solutions, also, will more readily find acceptance than others. All will require instrumental tools for appropriate formulation and testing: reasoning from cause to effect, rather than from faith; trial and error; experimentation.

This is not a matter of imposing one's beliefs upon others but, rather, of communication and demonstration. Mainstream economics has achieved success in recent years in having its program adopted not because it "imposed" its preferred social ethic of individualism, and it *is* a *social* ethic, but because it was successful in convincing opinion leaders, and through them the populace, that its view of the world was the correct one. It did so partly by constant repetition, and partly by redefining and appropriating the discipline, but that is another story. Its message became the message of newspaper editorial and the promise of bipartisan political oratory. It is quick to attach responsibility for its policy failures to its usual targets—flawed regulation, say, or deposit insurance.

It is important that both the economic program of orthodoxy and the theoretical formulation on which it rests be subject to challenge. And this is part of the measure of the importance of this admirable and estimable work of Philip Klein, and that of others working in the same economic tradition.

Notes

1. Philip A. Klein, "Institutionalism As a School-A Reconsideration," *Journal of Economic Issues* 24 (June 1990): 381–388.

2. John R. Commons, *Institutional Economics* (Madison: The University of Wisconsin Press, 1961 [1934]); p. 73.

3. An early statement of this perspective is found in Milton Friedman, "The Methodology of Positive Economics," in *Essays in Positive Economics* (Chicago: the University of Chicago Press, 1953). Friedman states "... under a wide range of circumstances individual firms behave *as if* they were seeking rationally to maximize their expected returns ... and had full knowledge of the data needed to succeed in this.... Now, of course, businessmen do not actually and literally solve the system of simultaneous equations in terms of which the ... economist finds it convenient to express this hypotheses.... [But] unless the behavior of businessmen in some way or other approximated behavior consistent with the maximization of returns, it seems unlikely that they would remain in business for long...." (pp. 21–22, emphasis in original).

4. This includes a body of work often designated as the work of the Chicago School of economics. I have elsewhere suggested that a foundation stone of this structure of thought was a 1960 article of Ronald Coase. See Ronald E. Coase, "The Problem of Social Cost," in *The Firm, The Market and The Law* (Chicago: The University of Chicago Press, 1988 [1960]). For additional citations of work in this tradition see my "Economic Efficiency, The Economics Discipline and the 'Affected-With-A-Public-Interest' Concept," *Journal of Economic Issues* 24 (September 1990): 719–732.

3 THE METHODOLOGY OF INSTITUTIONAL ECONOMICS: A PRAGMATIC INSTRUMENTALIST PERSPECTIVE

Paul D. Bush

Institutionalists engage in a very active, ongoing dialogue about methodological issues. Their preoccupation with methodology is motivated in part by their critique of mainstream economics. Since institutionalists attempt to steer economic inquiry in a direction quite different from that followed by mainstream economists, the institutionalist critique of neoclassical thought requires that institutionalists be concerned with methodological issues. But there is a more profound reason for the institutionalist emphasis on methodological discourse. It arises out of the influence of the philosophy of pragmatism on institutionalist methodology. A fundamental tenet of pragmatism is that all propositions are subject to revision as theoretical and empirical inquiry moves forward. In order to remain alert to the possibility that such revisions may be required at any given stage of inquiry, methodology must be under constant scrutiny. Consequently, institutionalists are as interested in methodological issues arising in their own work as they are in those arising in their critique of orthodoxy.

The fundamental premise of this chapter is that the dominant themes in the methodological literature of American institutionalist thought can best be understood as an application of pragmatic instrumentalist philosophy to the study of economics.[1] The presumption is not that pragmatic instrumentalist philosophy *should* be adopted by all those who call themselves institutionalists, let alone that the term *institutionalist* should be restricted only to social scientists who openly subscribe to the pragmatic instrumentalist point of view. Such a view would be inconsistent with the methodological pluralism that is encouraged and practiced by American institutionalists in the pursuit of inquiry. The view taken here is that the most coherent methodological positions found in the institutionalist literature are derived from American pragmatic instrumentalist philosophy and that even positions that appear to have no grounding in this philosophical tradition are quite compatible with it. The task that lies ahead, then, is that of distilling the essence of the pragmatic instrumentalist philosophy and providing a demonstration of its relevance to institutionalist methodology.

The Philosophical Foundations of Institutionalist Methodology

Charles Sanders Peirce, William James, and John Dewey gave the original shape and form to philosophical pragmatism. Of these three, it is John Dewey whose work most directly influences contemporary American institutionalist methodology.[2] In regard to the two giants of the institutionalist literature, John R. Commons and Thorstein B. Veblen, Dewey's direct influence on John R. Commons is a matter of record set down by Commons himself.[3] In contrast, it appears that Veblen never commented in print on his views of Dewey's work. Yet they were colleagues at both the beginning and end of Veblen's professional career.[4] Dewey, on the other hand, did comment quite favorably on Veblen's work, clearly indicating that he and Veblen were working with similar philosophical concepts.[5] From Dewey's favorable comments on Veblen's work, we are entitled to infer that Dewey believed that Veblenians should find his instrumentalism compatible with Veblen's thought. This is precisely the view that Clarence E. Ayres adopted in his effort to integrate Veblenian social theory with John Dewey's philosophy of instrumental valuation.[6] It is clear that Ayres approached his reading of Veblen from the perspective of John Dewey's philosophy of pragmatic instrumentalism. This may also be said of Ayres's students and other institutionalists who have adopted Ayres's general methodological approach to institutional economics.[7] However, one need not be an Ayresian to recognize the seminal influence of John Dewey's philosophy on the literature of American institutionalism. For example, K. William Kapp, whose innovative work contributed significantly to the emergence of contemporary European institutionalism, emphasized the importance of the role played by the pragmatic philosophy of Peirce and Dewey in the formation of American institutionalist methodology.[8]

Dewey's version of pragmatic instrumentalism is the focus of the following commentary. Primary attention will be given to aspects of Dewey's thought that appear to be most pertinent to a number of issues that have arisen in recent years in the methodological literature of American institutionalism. Some years ago, prompted by a sense of frustration over the methodological confusion he perceived rampant in the institutionalist dialogue, Baldwin Ranson invited his colleagues to engage in a serious collective reading of Dewey's *Logic: The Theory of Inquiry* and *Theory of Valuation* as a way of trying to lay a foundation for setting things straight.[9] In some ways, this essay is a response to Ranson's invitation. What has been discovered in its preparation is how difficult the job is and how little can be accomplished in the space available. A proper elaboration of the arguments sketched here would require a work of greater breadth and depth. Since it has been impossible to provide an extension of the methodological arguments to detailed examples of substantive institutional analysis, this essay must be considered a prolegomenon to that kind of undertaking.

Rorty's Three Characterizations of Pragmatism

The philosophy of pragmatism has been refined and extended beyond the point where Dewey left it at the time of his death. Perhaps the most interesting and provocative of the contemporary philosophers who has taken pragmatism in new directions is Richard Rorty.[10] Although Rorty's approach to pragmatism may not be acceptable to all institutionalists working in the pragmatic instrumentalist tradition, the clarity with which he characterizes pragmatism provides a most useful starting point in this discussion of pragmatism as the philosophical foundation of institutionalist methodology. In his *Consequences of Pragmatism*, Rorty offers three "characterizations" of pragmatism, which can be summarized as follows:

1. "[P]ragmatism is . . . simply anti-essentialism applied to notions like 'truth,' 'knowledge,' 'language,' 'morality,' and similar objects of philosophical theorizing."[11]
   "There is no wholesale, epistemological way to direct, or criticize, or underwrite, the course of inquiry."[12]
2. "[T]here is no epistemological difference between truth about what ought to be and truth about what is, nor any metaphysical difference

between facts and values, nor any methodological difference between morality and science."[13]

3. "[T]here are no constraints on inquiry save conversational ones—no wholesale constraints derived from the nature of the objects, or of the mind, or of language, but only those retail constraints provided by the remarks of our fellow-inquirers."[14]

These three characterizations of pragmatism will be used to structure the following discussion. The first two characterizations might well have been written by Dewey, for they capture, without the necessity of extended interpretation, the essence of the dominant themes in Dewey's philosophy of inquiry and valuation. The third characterization is somewhat more problematic and will be the subject of a concluding remark at the end of this chapter. But until then, it will serve as a useful device for organizing the main themes to be pursued in the following remarks.

Rorty's First Characterization of Pragmatism

"There is no wholesale, epistemological way to direct, or criticize, or underwrite the course of inquiry."

Rorty's first characterization captures the idea that pragmatists do not believe that the formulation of eternal verities, first principles, or essences are of any assistance in the pursuit of inquiry. Pragmatism is "nonfoundationalist," to use a term that has achieved wide currency in recent years. A "foundationalist" epistemology, Brice R. Wachterhauser tells us, is the belief that "certainty . . . can be had . . . only if we can discover certain self-evident first truths that can act as a 'foundation' for all other knowledge-claims in the sense that all other knowledge-claims can be deduced from these foundational truths."[15] The rejection of "foundationalism" was, of course, a dominant theme in John Dewey's epistemological commentaries, which he highlighted in the title of the book he called *The Quest for Certainty*.[16] Dewey's view was that the quest for certainty had to be abandoned as the first step in freeing philosophy from the metaphysical constraints of its classical past.

Dewey included in his rejection of the quest for certainty not only those forms of "higher knowledge" presumably entailed in the absolutes of Platonic idealism but also the Cartesian dualism that makes a ". . . definite separation between the world in which man thinks and knows and the world in which he lives and acts."[17] Indeed, Dewey's attack on the idea that there is an opposition between "knowing and doing" was a hallmark of his critique of traditional philosophy. It is one of a whole panoply of dualisms that Dewey attempted to expunge from philosophical discourse. The knowing–doing dualism gave rise to what Dewey called the "spectator theory of knowledge."

> The common essence of all these theories, in short, is that what is known is antecedent to the mental act of observation and inquiry, and is totally unaffected by these acts; otherwise it would not be fixed and unchangeable. This negative condition, that the processes of search, investigation, reflection, involved in knowledge relate to something having prior being, fixes once for all the main characters attributed to mind, and to the organs of knowing. They *must* be outside what is known, so as not to interact in any way with the object to be known. . . . A spectator theory of knowledge is the inevitable outcome.[18]

The alternative to the spectator theory of knowledge regards the practical activity of the inquirer as critical to the process of inquiry and the creation of knowledge. Dewey says, "[I]f we see that knowing is not the act of an outside spectator but of a participator inside the natural and social scene, then the true object of knowledge resides in the consequences of directed action."[19] Kant was among those foundationalists whose philosophy rested on the quest for certainty. According to Dewey, "[T]here is nothing hypothetical or conditional about Kant's forms of perception and conception."[20] He goes on to say that "[t]hey work uniformly and triumphantly; they need no differential testing by consequences. The reason Kant postulates them is to secure universality and necessity instead of the hypothetical and the probable."[21] Thus, while Kant had managed to "shift the authorship" for knowledge from the divine to human reason, he did so in such a way as to leave the quest for certainty intact.[22]

The Problematic Situation, the Process of Inquiry, and Warranted Assertions

The alternative to foundationalism is a contextualist approach in which knowledge is not deduced from first principles, but is developed out of a consideration of the context of which a purported fact or idea is considered to be a coherent part. For Dewey the relevant context was the "problematic situation," which arises out of the effort to apply inquiry to what he called an "indeterminate situation." An indeterminate situation is a precognitive state of affairs in which individuals have a sensed awareness that something is wrong. The situation gives rise to doubt, which is the starting point of inquiry. But the indeterminate situation is not itself a mental condition. "The indeterminate situation," Dewey says, "comes into existence from existential causes, just as does, say, the organic imbalance of hunger."[23] He goes on to say that "[t]here is nothing intellectual or cognitive in the existence of such [indeterminate] situations, although they are the necessary condition of cognitive operations of inquiry. In themselves they are precognitive."[24] A problematic situation, on the other hand, is a cognitive construction which comes into focus as inquiry is brought to bear on an "indeterminate situation." In other words, problems do not define themselves precognitively; the conceptualization of a problem requires all of the theoretical and observational tools of coordinated inquiry. If inquiry is successful, the indeterminate situation is transformed into a "determinate whole," and inquiry is terminated "in the institution of conditions which remove need for doubt."[25]

According to Dewey, "knowledge" is "the product of competent inquiries."[26] But he was reluctant to use the term *knowledge* because of all the metaphysical connotations the term carries in traditional philosophy. He preferred to speak of successful inquiry as producing "warranted assertions." In selecting this language he sought to emphasize the idea that inquiry is an ongoing process. Warranted assertions are beliefs that function as the starting point for the next stage of inquiry. "There is," he says, "continuity in inquiry. The conclusions reached in one inquiry become the means, material and procedural, of carrying on further inquiries."[27] But he insists that this does not mean that warranted assertions, once established, are themselves beyond further scrutiny; accordingly, he says that "there is no belief so settled as not to be exposed to further inquiry."[28] Such a notion is the antithesis of foundationalism.

It should be observed that if the pursuit of inquiry is not grounded in some set of ultimate first principles, neither is its goal the acquisition of universal truths that once discovered would remain fixed and immutable. "The problem of knowledge," Dewey says,

> . . . is the problem of discovery of methods for carrying on this enterprise of [the redirection of experience]. It is a problem never ended, always in process; one problematic situation is resolved and another takes its place. The constant gain is not in approximation to universal solution but in betterment of methods and enrichment of objects experienced.[29]

There is, then, no teleological law that requires the pursuit of inquiry to achieve some sort of definitive finality in order to meet an epistemological standard of adequacy. The value of knowledge is not to be appraised in terms of its approximation to an ultimate, comprehensive truth; rather, it is to be appraised for the instrumental capacity it posesses for the solution of problems.

The Rejection of Foundationalism in Institutionalist Methodology

Beginning with Thorstein Veblen's critique of orthodox economics at the turn of the century, institutionalists have been critical of what they perceive as the foundationalist character of classical (and neoclassical) methodology. Veblen's critique of orthodox economics pointed to the untenable logic of natural law theory. The "first principles" of natural law theory constituted the foundation on which all generalizations of economics were to be built. Among the substantive errors nurtured by this natural law point of view was the belief that economic processes tended in the long run to achieve a state of "definitive normality," defined analytically as an equilibrium; that is to say, as Veblen put it, economic processes "must be apprehended in terms of a consistent propensity tending to some spiritually legitimate end."[30] Such a conception is antithetical to the evolutionary point of view as Veblen conceived it.

Although much of the rhetoric of natural law theory has been expunged from the discourse of contemporary neoclassical thought, the "foundationalist" epistemology remains intact. The Cartesian dualisms separating knowing from doing, subject from object, fact from value, and theory from practice, among others, continue to form the epistemological foundations of neoclassical thought. These dualisms are taken as metaphysical premises that are not subject to revision through critical inquiry. It matters not whether the neoclassical economist professes to be a positivist or a Popperian in methodological orientation because Cartesianism is common to both.

In the constant methodological surveillance that institutionalists maintain over their own literature, nothing raises a red flag quicker than the suspicion that a colleague may have inadvertently slipped into foundationalist thinking. One such case has recently attracted considerable attention. It came to the surface when Wendell Gordon charged that Marc Tool's formulation of the "social value principle" amounted to nothing less than the promulgation of an "eternal verity."[31] Tool vigorously denies that he intended the social value principle to be taken as an eternal verity, underscoring his own belief in the pragmatic instrumentalist position that no proposition is, or should be, protected from inquiry and revision. He has been quite explicit in stating his view that others should not read into the principle that which he did not intend to put in it or that which it does not logically entail. His response to Gordon is contained in his essay on "The Theory of Instrumental Value," which appears in this book.[32] This controversy is instructive on several levels, some elements of which will be considered in the subsequent discussion of the value problem; but at this juncture it is of interest because it illustrates the intensity with which institutionalists attempt to eschew foundationalism. Whatever differences may exist between them on other issues, Gordon and Tool agree on one important methodological point: namely, there can be no more serious charge made against an institutionalist than the allegation that his/her analysis rests implicitly on the notion of essences, first causes, or eternal verities of any sort. That an institutionalist would *knowingly* engage in foundationalist reasoning is not even contemplated as a remote possibility.

Dewey's Rejection of Subjectivism

Dewey was particularly concerned that the process of inquiry in which an indeterminate situation is transformed into a unified one not be misconstrued as a purely "mental" operation. He argued that "inquiry effects *existential* transformation and reconstruction of the material with which it deals."[33] Since "the transformation is existential and hence temporal, . . . the objective subject-matter of inquiry undergoes temporal modification."[34] In presenting this argument Dewey takes pains to avoid any misconception that he may be talking only about a transformation of the "subjective" perceptions of the inquirer. He is intent upon drawing a contrast between his conception of the experimental nature of inquiry and the "subjectivist" views that permeate what he calls the "traditional theory."

> The latter holds that such modifications as may occur in even the best controlled inquiry are confined to states and processes of the knower—the one conducting the inquiry. They may, therefore properly be called "subjective," mental or psychological, or by some similar name. They are without objective standing, and hence lack logical force and meaning. The position that is here taken is to the contrary effect: namely, that beliefs and mental states of the inquirer cannot be legitimately changed except as existential operations, rooted ultimately in organic activities, modify and requalify objective matter.[35]

This notion that inquiry involves an existential transformation of the object of inquiry is key to Dewey's conception of experimental science, and it lays the philosophical foundation for the institutionalist view that the solution to social problems involves institutional change in historical time. These remarks are also diagnostic of Dewey's philosophical realism, a matter that will be taken up in a later subsection of this chapter.

Factual Propositions are Theory-Laden

It is clear that Dewey did not believe that the facts speak for themselves. For Dewey, inquiry requires empirical evidence; but to qualify as evidence, factual propositions must be functional within the scope of the theory developed to guide the solution of the problem under consideration. "Their function is to serve as evidence and their evidential quality is judged on the basis of their capacity to form an ordered whole in response to operations prescribed by the ideas they occasion and support."[36] Throughout his *Logic: The Theory of Inquiry* Dewey discusses the "conjugate relation" that must hold between the empirical and theoretical dimensions of inquiry. Thus, he says: "Observation of facts and suggested meanings or ideas arise and develop in correspondence with each other."[37] He expands on this ideas as follows:

> Inquiry demands . . . operations of both observation and ideation. There would be no control of the process of inquiry if each of these operations were not expressly formed with reference to the other. . . . in controlled inquiry, the entire object [of theoretical formulations] is to obtain *that* meaning or conceptual structure which is best adapted to instigate and direct just those operations of observation that will secure as their consequence just those existential facts that are needed to solve the problem in hand.[38]

This conjugate correlation between ideas and facts clearly entails the notion that factual propositions are theory-laden since a theoretical formulation is required to transform data into evidence.[39] Equally important, however, is the corollary that theoretical formulations that fail to contribute to the end-in-view of providing a unified whole, including empirical observations that lead to that end, must be abandoned in favor of alternative hypotheses that do.

Dewey and the Correspondence Theory of Truth

Dewey's conception of the "conjugate correlation" between ideas and facts raises the issue of the "correspondence theory of truth." Dewey clearly rejected the correspondence theory of truth which holds that knowledge is achieved through the accuracy of representation of nature and entails the view that philosophy is, as Rorty puts it, "a mirror of nature."[40] Central to Dewey's objection to the traditional formulation of the "correspondence" theory is that it is premised on the Cartesian objective–subjective dualism. According to the standard formulation, the truth of a proposition (which is subjective) is established if it "corresponds" to the facts (which are objective). Among the many commentaries on the "correspondence theory of truth" to be found in Dewey's works, probably the most interesting is one that appears in *Problems of Men*, for it not only captures his critique of the theory, it also illuminates the meaning of his conception of the "conjugate correlation"of ideas and facts. In it, Dewey professes to subscribe to a correspondence theory of his own formulation that is quite different from that found in the traditional literature. He puts the matter as follows:

> . . . my own view, takes correspondence in the operational sense it bears in all cases except the unique epistemological case of an alleged relation between a "subject" and an "object"; the meaning, namely, of *answering*, as a key answers to conditions imposed by the lock, or as two correspondents "answer" each other; or, in general, as a reply is an adequate answer to a question or a criticism—as, in short, a *solution* answers the requirements of a *problem*. On this view, both partners in "correspondence" are open and above aboard, instead of one of them being forever out of experience and the other in it by way of "precept" or whatever. Wondering at how something in experience could be asserted to correspond to something by definition outside of experience, which it is, upon the basis of epistemological doctrine, the sole means of "knowing," is what originally made me suspicious of the whole epistemological industry.
>
> In the sense of correspondence as operational and behavioral (the meaning which has definite parallels in ordinary experience), I hold that my *type* of theory is the only one entitled to be called correspondence theory of truth.[41]

In spite of the rhetorical stance he takes to make his point in this passage, Dewey does not, in fact, subscribe to any form of a "correspondence theory of truth" which is translatable into the vocabulary of traditional philosophical discourse. But his use of the notion of "answering" offers profound insight into his meaning of the term *conjugate correlation*. Although the matter cannot be pursued here, it should also be noted that Dewey's remark about his suspicions of the "epistemological industry" provides support for Richard Rorty's overall interpretation of Dewey as a nonepistemological philosopher who believed that "if scientific inquiry could be seen as adapting and coping rather than copying, the continuity between science, morals, and art would become apparent."[42]

Correspondence, Coherence, and Holism

In philosophy the correspondence theory of truth, espoused primarily by empiricists, is contrasted with the coherence theory of truth, espoused primarily by idealists. If Dewey rejects the correspondence theory, does this mean that he embraces the coherence theory? The answer to this question would have to be that he does not—that is, not in the sense that coherence theories have been formulated in the idealist literature. The coherence theory of truth holds that the truth of a proposition can only be determined by establishing whether it coheres with other propositions we already know to be true. The traditional defense of the coherence theory requires that one rely upon the metaphysical preconceptions of idealism, which, as has already been indicated in the above discussion of Dewey's views on Kant, pragmatists are unwilling to do. Rorty has suggested that Dewey's pragmatic philosophy makes it possible to view correspondence and coherence theories of truth as "noncompeting trivialities," thereby permitting us to get beyond "realism and idealism."[43]

But just as Dewey's theory of inquiry incorporates his conception of correspondence as a conjugate correlation of ideas and facts, it also incorporates his conception of coherence as a necessary characteristic of "warranted assertions." Dewey's conception of the continuity of inquiry incorporates notions of coherence and holism. The continuity of inquiry signifies that warranted assertions build on one another to achieve a coherent pattern that produces a unified whole. Speaking of the role of inferred ideas in inquiry, Dewey says that they must be validated by their capacity "to order and organize particulars into a coherent whole."[44]

The prominence of the idea of coherence in Dewey's theory of inquiry produces a distinctive holistic methodology in problem solving. J.E. Tiles has observed that

> . . . Dewey's philosophy is characterized by a disregard for the problems generated by attempts to treat truth in terms of correspondence, and by a holist perspective which prizes genetic accounts, particularly those which reveal progressive functional differentiation within an organically structured whole.[45]

Abraham Kaplan has pointed out that holism involves development and use of "pattern models" in inquiry. In a pattern model, he says, ". . . something is explained when it is so related to a set of other elements that together they constitute a unified system."[46]

Dewey's holistic perspective on the continuity of inquiry fully anticipated what has come to be called the Duhem–Quine thesis, which states that empirical tests cannot confirm or disconfirm a hypothesis in isolation from the cluster of related hypotheses to which it belongs and upon which it depends for its meaning and significance. Pierre Duhem put it this way: "an experiment in Physics can never condemn an isolated hypothesis but only a whole theoretical group."[47] In his famous essay on the "Two Dogmas of Empiricism," Willard Van Orman Quine makes the following observation about the "dogma" of "reductionism":

> The dogma of reductionism survives in the supposition that each statement, taken in isolation from its fellows, can admit of confirmation or information at all. My countersuggestion . . . is that our statements about the external world

> face the tribunal of sense experience not individually but only as a corporate body.[48]

The Duhem–Quine thesis clearly undermines the reductionism of positivism by offering a pragmatic holistic conception of the testing of hypotheses.[49] As such, the Duhem–Quine thesis is consistent with Dewey's conception of the process.

Holism, Inductively Formulated, and Deductively Formulated Models

Holism and pattern models have been correctly identified as diagnostic characteristics of institutionalist methodology by many commentators.[50] But the thrust of their commentaries has often led to the impression that reliance on pattern models must necessarily involve the rejection of deductive models because of the belief that the two approaches are inherently incompatible. For example, this appears to be the position advanced by Yngve Ramstad in what is otherwise a splendid treatment of the holistic methodology employed by John R. Commons.[51] To the extent that holism is associated in the minds of institutionalists with inductive methods, the incompatibility of holistic and deductively formulated models reinforces a long-held view among many institutionalists that their rejection of the neoclassical deductively formulated "covering law" models leaves no place for hypothetico-deductive models in their own methodology.[52] This view appears to be based on a serious misconception of the compatibility of pattern models with deductively formulated models.

Abraham Kaplan offered a lucid discussion of this matter in his book, *The Conduct of Inquiry*. In that work Kaplan set forth the nature of pattern models and compared them to hypothetico-deductive models.[53] Among the many profound insights he offers in that discussion is the view that pattern models and deductively formulated models need not be taken as mutually exclusive (or incompatible) intellectual strategies. On the contrary, he demonstrates that one may subsume the other. The importance of this demonstration for institutionalist methodology is that pattern models may very well be compatible with hypothetico-deductively formulated models, and that the appearance of deductively formulated models within the institutionalist literature would not constitute an abomination of the institutionalist methodology. This is not to say that institutionalists should, therefore, abandon their critique of neoclassical hypothetico-deductive models; but it does suggest that hypothetico-deductive models constructed for the purpose of exploring the implications of institutionalist pattern models may very well be a badly neglected method of inquiry in the institutionalist literature. In other words, hypothetico-deductive models are not, in themselves, the problem. It is when the "hypotheticals" are formulated in aprioristic terms, or when they are treated as foundationalist covering laws that they become incompatible with the pragmatic instrumentalist approach to institutionalist methodology.[54]

But this point does not seem to be fully appreciated in two major methodological commentaries widely cited by institutionalists. Paul Diesing took Kaplan's treatment of pattern models as a point of departure for his discussion of holism.[55] Although he is somewhat skeptical that pattern models and deductive models can be made as compatible as Kaplan suggests, he grants that they may be compatible in some cases. It appears that Diesing's skepticism regarding their compatibility is premised on his rather narrow treatment of deductive models in terms of the strict positivist conception of covering law models. Both Kaplan's and Diesing's works are featured prominently in Charles K. Wilbur's and Robert S. Harrison's widely cited article, "The Methodological Basis of Institutional Economics: Pattern Model, Story-telling, and Holism." But Wilbur and Harrison tend to follow Diesing more closely than Kaplan on the question of the compatibility of pattern and deductive models. Indeed, they seem not to grant any compatibility at all when they argue that pattern models may be appropriate for some problems of interest to institutionalists but that "[t]he formal models of standard economics have their use, even by institutionalists, for certain types of problems."[56] The separation of types of problems in this remark indicates not a compatibility of pattern and deductive models, but rather their mutually exclusive use in treating different types of problems. The Wilber and Harrison view is clearly evident in Yngve Ramstad's treatment of holism, where holism and deductively formulated ("formalist") models are treated as fundamentally incompatible.

The Relation of Knowledge to Reality in Dewey's Thought

This discussion of Dewey's theory of inquiry must take into account a rather serious error of interpretation of Dewey's philosophy contained in a widely cited essay on institutionalist methodology. It appears in Philip Mirowski's "Philosophical Basis of Institutional Economics."[57]

Mirowski states: "Dewey's crusade was to argue against the idea of truth as accuracy of representation, which took the form in his later life of an insistence *that reality could not exist prior to and independent of the process of inquiry*."[58] The words italicized [by this writer] attribute to Dewey a view that he did not hold. Indeed, he held just the opposite view. Mirowski's citation to Dewey on this point is Joseph Ratner's compendium of Dewey's works.[59] The excerpt in Ratner's compendium is taken from Dewey's *The Quest for Certainty*, pages 32–37, the source of Mirowski's interpretation being found on page 35. Mirowski's misreading is traceable to Dewey's sentence, which reads: "As long as the notions persist that knowledge is a disclosure of reality, of reality prior to and independent of knowing, and that knowing is independent of a purpose to control the quality of experienced objects, the failure of natural science to disclose significant values in its objects will come as a shock." This statement *is* supportive of the first clause of Mirowski's sentence, preceding the comma; but it is not supportive of the clause following the comma, that is, the words italicized. Dewey's remark does not say, as Mirowski insists, that reality cannot exist independent of inquiry. The passage is Dewey's characterization of the traditional philosophical view that one can possess a "knowledge" of "reality" that is independent of the process of "knowing," as Dewey defines the term. The passage is not an argument in support of, or in negation of, the notion that reality exists independent of inquiry. It is not an ontological commentary; rather it is a characterization of knowledge that presumably possesses an a priori conception of reality. *The Quest for Certainty* contains a number of comments by Dewey that clearly support the interpretation given here of the sentence in question. The following should suffice to make the point: 1) "The world we experience is a real world. But it is not in its primary phases a world that is known, a world that is understood, and is intellectually coherent and secure"[60]; 2) "Knowledge then does not encompass the world as a whole. But the fact that it is not coextensive with experienced existence is no defect nor failure on its part"[61]; 3) "Not all existence asks to be known, and it certainly does not ask leave from thought to exist."[62] These three comments clearly indicate that Dewey believed in a reality that is independent of inquiry.

On a closely related point concerning Dewey's conception of reality, George R. Geiger makes the following observation concerning Dewey's concept of "experience": "It cannot be repeated too often that experience is not a veil coming between organism and environment which is itself natural and existential, that what is experienced is not simply more experience but a natural and real world."[63] The point to be made with this citation is that if Mirowski's interpretation of Dewey's view of reality were accepted, it would be difficult, if not impossible, not only to understand Dewey's conception of the process of inquiry but also to make sense of other dimensions of his philosophy, such has his treatment of experience.

J.E. Tiles has observed that "[i]t is . . . unhelpful to label Dewey simply as an 'anti-realist'. It invites the assumption that somehow Dewey was opposed to reality rather than being opposed to a variety of (mis)-conceptions about our relation to reality, which happen to label themselves 'realism'."[64] As Tiles points out, "Dewey insisted on the right of his own version of pragmatism to be regarded as a 'realism.' "[65]

As indicated in an earlier subsection of this essay, the realism of Dewey's philosophy is manifest in his theory of inquiry. It is instructive to note that in *Logic: The Theory of Inquiry*, Dewey discusses matters pertaining to his "realism" in a chapter entitled the "The Existential Matrix of Inquiry."[66] To reiterate, inquiry arises in response to an indeterminate situation which gives rise to doubt. But Dewey emphasizes that "[*w*]*e* are doubtful because the situation is inherently doubtful."[67] Through inquiry we are able to formulate a "problematic situation" which may be amenable to solution. In developing a solution for the problematic situation, Dewey says ". . . inquiry effects *existential* transformation and reconstruction of the material with which it deals; the result of the transformation, when it is grounded, being conversion of an indeterminate problematic situation into a determinate resolved one."[68] What is being transformed here is not a state of mind but the existential circumstances that gave rise to the indeterminate situation.

Consistent with Dewey's views on the matter, institutionalist methodology is based on realist foundations. It incorporates an ontological hypothesis that logically entails, among other things, the view that society as a system of institutions is real and not merely a figment of the intellectual imagination; that continuity in human experience is not only a convenient theoretical construct but is a real process, the disruption of which has consequences independent of our ability to conceptualize them in deterministic mathematical models; that social and individual value formation are real processes and, as such, must be subject to investigation rather than postulation; that the process of institutional change is not merely a matter of shifting ideologies, or changes in linguistic conventions, but changes in real habits of behavior that have real consequences which may or may not be captured in discourse; that physical and cultural processes are part of a contingent universe that guarantees nothing, thereby imposing the necessity of choice on the human agent; and, finally, that human choices have real consequences for the physical and cultural processes of which they are a part.

Pragmatic Instrumentalism and Positivism

It would hardly seem necessary to belabor the point that pragmatic instrumentalism as formulated by Dewey is fundamentally incompatible with logical positivism and logical empiricism, but there are indications that some institutionalists have succumbed to a misreading of the meaning and significance of Dewey's position on positivism. Two cases come immediately to mind. One is Mirowski's favorable citation[69] of H.S. Thayer's view that the decline of pragmatism in the 1940s was due, in part, to Dewey's "alliance with the logical positivists" which is reflected in his *Theory of Valuation*.[70] The other is James A. Swaney and Barry Premus's assertion that "[t]he methodology of logical positivism is capable of contributing to effective public policy formation" and that "[w]hile not generally considered to be in the school of logical positivism, John Dewey's methodological approach more nearly approximates natural science logical positivism than does [the methodology of self-proclaimed positivists in economics].[71] Space does not permit a lengthy commentary on either of these misinterpretations of Dewey. However, a brief reflection on Dewey's own critique of positivism should indicate the foundation upon which a critique of Mirowski and Swaney and Premus might be based. To this end the following passage from Dewey's *Logic: The Theory of Inquiry* is quoted in full.

> [Positivism] inherited from traditional empiricism its contempt for general ideas and for theories that pretend to be anything else than summary records of ascertained facts. Its logic has no recognized place for hypotheses which at a given time outrun the scope of already determined "facts," and which, indeed, may not be capable of verification at the time or of *direct* factual verification at any time. . . . the history of science shows that many hypotheses have played a great role in the advancement of science which were at the time of their origin purely speculative, and would have been condemned by a consistent positivism as merely "metaphysical"; e.g., the ideas of the conservation of energy and of evolutionary development. This history of science . . . shows that the verifiability (as positivism understands it) of hypotheses is not nearly as important as is their directive power. As a broad statement, no important scientific hypothesis has ever been verified in the form in which it was originally presented nor without very considerable revisions and modifications. The justification of such hypotheses has lain in their power to direct new orders of experimental observation and to open up new problems and new fields of subject-matter. In doing these things, they have not only provided new facts but have often radically altered what were previously taken to be facts. . . . [In spite of positivism's] claims to be strictly scientific, [it] has been in some respects the heir of an older metaphysical view which attributed to ideas inherent truth-falsity properties . . . . On this ground alone, the positivistic theory of knowledge falls short.[72]

The thrust of these comments—as well as others that Dewey makes on this issue in many of his later writings—is that he regarded the capacity of a hypothesis to offer coherence and understanding as more important than its ability to formulate descriptive propositions that could be tested by their correspondence with the facts. This is not to say that he regarded prediction as being unimportant; on the contrary, that would be inconsistent with his view that warranted assertions must be evaluated in terms of their consequences. To anticipate the consequences of adopting a given proposition or course of action, one must have the capacity to predict. The critical observation to be made, then, is not that predictions are inconsequential to the processes of inquiry, but that they are not in themselves the definitive test of the warrantability of hypotheses.[73]

Equally important to an understanding of the chasm that exists between Dewey and the positivists is his rejection of the normative–positive dualism upon which positivism is grounded. A discussion of Dewey's theory of valuation shall be taken up in the next section of this chapter, and the difference between positivism and pragmatic instrumentalism will be further discussed there. Earlier comments on Dewey's view that factual propositions are theory-laden and his anticipation of what has become known as the Duhem–Quine thesis reveal other aspects of his thought that set his philosophical position in direct opposition to positivism.

Thus rumors of Dewey's alliance with "positivism" cannot be taken seriously. Since Mirowski did not really press the point, his comment, having been noted, can be set aside until some future date when it is pursued by him or others with greater vigor. The implications of the Swaney–Premus thesis for institutionalist methodology is somewhat more troublesome. It reflects a lack of familiarity and/or impatience with the pragmatic instrumentalist approach to inquiry and invites institutionalists to try a little logical positivism when the going gets rough. As the themes developed in this chapter clearly indicate, the present writer must reject such a notion out of hand on the grounds that logical positivism and pragmatic instrumentalism are fundamentally incompatible. In reference to the Swaney–Premus paper, it must be noted with some emphasis that in the ten years subsequent to the publication of "Modern Empiricism and Quantum-Leap Theorizing in Economics," Swaney has abandoned in his own work anything resembling a logical positivist methodology and has formulated an institutionalist approach to environmental economics[74] that stands on all fours with the pragmatic instrumentalist methodology of writers such as Marc Tool.[75]

Dewey, Popper, Friedman, and Instrumentalism

If the use of the term *instrumentalism* in economic methodology were confined to discussions of the instrumentalism of Dewey and the kind of interpretation given to it in this essay, it would be possible to close this section with the above remarks. But, alas, the world is not that simple. The complications arise in the efforts that have been undertaken over the years to make some sort of coherent sense of Milton Friedman's essay on "The Methodology of Positive Economics."[76] Two approaches contribute to the confusion: the first is Lawrence A. Boland's effort to demonstrate that Friedman's methodology is "instrumentalist" in the sense given to the term by Karl Popper; and the second is found in two separate attempts to show that Friedman is a *Deweyan* instrumentalist. Both approaches cause considerable consternation to American institutionalists because they regard Friedman's methodology to be the antithesis of institutional economics and fundamentally incompatible with Dewey's pragmatic instrumentalist philosophy.

In the case of Boland, the institutionalist's displeasure is aroused by what appears to be the preemption of the term instrumentalism to mean something quite different than what they and pragmatic instrumentalist philosophers mean by the term.[77] In his exegesis of Friedman's methodology, Boland uses the term instrumentalism as it is defined by Karl Popper. Popper uses the term to describe the notion of a theory developed by members of the Vienna Circle—Ernst Mach, Ludwig Wittgenstein, and Moritz Schlick. "['Instrumentalism'] is the view," he says, "that a theory is *nothing but* a tool or instrument for prediction."[78] To the dismay of Deweyan instrumentalists, this definition of instrumentalism has enjoyed wide currency in the literature of the philosophy of science. Given the decline of interest in Dewey's philosophy in that literature, it appears that there is no great sense of urgency to remind the world that Dewey's instrumentalism exists and that it means something quite different. While the substance of Boland's rationalization of Friedman's methodology has aroused a critical response from institutionalists—for example, Ken Dennis[79]—his use of Popper's meaning of instrumentalism does not commit Boland to the view that Friedman is a *Deweyan* instrumentalist.[80] In his *Methodological Foundations of Economic Method*, Boland states very clearly that instrumentalists (as Boland defines Friedman) reject "pragmatism."[81] Although he makes no reference whatsoever to Dewey in this discussion, presumably Dewey would be counted among those whom Boland defines as pragmatists. Institutionalists would have no difficulty agreeing with the proposition that the views of instrumentalists as defined by Boland (following Popper) are incompatible with Deweyan pragmatic instrumentalism. But it is not clear that Boland and institutionalists hold the same conception of pragmatism. Boland defines pragmatism as the belief that "[w]hatever 'works' is true."[82] As the present commentary clearly implies, this is an unacceptable characterization of pragmatism. Boland could rebut this comment by citing Dewey's own words. In *Reconstruction in Philosophy*, Dewey does make the remark: "The hypothesis that works is the *true* one. . . ."[83] Such unguarded rhetorical flourishes plague efforts to interpret Dewey and give rise to all sorts of possible hermeneutical convolutions. The critical word in this statement is, of course, "works." If one leaves this word undefined, as Boland does, Dewey's remark is itself a trivialization of pragmatism. What Dewey meant by "works" in this comment is the subject of much of his later writing, such as *Logic: The Theory of Inquiry* and *Theory of Valuation*.

Passing over Boland's characterization of pragmatism, a matter of more immediate interest is the curious interpretation he gives to Friedman's instrumentalism. As defined by Popper, instrumentalism is a view that he (Popper) specifically rejects. Nevertheless, Boland (and his colleague William J. Frazer) argue that Friedman's instrumental methodology is compatible with Popperian falsificationism.[84] Presumably, the apparent contradictions in this line of reasoning are resolved by noting that Friedman's ideas are confined to the realm of methodology whereas Popper's constitute a full-blown philosophy of science. It is beyond the scope of this chapter to render a critique of Boland's interpretation of Friedman's methodology, and no further characterization of his position will be offered here. Yet it should be noted that Boland reports that Friedman affirms that his characterization of Friedman's methodology is "entirely correct."[85] However, the exact import of this affirmation has been called into question by Hirsch and de Marchi who dispute Boland's interpretation of Friedman and argue that Friedman *is*, in fact, a *Deweyan* instrumentalist. Furthermore, they quote Friedman's affirmation that *their* interpretation has persuaded Friedman that his "methodological views are almost identical with those of John Dewey."[86] The plot thickens.

Before turning to the Hirsch and de Marchi treatment of Friedman, a brief comment on another scholar's claim that Friedman is a Deweyan instrumentalist is worth noting because it rests, in part, on Boland's interpretation of Friedman. James R. Wible argues that "Friedman's instrumentalism can be taken as a narrow, methodological special case of John Dewey's instrumentalism."[87] Wible accepts Boland's interpretation of Friedman's instrumentalism as being "a special case of Popperian philosophy of science."[88] He then adds to this premise the argument that "Dewey and the pragmatists" are to be found in the "same philosophical domain as the contemporary realists," including Popper.[89] Not surprisingly, this incredible wedding of the philosophies of Dewey and Popper aroused vigorous criticism from institutionalists.[90] To summarize to this point, in

Boland we have Popper's despised instrumentalism made compatible with Popper, and in Wible we have Popper made compatible with Dewey; all this in the effort to make some sort of philosophical sense out of Friedman's methodological essay.

The Hirsch and de Marchi effort to make Friedman into a Deweyan instrumentalist is at least free of the intellectual baggage of the Boland thesis, which they specifically reject as being philosophically inept.[91] For the most part their reading of Dewey is far superior to that of Wible's, but it is not sufficiently astute to dissuade them from undertaking what can only be described as a tortured effort to impute the legitimacy of Dewey's instrumentalism to Friedman's philosophically incorrigible methodological ruminations. A detailed critique of the Hirsch and de Marchi thesis is beyond the scope of this essay, but a brief comment on some aspects of their use of Dewey should indicate the line of attack a detailed critique by the present writer would take.

Hirsch and de Marchi attempt to provide a philosophical rationalization for Friedman's contention that an "important" hypothesis must be based on descriptively false assumptions[92] by calling upon Dewey's view that ". . . a hypothesis does not have to be true in order to be highly serviceable in the conduct of inquiry."[93] In a later comment on the concept of disconfirmation, they attempt to reinforce their support of Friedman's "unrealism" view by citing a portion of the long paragraph quoted earlier in this chapter where Dewey emphasizes the "directive power" of hypotheses over their verifiability. In both instances Hirsch and de Marchi misuse Dewey in an effort to rationalize Friedman's position. The context for the first citation is an argument that Dewey sets forth on the provisional character of hypotheses and the danger of taking hypotheses as " finally true," which leads to the obstruction of inquiry. There is no logical equivalence between the proposition that "a hypothesis need not be true in some final sense in order to be useful" and the proposition that "to be useful a hypothesis must rest upon unrealistic assumptions." Hirsch and de Marchi's second use of Dewey on the relative importance of the verifiability of hypotheses as compared to their "directive power" does not support Friedman's unrealism thesis; it is, instead—as indicated in the discussion above—a rejection of the positivist's theory of verification and knowledge. Dewey's rejection of positivism does not imply the kind of argument Friedman sets forth: namely, "to be important . . . a hypothesis must be descriptively false in its assumptions."[94] To suggest that such a notion can be validly inferred from any of the arguments in Dewey's *Logic: The Theory of Inquiry* would require that we ignore his insistence on the conjugate relation between observation and ideation,[95] his specific rejection of the "metaphysical individualism"[96] that underlies Friedman's methodological individualism, and, most importantly, his "holistic" conception of how warranted assertions are established in the process of inquiry.[97] Finally, Friedman's fictionalist, "as if" methodology conflates explanation and prediction, which by implication denies that there can be explanation without prediction (as in the case of the evolutionary hypothesis) or prediction without explanation (as in the case of Ptolemy's geocentric theory of the universe on which terrestrial navigation was based for over 1,000 years).[98]

But perhaps the most painful intellectual contortions in the Hirsch and de Marchi treatise are to be found in their attempt to reconcile Friedman's enthusiastic embrace of the normative–positive dualism with Dewey's explicit rejection of it.[99] Hirsch and de Marchi are well aware that they face a formidable task in making Friedman compatible with Dewey on normative issues. To accomplish this task, they adopt a two-step intellectual strategy. First, they deny that the normative–positive dualism is very important in Friedman's thinking. Accordingly, they write: "While Friedman in 'Positive Economics' seems to lean heavily on the normative-positive dualism, if we were to judge from the quoted statement [that among "disinterested citizens" there are few differences on fundamental values] we would have to conclude that in his way of thinking this dichotomy is not very meaningful."[100] Moreover, they argue, Friedman sees little use for normative analysis not only in *positive* economics but in *policy* analysis as well. They put it this way: "As we have seen, in 'Positive economics' he seems to see little if any value in normative analysis, not only for the pure economic scientist (positive economist), but even for the political economist whose chief interest is policy."[101] This illogical line of argument embodies the second intellectual strategy of drawing a distinction between "positive economics" and "political economy," which itself rests upon a use of the means–ends variant of the normative–positive dualism that Dewey clearly rejected in all of his philosophical commentaries. In spite of Hirsch and de Marchi's sustained and tenacious effort to make Friedman a Deweyan instrumentalist, American institutionalists can remain secure in their belief that pragmatic instrumentalism is incompatible with the Friedmanian version of neoclassical methodology.[102]

The Institutionalist Critique of Friedman's Methodology

A pragmatic instrumentalist critique of Friedman's position focuses on his conflation of explanation and prediction. From the pragmatic instrumentalist perspective, Friedman would not improve the validity of his position by changing his view on the reality of assumptions if he continued to insist that prediction is the test of explanation. While a due concern for the conjugate correlation between theory and evidence requires the pragmatist instrumentalist to reject Friedman's bald assertion that we need not concern ourselves with the realism of assumptions in the formulation of economic theories, the fundamental philosophical error lies in his narrow conception of "explanation" in scientific discourse.

Thus, from the pragmatic instrumentalist perspective, a meaningful critique of neoclassical (or Austrian) thought cannot be sustained solely on the charge of a lack of realism. As the arguments set forth above indicate, the pragmatic instrumentalist view does not preclude the possibility that some propositions of a theory may not be directly testable against the facts of experience; nor does it preclude the possibility of the *appearance* of apriorism in those warranted assertions that are so settled that they can be accepted as points of departure for further inquiry. What is required is an evaluation of the consequences for inquiry if the propositions in question were adopted as settled propositions at a given stage in inquiry. In other words, all propositions that enter into theoretical formulations must be evaluated in terms of their impact on the continuity of inquiry. It must be determined whether propositions will extend or truncate the process of inquiry. If it is judged that they would truncate inquiry, as in the case of first principles, ultimate ends, eternal verities, and so forth, then on pragmatic instrumentalist grounds they must be rejected.

Moreover, the question of realism would be considered within the context of what Dewey called the conjugate relationship (or correlation) of observation and ideation. In other words, facts become evidence only through the mediation of inquiry which involves the evaluation of the capacity of factual propositions to contribute to the unified whole, which is the end-in-view of inquiry. This holistic orientation is crucial to the issue of the realism of assumptions because it clearly requires that the assumptions in question be consonant with the cluster of related hypotheses and warranted assertions that contribute to the coherence of the theory of which the hypothesis in question is an organic component. Thus, while the determination of a lack of realism cannot be based merely on the question of the direct verification of certain theoretical propositions contained within a given hypotheses, the question of the realism of the assumptions is not by any means a matter of indifference to the pragmatic instrumentalist.

On the basis of the foregoing considerations it is clear that the pragmatic instrumentalist position entails the view that knowledge and human interests are inextricable. This aspect of Dewey's philosophy has been the subject of extended commentary by Richard Rorty, who views it as a major consequence of Dewey's rejection of the "spectator view of knowledge."[103] The spectator view of knowledge requires the Cartesian separation of knowing and doing, and the rejection of this dualism clearly implies the rejection of value-knowledge dualism as well, which brings us to Rorty's second characterization of pragmatism.

Rorty's Second Characterization of Pragmatism

"There is no epistemological difference between truth about what ought to be and truth about what is, nor any metaphysical difference between facts and values, nor any methodological difference between morality and science."

The Rejection of the Knowing–Doing Dualism is the Foundation of Dewey's Value Theory

Dewey's rejection of the Cartesian knowing—doing dualism logically entails his rejection of the value-knowledge dualism in all of its forms. This makes his theory of valuation a special case of his general theory of knowledge. He develops this point as follows:

> . . . in calling my theory on this matter [i.e., values and valuations] a special case of my *general* theory [of knowledge] I intend to call attention to the fact that I have denied that as judgments, or in respect to method of inquiry, test and verification, value-judgments have any peculiar or unique features. They differ from other judgments, of course, in the specific material they have to do with. But in this respect inquiries and judgments about potatoes, cats, and molecules differ from one another. The genuinely important difference resides in the fact of the much greater *importance with respect to the conduct of life-behavior* possessed by the special subject-matter of so-called value-judgments.[104]

What Dewey is saying here is quite remarkable. His theory of value and valuation is *incorporated* in his theory of knowledge; it is not isolated and set aside from it, as is the case in positivist philosophy. Unlike the positivists, who insist upon maintaining a philosophical chasm between knowledge and values, Dewey takes the position that values are a form of knowing. More importantly, valuations are essential to the process of inquiry that produces warranted assertions.

The Logic by which Dewey Incorporates Values within the Realm of Knowledge

The logic by which he reaches this conclusion may be roughly approximated as follows: the rejection of the knowing–doing dualism places "doing" within the process of inquiry. What this means is that practical judgments of "what should be done" are essential to the process of inquiry.[105] "There is," he says, "no inquiry that does not involve judgments of practice."[106] Judgments of practice are made at all the critical junctures of inquiry. Accordingly, he says:

> The scientific worker has continually to appraise the information he gathers from his own observations and from the findings of others; he has to appraise its bearing upon what problems to undertake and what activities of observation, experimentation and calculation to carry out. While he "knows" in the sense of understanding, systems of conceptual materials, including laws, he has to estimate their relevancy and force as conditions of the particular inquiry undertaken.[107]

Judgments of practice direct the behavior of the inquirer both in the formulation of hypotheses and in the testing of their consequences. Thus, the warranted assertions that are the outcome of competent inquiry cannot be formulated without judgments of practice.

Dewey incorporates valuations (involving value judgments) into this conception of inquiry by arguing that "judgments of value" are a form of practical judgments. Accordingly, he says, "my theme is that a judgment of value is simply a case of practical judgment, a judgment about the doing of something."[108] It is by this line of reasoning that inquiry logically entails value judgments.

Dewey uses the terms *valuation*, *judgments about values*, and *value judgments* synonymously. The distinction he is most concerned about making, however, is that between "prizing" and "appraising" (or between "valuing" and "valuation)."[109] Prizing (or valuing) is a matter of "direct, active, noncognitive experience,"[110] whereas the appraisal (or valuation) is a matter of judgment based on a conscious awareness of an intellectual process by which a standard of judgment is formulated and applied in a situation requiring an appraisal.

Prizing (or valuing) is not, in Dewey's view, a matter of judgment. Prizings "have their immediate source in biological modes of behavior and . . . owe their concrete content to the influence of cultural conditions."[111] They are, in other words, manifestations of conditioned behavior that is, for the most part, habitual and not premised upon reflection and inquiry. As behavior, prizing is subject to empirical investigation; it is not something that is confined to some sort of private, "subjective" realm (such as "mind"), which lies beyond the reach of systematic inquiry and critique. The act of prizing (or of valuing or of enjoyment or of desire) is a fact of behavior subject to inquiry and critique.

The Significance of Rejecting the Objective–Subjective Dualism in Value Theory

In Dewey's view values are part of nature, and their origins and character should not be extracted from nature through the use of the ontological objective–subjective dualism.[112] A separation between the objective and subjective realms, he says,

> ... could exist only if the personal attitudes ran their course in a world by themselves. But they are always responses to what is going on in the situation of which they are a part, and their successful or unsuccessful expression depends upon their interaction with other changes. Life activities flourish and fail only in connection with changes of the environment. They are literally bound up with these changes; our desires, emotions, and affections are but various ways in which our doings are tied up with the doings of things and persons about us. Instead of marking a purely personal or subjective realm, separated from the objective and impersonal, they indicate the non-existence of such a separate world. They afford convincing evidence that changes in things are not alien to the activities of a self, and that the career and welfare of the self are bound up with the movement of persons or things.[113]

However, as the previous discussion has indicated, the separation of the objective from the subjective is common to both the empiricist and idealist traditions in philosophy.

The reliance on this Cartesian dualism has led philosophers, in particular positivists, to adopt what Dewey calls a "metaphysical individualism." He develops this idea as follows:

> ... the notion that an adequate theory of human behavior—including particularly the phenomena of desire and purpose—can be formed by considering individuals apart from the cultural setting in which they live, move, and have their being—a theory which may justly be called metaphysical individualism—has united with the metaphysical belief in a mentalistic realm to keep valuation-phenomena in subjection to unexamined traditions, convention, and institutionalized customs. The separation alleged to exit between the "world of facts" and the "realm of values" will disappear from human beliefs only as valuation-phenomena are seen to have their immediate source in biological modes

of behavior and to owe their concrete content to the influence of cultural conditions.[114]

"Metaphysical individualism" is clearly the philosophical foundation upon which the "methodological individualism" of neoclassical and Austrian thought is based. Methodological individualism is grounded precisely in the subjectivism Dewey attributes to metaphysical individualism: namely, "It has its roots in the notion that the consciousness of each person is wholly private, a self-enclosed continent, intrinsically independent of the ideas, wishes, purposes of everybody else."[115]

The consequences of this subjectivistic approach to values in economics is precisely what Dewey alludes to in the above passage: fruitful inquiry into the nature of values (and valuation) in neoclassical and Austrian thought is blocked, thereby keeping "valuation-phenomena in subjection to unexamined traditions, convention, and institutionalized customs." The institutionalist critique of utility theory (both cardinal and ordinal) and Austrian subjective cost theory is based on the view that such formulations, relying on the Cartesian objective–subjective dualism, prevent the economist from examining those cultural processes of value formation that lie at the heart of economic valuation. This is the common theme that runs through all institutionalist criticisms of the "apriorism" they find in mainstream and Austrian theory.

Returning now to Dewey's conception of appraisal (or valuation), the first thing to note is that it involves judgments about prizings or valuings. It is necessary, according to Dewey, to be able to distinguish between what is desired and what is desirable; otherwise the use of intelligence in human affairs is futile. Accordingly, he says, "[t]o make a valuation, to judge appraisingly, is then to bring to conscious perception relations of productivity and resistance and thus to make value significant, intelligent and intelligible."[116] In other words, to engage in appraisal or valuation, it is necessary to subject valuing to inquiry. Moreover, it is critical to human well-being that inquiry produce conceptions of value that sustain the continuity of inquiry and offer a normative frame of reference for the problem-solving processes of the community. Dewey puts the matter this way:

> When theories of values do not afford intellectual assistance in framing ideas and beliefs about values that are adequate to direct action, the gap must be filled by other means. If intelligent method is lacking, prejudice, the pressure of immediate circumstance, self-interest and class-interest, traditional customs, institutions of accidental historical origin, are *not* lacking, and they tend to take the place of intelligence. Thus we are led to our main proposition: *Judgments about values are judgments about the conditions and the results of experienced objects; judgments about that which should regulate the formation of our desires,*

> *affections and enjoyments*. For whatever decides their formation will determine the main course of our conduct, personal and social.[117]

Thus appraisal (valuation) arises in the process of inquiry and requires the formulation of standards of judgment. It should be noted that Dewey's treatment of the distinction between valuings and valuation lies at the philosophical heart of the distinction that institutionalists draw between "ceremonial" and "instrumental" valuation. Indeed, the passage cited above is both substantively and rhetorically resonant with arguments offered repeatedly by Ayres, Foster, Tool, and other institutionalists who have commented on this distinction.

Judgments of Value Are Formed within the Process of Inquiry

Dewey distinguishes between values brought in from outside inquiry and valuations and standards of judgment formed within inquiry. When values are regarded as existing in a realm beyond knowledge, it makes perfectly good sense to exclude them from inquiry. This is true whether they take the form of absolutistic moral injunctions or some sort of "subjectivistic" set of preferences. In Dewey's view, values so conceived do not have the logical capacity to function as standards of judgment in inquiry. But the exclusion of such values does not mean that all forms of valuation must be excluded from inquiry. The way he develops this point is worth quoting at length.

> The soundness of the principle that moral condemnation and approbation should be excluded from the operations of obtaining and weighing material data and from the operations by which conceptions for dealing with the data are instituted, is, however, often converted into the notion that all evaluations should be excluded. This conversion is, however, effected only through the intermediary of a thoroughly fallacious notion; the notion, namely, that the moral blames and approvals in question *are* evaluative and that they exhaust the field of evaluation. For they are *not* evaluative in any logical sense of evaluation. They are not even judgments in the logical sense of judgment. For they rest upon some preconception of *ends* that *should* or *ought* to be attained. This preconception excludes ends (consequences) from the field of inquiry and reduces inquiry at its very best to the truncated and distorted business of finding out means for realizing objectives already settled upon. Judgment which is actually judgment (that satisfies the logical conditions of judgment) institutes means-consequences (ends) in *strict conjugate relation* to each other. Ends have to be adjudged (evaluated) on the basis of the available means by which they can be attained just as much as existential materials have to be adjudged (evaluated) with

> respect to their function as material means of effecting a resolved situation. For an end-in-view is itself a means, namely, a procedural means.[118]

In this statement Dewey links together the role of valuations in inquiry with his conception of the means–ends continuum. If one rejects the view that the ends of inquiry are not given a priori, then valuation is inherent in the process of inquiry. He lays specific emphasis on this point in his discussion of social theory.

> Evaluative judgments, judgments of better and worse about the means to be employed, material and procedural, are required. The evils in current social judgments of ends and policies arise, as has been said, from importations of judgments of value from outside inquiry. The evils spring from the fact that *the values employed are not determined in and by the process of inquiry*: [italics mine] for it is assumed that certain ends have an inherent value so unquestionable that they regulate and validate the means employed, instead of ends being determined on the basis of existing conditions as obstacles-resources. Social inquiry, in order to satisfy the conditions of scientific method, must judge certain objective consequences to be the end which is *worth* [Dewey's italics.] attaining under the given conditions. But, to repeat, this statement does not mean what it is often said to mean: Namely, that ends and values can be assumed outside of scientific inquiry so that the latter is then confined to determination of the means best calculated to arrive at the realization of such values. On the contrary, it means that ends in their capacity of values can be validly determined only on the basis of the tensions, obstructions and positive potentialities that are found, by controlled observation, to exist in the actual situation.[119]

It is clear from these remarks that Dewey does not believe that values are contaminants of inquiry, impairing objectivity in some sense. Objectivity in inquiry *is not* a matter of excluding valuations from inquiry; on the contrary, it is a matter of determining what kinds of valuations are appropriate by assessing the consequences they have for the continuity of inquiry. In Dewey's view it is when values are *not* determined *in and by* the process of inquiry that they introduce unwarranted and uncontrollable biases into inquiry and disrupt its continuity.

Valuations Are Required For the Determination of Factual Propositions

This point has particular relevance for the determination of the facts in any given inquiry. Contrary to the positivist view that the determination of facts inquiry must be confined to a strict observance of the positive–normative dichotomy, Dewey argues that valuations are critical to the determination of what the relevant facts are. He develops this idea as follows:

> The notion that evaluation is concerned only with *ends* and that, with the ruling out of moral ends, evaluative judgments are ruled out rests, then, upon a profound misconception of the nature of the logical conditions and constituents of all scientific inquiry. All competent and authentic inquiry demands that out of the complex welter of existential and potentially observable and recordable material, certain material be selected and weighed *as* data or the "facts of the case." This process is one of adjudgment, of appraisal or evaluation. On the other end, there is, as has been just stated, no evaluation when ends are taken to be already given. An idea of an end *to be* reached, and end-*in-view*, is logically indispensable in discrimination of existential material as the evidential and testing facts of the case. Without it, there is no guide for observation; without it, one can have no conception of what one should look for or even *is* looking for. One "fact" would be just as good as another—that is, good for nothing in control of inquiry and formation and in settlement of a problem.[120]

As stated earlier, Dewey did not believe that the facts "speak for themselves"; which is to say, all factual propositions in science are theory-laden. It is now clear from the above line of argument that the theoretical frame of reference in which facts are converted into evidence is a normative frame of reference.

The Community of Inquiry and the Values of Science

There is yet another sense in which Dewey's theory of inquiry entails normative considerations. It arises in connection with Dewey's concurrence with Peirce's view that "the method of modern science . . . has been made social."[121] As Dewey puts it: "An inquirer in a given special field appeals to the experiences of the community of his fellow workers for confirmation and correction of his results."[122] In other words, the process of verification requires the correlation of behavior among the practitioners in a given field of inquiry, and, by implication, in science in general. However, this requires that values are used as standards of judgment by which behavior is correlated.[123] Both Charles S. Peirce and Jacob Bronowski have commented on the kinds of normative considerations involved in the correlation of scientific behavior. Peirce asserts that one should "not block the way of inquiry."[124] And Bronowski states that an overriding moral injunction in science is that "we ought to act in such a way that what is true can be verified to be so."[125] "The values of science," Bronowski says, "derive neither from the virtues of its members, nor from the finger-wagging codes of conduct by which every profession reminds itself to be good. They have grown out of the practice of science, because they are the inescapable conditions for its practice."[126] Note how closely Bronowski's language parallels that of Dewey's regarding the notion that those values that are the legitimate bases of inquiry must be "determined in and by the process of inquiry."[127] These observations lead to the conclusion that "verification," "disconfirmation," "falsification," or whatever other name the process might be called is ultimately based on a system of values which is required to correlate the behavior of scientists in their collective effort to arrive at warranted assertions. The "demarcation" between "science" and "nonscience" is not to be found in a distinction between "objectively verifiable" and "nonverifiable" domains, but in the types of value systems that guide the formulation of propositions in each. "Metaphysical" systems of thought rely on standards of judgment (values) that are imposed on inquiry from without; "scientific" systems of thought rely upon values that are determined in and by the process of inquiry.

The Normative Character of Institutionalist Methodology

Dewey's theory of valuation was a work in progress throughout the latter part of his life. Even scholars sympathetic to Dewey's philosophical research program concede this point, noting that much work beyond his own contributions needed to be done to bring the theory of instrumental valuation to completion.[128] It was to be expected that those American institutionalists working in the pragmatic instrumentalist tradition would attempt to carry Dewey's research program forward in the field of political economy. This effort is manifest in both their methodological and substantive inquiries. To acknowledge this effort is not to suggest that it has been met with uniform acceptance among all institutionalists or that it has (or should) become the cannonical form of institutional economics in the United States or abroad. Nevertheless, the development and application of the theory of instrumental valuation is a dominant characteristic in "neoinstitutional" economics (i.e., American institutional economics in the post-World War II period developed primarily under the influence of the teaching of Clarence E. Ayres).[129] The comments that follow provide a brief sketch of the author's understanding of how the theory of instrumental valuation is worked out in the methodological and substantive research of the neoinstitutional literature.

At the methodological level of discourse, instrumental valuation requires that a clear distinction be drawn between prizings, value judgments, and valuations. Dewey's definition of prizings is adopted in drawing these distinctions. A prizing or desire is a taste or preference unmediated by inquiry into whether what is desired is desirable. Habituated patterns of unexamined tastes and preferences acquired through cultural conditioning would fall into this category. There is uniform agreement among institutionalists (of whatever persuasion on the theory of valuation) that such valuings must be excluded from methodological discourse on the grounds that they would have the same degenerative effect on inquiry as the a priori acceptance of ultimate values or eternal verities. Such values would indeed constitute a source of bias that would compromise the objectivity (however defined) of inquiry.

But is it really possible to eliminate completely such sources of bias from inquiry? The pragmatic instrumentalist response would have to be: probably not. This response, in itself, obviously distances the pragmatic instrumental institutionalist from any kind of "positivist" intellectual strategy that presumes that objectivity can be obtained through the elimination of values from inquiry. This does not mean, however, that the pragmatic instrumental institutionalist is willing to consider the Diltheyan alternative, which is to adopt the view that the methods of knowing in natural and social sciences are fundamentally different.[130] Pragmatic instrumentalists distance themselves from those versions of Continental hermeneutic philosophy that allow for *wertfreiheit* in the natural sciences while postulating a linguistically and historically value-embedded mode of knowing for the social sciences. From the point of view of the pragmatic instrumentalist, this intellectual strategy is unacceptable because, as the foregoing discussion of Dewey's philosophy indicates, the pragmatic instrumentalist view of science does not grant that "scientific" inquiry, whether in the natural or the social sciences, is value-free. Where, then, does this leave the issue?

To put the issue in perspective, we must consider the two other value terms introduced above: *value judgments* and *valuations*. For methodological purposes, a distinction must be drawn between them. This involves amending Dewey's terminology but not his conceptualization of the normative issues involved. The term *value judgment* will be defined more narrowly than it is in general methodological discourse (including Dewey's commentaries) where the term is a catchall for any kind of normative proposition. For purposes of this discussion, a value is a standard of judgment, and a value judgment involves the selection of a standard of judgment (value), which, in turn, is used as a standard by which valuations are made. The term *valuation*, involves the application of a standard of judgment (a value) in making choices. Thus, a value judgment is logically prior to a valuation.[131]

The traditional view that valuations as normative propositions must come to rest either on some ultimate value, or, in the alternative, amount to little more than an expression of prizings or desires ("emotional ejaculations") blocks inquiry into valuations and provides the basis for the belief that value judgments loosely defined must be excluded from scientific inquiry on pain of losing any semblance of objectivity. It must be granted that if the process by which valuations are formed *is* excluded from the discussion, then disputes over valuations *are* futile. The pragmatic instrumental view takes a different approach, as already indicated in the foregoing discussion of Dewey. Let us reiterate that approach using the new definitions just introduced. Properly conducted, scientific inquiry involves a systematic, critical formulation of value judgments that render values to serve as standards of judgment in the myriad valuations that the scientist undertakes at all stages of inquiry. As H.H. Liebhafsky has characterized it, this is a self-correcting process because the valuations are assessed in terms of their consequences for maintaining the continuity of inquiry.[132] In other words, the process of instrumental valuation is the mode of valuation that emerges from and gives direction to scientific inquiry. As Ayers puts it: "The values which emerge from this instrumental process derive their significance from that process."[133] When the mode of valuation itself is under systematic, critical scrutiny, it is more likely that those inappropriate valuings styled above as prizings or desires can be minimized, if not entirely eliminated, from inquiry. Such valuings lack instrumental warrant precisely because they emerge from habituations which are themselves generated outside the process of inquiry. As such, a methodology that affords rigorous attention to the character of the instrumentally warranted normative propositions used in inquiry provides the means by which prizings and desires can be identified and rooted out.

What must be emphasized is that objectivity is not achieved by eliminating normative propositions from inquiry. On the contrary, objectivity requires the self-conscious application of the instrumental mode of valuation to each step or phase of inquiry. Thus, values as such *are not* contaminates of inquiry; instrumentally warranted values are the necessary standards by which choices are made in the process of inquiry.[134]

Scientific Inquiry as an Institutional Arrangement

As indicated in the foregoing discussion of the views of Dewey, Pierce, Bronowski, and Kaplan, scientific inquiry is a *social* process. This "knowing and doing" process, as Dewey says, involves "judgments of practice" that imply the doing of things in a social context that requires the correlation of behavior among scientists. Accordingly, instrumentally warranted values function as standards of judgment by which behavior is correlated in the conduct of inquiry.

This methodological observation raises an important substantive matter which plays a prominent role in institutional analysis, the concept of an "institution." J. Fagg Foster and his students define an institution as "a set of socially prescribed patterns of correlated behavior, wherein patterns of behavior are either ceremonially warranted or instrumentally warranted."[135] The "warrant" of a behavioral pattern depends on the mode of valuation by which the behavior is correlated. If the mode of valuation is ceremonial, the value that serves as a standard of judgment for correlating behavior is habituated by common practices of the community that are regarded as being beyond inquiry and accepted as cultural givens. The validity of such values is established through considerations of authenticity, tradition, and invidious distinctions among the populace, and are mystified by ideology. Validity is symbolized by "ceremonial adequacy." If the mode of valuation is instrumental, the value that serves as a standard of judgment for the correlation of behavior is validated by its consequences and subject to continuous scrutiny through the application of the community's technological processes out of which it has emerged. A working hypothesis of the theory of institutional change (as it has evolved out of the works of Veblen, Dewey, Ayres, Foster, and Tool) is that all institutions will exhibit varying mixes of ceremonially warranted and instrumentally warranted behavior.

In applying these analytical concepts to the foregoing methodological discussion, to the extent that scientific inquiry can be regarded as a social process, it is an institutionalized process. Furthermore, the arguments presented above concerning the role of values in scientific inquiry presume that instrumentally warranted patterns of behavior are dominant in scientific enterprise. Notice the use of the word *dominant*, for it pertains to the question of whether prizings and desires and other forms of noninstrumental values can be eliminated from scientific inquiry. Once again, the answer to this question is: not entirely. But the presumption is that the dominance of instrumentally warranted patterns of behavior in scientific activity and the self-correcting character of the instrumental mode of valuation will minimize their presence.

In regard to the specific stages of inquiry at which values play a role in inquiry, pragmatic instrumental institutionalists would argue that all stages of inquiry have a normative dimension, including but not limited to: 1) the identification of problems for inquiry as an expression of human interests; 2) the choice of an appropriate logic (or logics) to be used in the formulation of theoretical concepts; 3) the choice and application of a standard (or standards) of relevance in the process of abstraction; 4) the choice of appropriate techniques of empirical observation; 5) the choice and application of a standard (or standards) of statistical significance; 6) the choice of technique (or techniques) by which linguistic and historical dimensions of both the problem and the investigator are to be brought to the fore and subjected to critique; and 7) the choice and application of standards by which to monitor and clarify discourse among the community of scholars involved in the inquiry. Gunnar Myrdal captured the flavor of the foregoing enumeration in his remark that

> . . . [f]acts do not organize themselves into concepts and theories just by being looked at; indeed, except within the framework of concepts and theories, there are no scientific facts but only chaos. There is an inescapable *a priori* element in all scientific work. Questions must be asked before answers can be given. The questions are all expressions of our interest in the world; they are at bottom valuations. Valuations are thus necessarily involved already at the stage when we observe facts and carry on theoretical analysis, and not only at the stage when we draw political inferences from facts and valuations.[136]

It is on the basis of such considerations that Jerry Petr correctly notes that institutional economics is "values-driven."[137]

Rorty's Third Characterization of Pragmatism

"[T]here are no constraints on inquiry save conversational ones—no wholesale constraints derived from the nature of the objects, or of the mind, or of language, but only those retail constraints provided by the remarks of our fellow-inquirers."

The Problem of Choosing Among Competing Paradigms

An issue that has preoccupied the literature of the philosophy of science in the post-World War II period is the question of how to choose among competing theories.[138] Two points of view have tended to dominate in this debate among mainstream economists: the verificationists (who subscribe to the positivist view) and the falsificationists (who subscribe to Popper's view). Both of these positions presume that there is a philosophical court of last resort to which the issue can be appealed. In other words, both presume that there are metaphysical foundations, couched either in a language of sense data or, at least, a common vocabulary, upon which the definitive criteria for choosing among theories can be based. This common assumption has been attacked from two different (but similar) positions.

One line of attack arises out of the Kuhnian analysis of the structure of scientific revolutions.[139] Although he did not fashion his analysis to deal with economics, Kuhn's discussion of "normal science" is a precise description of the dominant influence that neoclassical thought exerts on economics. What is particularly disconcerting about Kuhn's analysis to those who subscribe to foundationalist views of science is his thesis that the dominance of a particular scientific paradigm, which gives shape and form to the "normal science" in a field, is less a matter of the application of metaphysical criteria to an evaluation of the paradigm's scientific credentials as it is a matter of the historical development of the practice of science in that field. Although the meaning of his position has elicited considerable confusion, debate, and criticism, Kuhn advances the argument that there are no ultimate philosophical grounds upon which competing scientific paradigms can be judged. In short, it is his view that the unique character of the vocabulary of each scientific paradigm is such as to make competing paradigms "incommensurable."[140]

The other line of attack on the notion that metaphysical grounds can be found for choosing among alternative scientific theories arises out of the literature of philosophical hermeneutics, particularly in the works of European scholars. Although the term *hermeneutics* has been given different meanings in a variety of different contexts, reflecting the fact that widely disparate types of intellectual activity are carried on in its name, there appears to be general agreement among those engaged in hermeneutical studies that the term refers to the theory of interpretation.[141] Philip Mirowski has defined hermeneutics as "the theory of the process of interpretation, be it of a text, a doctrine, or a phenomenon, by a self-identified community of inquiry."[142] Hemeneutical philosophers emphasize the "historicity" and the "linguisticality" of knowledge.[143] According to Wachterhauser, they "argue that language and history are always both conditions and limits of understanding."[144] "Historicity" entails the ontological notion that who we *are* cannot be traced to "a human nature that is the same in all historical circumstances."[145] Moreover, hermeneutical scholars believe "that the very meaning and validity of any knowledge-claim is inextricably intertwined with the historical situation of both its formulators and evaluators."[146] "Linguisticality" entails the idea that all human understanding is bounded by "language that itself has limitations and blind spots and hence awaits its own critique."[147] The combined effects of the historicity and linguisticality of human understanding make it entirely possible that different "self-identified communities of inquiry" cannot find a common intellectual ground upon which directly to compare or judge their competing knowledge-claims. In the case of economics, this means that it may not be possible to find a common theoretical language by which competing paradigms of inquiry can be compared and judged.

There are many important areas of consideration shared in common by Kuhn and hermeneutical philosophers, and in the more advanced stages of Kuhn's argument it may well be that his position is essentially the same as the hermeneutical perspective. The Kuhnian and hermeneutical perspectives are treated here (perhaps somewhat arbitrarily) as separate approaches primarily because they have evolved in separate literatures; the Kuhnian in the history of science, the hermeneutical in the broad reach of Continental philosophy across the sciences and humanities. But the essential point is that Kuhn and the hermeneutical philosophers both pose a challenge to the idea that there is some transcendental set of criteria by which competing scientific paradigms can be compared and judged for their essential validity.

According to Richard Rorty, the kinds of positions taken by Kuhn and many (but not all) hermeneutical philosophers amounts to a rejection of the notion that either science or philosophy can be a "mirror of nature."[148] Rorty himself speaks of the escape from "epistemology." As traditionally conceived from the time of the Greek philosophers (with the important exception of the pragmatists and a few others), epistemology has been understood to embody foundational principles upon which all reliable knowledge is based. If science is, indeed, a mirror of nature, then it is just a matter of discovering the transcendental vocabulary that best represents it. If such a vocabulary does exist, then it is possible to reckon all knowledge-claims in terms of it, and it becomes possible to choose among competing scientific paradigms on the basis of this philosophical court of last appeal. But the pragmatists, particularly Dewey, abandon this "spectator theory of knowledge" for a process of inquiry in which the standards used to evaluate knowledge-claims are generated from within the process of inquiry itself rather than from without. To reiterate Rorty's first characterization of pragmatism: there is no wholesale, epistemological way to direct, or criticize, or underwrite the course of inquiry.

The Institutionalist Position

We are now at a point in the discussion where we can consider the position institutionalists have taken on the question of the choice of theories. Over the years, various institutionalists have provided an array of views on the issue. Indeed, in spite of the influence of philosophical pragmatism on the institutionalist literature, one can find different institutionalists toying with just about every philosophical position mentioned above: logical empiricism, Kuhnian paradigmatics, Popperian falsificationism, and philosophical hermeneutics. But perhaps the most common deviation from pragmatic instrumentalist position in the institutionalist literature is empiricism. The repeated stress on the issue of realism in the institutionalist critique of neoclassical thought has often been premised on the kind of empiricist epistemology that Dewey explicitly rejected. The charge of a lack of realism in the basic postulates of neoclassical thought is often presented as if a straightforward appeal to the facts would provide definitive grounds for the rejection of neoclassical postulates. Such commentary continues to rattle about the back corridors of the institutionalist literature.

The most charitable thing that can be said about such arguments is that institutionalists tend to err on the side of empiricism rather than idealism when they inadvertently backslide into the Cartesian vice of dualistic thought.[149] This reflects their assiduous effort to avoid the errors of apriorism, which they believe are diagnostic of the difficulties inherent in neoclassical methodology. To the extent that their aversion to apriorism is based on the argument that all assumptions of a theory must be descriptively accurate of some existential phenomenon, they presume, in effect, that a fact can kill a theory, and descend into a kind of naive empiricism (or ultra-empiricism as Machlup would have called it).[150] Nevertheless, the apriorism of both neoclassical and Austrian economics is vulnerable to the kind of criticism Dewey used against Kant. Thus institutionalists can be pardoned for erring on the empiricist side when they reject Lionel Robbins's assertion that the postulates of economics "are so much the stuff of our everyday experience that they have only to be stated to be recognized as obvious."[151] Those things that need only to be stated in order to be recognized as obvious are propositions unmediated by inquiry, and, as such, they are as close as one gets to self-evident propositions in the context of any discussion that purports to have empirical significance. If such propositions are effectively insulated from the possibility of critique and revision, they would indeed be regarded by pragmatic instrumentalists as beyond the scientific pale. Having made this point with respect to Robbins's thinking, it is probably unnecessary to repeat these arguments with respect to the purest form of apriorism still exerting influence on the contemporary Austrian literature: namely, the neo-Kantian apriorism of Ludwig von Mises.[152] Mises's "praxeology" is based upon Kantian foundationalism which postulates that there are logical categories of mind that offer irrefutable, a prior propositions about human action that possess apodictic truth. In other words, the fundamental premises of praxeology take the form of synthetic a priori propositions. Unlike Lionel Robbins who believed that empirical investigations might establish the "applicability" of economic theory based on self-evident premises, von Mises abjures even this limitation on the universal applicability of adpodictically certain postulates of praxeology. According to von Mises, the only flaws that might appear in praxeology would take of the form of errors in logical deduction. From an institutionalist perspective, Lionel Robbins is a paragon of reasonableness when compared to von Mises.

Finally, the pragmatic instrumentalist view on the choice of theories in economics (or any of the social sciences) comes down to this: competing theories must be judged on their capacity to transform an indeterminate situation into a unified whole; that is, they must be evaluated for their capacity to contribute to the problem-solving processes of real, living communities. It should be noted that the pragmatic instrumentalist view shifts the ground of the theory choice debate from the realm of knowing to the realm of knowing and doing. Given the prevalence of Cartesianism in the philosophy of science in general, and in economic methodology in particular, the theory choice debate is preoccupied with the question of competing knowledge-claims within a realm of discourse that typically separates knowing from doing (in Dewey's sense of these terms). The pragmatic instrumentalist view of the matter eschews the search for formal criteria by which to select among competing theories and focuses instead on a means–ends continuum in which theories are viewed as a means to the ends-in-view of inquiry. But it must be recalled that for Dewey inquiry is not confined to a realm of knowing that is somehow ontologically distinct from the realm of doing. Both the conduct of inquiry and the application of its outcomes to the problem-solving processes of the community combine knowing *and* doing. Thus competing theories ultimately must be evaluated for their potential to contribute to the problem-solving activities of the community.

A Concluding Comment

A number of philosophers have called into question Rorty's use of Dewey in setting forth his version of pragmatism. It is frequently argued that Rorty completely rejects Dewey's conception of science, even though he finds Dewey's rejection of the spectator theory of knowledge most useful for his (Rorty's) own philosophical agenda. Rorty interprets Dewey as abandoning "epistemology" in favor of hermeneutics, the search for "truth" in favor of a search for ways of "coping," and "objectivity" in favor of a notion of "solidarity." For Rorty, this comes down to a matter of substituting "conversation" for "verification" or "falsification," and so forth. As one of the world's most interesting and provocative philosophers, Rorty has stirred up a good deal of controversy, the dimensions of which cannot be easily summarized in this essay.[153] Suffice it to say, it has been a calculated philosophical risk to feature Rorty's three characterizations of pragmatism in the structure of this chapter. This is particularly true of the third characterization. Rorty's view that "there are no constraints on inquiry save conversational ones" carries with it formidable ontological, epistemological, and axiological implications, none of which can be explored here.[154]

Nevertheless, there is a generosity and openness in Rorty's notion of "conversation" that captures very nicely an important aspect of institutionalist methodology. It is the inclination toward methodological pluralism exhibited in pragmatic instrumentalist aversion to professional dogmatism and ideological (paradigmatic) rigidity. Pluralism in the sense that the term is being used here is not synonymous with eclecticism. Pragmatic instrumentalists place too high a value on coherence to be eclectic in their methodology. It is rather the basic pragmatic doctrine that no proposition is beyond revision that keeps open institutionalist discourse and permits the institutionalist to engage in genuine dialogue with all who would care to join in, including neoclassicists, Austrian marginalists, Marxists, critical theorists, and others.

In recent years this "conversational" openness has permitted American institutionalists to form strong intellectual bonds with a new and energetic group of evolutionary economists in Great Britain and on the Continent. One of the most exciting discoveries in this trans-Atlantic dialogue is the remarkable degree of intellectual congruity between American institutionalists of the pragmatic instrumentalist perspective and British and Continental evolutionary economists. A case in point is to be found in the work of Geoffrey Hodgson, who is the founding Secretary-Treasurer of the European Association for Evolutionary Political Economy (EAEPE). Hodgson's book, *Economics and Institutions: A Manifesto for a Modern Institutional Economics*,[155] sets forth both a critique of orthodoxy and an agenda for the development of an institutionalist alternative that closely parallels the pragmatic instrumentalist methodology characterized in this chapter; yet Hodgson makes only one reference to Ayres and no mention at all of Dewey. Hodgson's work and that of his colleagues in EAEPE provide an interesting case of an intellectual convergence (with American institutionalism) of two quite independent philosophical traditions in economic methodology. This is not to suggest that the European evolutionary institutionalists are likely to embrace American institutionalism (the pragmatic instrumentalist variety or otherwise) or that American institutionalists will find that all the Europeans are doing to be to their liking. Nevertheless, the intellectual cross-fertilization is well under way and a new worldwide institutionalist literature is in the offing.

Acknowledgments

The author would like to acknowledge the patience, moral support, and insightful editorial commentaries provided by Marc Tool during all phases of the preparation of this chapter. It could not have been completed without his personal and professional generosity. He is, of course, absolved of any responsibility for the deficiencies that remain.

In addition, the author would like to thank Dr. Jo Ann Boydston and The Center for Dewey Studies and the Southern Illinois University Press for permission to use quotations from *The Works of John Dewey*.

Notes

1. The term *pragmatic instrumentalist* is taken from Dewey's use of the term in *The Quest for Certainty* in Jo Ann Boydston, ed., *The Later Works of John Dewey, 1925–1953, Vol. 4: 1929* (Carbondale: Southern Illinois University Press, 1984, footnote, p. 30. It is hoped that by using "pragmatic" to modify "instrumentalist" one can clearly differentiate between Dewey's use of "instrumental" and Karl Popper's use of the term in his philosophy of science. See Karl Popper, *The Logic of Scientific Discovery* (New York: Basic Books, 1959), footnote, p. 59. Alas, the failure to make this differentiation between the Deweyan and Popperian uses of the term has led to considerable intellectual mischief, a matter that will be taken up later in a comment on Friedman's "instrumentalism." One must also differentiate between Dewey's use of the term from that of Jürgen Habermas. Habermas confines the term *instrumental* to the *technical cognitive interest* which he distinguishes from "practical" and "emancipatory" human interests. In contrast, Dewey's use of *instrumentalism* spans the three realms of human interests identified by Habermas. See Jürgen Habermas, *Knowledge and Human Interests*, trans. Jeremy J. Shapiro (Boston: Beacon Press, 1971), pp. 308–311. For a discussion the Habermasian usage, see Jon D. Wisman, "Toward a Humanist Reconstruction of Economic Science," *Journal of Economic Issues* 13 (March 1979): 19–48; and "Economic Knowledge, Evolutionary Epistemology, and Human Interests," *Journal of Economic Issues* 23 (June 1989): 647–656.

2. There is no intention here to diminish the importance of Peirce's philosophical influence on institutionalist methodology. Philip Mirowski, for one, suggests that while Dewey has, indeed, had a greater influence than Peirce on institutionalist methodology, Dewey's

dominance must be regarded as a basic weakness in the institutionalist literature. He argues that the viability of institutionalism will depend on whether the "hermeneutical" perspective of Peirce can be substituted for the views of Dewey in guiding the methodology of institutional thought in the future. See Philip Mirowski, "The Philosophical Basis of Institutional Economics," *Journal of Economic Issues* 21 (September 1987): 1001–1038; and the author's critical comment on this piece, Paul D. Bush, "Institutionalist Methodology and Hermeneutics: A Comment on Mirowski," *Journal of Economic Issues* 23 (December 1989): 1159–1172. For two views of Peirce's influence on institutionalist methodology that are quite different than Mirowski's, see Alan W. Dyer, "Veblen on Scientific Creativity: The Influence of Charles S. Peirce," *Journal of Economic Issues* 20 (March 1986): 21–41; and H.H. Liebhafsky, "Peirce on the Summum Bonnum and the Unlimited Community," *Journal of Economic Issues* 20 (March 1986): 5–20.

3. John R. Commons, *Institutional Economics*, Vol. I and II (Madison: University of Wisconsin Press, 1961 [1934]), p. 150.

4. Both studied at Johns Hopkins as graduate students under Peirce. They both taught at the University of Chicago from the late 1890s until 1904 (Veblen, 1892–1904, and Dewey, 1894-1904) and at the New School for Social Research, where Veblen held his last academic post. See Joseph Dorfman, *Thorstein Veblen and His America*, 7th ed. (Clifton: Augustus M. Kelly, 1972), p. 449; and H.H. Liebhafsky, "An Institutionalist Evaluation of the Recent *Apparently*, But Only Apparently Fatal Attack on Institutionalism," *Journal of Economics Issues* 22 (September 1988): 837–851. The Liebhafsky article contains a discussion of the relationship of Veblen and Dewey to Peirce and Ayres.

5. Dorfman, *Thorstein Veblen and His America*, p. 450.

6. C.E. Ayres, *Toward a Reasonable Society* (Austin: University of Texas Press, 1961), pp. 29–32. Rick Tilman documents in some detail the strong intellectual ties between Dewey and Ayres as expressed in their correspondence. See Rick Tilman, "New Light on John Dewey, Clarence Ayres, and the Development of Evolutionary Economics," *Journal of Economic Issues* 24 (December 1990): 963–979. Dewey made direct reference to Ayres's *Theory of Economic Progress* (Chapel Hill: University of North Carolina Press, 1944) as a study that incorporated an approach to values and valuations which Dewey regarded as pertinent to his own inquiries. See John Dewey, "Some Questions about Value," in Jo Ann Boydston, ed., *The Later Works of John Dewey, 1925–53, Vol. 15: 1942–48* (Carbondale: Southern Illinois University Press, 1989), p. 108, footnote 6; and "By Nature and by Art," *ibid.*, p. 89, footnote 3. Ayres participated in Ray Lepley's symposium on Dewey's theory of value in which there is considerable discussion among Dewey, Ayres, and others (e.g., George R. Geiger) concerning the interrelationship between Dewey's and Ayres's views on values in culture and on their role in inquiry. See Clarence E. Ayres, "The Value Economy," in Ray Lepley, ed., *Value: A Cooperative Inquiry* (New York: Columbia University Press, 1949), pp. 43–63. For the criticisms and rejoinders relevant to Ayres's contribution, see pages 302–311, 321–333, and 415–423.

7. An important consequence of reading Veblen from this perspective is that a "normative" Veblen emerges from behind his well-known rhetorical stance of "Olympian detachment." For a brief characterization of the normative Veblen presented in the context of a commentary on David W. Seckler's *Thorstein Veblen and the Institutionalists* (Boulder: Colorado Associated University Press, 1975), see Paul D. Bush, "Radical Individualism vs. Institutionalism, I," *American Journal of Economics and Sociology* 40 (April 1981): 139–148; and "Radical Individualism vs. Institutionalism, II," *American Journal of Economics and Sociology* 40 (July 1981): 287–298. For Seckler's rebuttal to this characterization, see Seckler, "Individualism and Institutionalism Revisited: A Response to Professor Bush," *American*

Journal of Economics and Sociology 40 (October 1981): 415–425. Not all institutionalists who have an affinity for the ideas of Dewey and Ayres acknowledge the existence of a normative Veblen. See, for example, Wendell Gordon, "The Role of Institutional Economics," *Journal of Economic Issues* 18 (June 1984): 369–381, specifically, pages 378–379.

8. K. William Kapp, "In Defense of Institutional Economics," *Swedish Journal of Economics* 70 (March 1968): 1–18; reprinted in Warren J. Samuels, ed., *Institutional Economics*, Vol. I (Aldershot: Edward Elgar, 1988), pp. 92–107.

9. Professor Ranson made this invitation during his presidential address to the Association for Institutional Thought on April 27, 1984, in San Diego, California, at the 26th Annual Conference of the Western Social Science Association. His address was entitled "Activating AFIT: The Problems and a Possible Solution."

10. Some of Richard Rorty's most important works are: *Philosophy and the Mirror of Nature* (Princeton: Princeton University Press, 1979); *Consequences of Pragmatism* (Minneapolis: University of Minnesota Press, 1982); *Objectivity. Relativism, and Truth: Philosophical Papers*, Volume One (New York: Cambridge University Press, 1991); and *Essays on Heidegger and Others: Philosophical Papers*, Volume Two (New York: Cambridge University Press, 1991).

11. Rorty, *Consequences of Pragmatism*, p. 162.

12. *Ibid*.

13. *Ibid*., p. 163.

14. *Ibid*., p. 165.

15. Brice R. Wachterhauser, "Introduction: History and Language in Understanding," in Brice R. Wachterhauser, ed., *Hermeneutics and Modern Philosophy* (Albany: State University of New York, 1986), pp. 5–61; the quotation is at page 13. The use of the terms *foundationalism* and *foundationalist* in this philosophical context should not be confused with the term *philosophical foundations of*. . . . When the latter phraeseology is used, it simply refers to the philosohical underpinnings of a given methodological position; the philosophical foundations may or may not be foundationalist in character.

16. Dewey, *The Quest for Certainty*.

17. *Ibid*., p. 233.

18. *Ibid*., p. 19. Italics in the original.

19. *Ibid*., p. 157.

20. *Ibid*., p. 231.

21. *Ibid*.

22. *Ibid*., p. 229.

23. John Dewey, *Logic: The Theory of Inquiry*, in Jo Ann Boydston, ed., *The Later Works of John Dewey, 1925–53, Vol. 12: 1938* (Carbondale: Southern Illinois University Press, 1986), p. 111.

24. *Ibid*.

25. *Ibid*., p. 15.

26. *Ibid*., p. 16.

27. *Ibid*., p. 143.

28. *Ibid*., p. 16.

29. Dewey, *The Quest for Certainty*, p. 236.

30. Thorstein B. Veblen, "Why is Economics Not an Evolutionary Science?" in Thorstein B. Veblen, ed., *The Place of Science in Modern Civilisation* (New York: Viking Press, 1942 [1919]), pp. 56–81; the quotation is from page 61.

31. See Wendell Gordon, "The Role of Institutional Economics," pp. 369–381; and *idem*, "The Role of Tool's Social Value Principle," *Journal of Economic Issues* 24 (September 1990): 879–886.

32. A slightly different version of his reply to Wendell Gordon (and also to Anne Mayhew) appears in Marc R. Tool, "Instrumental Value an Eternal Verity? A Reply to Wendell Gordon," *Journal of Economic Issues* 24 (December 1990): 1109–1122; and *idem*, "Culture Versus Social Value? A Response to Mayhew," *Journal of Economic Issues* 24 (December 1990): 1122–1133. See Anne Mayhew, "A Critical Analysis of Tool's *Essays in Social Value Theory*," a paper read at the Annual Meetings of the Association for Institutional Thought, EI Paso, Texas, April 1987; and *idem*, "Culture: Core Concept Under Attack," *Journal of Economics Issues* 21 (June 1987): 587–603.

33. Dewey, *Logic: The Theory of Inquiry*, p. 161. Italics in the original.

34. *Ibid.*, pp. 121–122.

35. *Ibid.*, p. 161.

36. *Ibid.*, p. 117.

37. *Ibid.*, p. 113.

38. *Ibid.*, p. 136. Italics in the original.

39. More will be said about this below in the discussion of the role of value judgments in inquiry.

40. Rorty, *Philosophy and the Mirror of Nature*, p. 12.

41. Dewey, "Propositions, Warranted Assertability, and Truth," in Jo Ann Boydston, ed., *The Later Works of John Dewey, 1925–53, Vol. 14: 1941*, (Carbondale: Southern Illinois University Press, 1988), pp. 179–180. Italics in the original.

42. Rorty, *Consequences of Pragmatism*, p. 86.

43. *Ibid.*, p. 17.

44. Dewey, *Logic: The Theory of Inquiry*, p. 160.

45. J.E. Tiles, *Dewey* (New York: Routledge, 1988), p. 25.

46. Abraham Kaplan, *The Conduct of Inquiry* (San Francisco: Chandler Publishing Company, 1964), p. 333.

47. Pierre Duhem, "Physical Theory and Experiment," in Herbert Feigl and May Brodbeck, eds., *Readings in the Philosophy of Science* (New York: Appelton-Century-Crofts, Inc., 1953), pp. 235–252.

48. Willard V.O. Quine, "Two Dogmas of Empiricism," in Willard V.O. Quine, ed., *From a Logical Point of View*, 2nd ed., rev. (Cambridge: Harvard University Press, 1980 [1953]), pp. 20–46.

49. *Ibid.*, p. 79.

50. Allan G. Gruchy was the first to use the term *holism* in describing the methodology of institutional economics. See his *Modern Economic Thought: The American Contribution* (Now York: Prentice-Hall, 1947). An extensive discussion of holistic methodology in institutional economics is found in Charles K. Wilber and Robert S. Harrison, "The Methodological Basis of Institutional Economics: Pattern Model, Storytelling, and Holism," *Journal of Economic Issues* 12 (March 1978): 61–89. Discussions of holism and pattern models in the social sciences are undertaken by Kaplan, *The Conduct of Inquiry*, pp. 327–328; and Paul Diesing, *Patterns of Discovery in the Social Sciences* (New York: Aldine, 1971), pp. 157–167. For a sophisticated treatment of holism in general, and with respect to John R. Commons's thought in particular, see Yngve Ramstad, "A Pragmatist's Quest for Holistic Knowledge: The Scientific Methodology of John R. Commons," *Journal of Economic Issues* 20 (December 1986): 1067–1105.

51. Ramstad, "A Pragmatist's Quest for Holistic Knowledge . . . ," p. 1097.

52. For a discussion of the preoccupation with "induction" in institutional economics and the failure to develop formal models "to guide observation and experience," see James I. Sturgeon, "Induction and Instrumentalism in Institutional Thought," *Journal of Economic Issues* 18 (June 1984): 599–608, especially, page 604.

53. Kaplan, *The Conduct of Inquiry*, pp. 335–338.

54. An exmple of the use of a hypothetico-deductively formulated model in institutional economics is found in Paul D. Bush, "An Exploration of the Structural Characteristics of a Veblen–Ayres–Foster Defined Institutional Domain," *Journal of Economic Issues* 17 (March 1983): 35–66. Ramstad has criticized the approach taken in that article as being incompatible with a holistic methodology. See Ramstad, "A Pragmatist's Quest for Holistic Knowledge . . . ," p. 1097 and footnotes 12 and 51. "It is my suspicion," he says, "that Bush's ingenious effort to formalize such qualitative and evolving concepts as 'social values,' and then to combine them into concepts such as 'ceremonial encapsulation' or into quantitative indexes such as the 'index of ceremonial dominance,' will ultimately prove sterile" [footnote 15]. While the author is sympathetic to Ramstad's concerns with respect to the perils of both "formalism" and "quantification," he does not believe that the model he set forth in the 1983 article is incompatible with holistic methodology. Indeed, every effort was made to indicate that the "hypothetical" portion of the model was derived from the rich theoretical and empirical insights found in the pattern models of Veblen, Dewey, Ayres, and Foster. In regard to the question of sterility, that is a matter that can only be settled through further inquiry.

55. Diesing, *Patterns of Discovery* . . . , pp. 156–67.

56. Wilbur and Harrison, "The Methodological Basis of Institutional Economics," p. 85.

57. Mirowski, "The Philosophical Basis of Institutional Economics."

58. *Ibid*., p. 1016.

59. Joseph Ratner, ed., *Intelligence in the Modern World: John Dewey's Philosophy* (New York: The Modern Library, 1939), p. 308.

60. Dewey, *The Quest for Certainty*, p. 235.

61. *Ibid*., p. 236.

62. *Ibid*.

63. George R. Geiger, *John Dewey in Perspective* (New York: Oxford University Press, 1958), p. 84.

64. Tiles, *Dewey*, p. 142.

65. *Ibid*.

66. Dewey, *Logic: The Theory of Inquiry*, pp. 30–47.

67. *Ibid*., p. 109. Italics in the original.

68. *Ibid*., p. 161.

69. Mirowski, "The Philosophical Basis of Institutional Economics," p. 1163.

70. *Ibid*., p. 1034, footnote 7. See John Dewey, "Theory of Valuation," in Jo Ann Boydston, ed., *The Later Works of John Dewey, 1925–53, Vol. 13: 1938–39* (Carbondale: Southern Illinois University Press, 1988), pp. 191–251. The author has commented on Mirowski's use of Thayer's observation about Dewey's "alliance with the logical positivists" in Bush, "Institutionalist Methodology and Hermeneutics: A Comment on Mirowski," p. 1163.

71. James A. Swaney and Robert Premus, "Modern Empiricism and Quantum-Leap Theorizing in Economics," *Journal of Economic Issues* 16 (June 1982): 713–730; reprinted in Alfred S. Eichner, ed., *Why Economics is Not Yet a Science* (Armonk, NY: M.E. Sharpe, 1983), pp. 41–60; the words quoted are on pp. 47–48. See Crossland's and Weinel's critique of Swaney and Premus [Philip P. Crossland and Ivan Weinel, "Modern Empiricism and Quantum Leap in Economics: A Comment," *Journal of Economic Issues* 17 (December 1983): 1129–1138] and Swaney's and Premus's reply [James A. Swaney and Robert Premus, "Practice, Logic and Problem Solving: A Reply to Crossland and Weinel," *Journal of Economic Issues* 17 (December 1983): 1138–1142.]. Although this is an interesting exchange of views, the alleged association of Dewey with logical positivism is not mentioned.

72. Dewey, *Logic: The Theory of Inquiry*, pp. 512. Italics in the original.

73. Gladys Parker Foster offers a very clear discussion of the role of prediction in pragmatic instrumentalist thought in "Cultural Relativism and the Theory of Value: The Educational Implications," *American Journal of Economics and Sociology* 50 (July 1991): 257–267; see especially pages 262–265.

74. James A. Swaney, "A Coevolutionary Model of Structural Change," *Journal of Economic Issues* 20 (June 1986): 393–401; *idem*, "Building Instrumental Environmental Control Institutions," *Journal of Economic Issues* 21 (March 1987): 295–308; and James A. Swaney and Paulett I. Olson, "The Economics of Biodiversity: Lives and Lifestyles," *Journal of Economic Issues* 26 (March 1992): 1–25.

75. Marc R. Tool, *The Discretionary Economy* (Santa Monica: Goodyear Publishing Company, 1979) and *idem, Essays in Social Value Theory* (Armonk, NY: M.E. Sharpe, 1986).

76. Milton Friedman, "The Methodology of Positive Economics," in Milton Friedman, ed., *Essays in Positive Economics* (Chicago: University of Chicago Press, 1953), pp. 3–43.

77. See Lawrence A. Boland, "A Critique of Friedman's Critics," *Journal of Economic Literature* 17 (June 1979): 503–522; and Lawrence A. Boland and William J. Frazer, Jr., "An Essay on the Foundations of Friedman's Methodology," *American Economic Review* 74 (September 1983): 782–788.

78. Popper, *The Logic of Scientific Discovery*, p. 59.

79. Ken Dennis, "Boland on Friedman: A Rebuttal," *Journal of Economic Issues* 20 (September 1986): 633–660; and *idem*, "Boland on Boland: A Further Rebuttal," *Journal of Economic Issues* 21 (March 1987): 388–393.

80. Lawrence A. Boland, "Boland on Friedman's Methodology: A Summation," *Journal of Economic Issues* 21 (March 1987): 380–388.

81. Lawrence A. Boland, *The Foundations of Economic Methodology* (London: George Allen & Unwin, 1982), p. 145.

82. *Ibid*., p. 143.

83. John Dewey, *Reconstruction in Philosophy*, in Jo Ann Boydston, ed., *The Middle Works of John Dewey, 1899–1924, Vol. 12: 1920* (Carbondale: Southern Illinois University Press, 1982), pp. 169–170. Italics in the original.

84. Boland, "A Critique of Friedman's Critics," and Boland and Frazer, Jr., "An Essay on the Foundations of Friedman's Methodology."

85. Abraham Hirsch and Neil di Marchi, *Milton Friedman: Economics in Theory and Practice* (Ann Arbor: The University of Michigan Press, 1990), p. 6.

86. *Ibid.*

87. James R. Wible, "The Instrumentalisms of Dewey and Friedman," *Journal of Economic Issues* 18 (December 1984): 1049–1070; the words quoted are on page 1065.

88. *Ibid*., p. 1060.

89. *Ibid.*

90. See H.H. Liebhafsky and E.E. Liebhafsky, "Comment on 'The Instrumentalisms of Dewey and Friedman," *Journal of Economic Issues* 19 (December 1985): 974–983; and James Webb, "Is Friedman's Methodological Instrumentalism A Special Case of Dewey's Instrumental Philosophy? A Comment on Wible," *Journal of Economic Issues* 21 (March 1987): 393–329.

91. Abraham Hirsch and Neil de Marchi, "Methodology: A Comment on Frazer and Boland, I," *American Economic Review* 74 (September 1984): 782–788; and *idem, Milton Friedman: Economics in Theory and Practice*, pp. 92–93.

92. Friedman, "The Methodology of Positive Economics," pp. 14–15.

93. Dewey, *Logic: The Theory of Inquiry*, p. 144.

94. Friedman, "The Methodology of Positive Economics," p. 14.

95. See Dewey, *Logic: The Theory of Inquiry*, pp. 113, 314, 485, and elsewhere.

96. Dewey, "The Theory of Valuation," p. 248.

97. Dewey, *Logic: The Theory of Inquiry*, pp. 16, 105–122.

98. The author originally offered this criticism in his "The Normative Implications of Positive Analysis," A paper presented to the Western Economics Association, Corvallis, Oregon, August 23, 1968; abstracted in the *Western Economic Journal* 6 (September 1968): 309.

99. The following criticism of this attempt anticipates the arguments of next section of this article, which will be devoted to a discussion of the normative dimensions of Dewey's theory of *inquiry* (and *knowledge*).

100. Hirsch and de Marchi, *Milton Friedman*, p. 273.

101. *Ibid.*

102. Bruce Caldwell's critique of Friedman's methodology, while not focused on the specific issues raised here, lends general support to the arguments set forth in this section. See Bruce Caldwell, *Beyond Positivism* (London: George Allen & Unwin, 1982), pp. 173–188. See also the Geoffrey M. Hodgson's discussion of the inadequacies of Friedman's methodology in Geoffrey M. Hodgson, *Economics and Institutions: A Manifesto for a Modern Institutional Economics* (Philadelphia: University of Pennsylvania Press, 1988), pp. 28–35.

103. Rorty, *Consequences of Pragmatism*, p. 164. However, K. Kolenda warns that Rorty may be giving too much credit to Dewey on this point. See K. Kolenda, "Rorty's Dewey," *Journal of Value Inquiry* 20 (1986): 57–62, especially page 61.

104. Dewey, "Valuation Judgments and Immediate Quality," in Jo Ann Boydston, ed., *The Later Works of John Dewey, 1925–1953, Vol. 15: 1942–48* (Carbondale: Southern Illinois University Press, 1989), pp. 70–71. Italics in the original.

105. Dewey, *Logic: The Theory of Inquiry*, p. 163.

106. *Ibid.*, p. 176.

107. *Ibid.*

108. John Dewey, *Essays in Experimental Logic*, in Jo Ann Boydston, *ed., The Middle Works of John Dewey, 1899–1924, Vol. 8: 1915* (Carbondale: Southern Illinois University Press, 1979), p. 29.

109. *Ibid.*, pp. 26–28. See also Dewey, "Theory of Valuation," pp. 194–195.

110. Dewey, *Essays in Experimental Logic*, p. 26.

111. Dewey, "Theory of Valuation," p. 249.

112. James Gouinlock, *John Dewey's Philosophy of Value* (New York: Humanities Press, 1972), pp. 10–11.

113. John Dewey, *Democracy and Education*, in Jo Ann Boydston, ed., *The Middle Works of John Dewey, 1899–1924, Vol. 9: 1916* (Carbondale: Southern Illinois University Press, 1980), p. 132.

114. Dewey, "Theory of Valuation," pp. 248–249.

115. Dewey, *Democracy and Education*, p. 306.

116. John Dewey, "Existence, Value, and Criticism," in Jo Ann Boydston, ed., *The Later Works of John Dewey, 1925–1953, Vol. 11: 1925* (Carbondale: Southern Illinois University Press, 1986), p. 321.

117. Dewey, *The Quest for Certainty*, pp. 211–212. Italics in the original.

118. Dewey, *Logic: The Theory of Inquiry*, pp. 489–490. Italics in the original.

119. *Ibid.*, pp. 496–497. Italics as indicated in quotation.

120. *Ibid.*, p. 491. Italics in the original.

121. *Ibid.*, p. 484, footnote 3.

122. *Ibid.*, p. 484.

123. The notion that values function as standards by which behavior is correlated has

been widely discussed in the institutionalist literature by J. Fagg Foster and his students. For a summary of this discussion, see Paul D. Bush, "The Theory of Institutional Change," *Journal of Economic Issues* 21 (September 1987): 1075–1116, reprinted in Marc R. Tool, ed., *Evolutionary Economics: Foundation of Institutional Thought*, Vol. I (Armonk, NY: M.E. Sharpe, 1988), pp. 125–166.

124. Charles S. Peirce, "The Scientific Attitude and Fallibalism," in Justus Buchler, ed., *Philosophical Writings of Peirce* (New York: Dover Publications, 1955), p. 54.

125. Jacob Bronowski, *Science and Human Values*, rev. ed. (New York: Harper & Row, 1965), p. 58.

126. *Ibid*., p. 60.

127. Dewey, *Logic: The Theory of Inquiry*, p. 496.

128. See, for example, George R. Geiger, *John Dewey in Perspective*, pp. 124–135; and Michael F. Sheehan and Rick Tilman, "A Clarification of the Concept of 'Instrumental Valuation' in Institutional Economics," *Journal of Economic Issues* 26 (March 1992): 197–208.

129. The meaning of the term *neoinstitutional*, like the term *instrumental*, has been obscured by usages that are incompatible with the meaning assigned to the term in the American institutionalist literature. The term neoinstitutional has been coopted by the so-called new institutionalists whose neoclassical methodology is fundamentally incompatible with what they call the old institutionalists (i.e., contributors to the standard American institutionalist literature). For a well-known specimen of the new institutional economics, see Richard N. Langlois, ed., *Economics as Process: Essays in the New Institutional Economics* (Cambridge: Cambridge University Press, 1986). The use of the term neoinstitutional as a synonym for the new institutional economics apparently enjoys wide currency in Europe. For example, one European neoclassical economist working in the new institutional economics mode who refers to his research program as neoinstitutional economics is Thrainn Eggertsson; see his *Economic Behavior and Institutions* (Cambridge: Cambridge University Press, 1990). Neoinstitutionalists of the old institutional economics variety, and those sympathetic to their exclusive claim on the neoinstitutionalist rubric, are highly critical of the new institutional economics and its cooption of the term institutional, neo, or otherwise. For a sample of this critical literature, see John Adams, "Reinventing the Mos: Neoclassical lgnorance of Institutionalism as a Source of Fame and Employment," a paper presented to the Fourth Colloquium of the Charles Gide Association, Marseilles, France, September 19 and 20, 1991; Geoffrey M. Hodgson, "Institutional Economic Theory: The Old versus the New," *Review of Political Economy* 1 (November 1989): 249–269, reprinted in Geoffrey M. Hodgson, *After Marx and Sraffra* (London: MacMillan, 1991), pp. 194–213; and Anne Mayhew and Walter Neale, "The Implicit Theory and Method of the Old (and Real) American Institutionalists," a paper presented to the Fourth Colloquium of the Charles Gide Association, Marseilles, France, September 19 and 20, 1991.

130. H.P. Rickman states that according to Wilhelm Dilthey, "the use of understanding [*verstehen*] provides the human studies with a method distinct from those of the physical sciences and thus frees them from subservience to the latter." See Wilhelm Dilthey, *Pattern and Meaning in History*, edited and introduced by H.R. Rickman (New York: Harper Torchbook, 1962), pp. 17–18.

131. Examples of the use of this distinction between "value judgment" and "valuation" are to be found in Paul D. Bush, "The Theory of Institutional Change," Edythe S. Miller, "Review of Wendell Gordon and John Adams, *Economics as a Social Science: An Evolutionary Approach,*" *Journal of Economics Issues* 24 (March 1990): 275–278; and Baldwin Ranson, "Review of Laurence H. Tribe, Corrine S. Schelling, and John Voss, editors, *When Values Conflict*," *Journal of Economic Issues* 12 (March 1978): 195–196.

132. It appears that Liebhafsky first used the term *self-correcting value judgments* in *The Nature of Price Theory*, rev. ed. (Homewood: Dorsey Press, 1968), p. 523. His elaboration on this idea is discussed by Warren Samuels in "Technology *vis-a-vis* Institutions in the *JEI*: A Suggested Interpretation," *Journal of Economic Issues* 11 (December 1977): 867–895; the discussion is found on pages 887–891. See also Anne Mayhew's use of Liebhafsky's notion in "Ayresian Technology, Technological Reasoning, and Doomsday," *Journal of Economic Issues* 15 (June 1981); 513–520.

133. C.E. Ayres, *The Industrial Economy* (Boston: Houghton Mifflin Company, 1952), p. 310.

134. A number of important issues arise in connection with the pragmatic instrumentalist view of the role of values in inquiry. Space does not permit their discussion here, but the author has attempted to address some of them in previous publications, two of which are: Paul D. Bush, "The Normative Implications of Positive Analysis"; and *idem*, "Reflections on the 25th Anniversary of AFEE: Current Philosophical and Methodological Issues in Institutional Economics," *Journal of Economic Issues* 25 (June 1991): 321–346. For a highly competent review of the pragmatic instrumentalist approach to the theory of valuation and its application in the institutionalist literature, see Steven R. Hickerson, "Instrumental Valuation: The Normative Compass of Institutional Economics," *Journal of Economic Issues* 21 (September 1987): 1117–1143; reprinted in Marc R. Tool, ed., *Evolutionary Economics: Foundation of Institutional Thought*, Vol. I (Armonk, NY: M.E. Sharpe, 1988), pp. 167–193. The most extensive development and application of the pragmatic instrumentalist value theory to institutional economics is to be found in the works of Marc R. Tool. See Tool, *The Discretionary Economy*, and *idem*, *Essays in Social Value Theory*. The pragmatic instrumentalist position acknowledges the possibility of an infinite regress in the means–ends relationship that exits between "value judgments" and "valuations." Contrary to the view held by many philosophers, pragmatic instrumentalists do not regard the possibility of an infinite regress as a deficiency of the theory. It is their view that, properly understood, all empirical and normative propositions are embedded in infinite regresses. On this issue, see Sidney S. Alexander, "Human Values and Economists' Values," in Sidney Hook, ed., *Human Values and Economic Policy* (New York: New York University Press. 1967), pp. 101–116; Paul D. Bush, "Reflections on the 25th Anniversary of AFEE: Current Philosophical and Methodological Issues in Institutional Economics," especially pp. 329–340; and Larry Dwyer, "The Alleged Value Neutrality of Economics," *Journal of Economics Issues* 16 (March 1982): 75–106.

135. For a discussion of the methodological significance of this definition of the term "institution," see Paul D. Bush, "On the Concept of Ceremonial Encapsulation," *Review of Institutional Thought* 3 (December 1986): 25–45. See also J. Fagg Foster's use of this conception of institutions in "The Effect of Technology on Institutions," *Journal of Economic Issues* 15 (December 1981): 907–913.

136. Gunnar Myrdal, *Objectivity in Social Research* (New York: Pantheon Books, 1969), p. 9. Myrdal's use of the term "*a priori*" should not be read to mean in some metaphysical sense "beyond inquiry." His use of the term is consistent with the pragmatic instrumentalist view that valuations are logically prior to the determination of the "facts."

137. Jerry L. Petr, "Fundamentals of an Institutionalist Perspective on Economic Policy," *Journal of Economic Issues* 18 (March 1984): 1–17; reprinted in Marc R. Tool, ed., *An Institutionalist Guide to Economics and Public* Policy (Armonk, NY: M.E. Sharpe, 1984), pp. 1–17.

138. See, for example, Mark Blaug, *The Methodology of Economics* (Cambridge: Cambridge University Press, 1980), pp. 1–51; Bruce Caldwell, *Beyond Positivism*, pp. 221–230; Paul

Feyerabend, *Against Method*, rev. ed. (London: Verso, 1988); Thomas S. Kuhn, *The Structure of Scientific Revolutions*, 2d ed. enl. (Chicago: University of Chicago Press, 1970), and *idem* "Reflections on My Critics," in Imre Lakatos and Alan Musgrave, eds., *Criticism and the Growth of Knowledge* (London: Cambridge University Press, 1970), pp. 231–278; Imre Lakatos, "Falsification and the Methodology of Scientific Research Programmes," in Imre Lakatos, *The Methodology of Scientific Research Programmes: Philosophical Papers, Volume I*, ed. John Worrall and Gregory Currie (Cambridge: Cambridge University Press, 1978), pp. 8–101; and Popper, *The Logic of Scientific Discovery*.

139. Kuhn, *The Structure of Scientific Revolutions*.

140. Kuhn, "Reflections on My Critics," pp. 266–277.

141. See, for example, John M. Connolly and Thomas Keutner, "Introduction: Interpretation, Decidability, and Meaning," in John M. Connolly and Thomas Keutner, trans. and eds., *Hermeneutics Versus Science? Three German Views: Essays by H.-G. Gadamer, E.K. Specht. W. Stegmüller* (Notre Dame: University of Notre Dame Press, 1988), pp. 1–67; Kurt Mueller-Vollmer, "Introduction: Language, Mind, and Artifact: An Outline of Hermeneutic Theory Since the Enlightenment," in Kurt Mueller-Vollmer, ed., *The Hermeneutics Reader* (New York: Continuum Publishing Company, 1985), pp. 1–53; and Wachterhauser, "Introduction: History and Language in Understanding," pp. 5–61.

142. Mirowski, "The Philosophical Basis of Institutional Economics," p. 1010.

143. Wachterhauser, "Introduction: History and Language in Understanding," pp. 7–10.

144. *Ibid.*, p. 6.

145. *Ibid.*, p. 7.

146. *Ibid.*

147. *Ibid.*, p. 10.

148. Rorty, *Philosophy and the Mirror of Nature*, pp. 12–13.

149. William Waller explores some related problems in William Waller, "Avoiding the Cartesian Vice in Radical Institutionalism: A Reply to Mayhew," *Journal of Economic Issues* 24 (September 1990): 897–901.

150. Fritz Machlup, "The Problem of Verification in Economics," *Southern Economic Journal* 22 (July 1955): 1–21; see especially pages 7–11.

151. Lionel Robbins, *An Essay on the Nature and Significance of Economic Science*, 2nd ed. (London: MacMillan and Co., Ltd., 1952 [1935]), p. 79.

152. See Ludwig von Mises, *Human Action* (New Haven: Yale University Press 1949); and *idem*, *The Ultimate Foundations of Economic Science* (New York: D. Van Norstrand, 1962).

153. For an excellent sample of critical commentaries of Rorty's work, see Alan Malachowski, ed., *Reading Rorty* (Oxford: Basil Blackwell, 1990). See also K. Kolenda, "Rorty's Dewey"; and *idem*, *Rorty's Humanistic Pragmatism* (Tampa: University of Southern Florida Press, 1990).

154. Unfortunately, the limits of space have not permitted a review of and response to the substantial body of literature critical of pragmatic philosophy. That task must remain for a later undertaking. Such an undertaking should include a discussion of some of the more interesting and relevant commentaries, such as: Roy Bhaskar, "Rorty, Realism and the Idea of Freedom," in Alan Malachowski, ed., *Reading Rorty* (Oxford: Basil Blackwell, 1990), pp. 198–232; Martin Hollis and Edward J. Nell, *Rational Economic Man* (London: Cambridge University Press, 1975), pp. 152–169; and Max Horkheimer, *Critical Theory*, trans. Matthew J. O'Connell et al. (New York: Herder and Herder 1972).

155. Hodgson, *Economics and Institutions*.

Commentary by Geoffrey M. Hodgson

Paul Dale Bush has written a timely and provocative chapter. Instead of the fashionable methodological pluralism presently and widely adopted by heterodox economists, he argues that the "pragmatic institutionalist" methodology developed by John Dewey and others is the most coherent alternative. He implies that the choice of a particular methodology cannot be evaded, and that in particular the pragmatic institutionalist methodology should be utilized.

One of the most commendable aspects of Bush's essay is its clear exposition of key aspects of Dewey's instrumentalism. There is much useful clarification, in the context of some modern interpretations and polemics. For instance, Bush presents an important critique of Philip Mirowski's interpretation of Dewey as an anti-realist: one who asserts that there is no reality prior to and independent of the process of inquiry. Bush shows that this is not the case and that Dewey accepted the pre-existence of an external reality. However, Dewey denied that knowledge of it can be independent of the process of inquiry into that reality. Bush argues convincingly that the pragmatism of Dewey in particular and institutionalist methodology in general are based on realist philosophical foundations.

Bush's essay is usefully structured around three propositions taken from Richard Rorty. However, the use of Rorty's work provides a difficulty for attempts to reconcile pragmatism with some brands of realism, such as the "critical realism" of Roy Bhaskar.

Nevertheless, this commentary first addresses the proposal by Bush that key elements of American pragmatism and modern realism could be usefully combined. In doing this we focus on the ontological questions involved in such a marriage. Furthermore, some problems relating to the proposed union will be briefly mentioned.

A second feature of this comment is a critical discussion of Rorty's proposition—quoted with approval by Bush—that "there is no epistemological difference between truth about what ought to be and truth about what is." It is argued that this proposition is highly problematic, and that some urgent clarification is necessary before it plays havoc on institutional economic writings in the future.

Pragmatism and Realism: A Proposed Intellectual Recombination

Bush's argument that the pragmatism of Dewey is based on realist philosophical foundations is important for a number of reasons. The demonstration that Dewey was a realist in the philosophical sense, along with the proposition that Charles Sanders Peirce[1] and other pragmatists were realists too, provides an important connection between American pragmatism and the current revival of philosophical realism, centered on Europe.[2] This potential philosophical recombination is particularly auspicious because it encompasses economic methodologists—such as Tony Lawson—who are working broadly in the new European institutionalist tradition of economics.

One of the strong links between pragmatists such as Peirce and Dewey and modern realists such as Bhaskar is their attempts to formulate a sophisticated naturalism as an alternative to Cartesian dualism. A realist cannot support the proposition that either human society or human ideas are completely separable from their foundation in nature. Yet much of social science today proceeds as if this proposition were true. In contrast, both naturalists and realists agree that nature, matter, and mind are all real, and not divided by any Cartesian boundary. However, this does not imply a single-level explanation or a reductionist dissolution of one level into the other.

These ontological similarities should be emphasized. Indeed, the stress on the general importance of ontological questions is one of the key features of the realism of Bhaskar and others. However, by concentrating on epistemology, Bush leaves ontological questions to one side. Moreover, the philosophical writings of Dewey, which are so inspirational for Bush, have much less to say about ontology than those of his predecessor Peirce.

Realism and the Precedence of Ontology

Accordingly, one of the first results of the proposed intellectual recombination of modern realism with American pragmatism would be to promote a revival of interest in the naturalistic and indeterministic ontology of Peirce. It is possible that some of Peirce's ontological insights may prove to be foundational for a modern evolutionary economics.[3]

A discussion of ontology in this context cannot be complete, however, without some mention of the more fully developed organicism of Alfred North Whitehead. The naturalistic philosophy of Whitehead is notable for its rejection of both Cartesian dualism and reductionism, positing a multileveled ontological hierarchy. Indeed, Whitehead provides an important linkage between some of the aforementioned philosophers. Notably, in a work published in 1929 he acknowledged an intellectual debt both to "English and American Realists" and also to Bergson, James, and Dewey.[4]

With Whitehead the proposed philosophical network widens considerably. In particular, the leading institutionalist John Commons referred to Whitehead and seems to have been strongly influenced by his organicism.[5] In addition, there is a personal and intellectual connection between Whitehead and John Maynard Keynes. Keynes came under the influence of Whitehead in Cambridge in the first decade of the 20th century, before Whitehead's transfer to London in 1910 and his emigration to the United States in 1924. As well as his ventures into logic and mathematics, Whitehead promoted an organicist philosophy. The institutionalist Allan Gruchy noted the organicist quality of Keynes's thinking as early as the 1940s, heralding the much later philosophical interest in Keynes, where a number of writers have noted the organicist thinking in Keynes's *General Theory*. It is reasonable to suggest that Whitehead is partly responsible for this feature.[6]

Organicist views were expressed by one of the few English economists who could reasonably be described as an institutionalist, namely John A. Hobson, a person who interchanged ideas with both Veblen and Keynes. Hobson wrote: "An organized unity, or whole, cannot be explained adequately by an analysis of its constituent parts: its wholeness is a new product, with attributes not ascertainable in its parts, though in a sense derived from them."[7]

In an organicist ontology, relations between entities are internal rather than external, and the essential characteristics of any element are outcomes of relations with other entities. This relates to the central question in social theory as to whether structure can be represented simply as the property of the interactions between given individuals. Organicism denies that individuals can be treated as elemental or immutable building blocks of analysis. Just as society cannot exist without individuals, the individual does not exist prior to the social reality. Individuals both constitute and are constituted by society. We often hear the truism that society is composed of individuals. The organicist does not deny this, but insists that individuality is itself a social phenomenon.

Organicist views are sometimes described as "holistic" by institutionalist writers.[8] However, the use of the word *holism* is problematic. It is sometimes taken as the view that wholes can be understood without reference to parts. There is a danger that holism itself becomes one-sided and perhaps even reductionist: in social analysis a mirror image of methodological individualism. I am in complete agreement with Bush that holism should not be taken as a denial of deductive models and methods. To go further, just as an understanding of wholes is necessary to comprehend the parts, the parts and their relations have to be diagnosed to understand the wholes.

Overall, these problems and ambiguities in the term holism suggest that organicism might be a better touchstone for institutionalist methodology. It might be advantageous to counterpose the atomism and reductionism of orthodox economic theory with an organicist ontology, rather than the much abused notion of holism.[9]

Are There Anti-Realist Strains in Pragmatism?

Although Bush has made a strong case that Dewey was a realist, there are still problems in some pragmatist writings from a realist perspective. For instance, Peirce's definition of reality as "the dynamical reaction of certain forms upon the mind of the community"[10] would not be acceptable to many realists. Here Peirce seems to identify reality with states of mind, not with the world "out there." Indeed, there is a hermeneutical strain in pragmatism, and the reconciliation of hermeneutics with modern realism remains a difficult and open question.

Accordingly, Bhaskar has similarly criticized the pragmatism of Rorty.[11] Bhaskar sees Rorty as defining being in terms of knowledge, thereby denying the precedence of ontology. A similar criticism could be made of some of Peirce's formulations. Bhaskar admits that Rorty's pragmatism helps us understand the historicity of scientific and other knowledge, but it does not address the reality of its objects. Bhaskar's critique is well taken, and it means that much investigatory and critical work needs to be done to see if realism and pragmatism can be fully reconciled. One great merit of Bush's article is that he has announced the project leading to the eventual possible reconciliation between realism and pragmatism, and has made a prima facie case that it is possible.

The Problem of the Fact–Value Distinction

We now turn to a different issue: Bush's approving adoption of Rorty's statement that "there is no epistemological difference between truth about what ought to be and truth about what is." In my view this statement is unacceptable. Furthermore, it points to a malaise on the question of facts and values that seems to afflict much institutionalist writing today.

This is not to say that the mainstream economists' position on the distinction between facts and values should be accepted. Orthodox economists assume that a watertight distinction is possible between value-free, or positive, statements on the one hand, and value-laden, or normative, statements on the other. But rejection of the hermetic fact–value distinction does not mean that we should accept Rorty's proposition that there is *no epistemological difference* between truth about what ought to be and what is.

Rorty is saying, quite literally, that there is no difference between knowing an "is" and knowing an "ought." This is manifestly unacceptable, and means abandoning any distinction whatsoever between science and ideology. Yet knowing that blacks have a poor deal in the ghettos of Los Angeles is not the same thing as knowing that blacks ought to retain that station in life. Rorty, I fear, is being provocative and extreme for the sake of it, but at the cost of his own considerable philosophical reputation. If there is no epistemological difference between positive and normative statements, then we are led into a conservative cul-de-sac where we may derive an ought from an is. If an is is equivalent to an ought, then whatever is, is, and ought to be.

Furthermore, Rorty's proposition ignores the possibility of an inversely charged moral judgment. A conservative may derive an ought from an is, but the nihilist, with equivalent philosophical credentials, may derive an "ought not" from an is. Why didn't Rorty write: "there is no epistemological difference between truth about what *ought not* to be and truth about what is," or "there is no epistemological difference between truth about what ought to be and truth about what *is not*"? If the fact–value distinction entirely disappears, we must do contest with all these mutually irreconcilable statements.

The polar opposite position to that of Rorty on this question is David Hume's famous argument that we can *never* derive an ought from an is. But much subsequent philosophical discussion has shown that Hume's statement, while having a realm of validity, is not strictly or universally true. Faced with a decision between an untried and uncertain option, on the one hand, and one that is well tried and traditional, on the other, it is often reasonable to opt for that with which we are familiar, and to reject change. In fact, even the most radical thinkers do this all the time. In an uncertain world we are always relying on the safety of precedent. In that sense, people do often derive an ought from an is, and in some circumstances it is quite reasonable to do so.

Emphatically, however, this does not mean that we can *always* or generally derive and ought from an is. Neither does it mean that there is no distinction between positive and normative statements. The fact that people do often derive an ought from an is does not mean that the social scientist should necessarily do so as well. In fact, Veblen made a similar point, writing as long ago as 1899:

> In their discourse and in their thinking, men constantly and necessarily take an attitude of approval or disapproval toward the institutional facts of which they speak, for it is through such everyday approval or disapproval that any feature of the institutional structure is upheld or altered. It is only to be regretted that a trained scientist should be unable to view these categories in a dispassionate light, for these categories, with all the moral force with which they are charged, designate the motive force of cultural development.... A scientist inquiring into cultural growth, and an evolutionist particularly, must take account of this dynamic content of the categories of popular thought as the most important material with which he has to work. Many persons may find it difficult to divest themselves of the point of view of morality or policy, from which these categories are habitually employed, and to take them up from the point of view of the scientific interest simply. But the difficulty does not set the scientific necessity aside. His inability to keep the cultural value and the moral content of these categories apart may reflect credit upon the state of such a person's sentiments, but it detracts from his scientific competence.[12]

A more tenable position than that of Rorty could be formulated on the basis of the following propositions:

1. Factual propositions are contaminated with values because of the inevitable value biases of the researcher.
2. Factual propositions are contaminated with values because the researcher must make a value judgment about what is important or valuable in order to do the research in the first place.
3. Factual propositions are contaminated with values because the researcher depends on resources, and the provision of these is in turn dependent on the value judgments and vested interests of corporate, political, or other social institutions.
4. Factual propositions in social science are contaminated with values because the researcher is a human agent and inevitably is part of the social system under investigation.

There are other propositions along these lines, but we need not extend our list any further. Note that propositions 1–4 above amount to the statement that "values are always" with us, but they do *not* amount to the idea that positive and normative statements are epistemologically equivalent.

It should be emphasized that Rorty alone is not responsible for the confusion. For instance, Clive Beed (1991, p. 470) sets out this "anti-positivist" proposition: "the distinction between positive and normative science is untenable." However, this notion is highly ambigious, depending on different possible meanings of "distinction between." For instance, as all positive statements are contaminated by values, then distinction between, in the sense of a complete, hermetic division, is clearly untenable. But this does not mean that we cannot classify statements between those that are broadly (although no wholly) positive, on the one hand, and those that are broadly (although no wholly) normative, on the other. We may reject rigid dualisms while maintaining criteria of classification. It would be a mistake to replace a Cartesian dualism with a homogenizing monism where all statements have the same epistemological status.

Gunnar Myrdal is well known for his emphasis on the inevitability of value judgments in social science. He wrote: "Valuations are present in our problems even if we pretend to expel them. The attempt to eradicate biases by trying to keep out the valuations themselves is a hopeless and misguided venture."[13] So far so good. But does this mean that Myrdal is saying that positive and normative statements are epistemologically indistinguishable? In fact he implies the opposite:

> Values do not emerge automatically from the attempt to establish and collect the facts. Neither can we allow the individual investigator to choose his value premises arbitrarily. *The value premises should be selected by the criterion of relevance and significance to the culture under study.*[14]

This passage clearly indicates that, for Myrdal, facts and values were not the same thing. Values do not "emerge automatically" from facts; neither is the choice of value premises an arbitrary matter. In short, Myrdal believed that "values are always with us," but he did not make the mistake of treating them as epistemologically equivalent to facts.

The Danger of Confusing Fact with Value

My brief remarks have not done justice to the complex question of the relationship between facts and values. Clearly, many orthodox economists have played ideological havoc—consider the history of monetarism, Laffer curves, rational expectations, and the like—while simultaneously and deceptively entertaining the dubious proposition of a value-free social science. But there is a dangerous, obverse error committed by many on the heterodox fringes. It takes several forms: the main one is to evaluate theories mainly or wholly in terms of their normative, rather than their analytical, content.

Many examples of this latter error may be found. For instance, several heterodox economists have entirely dismissed the brilliant insights of Friedrich Hayek—one of the greatest economists of the 20th century—simply because of his unpalatable policy conclusions. Another case is the frequent dismissal of neoclassical economics, not because of its analytical limitations but because of the supposed conclusion that it supports a free-market policy.[15] Other instances can be found in frequent heterodox attempts to classify economic theories primarily with ideological categories, such as the vague and imprecise trichotomy of "conservative," "liberal," and "radical", rather than in terms of their core assumptions and theories.

Instances of such error are legion in the history of heterodox economic theory. But I am personally with Veblen in rejecting the idea that theories can and should be evaluated through ideological lenses. If an attempt is made to engender a more "scientific" attitude—to use Veblen's word—then the heterodox offender can and often will resort to Rorty-like statements in his or her defense. It is important that such ripostes are not accepted. The idea of the epistemological equivalence of fact and value has highly damaging results. It would be much more advisable to follow the more careful statements of Veblen or Myrdal.

In summary in social science, statements about fact are always contaminated with values. But this does not mean that factual statements and judgments of value are epistemologically equivalent. If they are, then we might as well pack our scientific bags and become political agitators instead. Nothing will endanger the current revival of institutional and evolutionary economics more than the adoption of such a course of action by its leading protagonists. This does not mean that, as scientists, we can or should abandon any commitment to appropriate values. We have the personal examples of Keynes, Myrdal, Kapp, and many others to follow in this regard.

Notes

1. On Peirce's realism see Boler (1963).
2. See, for instance, Aronson (1984), Bhaskar (1975, 1979, 1986, 1991), Chalmers (1985), Harré (1986), Kanth (1991), Leplin (1984), Manicas (1987), Sayer (1984). Two realists who have concentrated on the philosophy of economics are Lawson (1987, 1989) and Mäki (1989, 1991).

3. See Hodgson (1983) for a more extensive discussion of this point.

4. Whitehead (1929, p. vii).

5. Commons (1934, pp. 17, 96).

6. Allan Gruchy (1948) foreshadowed a now widespread discussion of the organicist quality Keynes's thought, involving Brown-Collier (1985), Brown-Collier and Bausor (1988), Carabelli (1985, pp. 164–168; 1988; 1991), Dow (1985, 1990), Fitzgibbons (1988, pp. 18–21), Hamouda and Smithin (1988), Lawson (1985, pp. 923–924), O'Donnell (1989, pp. 127–136, 177–178), Rotheim (1989–1990), and Winslow (1986, 1989). But Bateman (1989) and Davis (1989, 1989–1990) deny that Whitehead had a significant influence on Keynes.

7. Hobson (1929, p. 32).

8. See, for instance, Wilber and Harrison (1978).

9. Since Keynes, Whitehead has had a negligible influence on economics, reflecting the resurgence of mechanistic and atomistic views in the postwar period. One exception, however, is the work of Nicholas Georgescu-Roegen (1971), particularly in regard to such concepts of purpose and time. With his idea of the hierarchic ordering of the real world, Whitehead also had a strong personal influence on pioneering systems theorists such as James Miller (1978).

10. Peirce (1935, pp. 433–434).

11. See Bhaskar (1991).

12. Veblen (1934, pp. 30–31).

13. Myrdal (1958, p. 131).

14. Myrdal (1958, p. 134).

15. I have argued elsewhere (Hodgson, 1992) that neoclassical theory does not adequately represent a market system and corresponds more exactly to a mythical, centralized economy. Hence quite different ideological ramifications can—and have been—grafted onto neoclassical theory. The reasons why neoclassical theory should be rejected are mainly analytical rather than ideological.

References

Aronson, J. *A Realist Philosophy of Science* (Basingstoke: Macmillan, 1984).

Bateman, Bradley W. " 'Human Logic' and Keynes's Economics: A Comment," *Eastern Economic Journal* 15 (January–March 1989): 63–67.

Beed, Clive. "Philosophy of Science and Contemporary Economics: An Overview," *Journal of Post Keynesian Economics* 13 (Summer 1991): 459–494.

Bhaskar, Roy. *A Realist Theory of Science*, 2nd ed. (Leeds: Leeds Books), 1978 [1975]. Brighton, Harvester.

Bhaskar, Roy. *The Possibility of Naturalism: A Philosophic Critique of the Contemporary Human Sciences* (Brighton: Harvester), 1979).

Bhaskar, Roy. *Scientific Realism and Human Emancipation* (London: Verso), 1986.

Bhaskar, Roy. *Philosophy and the Idea of Freedom* (Oxford: Basil Blackwell), 1991.

Boler, J.F. *Charles Peirce and Scholastic Realism: A Study of Peirce's Relation to John Duns Scotus* (Seattle: University of Washington Press, 1963).

Brown-Collier, E.K. "Keynes' View of an Organic Universe: The Implications," *Review of Social Economy* 43 (1985): 14–23.

Brown-Collier, E.K. and Bausor, R. "The Epistemological Foundations of the General Theory," *Scottish Journal of Political Economy* 35 (August 1988): 227–241.

Carabelli, Anna M. "Keynes on Cause, Chance and Probability," in A. Lawson and H. Pesaran, eds., *Keynes' Economics: Methodological Issues* (London: Croom Helm, 1985), pp. 151–180.

Chalmers, Alan F. *What is This Thing Called Science?* (Milton Keynes: Open University Press, 1985).

Commons, John R. *Institutional Economics—Its Place in Political Economy* (New York: Macmillan, 1934). Reprinted 1990 with a new introduction by M. Rutherford (New Brunswick: Transaction Publishers).

Davis, John B. "Keynes on Atomism and Organicism," *The Economic Journal* 99 (December 1989): 1159–1172.

Davis, John B. "Keynes and Organicism," *Journal of Post Keynesian Economics* 12(2) (Winter 1989-90): 308–315.

Dow, Shiela C. *Macroeconomic Thought: A Methodological Approach* (Oxford: Basil Blackwell, 1985).

Dow, Shiela C. "Beyond Dualism," *Cambridge Journal of Economics* 14 (June 1990): 143–157.

Fitzgibbons, Athol. *Keynes's Vision: A New Political Economy* (Oxford: Clarendon Press, 1988).

Georgescu-Roegen, Nicholas. *The Entropy Law and the Economic Process* (Cambridge, MA: Harvard University Press, 1971).

Gruchy, Allan G. "The Philosophical Basis of the New Keynesian Economics," *Ethics* 58 (July 1948): 235–244.

Hamouda, Omar F. and Smithin, John N. "Some Remarks on 'Uncertainty and Economic Analysis," *The Economic Journal* 98(1) (March 1988): 159–164.

Harré, Rom. *Varieties of Realism* (Oxford: Basil Blackwell, 1986).

Hobson, John A. *Wealth and Life: A Study in Values* (London: Macmillan, 1929).

Hodgson, Geoffrey M. *Economics and Institutions: A Manifesto for a Modern Institutonal Economics* (Cambridge: Polity Press, 1988).

Hodgson, Geoffrey M. "The Reconstruction of Economics: Is There a Place for Neoclassical Theory?" *Journal of Economic Issues* 26 (September 1992): 749–767.

Hodgson, Geoffrey M. *Economics and Evolution: Bringing Life Back into Economics* (Cambridge: Polity Press, 1993).

Kanth, Rajani K. "Economic Theory and Realism: Outlines of a Reconstruction," *Methodus* 3 (December 1991): 37–45.

Lawson, Antony. "Uncertainty and Economic Analysis," *The Economic Journal* 95 (December 1985): 909–927.

Lawson, Antony. "The Relative/Absolute Nature of Knowledge and Economic Analysis," *The Economic Journal* 97 (December 1987): 951–970.

Lawson, Antony. "Abstrction, Tendencies and Stylised Facts: A Realist Approach to Economic Analysis," *Cambridge Journal of Economics* 13 (March 1989):

59–78. Reprinted in A. Lawson, J.G. Palma, and J. Sender, eds., *Kaldor's Political Economy* (London: Acdemic Press, 1989).

Leplin, Jarrett ed. *Scientific Realism* (Berkeley: University of California Press, 1984).

Mäki, Uskali. "On the Problem of Realism in Economics," *Ricerche Economiche* 43 (gennaio-giugno 1989): 176–98.

Mäki, Uskali. "Practical Syllogism, Entrepreneurship, and the Invisible Hand," in D. Lavoie, ed., *Economics and Hermeneutics* (London: Routledge, 1991, pp. 149–176.

Manicas, P.T. *A History and Philosophy of the Social Sciences* (Oxford: Basil Blackwell, 1987).

Miller, James G. *Living Systems* (New York: McGraw-Hill, 1978).

Myrdal, Gunnar. in P. Streeten, ed., *Value in Social Theory: A Selection of Essays on Methodology* (New York: Harper, 1958).

O'Donnell, Rodney M. *Keynes: Philosophy, Economics and Politics* (London: Macmillan, 1989).

Peirce, Charles Sanders. in C. Hartshorne and P. Weiss, eds., *Collected Papers of Charles Sanders Peirce, Volume VI, Scientific Metaphysics* (Cambridge, MA: Harvard University Press, 1935).

Rotheim, Roy J. "Organicism and the Role of the Individual in Keynes' Thought," *Journal of Post Keynesian Economics* 12 (Winter 1989–90): 317–326.

Sayer, Andrew. *Method in Social Science: A Realist Approach* (London: Hutchinson, 1984).

Veblen, Thorstein B. in L. Ardzrooni, ed., *Essays in Our Changing Order* (New York: Viking Press, 1934).

Whitehead, Alfred N. *Process and Reality: An Essay in Cosmology* (Cambridge: Cambridge University Press, 1929).

Wilber, Charles K. and Harrison, Robert S. "The Methodological Basis of Institutional Economics: Pattern Model, Storytelling, and Holism," *Journal of Economic Issues* 12 (March 1978): 61–89. Reprinted in W.J. Samuels *Institutional Economics*, vol. 2. (Aldershot: Edward Elgar 1988).

Winslow, Edward A. " 'Human Logic' and Keynes's Economics," *Eastern Economic Journal* 12 (October–December 1986): 413–430.

Winslow, Edward A. "Organic Interdependence, Uncertainty and Economic Analysis," *The Economic Journal* 99 (December 1989): 1173–1182.

4 THE THEORY OF INSTRUMENTAL VALUE: EXTENSIONS, CLARIFICATIONS

Marc R. Tool[1]

Institutional economists have long argued that social value theory is and must be an integral part of economic inquiry. They have recognized that inquiry, addressed directly or indirectly to problem analysis, is purposive in the normative sense. To define an economic problem is to distinguish between "what is" and "what ought to be." Constructs of social value are employed, then, in identifying the social significance of economic inquiry. In recent years, institutional economists have contributed to a theory of instrumental social value. In this chapter, I explore elements and attributes of this theory of instrumental value and, in particular, present recent extensions and theoretical clarifications of this value theory.

Heterodox scholars have followed Gunnar Mydal's admonitions[2] of a generation ago and placed inquiry into social value theory generally, and criteria of economic judgment more specifically, on the agenda for inquiry as necessary components of any approach claiming comprehensive coverage and relevance to problem solving. Warren Samuels has recently reiterated this call.[3] "Economics is normative," he suggests, "because the economy is normative.[4] . . . economists should, as Gunnar Myrdal had long maintained, strongly endeavor to make the normative and valuational premises of their work explicit."[5] Among other scholars responding are Mark Lutz and the social economists,[6] and Amitai Etzioni and the socioeconomists.[7] But it is to the work of institutionalist economists in the Veblen–Dewey–Ayres tradition that I turn here.

The purpose of this chapter, then, is to explore the current status of the distinctively institutionalist contribution of the theory of instrumental value. In the first part, for readers unfamiliar with this institutionalist position, I briefly review the principle of instrumental value and identify some of its distinguishing characteristics. In the second part, I consider some extensions and refinements of the theory of instrumental value, particularly those of Paul D. Bush. In the third part, I pursue clarifications of the institutionalist's value position, as I understand it, in light of recent criticism by Wendell Gordon and Anne Mayhew. The chapter closes with some summary observations.

The Theory of Instrumental Value: A Reprise

On my reading, the normative construct most frequently used by institutionalists is the instrumental[8] principle of social value as it has emerged in this century, and especially in the last few decades.[9] This instrumental principle originated in the writings of John Dewey[10] and Thorstein Veblen; it was developed by Clarence Ayres[11] and Fagg Foster,[12] and amplified by their students.

Veblen's principle contribution was the formulation of what has come to be called the "Veblenian dichotomy"[13]; it appears in a variety of forms in all of his major works. A representative formulation is found in his *Leisure Class*: "Institutions . . . may be roughly distinguished into two classes or categories, according as they serve one or the other of two divergent purposes of economic life[:] . . . acquisition or production . . . pecuniary or industrial [activity] . . . [an] invidious or non-invidious economic interest."[14] Other examples of the dichotomy include "salesmanship" versus "workmanship," "vested interests" versus the "common man," "sabotage" versus "community serviceability," and "conscientious withdrawal of efficiency" versus "inordinately productive enterprise."[15] In the following pages, the emergent form of this dichotomy will be a distinction between invidious (or ceremonial) behavior and instrumental (or technological) behavior. The pages of *The Journal of Economic Issues* contain numerous contributions to and clarifications of instrumental value criteria[16] and their application to problem areas.[17]

Instrumental Social Value Principle

My efforts to review, synthesize, and assess the contributions of Veblen, Dewey, Ayres, and Foster, to which others contributed, has led to the following formulation of the instrumental value principle: do or choose that which provides for "the continuity of human life and the noninvidious recreation of community through the instrumental use of knowledge."[18] The four primary conceptual components of this principle can be elaborated as follows:

The continuity of human life. On an earlier occasion I wrote:

> The whole of the human experience is with process, the social process. There is no human history except of evolutionary movement of human organisms and of the culture such persons create and preserve. "Continuity" in the value premise is grounded in this fact and asserts the obvious as an 'ought'—that the continuance of human life is a precondition for the pursuit of all earthly concerns including the creation and use of all social value theory.[19]

As James Swaney observes: "'Continuity of human life' implies that a balanced diet for malnourished people should come before luxury automobiles; that one human's right to live should come before another's right to bear arms; and that the human community must live within its ecological means."[20] Swaney continues with an environmental focus: "A threat to any ecosystem is a threat to the human community, because the ecology of every living thing on earth is connected to the ecology of every other living thing on earth, including people."[21] The continuity of human evolution is clearly interdependent with ecological evolution. In view of environmental threats of meltdowns, acid rain, "greenhouse effects," and the like, a continuously relevant social value principle must include provision for "the continuity of human life" in coevolutionary congruity with biotic continuity.

If the focus is shifted to economic concerns, real and growing threats to "the continuity of human life" are readily apparent: financial and real income austerity measures imposed to meet the debt crises of newly developing countries are impoverishing large numbers of people. The increase in income inequality[22] and the emergence of an underclass in the United States, in consequence of the Reagan revolution, reflect growing poverty and increased threats to those with the least discretion over their own well-being. The economic implications of the rapidly spreading AIDS epidemic in undeveloped and developed countries reminds us all of our mutually shared hazards. Obviously, analytical recognition of the significance of this value component is a precondition for application of the other facets of this social value principle.

The re-creation of community. This second component of the instrumental value principle acknowledges and incorporates the long demonstrated recognition that people build cultures and live only in community with others. People are, quite naturally, social animals. Since there is no significant human life outside community, communal and cultural continuity is everywhere a priority concern. Institutions are prescribed or proscribed patterns of correlated behavior and attitudes that coordinate life in community. They specify—as codes, rules, laws, customs—what can and cannot be done. When these existing prescriptive arrangements are perceived as failing to provide adequately for the flow and quality of real income, given the level of understanding evident, the community has a *problem*. The character and continuity of the community is threatened. Resolution of the problem consists of recasting that part of the institutional structure understood to be the source of the impairment. *The continuing task is the re-creation of community through institutional adjustment.* As Paul D. Bush reminds us, "social problems arise when the institutional structure is unable to accommodate the noninvidious application of instrumentally warranted knowledge to the support of the life processes of the community."[23] Institutions, or elements thereof, that have become significantly ceremonial and inefficient in their operation, are candidates for modification or abandonment.

Pursuit of noninvidious change. This third component addresses the *character* of institutional change required to re-create community. How does a community know what sorts of adjustments to recommend or make? How can "what is wrong" be identified? Answers are found, as was indicated above, in the concepts of ceremonially or invidiously warranted behavior.

"Invidious" is here used generally in the Veblenian sense. As he put it, invidious means "a comparison of persons with a view to rating and grading them in respect of relative worth or value."[24] Invidious distinctions, then, are reflected in judgments of worth or merit rooted in race, creed, gender, ancestry, ethnicity, wealth, ownership, power, tradition, and the like. Invidious judgments discriminate and denigrate on the basis of observed, or attributed, differences among individuals. Such differences generate class, status, rank, income, discretion, and participatory distinctions within communities. Those groups and individuals against whom invidious discrimination is directed are denied options, entitlements, and the full development of their capabilites (for example, access to education, occupation, or income). In consequence, the development of individuals' creative potential and productive capacities (and their sense of self-worth) are arrested or eroded. Their individual and collective contributions to the provisioning process (to speak only of economic considerations) are impaired significantly. Given contemporary levels of interdependence, invidiously to cripple a part is to cripple the whole community. "The one luxury which the rich cannot afford is the poverty of the poor."[25]

The constructive potential of the instrumental principle is eroded, perverted, or denied by the design and retention of ceremonially warranted behavior in institutions that create or perpetuate the invidious use of such distinctions.[26] The overriding efforts of vested interests to retain their power may preclude any adjustments at all. Race and gender discrimination may remove major segments from discretionary roles in institutional change. Slavish observance of customary working rules may preclude the enhancement of real income flows through technological innovation.

The instrumental use of knowledge. This last component of the instrumental value principle stipulates that problem resolution through institutional adjustments (choices) can most effectually occur when the design and implementation of such structure reflects judicious use of causally explanatory knowledge. "Instrumental use" means appropriate and effectual recourse to evidentially grounded and logically coherent products of prior inquiry. An exploratory example will help explain this component of the instrumental value principle.

As this is being written, there is in the United States extensive public deliberation concerning the adequacy, efficiency, and costs of providing medical care for the community. The central task, as an institutionalist would describe it, is to re-create institutional structure to ensure that all those who need medical care may have adequate access to it. Physical impairments, as defined by the prevailing state of medical knowledge, determines "need." An instrumental use of knowledge would involve an extensive analysis of what segments of the community now receive, or do not receive, comprehensive and adequate care. The knowledge fund for the treatment of the ill and impaired is enormous and growing. How can that knowledge be made available, humanely and efficiently, to those afflicted?

Among the inquiry questions an institutionalist might pose are the following. *Regarding access*: To what extent is access to care denied by prices charged? Are existing health plans deficient in coverages offered? How should the allocation of care be arranged and on what criteria of entitlement? *Regarding control*: Where should discretion over access to care reside? Who should control the introduction of new medical technologies and drugs? Has the corporate merger movement into medical delivery systems imposed pecuniary judgments on medical practitioners?

Are public controls needed over administered pricing of medical care and products?

Institutionalist judgments would be grounded in recognition of the continuing community responsibility to provide adequate and quality medical care for its members. Instrumentally oriented reformers would be committed to the maximal use and appraisal of warranted knowledge regarding past institutional experience (local, national, and international) with medical care systems. They would create and test options for institutional adjustment. They would seek accountability for those exercising control over health programs and delivery systems.

To whatever extent, if any, these institutionally diagnostic and restorative judgments—instrumental uses of warranted knowledge—are intruded upon, for example, 1) by power centers that deny access to care based on invidious discrimination, 2) by those who adamantly insist on the use of "free market" allocations of care, or 3) by those who place control over care in the hands of corporate-medical vested interests, instrumental use of knowledge is impaired or aborted. Institutional problems of health care delivery will remain inadequately addressed.

In summary, the simultaneous and interdependent synthesis of these four components of the instrumental value principle constitutes instrumental criteria of social value. This instrumental value principle is offered as a way of coming to understand and appraise the character and causal determinants of economic problems. Its inquiry function is to provide criteria with which an investigator can approach social and economic analysis. As theory, it suggests how problems may be identified, what sorts of evidence to seek, how to arrange it for analysis, how to identify and track causal determinants of problems, and perhaps, what sorts of institutional adjustments could constitute solutions. The instrumental principle suggests a fresh and defensible meaning for "economic reform"

Instrumental Valuation

I now offer some summary observations that characterize the instrumental value principle, and reaffirm its theoretical cogency and its relevant applicability to problem identification, analysis, and resolution. Given present constraints, these observations must be brief.

1. As Veblen, Dewey, and Ayres made very clear, the instrumental social value principle is derived from reflections on the continuum of human experience, the social process itself in all its complexity, the evolutionary development of cultures and peoples. It is a construct of inquiry that

incorporates and cultivates peoples' ability to reason in causal terms about matters of fact. The origin of the value principle is to be found in the historical application of reason to experience and is reflected in the creation of the technological continuum itself.[27] This continuum—the cumulative "increase and diffusion of knowledge among men"—is pursued by tool and idea combinations in quest of causal understanding of observable realities. The instrumental value principle is a processual construct, in accord with the evidential social reality to which it is addressed.

The instrumental value principle may not be characterized as taxonomic, telelogical, or hedonistic as Veblen characterized neoclassical utility theory in his *The Place of Science*.[28] Not taxonomic: the instrumental value principle is not concerned with sorting out, naming, and classifying a static conceptual universe; it is an evolutionary construct addressed to an understanding and appraisal of cumulative causation. Not teleological: this principle incorporates no notion of an inherent ameliorative trend, no idea that ends are immanent in nature; rather, ends are causal and provisional outcomes. Not hedonistic: this principle posits no "lightening calculator of pleasures and pains," no "homogeneous globule of desire of happiness," no "passive and . . . inert and immutably given human nature."[29] It sees people as discretionary agents, as conditioned by and conditioners of culture, and as appliers of value theory.

2. The instrumental value principle does not rest on nonevidential or unreasoned sources of information or insight. It has no recourse to, neither does it depend on, intuitively revealed knowledge that is private and beyond grounding or demonstration. Instrumentally warranted knowledge is amenable to empirical check or verification.

In instrumental value theory, no given, antecedent natural laws deterministically pattern or constrain behavior: instrumental theory reflects a quest for and assessment of observable regularities of actual behavior, rather than a tacit acceptance of observable regularities of a presumed natural order. No presumptions are made of a continuous movement toward equilibrium conditions as a normative good or of a fortuitous and autogenetic emergence of capitalist institutions.

Instrumental value theory rests on warranted perceptions that human beings create and sustain forms and products of knowing. Changes in the structural fabric of a society are a consequence of human deliberation and agency. They may subsequently be viewed as erroneous or flawed.

3. The instrumental value principle reflects the philosophic and analytic rejection of the positive–normative dualism in all of its forms: means versus ends, real versus ideal, explanation versus evaluation, description versus prescription, objective versus subjective, science versus art, economics versus

ethics, truth versus goodness. It hosts no fact–value dualism. As William Waller has observed, ". . . both sides of the dualism are treated as separate realms of reality. Institutionalist reject this separateness and argue that both sides of the dualism in fact are different aspects of the same unified reality."[30] Instrumental value theory offers a "remedy" for, as Ayres put it, "the pestilence of moral agnosticism."[31]

4. Moreover, the instrumental value principle is not ethically relative; it does not convert mores into criteria nor defer to a "mores nihilism."[32] Neither is it an ethical absolute; it does not elevate an "Absolute Truth" (e.g., Divine Right or power retention) to the status of an exclusive judgmental premise. It provides no eternal verity (see comments on Gordon below).

The acceptance of "given wants" reflects use of value theory that is ethically relative. Since all economies do and must distinguish between admissible and inadmissable wants, any willingness uncritically to accept market satisfaction of wants evades judgmental responsibility. As Joan Robinson observes: "How do we decide what preferences should be respected and what restrained unless we judge the preferences themselves?"[33]

Furthermore, scholars' claiming a position of ethical relativism vis-a-vis judgments among preferences may, if compelled to make choices, fall back on an unanticipated use of ethically absolutist criteria. An unreflective decision to perpetuate the status quo is an example. "What is" is reaffirmed as "what ought to be." The instrumental value principle does not enshrine the status quo. However, an institutionalist, if confronted with limited and invidiously warranted alternatives, might recommend retention of the status quo as the more instrumental choice.

5. The instrumental value principle incorporates no recommended institutional structure; it provides criteria for choosing among alternative structures. Of course, all societies do and must utilize existing institutions, and/or create new institutions, to correlate behavior for a myriad of purposes. But the instrumental value principle does not recommend or imply, for example, a *particular* pattern of ownership, of governance, of market exchange, or of productive associations. Accordingly, it is neither identified with nor supportive of any of the Grand Alternatives, the isms of political economy—capitalism, socialism, communism—all of which do offer timeless, institutionally defined economic models. It is addressed to an assessment of prevailing *conditions* of institutional malperformance; it does not point *direction* to the adoption or restoration of a pre-packaged institutional recipe or ism model. The "constants" of the instrumental value principle are not institutional forms; they are experience-derived canons or tenets of processual inquiry that are themselves amenable to revision as the noninvidious ends or inquiry are pursued.

6. I see the instrumental value principle as a judgmental standard for inquiry and conduct addressed wholly to actual problems facing real people. The instrumental value principle is a product of human inquiry; it reflects and draws its significance from the problem-solving experience of a community. That problem-solving experience involves repeated formulations of a difference between "what is" and "what ought to be."[34] Identified problems, using the "is–ought" distinction of instrumentalists, might include, for example: 1) a fundamental deterioration in the availability of real income; 2) an incompacitated, archaic, and self-serving bureaucratic leadership; 3) a breakdown in the education of the young for adulthood; 4) as noted above, the denial of access to adequate medical care to large segments of the community; or 5) any other new circumstance that is understood to be of such potential significance, in the instrumental sense, that it requires reflection on the adequacy of accepted behavior forms. "Ought" they to be continued? Should they be adjusted or abandoned? As this is being written, such pressures for change are faced by Eastern Europeans in the recomposition of their economic systems, by black leaders in South Africa seeking the abandonment of apartheid and the restructuring of their political economy, and by those seeking to restore the infrastructure and productivity of the American economy.

7. The employment of the instrumental value principle requires careful and extensive inquiry in any particular problematic context. It offers no shortcuts, no panaceas, no prefigured or simple solutions. Its sources are neither "black magic" nor "black boxes" (see comment on Gordon below). The theory of instrumental value gives direction to inquiry by indicating what kinds of questions to pose, what sort of evidence to seek, and how to arrange it for analysis. It does not provide preanalytic "answers." There is nothing routine or automatic about instrumental value analysis. But it does, I think, provide practical, pragmatic, and relevant judgmental criteria for problem analysis.

8. Finally, the instrumental value principle serves no special economic interest group, political power system, social class, or national or ethnic people. It is not ethnocentric. But the principle may well have some pan-cultural and pan-temporal relevance in its present formulation.

Extensions of Instrumental Value Theory

The Role of the Instrumental Value Principle in Inquiry

I begin these observations on extensions and refinements of the instrumental social value principle with a consideration of the role this principle plays in inquiry. The fundamental contention made here is that modern inquiry incorporates instrumental value theory as primary judgmental premises. It is my view that modern methods of social inquiry, that convey credibility, are persuasive, and have applicability, are those held to account, in the main, by the instrumental value principle. As Paul D. Bush observes: "instrumentally warranted values are inherent in the processes of scientific inquiry."[35] The argument here is that *the process of valuation that guides scientific inquiry is the process of instrumental valuation*. Most contemporary institutionalists, as I view their scholarly work, are practicing instrumentalists.

I have often contended that if inquiry is purposive, it is value-laden. Institutionalists, beginning with Veblen, have identified the purposiveness of inquiry with pursuit of the *continuity of the life process*. Veblen identified continuing and constructive human proclivities—he called them "instincts"—as "idle curiosity," the "instinct of workmanship," and the "parental bent."[36] These proclivities for acquisition of knowledge and understanding, for "taking pains—a disposition to do the next thing and do it as well as may be," and concern for the "well-being of the incoming generation," are implied in purposive social inquiry. (I note in passing that Veblen's "idle curiosity" does not disclaim purposiveness of inquiry; joined with the other two "proclivities," it implies doubt and invokes inquiry.)

Similarly, the purposiveness of inquiry implies the *reconstruction of community*. Social and economic inquiry in particular is addressed by institutionalists to the resolution of problems, to the use of policy initiatives to reconstitute the social and economic institutional fabric to achieve a more adequate and efficient provisioning process and more equitable distribution of the material means of life. There would be general agreement among modern scholars that any judgments affecting inquiry that reflected *the employment of invidious discrimination* would have the effect of corrupting inquiry and destroying its integrity and usefulness. The quest for tentative truth is compromised, for example, by invidious deference to rank, status, or authority (academic or political), or by gender or race discrimination. Scholars have long understood that "argument by authority" does not, as such, establish truth-status for any contention. Veblen regarded the distructive proclivities of "predation" and "emulation" particularly as a continuing threat to life process.[37] Predatory and emulative judgments and behavior may well defeat the purposiveness of inquiry, destroy the integrity and credibility of the results of inquiry, and mischieveously misdirect both scholarly inquiry and policy adjustments. Doubts, instead of being allayed or resolved, are enhanced. Problems remain unresolved; indeed, they may well worsen in consequence.

But the primary focus here must be on the final component of the instrumental value principle—*the instrumental (creation and) use of warranted knowledge.*

Value judgments initiate inquiry; value judgments guide inquiry. Inquiry is initiated by the emergence of doubt.[38] Doubts may arise in the making of judgments concerning the adequacy of existing explanations or the tolerability of perceived conditions or circumstances. Why are there more persons living in poverty? How can environmental destruction be reduced? Why did public regulation of the savings and loan industry fail? We appraise theoretical accounts and find them to be inadequate or unconvincing. We examine implemented policies and lament their destructive consequences.

Inquiry is a deliberative means employed to reduce or resolve doubt concerning both the "is" and the "ought to be," to restore congruity of understanding and experience. We ask why? And how so? To get credible answers, we must search for causal linkages and determinants. But in every facet of inquiry—from the framing of an initial question, to the culminating and provisional choice of the hypothetical account that most completely explains the causal phenomena under review—choices are made continuously. Every choice made requires use of criteria of judgment. Every such use is the making of value judgments. Judgmental standards or criteria must be employed to provide a basis for selecting one option over one or more other options at every point or stage of the inquiry process. It is my contention that *the process of instrumental valuation provides the primary judgmental standards for modern causal inquiry.*

Choices that function to advance and facilitate the inquiry process to reach its provisional conclusion reflect use of instrumental judgments. In choosing and judging the grounding and relevance of assumptions, the directive hypotheses created and employed, the pertinence of evidential material, the assessment of the appropriateness of tools used, of theories employed, of evidential tests conducted, of coherence achieved, of inferences drawn (both deductive and inductive), the researcher must choose what is instrumentally required, what will demonstrably function, for the continuum of inquiry to proceed and for tentative and warrantable conclusions to be derived.

But how, in the formulation of instrumental judgments, are pertinence and appropriateness identified? The term *instrumental* connotes means–consequences connections. The continuing inquiry question is how can ideas, principles, constructs, and hypotheses *function* as means to achieve consequences as ends-in-view. *Instrumental valuing* encompasses the knowledge-guided use of "tool-and-skill configurations"[39] as means to transform an indeterminate situation—don't know, don't understand, can't explain, can't act—into a more ordered and determinate end-in-view where consequences are observed, causal understanding is enhanced, connections are disclosed, unknowns become knowns, questions are answered, and some congrency between expectations and outcomes is achieved. Which instruments or constructs are instrumentally useful and are serviceable in the pursuit of inquiry? Which are demonstrably necessary or needed? Answers must be generated. *Instrumental valuing* is not "merely" incidental to the judgment process; it is the heart of it. As the means are chosen in inquiry, so are the outcomes determined. Outcomes or consequences become means to further outcomes. A continuum of means–consequence linkages is disclosed. The "ought to be" is implicit in sustaining and enhancing the continum of inquiry itself.

In the continuity of modern inquiry, instrumental judgments tend to be corrected by the inquirer as the quest for understanding drives the process of inquiry and imposes successive and critical judgments of pertinence, and therefore significance, at every point or stage. Judgmental errors in inquiry tend to surface in the continuing interactive quest for what Dewey called "conjugate correspondence" of theory and fact, of causal accounting and evidential grounding, in the context of a coherent frame of reference. Evidential grounding is found to be insufficient; explanations are unable to account for observed results. Epistemological tests of correspondence and comprehensiveness are not met.[40] Coherence tests of connectedness and integration are unsuccessful. The *process* of conducting inquiry fosters the uncovering and correcting of unwarranted assumptions, illogical constructs, disjunctions in coherence, or flawed connections. Instrumental valuing is inherent in the search for coherence, correspondence, appropriateness, and relevance. Instrumental value theory is an integral part of social and economic inquiry. The distinction between what is admissible and not admissible as credible inquiry and the tentative truths derived—the right and wrong of it—are identified through the instrumental valuing process.

Instrumentally warranted judgments, moreover, are reflected in the creation and/or selection of the relevant constructs and intellectual tools and techniques for inquiry. Such judgments define the need for, and direct the creation of, new conceptual tools as required to move the inquiry along. The creation of ideational/physical tools is an integral and highly creative part of the inquiry process generally. To unravel causal complexities, new instruments of observation may be required. To provide coherence of comprehension, new synthetic constructs may be needed. The interdependence of tool creation and theory refinement and expansion is well understood in the hard sciences (microscopes and the bacterial theory of infection, telescopes and theories of universe expansion). A similar interdependence is commonplace in economics: Maynard Keynes's aggregate supply and demand construct and his theory of income and employment,[41] Veblen's multiform dichotomy and his theory of business enterprise,[42] John Munkir's empirical connections-among-firms matrix and his theory of private sector centralized planning,[43] Gregory Hayden's social fabric matrix and his delivery and receipt analysis of social policy formation,[44] all illustrate the imaginative creation of analytical constructs that become operational tools of new theoretical analysis. The choice of a conceptual tool is determined by its ability to function appropriately to inform, and instrumentally to correct, in the role assigned.

In summary, the quest for tentative truth in causal inquiry reflects the effectual recourse to the methodological use of instrumental value theory to direct the conduct and patterning of inquiry. The scholarly concerns to explain and to appraise are interdependent and mutually supportive facets of institutionalist economic inquiry.

Social Value and Social Change: The Bush Contributions

In four articles since 1983,[45] Paul D. Bush has significantly extended and refined the theory of instrumental value. Building on earlier papers,[46] he provides 1) an exploration of the logical implications of the institutionalist dichotomy, 2) a theory of "ceremonial encapsulation," and 3) an analysis, from the instrumentalist perspective, of a cogent distinction between "progressive" and "regressive" social change. Our understanding of instrumental value theory and its pertinence for problem solving is materially enhanced by this work. I here briefly consider each of these three analytical contributions.

Logical Implications: Axiomatic Formulation. In the first of these four articles, Bush constructs "an analytical model of the institutional structure based on the rich theoretical and empirical implications of the Veblen-Ayres-Foster . . . institutionalist . . . dichotomy."[47]

That dichotomy "is contained in this distinction between the two modes of social valuation existing within the society."

> Ceremonial values are warranted by those mores and folkways that incorporate status hierarchies and invidious distinction as to the relative "worth" of various individuals or classes in the community. They rationalize power relationships and patterns of authority embedded in the status quo. Instrumental values are warranted through the systematic application of knowledge to the problem-solving process. They emerge from the processes of inquiry into causal

> relationships. As criteria for correlating behavior, they ensure causal continuity in the problem-solving process. . . . Although the value system is dichotomous, behavior is dialectical. A particular activity or behavior may have either ceremonial or instrumental significance, or it may possess *both* ceremonial and instrumental significance.[48]

The analytic focus of the model, then, is the manner in which these two modes of valuation interact in the correlation of behavior within institutional structures.

Bush derives his "deductively formulated model from the 'pattern theories' of the institutionalist paradigm." He acknowledges that institutionalists have made important analytical gains through the use of "pattern" models of inquiry,[49] but suggests that they have been reluctant to have anything to do with logico-deductivistic inquiry because of its aprioristic and dominating presence in neoclassicism. He wants to assist institutionalists to enhance the logical coherence of their analyses and to formulate analytical structures that will improve "the precision with which the paradigm may be applied" in the search for "a more precise statement of testable empirical hypotheses and a clearer delineation of policy issues."[50]

Accordingly, Bush formulates an axiomatic system of institutionalist constructs. "The 'artificial' language used to express the structural logic of the model is taken from the mathematical field of 'graph theory.'" This logic "may be the most appropriate to institutional analysis."[51] The model is comprised of ten axioms and eight theorems (sometimes with corollaries) deduced from the axiom set. Proofs are offered for all of the theorems introduced. While present constraints prevent review of the symbolic and graphic presentations, and the proofs offered, it is possible to get a sense of the model's character and significance through an abbreviated review of the major tenets. (What follows here is a mix of quoted and paraphrased statements; symbols have been deleted.)

Axiom 1: "An 'institution' is defined as set of socially prescribed patterns of correlated behavior."[52] It contains subsets of behaviors and correlating values.

Axiom 2: "The set of all values contains two disjoint subsets: ceremonially warranted values and instrumentally warranted values."[53] The value structure of the institution is dichotomous.

Axiom 3: "The set of all behaviors is formed by two subsets and their intersection. The two subsets are ceremonial behavior and instrumental behavior"; the intersection "is behavior having both ceremonial and instrumental significance."[54]

Axiom 4: For every behavior there is an associated value. "All behavior is rationalized according to the value structure of the institution."[55]

Axiom 5: Values are the "logical operators that 'correlate' behavior."[56] Correlations may be ceremonially or instrumentally "dominated." Instrumental behavior may be "encapsulated" by ceremonial behavior.

Theorem 1: "On the basis of Axioms 1 through 5, the set of all possible behavior patterns may be specified" and "partitioned into two subsets: the set of ceremonially warranted patterns of behavior and the set of instrumentally warranted behavior patterns."[57] Elements of the subsets are specified.

Axiom 6: "The institutional structure is defined as a set of ceremonial and instrumental patterns of behavior. . . . Institutional structure is neither purely ceremonial nor purely instrumental."[58]

Theorem 2: "On the basis of Axioms 1 through 6, the minimal institutional structure must take the form of one or the other of two sets of behavioral patterns as indicated." Ceremonial patterns of behavior are connected to instrumental patterns. Ceremonial "encapsulation" of instrumental behavior provides "the appearance of experiential warrant to ceremonial practices."[59]

Theorem 3: An "index of ceremonial dominance" is introduced. It "describes the value structure of the institution to the extent that it indicates the degree of dominance of ceremonial patterns of behavior over instrumental patterns of behavior."[60]

Axiom 7: "Dominance relations are transitive within the ceremonial and instrumental subsets of behavior patterns. Transitivity within ceremonial patterns reflects hierarchies based on invidious distinctions. Within instrumental patterns, transitivity reflects causal sequences."[61]

Theorem 4: "Ceremonial patterns dominate instrumental patterns of behavior within the institutional structure."[62]

Axiom 8: "The society's fund of knowledge is 'embedded' in the behavior patterns of its institutions. The knowledge fund is 'encapsulated' within ceremonially warranted patterns of behavior and 'embodied' in the instrumental patterns of behavior."[63]

Axiom 9: "A change in the fund of knowledge will be partly encapsulated within ceremonial patterns of behavior and partly embodied in instrumental patterns of behavior."[64]

Theorem 5: "For a given index of ceremonial dominance, an increase in the fund of knowledge will always result in less than the maximum feasible increase in instrumental behavior, that is, less than the maximum feasible level of technological innovation."[65]

Corollary to Theorem 5: "The lower the index of ceremonial dominance, the higher [will be the] level of technological innovation generated by an increase in the fund of knowledge."[66]

Theorem 6: "Structural change may occur without changing the index of ceremonial dominance, [but it] is *strictly* confined to ceremonial patterns of behavior." However, "changes in dominance relations among patterns of instrumental behavior are strictly the function of changes in either the fund of knowledge or the index of ceremonial dominance or both."[67]

Axiom 10: "A 'progressive' institutional change occurs when there is a decrease in the index of ceremonial dominance."[68]

Theorem 7: "For a given fund of knowledge, the necessary condition for technological innovation is a decrease in the index of ceremonial dominance, and the sufficient condition is that the increase in instrumental behavior results in a displacement of ceremonial behavior. . . . Technological innovation is accomplished by the displacement of a ceremonial pattern of behavior by an instrumental pattern of behavior."[69]

Theorem 8: "If a progressive institutional change occurs simultaneously with a change in the knowledge fund . . . the resulting technological innovation will be greater than that which occurs under conditions of the ceremonial encapsulation phase of institutional adjustment."[70]

Corollary to Theorem 8: "The index of ceremonial dominance [may decline] "not as a result of a 'displacement' of ceremonial behavior patterns by instrumental behavior patterns, but by the 'adding on' of instrumental patterns to the previously existing behavior set."[71]

Among the many implications one can draw from the foregoing analytical model, I note the following:

1. The behavioral structure that is the object of institutionalist inquiry tends to be exceedingly complex. The admixture of instrumental and ceremonial behaviors in institutions will vary in each problematic condition or circumstance investigated. Extensive empirical inquiry and assessment of the nature and performance of existing institutional arrangements is required.
2. Social value theory is, and must be, at the center of institutional problem-oriented inquiry. It is centrally embedded in the very logical structure of the analysis. It is no after-the-fact addendum.
3. The model provides an analytic map or template with which to establish and sustain logical coherence in the ordering of institutional inquiry. Yet the model itself remains an object of inquiry awaiting further development and refinement.
4. The model is free of the aprioristic unassailability of axiomatic formulations. It is rooted in and draws its credibility from its logical coherence, its evidential grounding, and its processual adaptability.

The Concept of Ceremonial Encapsulation. Having ordered value constructs logically, Bush turns, in the second of the four papers,[72] to a descriptive elaboration of a number of concepts formally introduced in his axiomatic model. Prominant among these is the "The Concept of Ceremonial Encapsulation," a newly emergent and most useful analytical construct.

At the outset, recall that the Veblenian dichotomy is embedded in Bush's concept of an institution. As Bush phrases it:

> . . . an "institution is defined as a set of socially prescribed patterns of correlated behavior. The "correlation" of behavior is prescribed by the value structure of society; that is, values function as criteria for the correlation of behavior within the institutional domain. The value structure, in turn derives its social warrant from one of two systems of value formation. Values are either ceremonially warranted or instrumentally warranted. The essence of the "institutional dichotomy" is contained in this distinction between the two modes of social valuation existing within the society.[73]

In this context, then, social prescriptions may be either ceremonially or instrumentally warranted. Indeed, institutions will display a mix of each of the two behavior patterns; no institution is wholly comprised of one or the other mode and warrant of behavior. Yet, both Veblen and Ayres took the view that ceremonial behavior patterns tend to dominate instrumental behavior patterns most of the time. Their contention is that:

> . . . while ceremonial practices cannot generate technological progress, they very clearly affect its direction and the rate of change by their degree of "permissiveness" with respect to technological innovation. The degree of ceremonial "permissiveness" is, then, a measure of the dominance of ceremonial practices over instrumental practices in the social structure.[74]

The concept of "ceremonial encapsulation," initiated independently by Bush and Louis Junker,[75] develops further "the logic of this dominance relationship," and in so doing extends and refines the institutionalist theory of institutional adjustment. According to Bush, "the process of institutional adjustment occurs in two analytically distinct phases." The first phase involves ceremonial encapsulation; the second constitutes progressive institutional change.

Institutionalists have long argued that the dynamic force that generates pressure for institutional adjustment is the growth of new knowledge and its application as technology through efforts to resolve problems. According to Bush's theory of ceremonial encapsulation, in the first phase of adjustment,

> . . . new knowledge will be incorporated into the institutional structure only to the extent that it can be made ceremonially adequate; that is, only to the extent

> that its incorporation can be accomplished without upsetting the existing degree of ceremonial dominance embedded in the value structure of the community.[76]

New knowledge and technology represent a threat to existing patterns of status and power. Ceremonial encapsulation operates to preserve the status quo that is ceremonially grounded; the existing pattern of invidiously warranted dominance is sustained. Efficiences of new instrumental behavior, where they pose no threat to existing ceremonial patterns of behavior, may be permitted. Where threat occurs, controls through legal constraints, exercise of property rights, discretion over financial resources, and/or sequestering of information will be used as means of encapsulation.

In the second phase of institutional adjustment, "progressive" institutional change occurs when, for a given state or fund of knowledge, "instrumentally warranted patterns of behavior displace ceremonially warranted patterns of behavior, thereby bringing about a change in the value structure of the community."[77] In this circumstance, there is a reduction in ceremonial dominance. Knowledge, that was at one time encapsulated, becomes embodied in instrumental patterns of behavior. As Junker thought of it, the use of knowledge passes from "encapsulation" to "liberation."[78]

Bush explains that the "first phase" ceremonial encapsulation that inhibits this "passing," occurs in one of three different forms: "past-binding," "future-binding," or the "'Lysenko' type."[79]

Past-binding is the familiar resistence to technological innovation, explored by Veblen and Ayres, that is rooted in the desire to protect the status quo and the power and status roles inbedded in it.

Future-binding encapsulation occurs in a setting where, as Bush observes,

> . . . the vested interests, seeking to impose and preserve a cultural hegemony that will nurture the values and attitudes most favorable to their own survival, will actively promote and control science and technology. . . . this kind of encapsulation . . . does not involve a resistance to technological innovation, but rather the active effort to develop, control, and choose among alternative technological paths through time; that is, it involves the selection among alternative "futures."[80]

Junker conducted extensive research into this form of encapsulation showing how "industrial clusters of giant corporations . . . effectively controlled scientific inquiry and influenced medical practices relating to the use of tobacco, food processing, and nutrition."[81] Similar demonstrations can be made with reference to the established energy corporations (especially petroleum) securing control over alternative energy technologies and processes.[82]

The third form of ceremonial encapsulation is the "Lysenko" type. It is named after an "agrobiologist" in the USSR in the 1930s, who, in purporting to demonstrate the genetic transmission of acquired characteristics, and with ideological and enthusiastic support of the Marxist state, placed regular biological inquiry in Russia in receivership for a generation.[83]

Here, "instrumentally warranted behavior is actually *reduced* [emphasis in original] through ceremonial encapsulation." Instrumentally warranted behavior patterns are *displaced and abandoned*, for example, in the pursuit of ideological utopias (economic isms), the advent of mind-controlling religious survivalists sects, or the deliberately contrived propagandistic paranoia over military preparedness. Warranted knowledge is withheld; instrumental behavior is denigrated; recourse to both psychological and physical coercion is predictable.

Progressive' versus "Regressive" Social Change. In Bush's analysis, to pursue Lysenko-like forms of ceremonial encapsulation, in which instrumentally warranted behavior is *supplanted* by ceremonially warranted behavior, is to introduce "*regressive*" institutional change.[84] In this case, the index of ceremonial dominance is *increased*. Ceremonial judgments are rationalized as if they are instrumentally warranted, and various information and communication controls are introduced to prevent disclosure of the fraudulent manipulation. "Big lie" campaigns pass off propaganda as warranted information; "photo opportunities" supplant deliberations and communications on issues.

Regressive change means deliberate recourse to, and the vigorous retention and probable extension of, invidiously warranted behavior—in pursuit or preservation of power, status, rank, income, or wealth—at the expense of instrumental behavior rooted in causal inquiry and the quest for problem-solving institutional adjustments.

Regressive change is not easily overcome and reversed, as Bush acknowledges, quoting Veblen: "History records more frequent and more spectacular instances of the triumph of imbecile institutions over the life and culture than of peoples who have by force of instinctive insight saved themselves alive out of a desperately precarious institutional situation."[85]

In direct contrast, "*Progressive* institutional change occurs when, *for a given fund of knowledge* [emphasis in original], ceremonial patterns of behavior are displaced by instrumental patterns of behavior."[86] Here, the index of ceremonial dominance is reduced. As noted, the theory of ceremonial encapsulation explains the *first* phase of institutional adjustment. The analysis that explains how ceremonial behavioral patterns are supplanted by instrumental ones, providing for progressive institutional change, accounts for the *second* phase of institutional adjustment.

This second phase is a consequence of the community's increasing awareness of the cumulatively causal understanding that occurs even under circumstances where new knowledge and technology are encapsulated by past-binding and future-binding values and behaviors. In both cases, where threats to the status quo can be well constrained, some new instrumental valuation and behavioral patterns are permitted. As these new instrumental judgments spread through the culture, reflecting a "demonstration effect" (Galbraith), they tend to erode or undermine confidence in other ceremonial and invidious behavioral patterns. Veblen's *Imperial Germany and the Industrial Revolution*[87] was among the first serious works by institutionalists to explain this sort of evolutionary change. In this work, Veblen considers the impact of the transfer of English technological and industrial behavioral modes on Germanic cultural traditions. To juxtapose matter-of-fact, machine-oriented habits of mind with concerns over prowess, exploit, and emulation would eventually lead to an erosion of the latter, he thought. Instrumental habits of mind, although encapsulated by traditional power centers, generally do, after a period of time, spread widely enough to produce less reliance on cerenomial patters of behavior.

Bush also reminds us of the significance of the interdependencies that exist between the growth of knowledge and the supplanting of ceremonial behavior with instrumental behavior. Increasing permissiveness in the inquiry process, generated by the lowering of the index of ceremonial dominance, permits an acceleration of the rate of growth of warranted knowledge. The latter, in turn, provides new and more extensive information about options for further progressive institutional adjustment. Acceleration of both the growth of knowledge and the rate of progressive institutional change can be expected as long as opportunities for the interactive inter-dependencies are permitted and encouraged.[88] Success in problem solving in one area generates incentives for further efforts at problem solving elsewhere.

Bush sees my formulation of the instrumental value principle (as noted above) as an "intellectual bridge . . . between the theory of institutional change and the theory of policy formation. . . . [I]t is an expression of 'progressive' institutional change under the condition of minimal dislocation. . . . Progress is to be found in any institutional change that 'provides for the continuity of human life and the noninvidious recreation of community through the instrumental use of knowledge.' "[89]

The invidious constraints on progressive change are well captured in Bush's consideration of the theory of ceremonial encapsulation. But there are nonceremonial constraints on progressive change as well. Bush, in the most recent of his papers in this area,[90] in which he draws on Fagg Foster's earlier work,[91] develops two of these in particular: the principles of "recognized interdependence" and of "minimal dislocation." Says Bush,

> The logic of the argument is clear. Since institutions are socially prescribed patterns of correlated behavior, the interdependence of human action is institutionally determined; and since institutional change requires new patterns of correlated behavior, the capacity of persons within institutions to understand and adapt to the new patterns will be an operative constraint on both the rate and direction of institutional change.[92]

Adaptation to new correlated patterns is difficult for two related reasons. First, the nature and scope of the new prescriptive arrangements are very likely to be exceedingly complex. Ceremonial or invidious patterns come in many forms, shapes, and varieties and in assorted combinations, the complexity of which makes it difficult to understand what changes are proposed and what consequences to expect. Second, since we all are creatures who internalize through habituation socially prescribed patterns of behavior, we are reluctant to modify those patterns until and unless we can anticipate what our particular circumstances will be following the changes, and are willing to consent to the changes being proposed. The success of introducing instrumentally warranted changes hinges on the provision of full information to those affected by the proposed structural changes and in the solicitation and receipt of their willingness to participate, given "recognized interdependence."

The second nonceremonial constraint on progressive change, in Bush's view, is found in the principle of "minimal dislocation." This principle specifies "that 'progressive' institutional change can occur only when the displacement of ceremonial patterns of behavior by instrumental patterns of behavior occurs in such a way as to preserve the continuity of the life processes of the community and minimizes the dislocation of instrumentally warranted patterns of behavior."[93] What Bush adds to this analysis is the implied logic that the constraint of minimal dislocation can only be met by careful and continuous *planning* of institutional change.

Extensive inquiry must disclose not only what centers of vested interest must be challenged but, just as importantly, what patterns of *instrumental* behavior elsewhere will be intruded upon by the proposed changes. The latter intrusions must be held to a minimum or those affected by the change will quickly abandon their tacit acceptance or their support for such changes. All change is disruptive; some disruption will involve existing instrumental arrangements. The latter must be minimized through careful planning.

Bush illustrates the enormous significance of *planning* structural change by referring to the largely successful historical efforts to introduce collective bargaining institutions to move adversarial labor-management relations from street battles to boardroom deliberations and to eliminate invidious discrimination in political, social, and economic participation through the civil rights movement. Careful planning to minimize dislocation is now required for "the demilitarization of the American economy and the combined global environmental threats of acid rain and the 'greenhouse' effect."[94]

In summary, Bush has analytically reshaped and extended the theory of instrumental value. He has demonstrated that instrumental value theory is logically coherent and capable of explaining complex social processes. He has generated new analytically useful constructs of an "index of ceremonial dominance" and (with Junker) "ceremonial encapsulation" and shown their analytical potency. He has provided a fresh and analytically grounded distinction between "progressive" and "regressive" institutional change. In consequence, instrumental value theory is at once more readily understandable, more analytically persuasive, and more applicable to policy considerations.

But within the house of institutionalists, some have published critiques of instrumental value theory and are apprehensive about its implications. On the assumption that some number of these criticisms are shared by others, I turn now to a consideration of several of these objections and reservations as expressed particularly by Wendell Gordon and Anne Mayhew, respectively.

Clarifications of Instrumental Value Theory

Instrumental Value an Eternal Verity? A Reply to Wendell Gordon[95]

In several recent publications, Wendell Gordon has raised serious and continuing questions about the character and use of the instrumental value principle discussed above.[96] In this section, I would like to respond to some of his reservations and intend thereby to contribute further clarification of the nature and significance of this institutionalist construct. First, I review and address Gordon's characterizations of the instrumental value principle and examine his evident ambivalence over value theory.

Gordon's characterizations of the instrumental value principle, my first concern here, include the following: "Tool *seems . . . to be alleging* the existence of an eternal verity in his social value principle."[97] Elsewhere he contends that Tool "*endorses* [emphases added] the existence of an eternal verity in his social-value principle."[98] He suggests "that institutionalists are capable by some sort of instinct or black magic of recognizing a maximum, a most efficient situation, a maximum product, a best result."[99] He argues, in contrast, that "a social value principle, criterion of judgment or value referent, which states a simple basic concept or two for use in judging instruments, ends, and values, is not a basic characteristic [of institutionalism]."[100] He views users of the instrumental principle as being "prone to [the] making of cavalier value judgments," as "carefree proliferators of value judgments," as offering judgments "coming out of a black box," as offering principles "of permanent validity which should guide all decision making," and of identifying "definitive, general purpose social values, criteria of judgment, or value referents."[101] Again, and finally, "Tool is offering the social value principle as a definitive or eternal verity or truth."[102] Gordon insists, to the contrary, that "there are no absolute or permanent values or eternal verities identifying values." One must "admit the possibility that no value can be alleged with certainty as applicable for all time and under all circumstances to all types of being."[103] Indeed, at one point, Gordon insists that "institutionalism . . . has no commitment to particular values. Institutionalism as institutionalism is value free."[104]

Is the instrumental principle an "eternal verity"? If by eternal verity is meant a fixedly given truth that is beyond inquiry and has no evidential grounding, or an ethical absolute that is rooted in some religious dictum, received doctrine, or otherwise unchallengable source, the instrumental principle is not an eternal verity. The instrumental principle is rather an inquiry product and remains subject to revision or abandonment by further inquiry. It has no standing except as an inquiry creation and tool for further inquiry and judgment. Its relevance is repeatedly tested by its incorporation in and guidance of inquiry and its use as a judgmental standard in problem solving. That the instrumental principle has in fact been a frequent basis for judgment is a factual assertion and subject to the usual checks for verification. I have suggested as much above.

Moreover, I find it curious that on a page where Gordon alleges that the instrumental value principle is an "eternal verity," he quotes the following passage of mine evidently to illustrate the *absence* of "absolute values" or "eternal values" in institutional analysis:

> "What sets off the . . . formulation of instrumental value theory from the social value theory of other belief systems is that it is derived exclusively from the experience continuum of people and that it articulates what often has historically been meant by progress, reform, or betterment. . . [instrumental] value theory is different in kind; it is a product of inquiry; it may be modified or

> replace by subsequent inquiry. . . . The formulation here is thus provisional and exploratory."[105]

I appear to be both charged with and absolved of offering an "eternal verity" principle.

As for the "eternal verity or *truth*" characterization, I have repeatedly contended, following Dewey, that "truth" is a *provisional* outcome of inquiry. What is derived is a *tentative* warrant to assert something, pending further inquiry. As I argued earlier in the chapter, the value principle generally reflected in modern causal inquiry is the instrumental principle. Interestingly, Gordon assumes "that institutionalism is committed to the scientific method and to inductive argument" and that "the scientific method is the logical process by which values are recognized and established or adopted by individuals and by society."[106] But surely he does not mean to suggest that, for example, the value premises of racial supremecy or the natural right to property are "recognized and established" as values by the logic of scientific inquiry. He does not acknowledge or recognize that the instrumental value principle guides choices made in the conduct of scientific inquiry.

The contention that the instrumental value principle "can be alleged with certainty as applicable for all time and under all circumstances to all types of being" is Gordon's not mine. I make no claims of universality. There are, no doubt, areas of human experience to which it does not apply. Rather, I have argued that it appears to be a judgmental principle presently available that provides criteria for revising institutional structure to actually resolve social and economic problems. And I am not unaware that the instrumental principle is itself required to distinguish a problem from a nonproblem and what constitutes a "solution." But it is not a "personal" judgmental principle; it does not derive from individual tastes or preferences. It is a widely shared judgmental principle among those in any community who wish, through causal analysis and consequent appraisal, to understand and remove the institutional determinants of obstructions and impairments in the provisioning process and in the discretionary mechanisms through which public policy is determined. Familiar programs to provide for continuity in income flows and to ensure uncorrupted political participation illustrate this quest.

I can therefore be somewhat sympathetic with Gordon when he says that "the general procedure for identifying or establishing values is the instrumental or self-correcting value judgment process," and when he contends that "the social value principle is best viewed as a value judgment as to the best value referent to be used in trying to evaluate the appropriateness of various other value judgments."[107] But to whom or to what does Gordon appeal in establishing the "best view" and the "best value" referent? Is not "best" at bottom still a matter of individual taste, preference, or subjective prizing, in his view? Through what inquiry process, if any, is "best" identified? Inquiry is required; a criterion is required. Gordon does not supply either.

What Gordon may have intended to imply, and in this I could join him, is that the instrumental principle offers different *kinds* of value criteria. It is, in inquiry, a judgmental principle used to assess principles of assessment. It is *fundamental* in that sense. But its standing is not rooted in or based on individual preferences. It is a processual construct; it is devoid of utilitarian, religious, institutional, or unexamined "feelings" content. It is a *continuously* relevant principle with which to appraise other noninstrumental value concepts in considering proposed solutions to social and economic problems. But it has no "eternal verity" standing.

Gordon backs away from the potent implications of the instrumental value principle. He conceives the scholar's role as limited to a *descriptive* characterization of "the way people behave" when they try to decide "what works best." Here his retreat to and preference for an individualistic and subjective conception of "what works best" reflects his continuing entrapment in the descriptive–prescriptive version of the positive–normative dichotomy. I would go further and argue that the instrumental principle seems at present to be a most useful criterion publically and effectually with which to identify what does "work best." The scholar's role is not, of course, to decide for the community what is best for the community; rather, it is to help the community understand why instrumental judgments are better than noninstrumental judgments where "better" is itself the object of inquiry. We cannot accept an unexamined pleasure or satisfaction as the meaning of what is "better."

Second, as I read Gordon's critique, I find a disturbing ambivalence permeating his analysis. He defines "value" as a "judgment made by an individual being or by an institution as to what is *desirable*, *estimable*, or *instrumental*"[108] [emphasis added]. Do all such characterizations have the same analytical standing? In other places, the term *useful* or *satisfying* is substituted for *instrumental*. [I note in passing that institutions as prescribed patterns don't judge; people do.] *Desirable* connotes that which is "worth seeking or doing as advantageous, beneficial or wise." *Estimable* connotes "worthy of esteem or respect; deserving good opinion." *Instrumental* connotes "serving as a means or intermediary determining or leading to a particular result." *Useful* connotes "capable of being put to use; serviceable for a beneficial end"; *satisfying* connotes "to be happy" or "to be a source of pleasure or gratification."[109]

The ambivalence arises in the inadvertent mixing of incommensurate characteristics: *desirable, estimable* and *satisfying* are judgments arising as unexaminable, nonevidential individual preferences or tastes as to what is worthy, makes one happy, one finds satisfying, and the like. *Instrumental* and *useful* characterizations are matters of observable and demonstrable causal linkages. Ethical relativism rooted in subjective utilitarianism permeates the former; causal and evidential judging is reflected in the latter. We have disclaim and claim. Says Gordon: "The instrumental value judgment process, as I see it, does not involve endorsing a type of cultural relativism in which 'anything goes' so long as some person or some culture believes it is desirable."[110] Thus the formulation of his view of value judgments *does in fact* defer to relativistic views of what is desirable, estimable, and satisfying. What is "desirable" is the ultimate and unassessed "ought to be." Subjective utilitarianism, give its relativistic ambivalence, may well become (as noted above) a screen to conceal the use of a de facto ethical absolute, that is, an eternal verity.

There *is also* an element of Cartesian dualism about this judgmental ambivalence. Edythe Miller, in her review of the value theory sections of the recent Gordon-Adams book,[111] makes this logical flaw evident:

> First, a distinction is drawn between subjects and objects, and means and ends, although the possibility of some overlap is acknowledged. It is contended that individuals or institutions (subjects) make value judgments. They make them about goods and services (objects), that are the ends-in-view. Technology and resources are the means to attain these ends-in-view. Value is assigned by the subject to the object (p. 85). It is maintained that when, in the institutionalist literature, "technology is referred to as a locus of value, it is in the sense that technology is an 'object' to which value is being assigned. Technology is valued because it is instrumental in implementing desired results" (p. 86).
>
> The case does not hold up. Goods and services are means, as well as ends. Individuals are acted upon, in addition to being actors. . . . Nevertheless, they maintain that value is a matter of individual taste.[112]

This subject–object dualism contributes to the ambivalence. (I return to this point below.)

Gordon's logical and judgmental unease occurs in another context as well. It relates to the question of whether this instrumental (or self-correcting) value judgment process "works" or not. He writes:

> . . . an individual . . . applies a value and a technique to the solution of a problem and subsequently makes an additional (value) judgment [I assume he means "valuation" as application, not "value" as criterion] as to whether the process worked. If one judges that it did not work, one may revise either the technique or the value. If it works, one still may hypothesize that some other technique might work better, or . . . that other values would be preferable.[113]

What is left unaddressed, of course, is the referential meaning of "worked." If a value judgment process is "self-correcting" there must be some way to distinguish between a "correct" and an "incorrect" outcome, to identify what "worked better" or did not "work" at all. Yet no standard of correctness, no meaning for "worked," is provided. We are not instructed on how the criterion of judgment was selected and on what grounds. We are left once again with nothing but recourse to individual preferences, the character of which is, for Gordon, not analytically accessible. An ethically relative "*anything goes*" prevails after all.

This ambivalence continues into Gordon's most recent criticism of what he perceives to be the instrumental value principle.[114] While he sees his position as reflecting acceptance of Dewey's processual means–ends–means–ends continuum, that converts ends into ends-in-view, he separates (mistakenly, in my view) the judging of means and the judging of ends. In judging means, one selects tools and instruments that are "appropriate" in reaching the end-in-view. In judging ends-in view, one seeks the "best solution," what is "satisfactory," what is "desirable." Although these judgments are perceived "as a package," and the "appropriateness of means and ends is reconsidered" as the inquiry process proceeds, Gordon provides no distinguishing criteria to apply in determining what is "best," "satisfying," "desirable," or "appropriate." When, for example, an individual makes a "judgment . . . that unemployment is undesirable, or that a higher salary is desirable, or that 'I do not like Joe'",[115] these are, in his view evidently, merely different ends-in-view. For Gordon, there is no available standard with which to judge the merits of pursuing one versus another end-in-view. Yet his own conception of a "self-correcting value judgment" *must* incorporate some way of distinguishing between a correct value judgment and an incorrect one. Credible criteria are required. The claim and disclaim continue.

Part of Gordon's problem, as I read his work, is that he continues to employ, although he claims otherwise, the conventional "merely means" referent for "instrumental," rather than the referent supplied by Dewey. Gordon's reference is to instrumental means used in achieving *otherwise* identified "ends-in-view." The latter are, for Gordon, defined by what is desirable or satisfying. He here reflects the objective (means)—subjective (ends-in-view) form of the positive–normative dichotomy. This permits him to argue that institutionalists address the "objective means" facet and describe how value assessments, of what is subjectively pleasant and satisfying, occur. For Gordon, accordingly, institutionalists must defer to such subjective judgments; they have no principle for the appraisal of principles of appraisal; institutionalism is value-free.

I read Dewey, in contrast, to have abandoned the objective–subjective dichotomy and for compelling reasons. The means-ends continuum is not an episode of selecting objective means to achieve subjective ends-in-view. The means–ends continuum embodies the acknowledged interdependencies of means *and* ends. They are cut from the same conceptual cloth. They are related precisely in the means–consequence sense. *Means chosen determine the character of outcomes realized.* From a genuinely processual pespective, consequences become means to further consequences in an endless continuum. The captions "means" and "ends" or "ends-in-view" are affixed by the inquirer; they have no original or independent standing. The instrumental value principle operates endemically through the whole inquiry process; it applies to means *and* ends-in-view.

As I observed above, if inquiry is purposive, it is value-laden. And Gordon does affirm the purposiveness of inquiry. But not, as he insists, just to satisfy subjective feeling states of notions of desirableness, but to expand warranted knowledge to achieve levels of understanding or causal phenomena that will permit genuine problem solving.

The instrumental value principle identifies the purposiveness of inquiry and facilitates pertinent problem analysis and resolution. Although we cannot here enter into a discussion of the demise of confidence in the positive–normative dichotomy generally, clearly the erosion of support for logical positivism, and Lord Robbin's version for economists of a "gulf fixed [between the normative and positive] which no stretch of the imagination can bridge over," brings into question any retentive use of the objective–subjective derivitive. Put differently and bluntly, Gordon exhibits a major contradiction in his concurrent claims for a "value-free" status for inquiry and for *purposiveness* of that inquiry.

Gordon's primary difficulty, as I read his work, is his inability to break free of the positive–normative dichotomy, discredited though it now is. His understandable apprehension over ethical absolutes and eternal verities has led him to accept subjectivistically grounded, ethically relative criteria of what is "desirable, estimable, and satisfying." Instrumental value theory, even in its present state of development, can, I think, provide more credible, powerful and applicable alternative criteria.

Culture versus Social Value? A Response to Anne Mayhew[116]

In two recent papers, Anne Mayhew also takes pervasive exception to my formulation and use of the instrumental value principle.[117] Her reservations will be addressed under two headings: 1) the character and significance of the instrumental value principle, and 2) the applicability or policy relevance of the instrumental value principle.

First, with regard to the character and significance of the instrumental value principle, Mayhew sees a basic conflict within institutionalist thought between those who, like the present author, emphasize "evaluation of institutions, evaluation of structures" through recourse to the instrumental value principle, in contrast to those (like Wendell Gordon) who emphasize "description and analysis of institutions, descriptions and analyses of cultures." "The conflict occurs," she argues, "when what is agreed by all institutionalists to be an aspect of human behavior—instrumental valuing—becomes as well a strategy for valuing and policy prescription by the analyst. Transforming the aspect of instrumental valuing into a suitable strategy for saying what ought to be, and making it the most important of the institutionalist tools, demotes the concept of culture."[118] She objects to "the instrumental aspect" being made both the "*source and measure* of human progress."

Mayhew arrives at this perception of a conflict through an interpretation of an earlier discussion of mine that employed a structure–function distinction.[119] It will be useful to examine this interpretation briefly.

To the following questions, Mayhew argues that I would answer yes: "Does the institutionalist 'dichotomy' provide the basis for value judgments? Does the 'dichotomy' tell us what ought to be as well as giving us a way of thinking about how people decide what ought to be?"[120] She infers my affirmative answer from her interpretation of my position as follows:

> Tool . . . answers . . . yes, because—if I have it right—there are universal human goals—"continuous functions"—that can serve as standards against which performance can be measured. Institutions are human devices ("discontinuous functions") that organize our efforts to achieve the continuous and universal goals. The structures or "particular ways of organizing economic activity are discontinuous; that is, the prescriptive arrangements, property rights, legal constraints, . . . and the like are all products of human decisions and hence are potentially discontinuous." He goes on to say that "[t]he function of producing food and fiber is continuous . . . the function of educating the young is continuous." Recognition of the continuous functions serves, in Tool's view, as the basis for judgment. If we recognize that a "discontinuous structure"—let us say the American mid-Western family farm—serves a continuous function of producing food, we can then judge its adequacy. The criteria to be applied are those that are continuous; false criteria are those that are discontinuous.[121]

While Mayhew is correct in her assertion of my affirmative answer to the questions posed, in my view she misconstrues the substance of the function–structure distinction, at least as I have tried to employ it. She mistakenly converts my characterizations of "continuous functions" into "universal goals . . . that serve as standards against which performance can be measured." The functions identified are broad *categories* of persistent human activity generally pan-culturally viewed and identified. Some will be reflected in all cultures; some may be significant only in modern industrial societies. When Walter Neale contends that "there can, of course, be no denying that every society must provide for the maintenance of its members, for teaching its offspring to speak, and so on," he implies what I have identified as continuing functions. Neale adds that "what is not so much denied as ignored, avoided, or evaded is the proposition that we can (even should?) list and account for these necessary functions."[122] I support the foregoing "proposition"; he evidently does not think it instructive to exploit the structure-function distinction for its explanatory usefulness. As for his "and so on," an indication that there are other continuing functional categories of activity, he does suggest elsewhere that "all peoples have instituted one or another set of rules for sorting out permissible and impermissible sexual partners," and that "the family is a highly variable 'universal.'"[123] I would restate these, respectively, as the continuing functions of providing for the reproduction of members of the community, and of providing for the maintenance and enculturation of the young. There are, of course, other such continuing functions.[124] If they are as central and significant as the provisioning process, they represent areas of activity that must be organized in a manner judged sufficiently adequate by the members of the community. Failing this, the social order disintegrates.

Providing for the continuity of the social order, and the culture created therein, is a pan-cultural social obligation. The organization of continuing functions is accomplished through the establishment of institutional structures that correlate behavior to serve social purposes as perceived and defined by members of that social order. That structure may be newly invoked or it may be so embedded in custom that no living person has knowledge of its origins. Origins are usually obscure, but changes in institutions can often be traced historically.[125] All initiations of structural arrangements are products of human agency. None are "natural" in the sense of being specified by natural law. They are "given" only in the sense that individuals are born into an existing culture and institutional configuration. They are in principle and in fact discretionary; they are products of choice or judgment. In the general sense, then, any such structure *is* discontinuous and replacemental as are other prescriptive and proscriptive patterns that organize social and economic activity. The structure–function construct draws the critical distinction that permits scholars to bring institutions, as such, onto the agenda for inquiry where their character and their supportive rationale can be analyzed and appraised with regard to their role and impact on the community.

Institutions, incorporating both instrumentally warranted and ceremonially warranted behavior, become objects of inquiry and appraisal and are subject to retention or abandonment at the discretion of the community, hopefully, through democratic processes. The instrumental value principle does permit one to judge the extent to which the prevailing institutional structure is warranted through effectual incorporation of the community's fund of reliable knowledge or is compromised and impaired by ceremonially constituted and warranted authority. The more instrumental the institutional performance, the more efficient and equitable the correlation of behavior. The more invidious the institutional performance, the less efficient and equitable the correlation of behavior. Bush's analysis of progressive versus regressive change (considered above) refines this distinction. The "continuous functions" cited, then, are not themselves criteria; they are foci of activity requiring organization and correlation through institutional arrangements. Institutionalists suggest that they be *appraised* through recourse to the instrumental value principle. It is my contention that all peoples do in some measure make such appraisals in ways that institutionalists would characterize as rational where "rational" means acquired capacity to comprehend causal phenomena. As Neale observes, "all people reason in the same technological (instrumental) way, at least some of the time."[126]

The foregoing does not demote "the concept of culture," as Mayhew has claimed. Neither is the analyst's descriptive characterizations of cultural complexities threatened. Institutionalists have long agreed that descriptive characterizations must be an important part of any serious inquiry into economic problems. The culture concept, accepted by virtually all institutionalists, is certainly one of the preeminent contributions of social research in this century. An understanding of interrelationships of the individual and culture is central to any analysis of social problems. Surely that idea is not under attack in the foregoing discussion.

But *descriptive characterizations are not value-free.* In order to "describe" we must employ criteria that delimit the relevant from the irrelevant and identify what is significant and worthy of description. Such criteria are clearly normative and must be justified by some valuational scheme. As Hayden observes, "there is no description that is not laden with values, beliefs, and philosophical decisions; facts more so than most analytical entities. . . . Facts must be created by humans who must make judgments about criteria, research, design, gathering techniques and so forth. By the time a fact is gathered, judgment has been stacked upon judgment, and criterion upon criterion."[127]

But to what "valuational scheme" may a scholar turn in rendering descriptions? Institutionalists tend to reject ethical relativism because of its inherent judgmental ambivalence, as noted above, and to reject ethical absolutism because of its inherent doctrinaire exclusiveness. The valuational scheme of institutionalists, in contrast, is embedded in the inquiry process itself. To reiterate, it conjoins the pursuit of knowledge and the valuation process. The instrumental value principle is a product of this union.

Given the foregoing, it becomes evident, then, that the existing institutional fabric of a culture will not itself serve as a judgmental standard; perserving the status quo is not, per se, an admissible criterion. *Existing* structure can hardly be defended as a criterion for choosing what structure *ought* to obtain when breakdowns or impairments in the provisioning process, attributable to existing structure, occur and are identified. The instrumental principle, as noted, does not incorporate structure; it provides criteria for choosing among structures.

Mayhew is, of course, correct in perceiving "instrumental valuing" as an *aspect* of cultural behavior; but my argument is that it is the *critical aspect* in the analysis and resolution of social and economic problems. I am not disturbed by her concern that the instrumental criterion be viewed as the "source and measure of human progress" if the universe of inquiry to which it is applied is the political economy of any given culture. I see the instrumental criterion as pan-culturally relevant, then, to the provisioning and policy determining processes of a social order. I leave to others the recommendation of criteria appropriate, for example, to assessment of contributions to the arts. I do suggest, that, in the universe of inquiry specified, the instrumental value principle, because of its distinctive character and grounding, is effectual and pertinent in problem analysis.

Second, with regard to the policy relevance of the instrumental value principle, I must take strong exception to Mayhew's critique. She argues that the instrumental value principle has no "operational applicability." Although Mayhew does not provide referential content for the phrase, I construe her meaning to be a concern over the applicability and policy relevance of instrumental value theory. She denies "that we can operationally define 'continuity,' 'instrumental effectiveness,' a process of 're-creating community,' or 'noninvidiousness' in ways that will allow us to judge the 'normative content' of analyses with 'scientific' confidence."[128] These terms are necessarily empty, in Mayhew's view.[129] She observes that I have not provided "operational definitions"; I have not "provided a list of characteristics that clearly serve to identify 'wrong conclusions.' "[130] She asks for that which, were it provided, she would reject.

Operational definitions are, in effect, particularistic judgmental formulations in a specific problematic context. The instrumental value principle directs inquiry to the kinds of evidence and the universe of problems to be addressed. What will be characterized as instrumental or ceremonial in a particular context is determined in and through inquiry. What is an instrumental use of knowledge at one time, or in one setting, may well, with the growth of knowledge be *subsequently* viewed as having become non-instrumental or even invidious.

It is ironic that in her critique Mayhew inadvertently makes just this point: She says, for example, that she does "not favor master race coercion, dogmatic reaffirmation of the *status quo*, or 'invidious buttressing of hierarchical economic power of elites,' " but that she "could be charged with favoring analyses 'validating discriminatory treatment of persons' because she supports 'discriminatory treatment for those with various 'handicaps'" so that their lives can be improved. She implies, with the latter comment, that a failure to marshall knowledge and resources to aid those whose handicaps prevent fuller participation represents invidious suppression.[131] This is an instrumental judgment.

Similarly, when, in my reference to "continuity of human life," I indicate that it includes a "concern for conditions that cater to and elevate distinctively human traits and capabilities to think freely, to create imaginatively," and so on, and suggest that "lower and higher education" contribute to this concern, Mayhew takes exception. She suggests that "*some* people are probably going to think more freely and create more imaginatively if they do *not* sit in college classrooms."[132] Of course, this is possible. But she provides no hint of an institutional setting that would provide for this circumstance. She does share the educational goals of fostering free and imaginative thinking and implies a need for instrumental reform in the conduct of some classes.

A final example: In the context of considering policy that addresses the problem of involuntary unemployment, Mayhew raises the matter of "retirement."[133] She implicitly applies an instrumental judgment when she says that "we have made *progress* [emphasis added] in redefining [retirement] as a more general right." But "at what age should a person be allowed to define themselves out of the labor force?" Should people be forced out at 65? Should people stay on the job as long as they wish? Should or must everyone be treated the same? Mayhew is correct when she suggests that the answers made in legislation in 1935 might not be acceptable in 1990. What has happened in the meantime? Our knowledge of labor force demands, demographic shifts, impact of retirement on people's longevity, productivity at advanced ages, and the like has increased. What was an instrumental judgment in the 1930s may need to be revised substantially in the 1990s. But the quest for full employment and noninvidious treatment of persons is not empty. As our understanding of means and consequences of discretionary action increases and is refined, the quality of our judgments in the instrumental sense can be enhanced. That is what Mayhew implies; she is instrumentally correct in that recognition. She has in effect made the continuity and noninvidiousness principle operationally feasible. She has refuted her own critique and eroded her own unease.

The "crucial test of operationality" [her phrase] is a simple derivitive of the inquiry process guided by an instrumentalist conception of the problem. When Mayhew says that she and I "agree on almost all . . . specific policy recommendations," she is correct. When she says that she "cannot see into the future, so. . . [she] cannot give specificity to the principles of continuity, instrumental effectiveness, re-creating community, or noninvidiousness,"[134] she is correct; no one can. The specificity is determined and defined in the context of application. However, the general referential content of the criteria contained in the principle is not obscure to Mayhew. She exhibits it throughout her essay. She does not support the views that "private property is the system God intended" or that "America became great because government stayed out of the economy." As noted, she does not favor "master race coercion, dogmatic reaffirmation of the *status quo*" or "invidious buttressing of hierarchical economic power of elites." She supports higher education that "is consistent with freedom of thought, creativity, and humaneness." She does not justify "our acceptance of 6% or 7% unemployment rates as inevitable or desirable." In all these decisions regarding what is and is not "desirable," she speaks not out of personal taste or preference but as an instrumentalist formulating analyses and judgments in specific problem contexts.

Other institutionalists have found the Veblenian dichotomy, and/or its more developed form as the instrumental value principle, relevant and applicable in problem identification and policy considerations, Mayhew's reservations notwithstanding. I close this section with a brief canvass of several:

Paul Dale Bush. Education: "The G.I. Bill was a productivity-increasing investment in human capital that contributed significantly to post-World War II economic growth . . . [it] substantially reduced the importance of such invidious criteria as social and economic status in the allocation of educational opoportunities.[135]

Energy: "The traditional means by which the community has allocated energy resources are no longer adequate to sustain the life processes of the community . . . "progressive institutional change" is required. "Ceremonial encapsulation of energy resources and development" has occurred through the "concentration and centralization of power in the oil industry."[136]

Louis J. Junker. Food and Nutrition: "While institutionalists have explored its [the ceremonial–instrumental dichtomy] theoretical power as an analytical tool, they have not adequately developed its eminently practical relevance for problem solving and policy formation. This paper is a contribution toward filling that gap in the institutionalist literature. . . . The study of the political economy of food, nutrition, and agriculture requires an ecologically oriented recognition of the principles and corollaries" of instrumental value theory.[137]

F. Gregory Hayden. Agriculture: "In considering consequences, [of agricultural policy] there is probably nothing that more exemplifies the Veblenian dichotomy, which distinguishes between substantive economics and pecuniary valuation, than the policies applied to agriculture and rural communities."[138]

James A. Swaney. Environment: "A holistic systems approach to environmental problems starts with the recognition that social systems coevolve with natural systems. . . . A flexible approach is responsive to and supportive of advances in scientific knowledge and their subsequent practical implementation. . . . Foster's principles of institutional adjustment" [based on instrumental value theory] are applied "to environmental policy." The principle of "coevolutionary sustainability" is added.[139]

John R. Munkirs. Industrial Structure: "The analytical frame of reference upon which the analysis [of centralized private sector planning] is founded is the Veblenian dichotomy as presented by Thorstein Veblen in his book *The Theory of Business Enterprise*, and as applied by Veblen to the U.S. economy."[140]

Accordingly, I reject the claim of Mayhew that the instrumental value principle is devoid of applicability to problem identification and policy analysis. I do agree that a substantial expansion of efforts at its application are desirable and will be instructive. The instrumental principle itself will benefit from further refinement, respecification, and clarification. We should welcome the opportunity so to engage.

Summary Observations

It is my view that institutionalists have responded to the appeal of Myrdal and Samuels and provided relevant normative theory as an integral part of the institutionalists' approach to economic inquiry generally. In this chapter, I have:

1. Reintroduced the instrumental value principle and explored its character.
2. Noted extensions to instrumental value theory through the identification of instrumental criteria as an inherent and crucial attribute of modern causal inquiry; explored Dale Bush's contributions to instrumental value theory in his axiomatic formulation of instrumental value, his co-authored construct of ceremonial encapsulation, and his analytical distinction between progressive and regressive social change.
3. Responded to Gordon's critique of instrumental value theory by disclaiming his eternal verity characterization for the principle and noting his inadvertent injection of ethically relative criteria into the judgmental process.
4. Responded to Mayhew's critique of instrumental value theory by refuting her claim that it is a threat to culture or that it demotes the concept of culture, and argued that the instrumental principle has applicability to real economic problems. I suggest that both Gordon and Mayhew are, in important respects, de facto instrumental theorists, their respective critiques of instrumental value theory notwithstanding.

It is my hope that these extensions and clarifications will stimulate new refinements, assessments, and applications. Of such elements does the inquiry process consist.

Notes

1. I would like to express my deep appreciation to Paul D. Bush for extensive comments on earlier drafts of this chapter. Remaining errors are my own, of course.

2. Gunnar Myrdal, *An International Economy* (New York: Harper & Brothers, 1956), pp. ix–x, 336–340; and *Value in Social Theory* (London: Routledge & Kegan Paul, 1958), pp. 206–230.

3. Warren J. Samuels, "An Essay on the Nature and Significance of the Normative Nature of Economics," *Journal of Post Keynesian Economics* 10 (Spring 1988): 347–354.

4. *Ibid.*, p. 348.

5. *Ibid.*, p. 353.

6. Mark Lutz, ed., *Social Economics* (Armonk, NY: M.E. Sharpe, 1990).

7. Amitai Etzioni, *The Moral Dimension* (New York: Free Press, 1988). See also a Symposium on "The Ascent of Socioeconomics," in *Challenge Magazine* 33 (January/February 1990): 31–52.

8. Institutionalists construe the referential content of "instrumental," as originated by John Dewey, to allude to a means–consequence interdependent *continuum* where as the means are chosen, the ends-in-view are determined, and where ends-in-view become instrumental means to further ends-in-view. They reject the dualism-based usage that is reflected in the writings of Milton Friedman and others, in which the expression "merely instrumental" reflects a logical divorcement of means and ends.

9. Marc R. Tool, *The Discretionary Economy: A Normative Theory of Political Economy* (Santa Monica, CA: Goodyear, 1979; Encore Edition, Boulder, CO: Westview Press, 1985). Marc R. Tool, *Essays in Social Value Theory: A Neoinstitutionalist Contribution* (Armonk, NY: M.E. Sharpe, 1986).

10. John Dewey, *Logic: The Theory of Inquiry* (New York: Henry Holt, 1938): *Theory of Valuation* (Chicago: University of Chicago, 1939).

11. Clarence E. Ayres, *The Theory of Economic Progress* (Chapel Hill: University of North Carolina Press, 1944).

12. J. Fagg Foster, "The Papers of J. Fagg Foster," *Journal of Economic Issues* 15 (December 1981).

13. For the theoretical and historical background of this formulation, see Tool, *Essays*, pp. 33–54; and William T. Waller, Jr., "The Evolution of the Veblenian Dichotomuy: Veblen, Hamilton, Ayres, and Foster," *Journal of Economic Issues* 16 (September 1982): 757–72.

14. Thorstein Veblen, *The Theory of the Leisure Class* (New York: Modern Library, 1934), p. 208.

15. Tool, *Essays*, pp. 36–37.

16. For example, Steven Hickerson, "Instrumental Valuation: The Normative Compass of Institutional Economics," *Journal of Economic Issues* 21 (September 1987): 1117–1143. Republished in Marc R. Tool, ed., *Institutional Economics I: Foundations of Institutional Thought* (Armonk, NY: M.E. Sharpe, 1988), pp. 167–193.

17. For example, Marc R. Tool, ed., *An Institutionalist Guide to Economics and Public Policy* (Armonk, NY: M.E. Sharpe, 1985), *passim.*

18. Tool, *Discretionary Economy*, pp. 274–314.

19. *Ibid.*, p. 293.

20. James A. Swaney, "Elements of a Neoinstitutional Environmental Economics," *Journal of Economic Issues* 21 (December 1987): 1740. Republished in Marc R. Tool, ed., *Evolutionary Economics, II: Institutional Theory and Policy* (Armonk, NY: M.E. Sharpe, 1988), pp. 321–361.

21. *Ibid.*

22. Joseph H. Pechman, "The Future of the Income Tax," *American Economic Review* 80 (March 1990): 1–20.

23. Paul D. Bush, "The Theory of Institutional Change, "*Journal of Economic Issues* 21 (September 1987): 1108. Republished in Tool, ed., *Evolutionary Economics I*, pp. 125–166.

24. Veblen, *Leisure Class*, p. 34.

25. Gilbert Seldes, quoted by Clarence E. Ayres in *The Industrial Economy* (Boston: Houghton Mifflin, 1952), p. 268.

26. Bush, "Theory of Institutional Change," *passim.*

27. Ayres, *Theory of Economic Progress*, p. 220.

28. Thorstein Veblen, "Preconception" essays, *The Place of Science in Modern Civilization* (New York: Russell & Russell, 1961), pp. 82–179 and *passim.*

29. *Ibid.*, p. 73.

30. William T. Waller, Jr., "Criticism of Institutionalism, Methodology, and Value Theory: A Comment on Langlois," *Journal of Economic Issues* 23 (September 1989): 873.

31. Clarence E. Ayres, *Toward a Reasonable Society* (Austin: University of Texas, 1961), pp. 39–52.

32. Ayres, *Theory of Economic Progress*, p. 209.

33. Joan Robinson, *Economic Philosophy* (Chicago: Aldine, 1962), p. 49.

34. See Tool, "The Compulsive Shift to Institutional Analysis," *The Review of Institutional Thought* 1 (December 1981): 17–39. Republished in Tool, *Essays*, pp. 181–202.

35. Paul D. Bush, "An Exploration of the Structural Characteristics of a Veblen– Ayres–Foster Defined Institutional Domain," *Journal of Economic Issues* 17 (March 1983): 37.

36. Discussed briefly in Tool, *Essays*, pp. 34–36.

37. *Ibid.*

38. Dewey, *Logic*, pp. 104 *ff.*

39. Ivan Weinel and Philip P. Crossland, "The Scientific Foundations of Technological Progress," *Journal of Economic Issues* 23 (September 1989): 797 *ff.*

40. Alfred S. Eichner, "Why Economics is Not Yet a Science," in Eichner, ed., *Why Economics is Not Yet a Science* (Armonk, NY: M.E. Sharpe, 1983), pp. 206–210.

41. John Maynard Keynes, *The General Theory of Employment, Interest and Money* (New York: Harcourt Brace, 1936).

42. Thorstein Veblen, *The Theory of Business Enterprise* (New York: Charles Scribner, 1904).

43. John R. Munkirs, *The Transformation of American Capitalism: From Competitive Market Structures to Centralized Private Sector Planning* (Armonk, NY: M.E. Sharpe, 1985).

44. F. Gregory Hayden, "Social Fabric Matrix: From Perspective to Analytical Tool," *Journal of Economic Issues* 16 (September 1982): 637–662; and "Organizing Policy Research Through the Social Fabric Matrix: A Boolean Digraph Approach," *Journal of Economic Issues* 16 (December 1982): 1013–1026.

45. Paul D. Bush, "An Exploration," pp. 35–66; "On the Concept of Ceremonial Encapsulation," *The Review of Institutional Thought* 3 (December 1986): 25–45; "Theory of Institutional Change," pp. 125–166; "The Concept of 'Progressive' Institutional Change and Its Implications for Economic Policy Formation," *Journal of Economic Issues* 23 (June 1989): 455–464.

46. Paul D. Bush "The Normative Implications of Positive Analysis," paper presented at the Western Economics Association, Corvallis, Oregon, 1968; "A Veblen–Ayres Model of Institutional Change," paper presented at the Western Economics Association, Anaheim, California, 1977; and "The Normative Implications of Institutional Analysis," *Economic Forum* 12 (Winter 1981–82): 9–32.

47. Bush, "An Exploration," p. 61.

48. *Ibid.*, p. 37.

49. Discussed by Charles K. Wilbur and Robert S. Harrison, "The Methodological Basis of Institutional Economics; Pattern Models, Storytelling, and Holism," *Journal of Economic Issues* 12 (March 1978): 61–90.

50. Bush, "An Exploration," p. 36.

51. *Ibid.*

52. Bush, "An Exploration," p. 39.

53. *Ibid.*

54. *Ibid.*, pp. 39–40.

55. *Ibid.*, p. 40.

56. *Ibid.*

57. *Ibid.*
58. *Ibid.*, p. 46.
59. *Ibid.*, pp. 46–47.
60. *Ibid.*, p. 51.
61. *Ibid.*
62. *Ibid.*
63. *Ibid.*, pp. 51–52.
64. *Ibid.*, p. 52.
65. *Ibid.*, p. 53.
66. *Ibid.*, p. 54.
67. *Ibid.*, pp. 54–55.
68. *Ibid.*, p. 56.
69. *Ibid.*
70. *Ibid.*, p. 58.
71. *Ibid.*, p. 59.
72. Bush, "Ceremonial Encapsulation,"
73. Bush, "An Exploration," p. 8.
74. Bush, "Ceremonial Encapsulation," p. 29.
75. *Ibid.*
76. *Ibid.*, p. 30.
77. *Ibid.*, p. 31.
78. *Ibid.*
79. *Ibid.*, pp. 33–37.
80. *Ibid.*, pp. 33–34.
81. Cited by Bush, *ibid.* See Louis J. Junker, "Nutrition and Economy: Some Observations on Diet and Disease in the American Food Power System," *The Review of Institutional Thought* 2 (December 1982): 27–58.
82. Staff Report to the Federal Trade Commission, *Concentration Levels and Trends in the Energy Sector of the U.S. Economy*, March 1974. [Thanks to Professor Ken Nowotny for this citation.]
83. Discussed by Bush, "Ceremonial Encapsulation," p. 34.
84. *Ibid.*, pp. 35–37; "Theory of Institutional Change," pp. 150–151.
85. Bush, "Theory of Institutional Change," p. 151.
86. *Ibid.*
87. (New York: Augustus M. Kelley, 1964).
88. Bush, "Theory of Institutional Change," p. 153.
89. Bush, "Concept of 'Progressive' Change," p. 459.
90. *Ibid.*, pp. 457–459.
91. Foster, "Papers," pp. 933–934, 941, 1001–1002, 1005–1006.
92. Bush, "Concept of 'Progressive' Change," p. 457.
93. *Ibid.*, p. 479.
94. *Ibid.*, p. 460.
95. A somewhat longer version of this section appeared in the *Journal of Economic Issues* 24 (December 1990).
96. Wendell C. Gordon, "The Role of Institutional Economics," *Journal of Economic Issues* 18 (June 1984): 369–381; with John Adams *Economics as Social Science: An Evolutionary Approach* (Riverdale, MD: The Riverdale Company, 1989), Chapter VII, "Theory of Valuation (Value Theory)," pp. 83–99; "The Role of Tool's Social Value Principle," *Journal of Economic Issues* 24 (September 1990): 879–885.

97. Gordon, "Role of Institutional Economics," p. 377.

98. Gordon and Adams, *Economics as Social Science*, p. 92.

99. *Ibid.*, p. 380.

100. Gordon, "Role of Tool's . . . Principle," p. 879.

101. *Ibid.*, pp. 880–881.

102. *Ibid.*, p. 881.

103. Gordon, "Role of Institutional Economics," p. 378.

104. *Ibid.*

105. Gordon and Adams, *Economics as Social Science*, p. 92; Tool, *Discretionary Economy*, p. 292.

106. Gordon, "Role of Institutional Economics," p. 372.

107. *Ibid.*, p. 379.

108. *Ibid.*, p. 371.

109. *Webster's Third New International Dictionary.*

110. Gordon, "Role of Institutional Economics," p. 376.

111. Gordon and Adams, *Economics as Social Science.*

112. Edythe S. Miller, "Review of Wendell Gordon and John Adams," *Journal of Economic Issues* 24 (March 1990): 276–277.

113. Gordon, "Role of Institutional Economics," p. 375.

114. Gordon, "Role of Tool's . . . Principle," *passim.*

115. *Ibid.*, p. 880.

116. A somewhat longer version of this section appeared in the *Journal of Economic Issues*, 24 (December 1990).

117. Anne Mayhew, "Culture: Core Concept Under Attack," *Journal of Economic Issues* 21 (June 1987): 587–603; "A Critical Analysis of Tool's *Essays in Social Value Theory*," paper presented at the Western Social Science Association, El Paso, Texas, April 1987. See also a critique of these papers by F. Gregory Hayden, "Institutionalism for What: To Understand Inevitable Progress or For Policy Relevance?" *Journal of Economic Issues* 23 (June 1989): 633–645.

118. Mayhew, "Culture: Core Concept Under Attack," p. 599.

119. Tool, *Discretionary Economy*, pp. 73–82.

120. Mayhew, "Culture: Core Concept Under Attack," p. 597.

121. *Ibid.*, p. 596.

122. Walter C. Neale, "Institutions," *Journal of Economic Issues* 21 (September 1987): 1195. Republished in Tool, ed., *Evolutionary Economics I*, pp. 227–256.

123. Walter C. Neale, "Absolute Cultural Relativism: Firm Foundation for Valuing and Policy," *Journal of Economic Issues* 24 (June 1990): 333–344.

124. I have attempted a provisional listing of continuing economic functions, Neale's comment notwithstanding. See my *The Discretionary Economy*, p. 108. It is of interest, in this connection, to recall that Bronislaw Malinowski formulated a tableau entitled a "List of Universal Institutional Types" in which fundamental integrative principles (somewhat corollary to my continuing functions) are presented as common cultural categories of any social order. Institutional forms are listed as varying over time and from culture to culture. The integrative principles represent "a set of universal problems," that are resolved by differing institutional forms. Institutional adjustment is affirmed; institutional structures are potentially discontinuous. See his A *Scientific Theory of Culture* (New York: Oxford University, 1960), pp. 62–66 and *passim*.

125. Neale, "Institutions," pp. 244–245.

126. Neale, "Absolute Cultural Relativism," p. 341.

127. Hayden, "Institutionalism for What?" p. 637.

128. Mayhew, "A Critical Analysis," p. 3.

129. *Ibid.*, p. 11.

130. *Ibid.*, p. 4.

131. *Ibid.*

132. *Ibid.*, p. 5.

133. *Ibid.*, p. 10.

134. *Ibid.*, p. 11.

135. Bush, "Concept of Ceremonial Encapsulation," pp. 37–41.

136. Paul D. Bush, "Analyzing the Energy Problem: Pecuniary Logic Versus Institutional Analysis," paper presented at the Western Social Science Association, Albuquerque, New Mexico, April, 1980, pp. 25–37 & *passim*.

137. Louis J. Junker, "Nutrition and Economy: Some Observations on Diet and Disease in the American Food Power System," *Review of Institutional Thought* 2 (December 1982): 27, 29, and *passim*.

138. F. Gregory Hayden, "A Geobased National Agricultural Policy for Rural Community Enhancement, Environmental Vitality, and Income Stabilization" in Tool, ed., *An Institutionalist Guide*, pp. 251 and passim.

139. James A. Swaney, "Building Instrumental Environmental Control Institutions," *Journal of Economic Issues* 21 (March 1987): 295–298 and passim.

140. John R. Munkirs, "Centralized Private Sector Planning: An Institutionalist's Perspective on the Contemporary U.S. Economy," *Journal of Economic Issues* 17 (December 1983): 932. The definitive work published later is his *The Transformation of American Capitalism*, (cited above). His argument is reiterated in "The Existence and Exercise of Corporate Power: An Opaque Fact," *Journal of Economic Issues 21* (December 1987): 1700–1701. Republished in Tool, ed., *Evolutionary Economics II*, pp. 261–288.

Commentary by William T. Waller and Linda R. Robertson

Tool's extensions and clarifications of instrumental value theory touch on what we believe will be the most important issues confronting institutionalists in the next decade. While the influence of Charles Peirce on Thorstein Veblen and John Dewey on C.E. Ayres gave institutionalists a significant head start in thinking about important questions in value theory and epistemology, other scholars have come to regard these questions as central to the human condition as well. These scholars have asked questions about the implications of the social construction of knowledge and the cultural construction of meaning that require us to rethink both our epistemological and operational understanding of instrumental valuation. Given this opportunity to provide extensive commentary on Tool's arguments, we will cast our comments in a framework that will allow us both to provide critical commentary where appropriate and to address the larger scholarly community mentioned above.[1]

It is only in explicit discussions of value theory that the nature of the economics discipline and its purpose come into clear relief. When we understand that the study of economics is the study of the social manifestations and consequences of valuational decisions, it becomes evident that Cartesian notions of objective scientific inquiry fundamentally miss something. The essential Aristotelian distinction that is relevant to this discussion is that between demonstrative and dialectical reasoning. Demonstrative reasoning is appropriate for the kind of reasoning most frequently associated among lay people with "scientific" inquiry; for instance, no reasonable, noncolor-blind adult schooled in English would disagree with the statement that a healthy deciduous tree has leaves that turn to shades of orange, red, and yellow at the end of the summer. Why do leaves change color? The answers represent demonstrative reasoning, because they explain the cause for an event which is regular, recurrent, and observable; hence, it can be demonstrated and is predictable. Descartes's rage for certainty led him to disqualify as "reasoning" any lines of inquiry into matters except those taken as "certain" (demonstrable).

A clear-eyed thinker would recognize that economics as a kind of inquiry is not a form of demonstrative reasoning, but a form of dialectical reasoning; specifically it is what Aristotle would call an ethical dialectic. It is a kind of inquiry that addresses what actions people ought to pursue in given circumstances—which is also (obviously) the realm of politics. The purpose of the inquiry is to consider what choices or policies, if adopted at a given time, would probably contribute to the greatest good for a given community. Such reasoning depends on a general teleological consensus—that is, a general agreement about what would constitute the "greatest good." Clearly such an end is debatable. The inherent debatability of the assumptions is what led Aristotle to call this kind of reasoning "dialectical" rather than "demonstrative." In context, the term *dialectical* referred to debate, to dialogue among those engaged in considering what was probably best.

The relevance of this way of describing economic inquiry to instrumental valuation, institutional economics, and Tool's extensions and clarifications is that it locates their purpose within a particular kind of discourse and a particular modality of reasoning.

The first part of Tool's essay which he characterizes as a reprise of his earlier discussions of instrumental valuation is itself an extension by elaboration of his earlier work. Of crucial importance in this extension is a reemphasis on the processual nature of instrumental valuation. The process of instrumental valuation is both contextual (and cultural) and evolving. The instrumental value principle identifies a valuational process and a valuational "location" from which analysis begins, but most importantly the "location" is itself the object of analysis and reevaluation by instrumental means. This is crucial to understanding how instrumental valuation, and as a result institutional economics, can be relativistic but not ethically agnostic, and be pan-cultural without slipping into ethnocentrism or abandoning the concept of culture.

The correspondence between instrumental valuation and ethical dialectical reasoning will be clear when we discuss the latter. Ethical dialectical reasoning is a deliberative mode for decision making about what is best for a given group, community, nation, or human beings, that entails dialogue as a necessary condition. Ethical dialectical reasoning begins with the statement of a proposition about a proposed action, policy, or social arrangement that might be true. The reasoning proceeds by the critical analysis of that proposition: provisional solutions, alternative proposals, evaluation of potential consequences, and questions are all posed. The critical examination leads to either new proposals or modifications of the old. An important aspect of this form of reasoning is that eventually the group engaged in this discourse chooses: not because they know with certainty that they have found the best solution, but because they must make a decision about what is the best policy. Their solution may or may not be "correct," but it is simply the best option currently available to them given the provisional character of knowledge. It is this uncertainty and the finite time in which to decide that leads to their ethical relativism. But this is neither moral agnosticism or, as critics of neopragmatism (especially critics of Rorty), often assert epistemological relativism. This is, in our view, a description of instrumental valuation.

Instrumental valuation is ethically relativist and must necessarily be so because ethical absolutes require certainty and ignore context. The absence of certainty requires a process solution (where the solution to the problem is a process of ongoing adjustment rather than a one-time correction) which will lead to relativism, but not moral agnosticism because eventually an ethical judgment is made, not because it is right (or true) but because it is the best we can do. Ignoring context is similarly impossible when the purpose of inquiry is to inform decisions to act. The criteria for evaluating what is a better choice of action depends on the circumstances in which the action is to take place. The circumstances in this case include both the cultural and environmental context. A potential solution, in order to be accepted by the discourse community (itself a group of people within a particular cultural context), must constitute both a viable and desirable course of action. A proposed solution will not be viewed as a genuine or viable alternative if it varies significantly with the culture's extant values.

But once a choice of action or policy is made, the discourse community employing instrumental valuation has "located" itself in valuational terms. They have provisionally accepted and implemented a particular set of values. This does not necessarily cloud their judgment or bias future valuational decisions because the "location" is itself subject to the same revision through the dialectical process that necessitated its choice in the first place. Hence, valuational decisions are provisional, and valuational location can change and possibly evolve. What remains constant is the teleological assumption; that is, the purpose of the discourse is to provide reasoned decisions that will contribute to the greatest good. The understanding of what that might be may change; but the ethical assumption that the ultimate reason for the inquiry is to provide a process for addressing problems is taken as given. Otherwise, there is no reason for the debate or inquiry to occur.

This teleological assumption provides a stable value location that grounds the inquiry. The provisional nature of particular valuational decisions and the realization that valuational "location" can change and possibly evolve also provides a stable—though not absolute—value location for further inquiry to use as a starting point; hence, the dialectic nature of the inquiry.

If the provisional character of this value location is forgotten, these values could reify and become ethical absolutes. It is through the provisional acceptance (which provides stability) and the required reevaluation and dialectical process (that insures the potential for change) that gives instrumental valuation its "relativist" flavor.

Ethical relativism does not, however, necessarily imply epistemological relativism. The status of knowledge developed through instrumental valuation and the technological process is provisional. But provisional is not the same as indifferent to the truth or falsity of the results. First, knowledge is socially constructed. In a nondualistic framework that denies the existence of distinction between objective and subjective knowledge, the status of knowledge is that of a cultural construct similar to other belief systems. Knowledge is neither absolute nor relative; it is in the process of becoming or evolving. This understanding of warranted knowledge as provisional and cultural does not deny the existence or even the importance of epistemological questions about the relationship between what we think we know of phenomena and "objective truth"; it simply is the wrong form of reasoning for questions of this sort. Put simply, probable knowledge is the result of dialectical reasoning from probable premises to probable solutions about the question of how persons, groups, or society ought to act. Traditional epistemological concerns are the province of demonstrative reasoning in a Cartesian framework. Dialectical reasoning concerns different but no less important epistemological questions about how we come to know provisionally, what the corrigibility of provisional knowledge is that results from a process of social and cultural construction and what causes an argument or proposition to convince people and more importantly move people to action?

The point to hold in mind is that the reasoning about probable premises is, in fact, a form of reasoning. The principles of logic, proof, and validity apply to the arguments about probable or desired outcomes. It is the test of logic that prevents such arguments from descending to the exchange of mere opinion, or to the manipulative strategies of the demagogue. What distinguishes reasoning about probable assumptions from reasoning about assumptions that are "certain" or "true" is the consciousness of the reasoner. When we consciously reason from probable assumptions in order to arrive at probable conclusions, we require ourselves to become highly aware of the social, political, historical, and ethical influences and constructs that we bring to the discussion. We further demand of ourselves the recognition that we can never be fully aware of those influences—that our knowledge and awareness of them are limited by our own capacities. In addition, we become more aware of the ways in which the "players" in a debate determine its nature. The assumptions to which the participants agree shape the inquiry itself, determine its direction to some extent, and have the effect of holding in abeyance or excluding other possible assumptions.

The point of these comments on Tool's "reprise" is to make clear that his emphasis on instrumental valuation as a process of inquiry—which is ultimately cultural bound but is sufficiently aware of its cultural context to be self-examining and self-critical of those bounds—constitutes a significant contribution by way of expansion and clarification. The form these introductory comments take is intended to introduce the taxonomy of dialectical discourse that will be useful in our reflections on Tool's evaluation of the contribution of Bush and his responses to Gordon and Mayhew.

The correct form of dialectical discourse is inextricably intertwined with the purpose of that discourse. Tool is clear about the purposeful nature of instrumental valuation: it is a practical, pragmatic, and relevant judgmental process for problem analysis. It is then an archetypal example of ethical dialectical reasoning. Interestingly, Bush's contribution, as described by Tool, is essentially based on moving institutional analysis and thus instrumental valuation into a merely logical framework. As already noted, logic and tests of validity are essential to inquiry into probable assumptions. But the recognition is granted that the premises are themselves limited or constrained by the categories chosen to begin the inquiry—categories that reflect the contingent and limited assumptions of those engaged in the inquiry. The application of the tests of logical reasoning can improve our understanding of the implication of any line of reasoning we choose to explore. More importantly, the application of logical analysis to the assumptions themselves can assist us in drawing epistemological conclusions; that is, an examination of the ways in which we assume certain categories and premises apply to widely differing circumstances can prove very profitable in revealing to us how widely (and often readily) we employ certain categorical assumptions to explain widely different phenomena.

But while logical inquiry can lead us to explore the logical consequences of certain lines of reasoning, and help us gain an insight into how language (categories) can itself construct meaning, logical inquiry alone is insufficient to economic inquiry; what is required in addition is a purpose which that logical examination serves. An example from the past will serve to illustrate this point. The philosophers of the Enlightenment—and intellectual wags ever since—have laughed at the scholastics for the question, "How many angels can dance on the head of a pin?" The answer to this question was pursued through logical tests and proofs. The question itself was generated by a serious issue at that time. The question was whether God is omnipotent or limited and constrained. If God is omnipotent, then an infinite number of angels can dance on the head of a pin, because God is not constrained by the laws of nature (physics). But if God is not only the cause of the laws of nature but is also constrained by them, then there is a limit to the number of angels who can dance on the head of a pin. The debate is one constructed along logical lines based on probable assumptions—because no could ever know for certain the nature or mind of God. But the issue was not merely one of idle curiosity; for instance, in a monarchical society, one that assumes the monarch represents some kind of divine investiture, the question of whether power is constrained by law has much to do with the way the society is constructed and maintained.

An examination of the scholastic debate indicates three things: 1) that logical proofs and tests are applied to premises that are taken as probable; such tests are not abandoned just because the premises are not "certain"; 2) an understanding of how the argument is constructed reveals the epistemological assumptions of those who frame the argument; and 3) the purpose for which the argument is undertaken gives the logical exercise its value; otherwise, it seems purposeless or absurd.

We would argue that Bush's contribution has two consequences: one identified by Tool and one he has overlooked. Bush's work on the logical structure of institutional analysis demonstrates its logical coherence and clarifies the implications of the extant definitions of the categories of analysis employed by institutional economists (in this case, ceremonial and instrumental valuation). In this regard it might make some possible but previously hidden combination or implication of our categories explicit. The consequence of Bush's move to the logical dialectical reasoning framework that is overlooked by Tool is the reification of the categories.

Tool correctly identifies that Bush's analysis demonstrates that institutional analysis is logically coherent by expressing it in an axiomatic framework. Moreover, we agree that Bush's analysis might contribute to making institutional analysis more readily understandable. But we disagree that ceremonial encapsulation is *generated* by the axiomatic presentation of institutional analysis, though we would agree that it is made explicit by Bush. The reason is that the concept of ceremonial encapsulation is a logical necessity within an axiomatic system that takes as axiomatic Foster's definition of an institution and an a priori concept of dominance. Recall that Foster's definition of an institution is: prescribed patterns of correlated human behavior with both instrumental and ceremonial functions or aspects. If all institutions (social structures) have both instrumental and ceremonial aspects and if one aspect can dominate the other, then ceremonial dominance over instrumental aspects (or ceremonial encapsulation) is a logical necessity. Similarly so is instrumental dominance of ceremonial functions that might lead to a notion of the instrumental embedding of ceremonial functions (instrumental encapsulation of ceremony?). Much of the rest of Bush's analysis focuses on the consequences of ceremonial dominance of instrumental functions. There is little if any mention or development of the similarly logical consequences of instrumentally embedded ceremonial aspects of behavior. Logically, prescribed and proscribed patterns of correlated human behavior that are ceremonially instrumental or instrumentally ceremonial are not precluded, in spite of the fact that most institutionalists would consider such terms oxymoronic.

The reason the above discussion is not part of Bush's original presentation or Tool's commentary is that both implicitly recognize the ethical dialectical nature of institutional inquiry. Moreover, the evaluational criteria of ethical discourse remain operational (providing desirable and viable solutions to real problems). Put simply, the latter logical constructions (instrumental ceremony) are not empirically useful in the real policy discussions that matter. Bush's contribution clarifies our categories and this helps us sharpen our analyses and label some previously unnamed, but empirically observed, phenomena in an analytically useful way. But this is not the only consequence of his axiomatic approach, and the other consequence is both serious and detrimental to the analytical structure of institutional economics and Tool's case for instrumental valuation as a necessary part of institutionalism.

The consequence to which we refer is reification of the categories of analysis. This manifests itself both methodologically and empirically. Reification occurs when an abstract category of analysis becomes the object of the inquiry rather than the existent phenomena under analysis for which the category was developed. For example, in neoclassical economics the dualistic separation of the individual from the social is accepted. As is typically the case, one side of the dualism is given priority—in this case, the individual. The concept is then reified so that economic analysis concerns itself with the behavior of abstract individuals and not real people. This is neither an argument against abstraction or categories. Categories are useful things, but when they are reified they become an impediment to inquiry.

We have already referred to reification of concepts or categories in the form of dualisms. Dualisms are logical constructions: they are mutually exclusive categories of phenomena that, taken together, include or exhaust all the phenomena. The empirical consequences of reification become apparent when we analyze gender. Male and female are biological categories into which the vast majority of the human race can reasonably and comfortably be included—this is not a dualism. But masculine and feminine are gender categories, socially constructed roles, that have been reified in our society to the detriment of a large number of people. Recent feminist scholarship has challenged this dualistic conception of gender.[2] Reification of dualistic gender roles has made the process of reconceptualizing our understanding of alternative gender identities and possibilities difficult. It will take considerable effort to eliminate our misunderstanding of gender, as anyone who attempts the comparatively simple task of degendering their prose immediately confronts, because the dualistic understanding of gender is now a part of the very structure of our language.

Instrumentalists, particularly Dewey, have long been critical of dualistic constructions of knowledge and reification. In our view the methodological consequence of Bush's axiomatic rendering of institutional analysis is that it reifies the categories of ceremonial and instrumental valuation. In his Axiom 2 Bush asserts a dualism. He closes off the possibility of opening up the dualistic construction in Axiom 5 where he postulates a one-to-one correspondence of value to behavior. Here he eliminates behavior correlated by a multiplicity of inconsistent values, and forgoes an explanation of behaviors resulting from accident, serendipity, impulse, thoughtlessness, habit, and most forms of novel (uncorrelated?) behavior. This does not cause problems in a logical system that makes no claim to isomorphic relationship to actual valuational practice and processes, but implicitly Bush (and all economists, since the purpose of economics is to say useful things about real economics) claims precisely this correspondence. By defining instrumental valuation only as a kind of logical inquiry rather than as a kind of ethical dialectical inquiry, Bush creates a contradiction similar to the one in which neoclassical economists find themselves. Bush is engaged in a type of discourse whose purpose is inappropriate for him and his audience. His mode of discourse constrains him to saying things about abstract categories when he wants to talk about cultural processes. Since we, including Bush, are talking about instrumental valuation as a process that human beings and communities are actually engaged in, the criteria for evaluating Bush's axiomatic rendering of institutional analysis should be its correspondence to actual valuational processes. The question then becomes empirical: Does instrumental valuation and ceremonial valuation exhaust the valuational processes available to individuals or society? William Waller has suggested elsewhere that human beings use a number of valuational processes both individually and collectively and that these processes include, but are not exhausted by, instrumental and ceremonial valuation.[3] We would argue, therefore, that Bush's analysis, although strictly speaking is not wrong, is seriously incomplete. But Bush's axiomatic system suggest a particular structure of valuation—a dualistic structure. This issue has been cogently addressed by James Swaney.[4] If ceremonial and instrumental valuation are mutually exclusive categories, but between them exhaust the possible valuational processes—in other words, if we construct a dualism—and if ceremonial processes are always regressive (bad) and instrumental processes are progressive (good), then we have constructed two tautologies. Ceremonial valuation is bad and instrumental valuation is good. The only thing that keeps institutionalists from creating an endless series of equivalent dualisms is the thing Bush's logical presentation leaves out—the cultural context in which the valuation processes (all of them) occur.

We believe that the concerns of Ann Mayhew that Tool responds to in his chapter are in many ways a result of the problems made explicit by and inherent in Bush's axiomatic approach. Specifically Mayhew is concerned with the implications of using the Veblenian dichotomy as a taxonomy for describing cultural processes, itself an evaluative act, then using the same categories as valuational processes for judging the efficacy of these same cultural processes toward achieving some predetermined goal. Mayhew is addressing the same logical problem articulated by Swaney in a different way. Mayhew would prefer to describe and analyze cultural processes and avoid invoking the valuational criteria necessarily implied by categorizing and labeling actual cultural processes as ceremonial or instrumental.

Tool addresses this problem well. His understanding of the role of instrumental valuation in institutional analysis is not axiomatic or linearly logical, which converts valuation into a static event; Tool's understanding is processual or dialectical. Tool sees the act of analysis as valuational. Moreover, he sees valuational criteria as provisional and subject to the same process of valuation as the actual analysis of the cultural processes. All meaningful discourse requires that the participants begin with at least one common premise that initially commands assent from all participants. In demonstrative discourse this premise has the status of a priori truth—what von Mises referred to as apodictic certainty. Dialectical discourse begins with at least one premise that all agree is probable—a much weaker starting point—but the dialectical nature of the discourse allows ongoing reevaluation of that initial premise as part of the conversation. Thus the description and analysis of cultural processes and the continuing evolution of the valuational criteria take place in a context where the internal dynamics of the cultural process intermingle and influence the understanding and valuational premises of the analyst in a simultaneous fashion—and what results from this process is a provisional evaluation that can become the initial point for further discourse. In fact, this is the kind of discourse in which Mayhew and Tool are currently engaged. Much of the difference between Mayhew and Tool results from the way their arguments appear when translated into the reified categories of logical dialectical discourse, and the reification makes their arguments unreconcilable. But Mayhew and Tool need not resolve problems that result only from the reification of categories within an axiomatic structure. Once logical dialectical discourse is recognized as inappropriate for institutional analysis, the logical problems resulting from reification within an axiomatic structure are irrelevant. The problems between Mayhew and Tools with respect to the practice of institutional analysis as ethical dialectical discourse are what is important. Neither Mayhew or Tool would find the reification of ceremonial or instrumental behavioral labels or categories as appropriate, nor would they find these categories universally exhaustive of all human experience.

It is in the area of actual practice of institutional research that Mayhew's critique is more telling and Tool's response less satisfactory. While Tool is correct that Mayhew's request for operational definitions in which we can have scientific (meaning demonstrative) confidence in a dialectical framework is not relevant, he has overlooked an element of Mayhew's critique. Ethical dialectical reasoning does require that institutionalists agree on provisional operational meanings of these terms, even while acknowledging the probable nature of the premise. These are the provisional or probable premises with which the discourse community of institutionalists begins its analysis. The work of Tool, Mayhew, Bush, Swaney, and others indicates that this area needs further exploration because the assent to these premises is more illusory than real—and that lack of genuine assent exists among those specifically addressing these questions. The questioning of the status and meaning of these probable premises is the daily work of institutionalists whose scholarly interest focuses on methodology, and as a result they are very aware of the premises' uncertain and probabilistic character. Other practitioners treat these premises as part of what Charles Whalen (following Joseph Schumpeter) refers to as the preanalytic vision of institutionalism.[5] The methodologically preoccupied institutionalist might object to the practitioner's lesser explicit concern with the probable character of the premises. In some cases both the methodologically preoccupied institutionalist and the applied practitioner have let the probable character of the premises so fade into the background that they seem naively to suggest that institutional analysis has a metaobjectivity absent in all other social (and for that matter scientific) analysis. But the applied practitioner *must* make some methodological and substantive assumptions to begin any sort of inquiry. The strength of institutional analysis is that the assumptions or premises are simultaneously reevaluated in the process of inquiry, not that they are never made.

The danger of concern to Mayhew is not Tool's position on instrumental valuation as much as it is that many applied practitioners proceed without explicitly examining their initial assumptions or premises while maintaining the view that their particular understanding is not only the shared understanding of the discourse community in which they participate, but in fact is a system of values that requires no justification beyond the context of that discourse community. It is this practice that Mayhew seems to consider the real danger. And while Tool's formulation avoids this problem *for Tool*, his understanding may not constitute the state of current practice within institutional economics and is probably inconsistent with the Bush approach to these same matters, thereby giving some credence to Mayhew's concerns.

Tool's response to Gordon we find very satisfactory. Gordon seems to want to avoid including instrumental valuation as a part of institutional analysis because he sees that the appropriate form for institutional analysis to take is that of demonstrative discourse. This would mimic the stance taken by orthodox economics and allow institutional analysis to embrace unreconstructed positivist rhetoric of science as neoclassical economics does. But this would limit institutional economics to descriptive activity while overlooking the valuational content of the process of description. Gordon seems to believe that institutional economics should be discourse characterized by demonstrative reasoning. Tool argues that institutional economics and instrumental valuations are a different form of reasoning, namely dialectical, with its focus on valuational processes rather than the demonstrative focus on static valuational acts so typical of neoclassical economics.

In conclusion we think Professor Tool's analysis of instrumental valuation extends and improves our understanding of the role of instrumental valuation in institutional economics. His greater emphasis on the process of inquiry, and the provisional nature of knowledge so gained, constitutes an important advance in institutional methodology. Moreover, this advance will improve institutional analysis. It will remind us to reconsider the radical character of the work of Peirce and Dewey on instrumental valuation. Both scholars pioneered the understanding of knowledge as socially constructed (meaning the process of inquiry is itself a cultural process). Peirce in his famous article, "How We Make Our Ideas Clear," is obviously connecting the process of inquiry to how we communicate our ideas—clearly identifying the unity of reasoning and discourse.[6] An understanding of this will facilitate institutionalists' ability to make use of interesting work in other disciplines (for example, rhetoric, feminist theory, feminist philosophy of science, literary criticism). But it should also generate a bit of humility with regard to the actual practice of institutional analysis. We are not morally agnostic; instead we are, to employ a characterization used by Walter Neale, absolute cultural relativists.[7] We have values. We use them in our work. We even provisionally accept them. But we also simultaneously reevaluate them within the context of our analyses. The conclusions of our analyses are themselves provisional. We avoid value absolutism through a process of continual reevaluation. With this understanding the views of Tool and Mayhew are, in our view, reconcilable. However, the differences between Gordon and Tool are at a fundamental level; they are differences over what the nature and purpose of economics ought to be. We believe Tool's position to be correct. We think Gordon's position reflects a very common understanding of what economics ought to be—in fact, it is the view extant among neoclassical economists—but we believe the rejection of the scientistic view embodied in this conception of economics to be the hallmark of institutionalism.

We find Tool's enthusiasm for Bush's axiomatic approach to be much more problematic. Bush's approach has been useful in suggesting interesting areas of inquiry. But we think transforming ethical dialectical discourse into a logical dialectical framework sacrifices the richness, complexity, and holism that are so important in institutional economics. Moreover, the general tendency to think of instrumental valuation in a noncontextual logical framework reduces instrumental valuation to an inappropriate dualistic, and rather vacuous, set of categories and encourages the practice of employing instrumental valuation as either an elemental human strategy or as an eternal verity creating the problems cited by Mayhew and Gordon.

Notes

1. We have noted elsewhere that scholars in critical rhetoric, feminist philosophy of science and literary criticism all grapple with these same issues. See William Waller and Linda Robertson, "Why Johnny (Ph.D., Economics) Can't Read," *Journal of Economic Issues* 24, (December 1990): 1027–1044.

2. Susan Bordo, *The Flight to Objectivity* (Albany: SUNY Press, 1987).

3. William Waller, "Criticism of Institutionalism, Methodology and Value Theory: A Comment of Langlois," *Journal of Economic Issues* 23 (September 1989): 876–877.

4. James A. Swaney, "Our Obsolete Technology Mentality," *Journal of Economic Issues* 23 (June 1989): 569–578. See especially Swaney's endnote number 9 on page 578.

5. Charles Whalen, "The Pre-analytic Visions of Institutional Economics," A paper presented at the annual meetings of the Association of Institutional Thought and the Western Social Science Association, Albuquerque, New Mexico, April 28, 1989.

6. Charles Peirce, "How We Make Our Ideas Clear," in Philip Wiener, ed., *Values in a Universe of Chance: Selected Writings of Charles S. Peirce* (Stanford, CA: Stanford University press, 1958), pp. 113–136. See also "Issues in Pragmatism," pp. 203–227, of the same volume.

7. Walter C. Neale, "Absolute Cultural Relativism: Firm Foundation for Valuing and Policy," *Journal of Economic Issues* (September 1990): 333–344.

5 INSTITUTIONAL ECONOMICS AND THE DUAL LABOR MARKET THEORY

Yngve Ramstad[1]

No one has put it better than Wesley Clair Mitchell: "The only reason, the only excuse, for the study of economic theory is to make this world a better place in which to live."[2] What Mitchell was insisting, of course, is that economic theory is most fundamentally an instrument for guiding the process of institutional adjustment in such fashion that "better" flows of real income will be produced. From this standpoint, accordingly, it becomes the task of the practicing economist to develop *valid* theories which can be used to devise or evaluate specific proposals for altering the institutions patterning specific subsystems of the market economy,[3] for example, the "labor market." For only if a theory, or the model through which it is expressed, is believed to be valid will policymakers be able to use it for institutional impact analysis,[4] that is, to anticipate (predict) whether, in the context of a concrete issue, proposed adjustments of existing rules or practices actually are likely to alter the future "economic" attainments (real incomes) of individuals or groups in a "good" way.

It has become standard practice to use the term *research program* in reference to the joint endeavor of a group of economists to transform a specific theoretical perspective (the "hard core") into valid models. Clearly, the vast majority of present-day applied economists participate in various "neoclassical" research programs. However, there has been a strong anti-neoclassical dissident tradition evident in American economic thought throughout the 20th century. Moreover, this dissident tradition was central to the early development of labor economics, a field in large part created during the first quarter of this century by many of the same individuals who were leading figures in the formation of the "institutional school."[5]

Against this background it is perplexing that there is in evidence today no discernable community of scholars among labor economists[6] pursuing an explicitly institutional research program[7]: present-day dissident labor economists refer to themselves either as neo-Marxists or as adherents of "dual labor market theory"—or in some cases as both. Even more perplexing is the absence in the labor economics literature of even a single article that carefully ties the first principles—or hard core—of any ongoing labor economics research program to the philosophical and theoretical literature of "mainstream" institutional economics.[8] Indeed, Michael Piore, the principal theorist of the dual labor market theory group, has not to my knowledge even once made reference, other than an occasional mention of John Kenneth Galbraith's *The New Industrial State*, to the philosophical and theoretical literature of mainstream institutional economics.

It appears to be the case, then, that mainstream institutionalists have failed absolutely to stimulate the development of an *explicitly* institutional theory of the labor market. Yet one must not jump to the conclusion that no such theory exists. For it is my judgment that the dual labor market theory, as articulated by Piore, does in fact manifest the institutional standpoint, that is, *is in fact an institutional conceptualization of the labor market*. Indeed, I believe the development of the dual labor market theory provides a striking example of what Marc Tool has referred to as the "compulsive shift toward institutional analysis" evident in 20th century economic thought.[9]

I am, of course, not the first to recognize the evident compatibility of the dual labor market theory with mainstream institutional economics. Still, I am not aware of even a single careful analysis showing exactly in what manner the dual labor market theory *in fact* manifests philosophical and theoretical propositions associated with the institutional standpoint and hence *is* in actuality an institutional theory of the allocation and pricing of labor. I will attempt such an analysis in what follows.

The chapter is organized as follows. I begin by establishing that mainstream institutional economists have failed completely to produce an explicitly institutional theory of the processes through which human productive effort is patterned (allocated) and rewarded in our present-day "market economy." I then outline the characteristics that a theory of these processes must reflect in order to be consistent with the standpoint reflected in the philosophical and theoretical literature of institutional economics. This task is made necessary by the reality, as noted already, that there exists no clear statement in either the labor or the contemporary mainstream institutional literature of the features that an *institutional* theory or conception of labor allocation and remuneration must possess.[10] For although it is clear that numerous institutional writers have produced holistic "general theories"[11] of the market system, or of particular subsystems within it, I am not aware of even a single analysis delineating the general features an institutional *model of market activity* capable of being used for institutional impact analysis—an institutional "microeconomics"—must possess. I next show that the dual labor market theory in fact reflects in almost every essential respect the perspective associated with the institutional standpoint and hence must be judged as an institutional theory. In making the case, I digress briefly to examine an important problem in institutional linguistics, namely, the borrowing of terms whose meaning is actually not fully detachable from the neoclassical framework itself.

The reader should keep in mind some important considerations. First, the literature pertaining to labor has grown to such proportions that it is beyond the capacity of any individual to be familiar with more than a small fraction of it. The following is based on a careful reading of what is clearly but a subset of the dual labor market theory literature—the attempts to articulate the "logic" of the dual labor market theory of Piore himself. Second, whereas the genesis and character of unions or government laws and regulations generally have been the objects of analysis for labor practitioners who might consider their work to be institutional in character, the present concern is with the essentials of an explicitly institutional conceptualization or theory of the process(es) through which human productive activity is allocated and rewarded in our present-day market society, that is, with the question of the "logic" and articulation of genuinely institutional models of the processes through which the activities of wage workers are patterned, and the appropriate remuneration for those activities established, in the present-day American setting. Finally, since there continues to be considerable controversy regarding defining features of *the* institutional approach to the analysis of economic questions, it is unlikely that all will agree with the synthetic characterization forwarded here.[12] Because my interpretation may be regarded by many as unconventional, I have included extensive documentation in order to establish that it is indeed rooted in the institutional literature writ large.

Has Mainstream Institutional Economics Produced a Theory of the Labor Market?

Of all the institutions patterning economic activity in a "market system," few, if any, would appear to be of greater importance than those relating to the utilization and remuneration of human productive effort, that is, of "labor." Institutional economics purports to be a theory of economic life.[13] Hence the question must be asked: Have mainstream institutional economists developed and articulated a distinctive, *policy-relevant* theory relating to the utilization and remuneration of labor in a market setting?[14]

In one respect, this is a curious question, given that a founder of the labor specialty, John R. Commons, was also a founder of institutional economics as well as one of its major theoreticians. Unfortunately, Commons, whose work can be understood to reveal an alternative conceptualization of the labor market, was singularly unable to communicate the logic of either his "volitional theory of value" or his "citizenship theory of labor" to others.[15] In spite of his enormous popularity with students, Commons also failed to leave behind an "invisible college" of scholars dedicated to a "research program" giving effect to his theoretical framework. Those who were influenced by Commons have during the decades since his death produced nothing, in my judgment, that, under even the most liberal interpretation, can be understood to constitute a coherent alternative to the neoclassical theory of labor utilization and pricing.

Regrettably, Commons's theoretical insights also have been largely ignored in the subsequent development of institutional theory, as second- and third-generation theorists of the institutional movement almost uniformly have found their inspiration in the ideas of Veblen, John Dewey, Clarence Ayres, and, sometimes, J. Fagg Foster.[16] So, while considerable progress has been made in clarifying and making more precise the logic of "instrumental valuing" and "instrumental value theory," and while attempts to use the ceremonial–instrumental dichotomy to analyze concrete issues can properly be understood to constitute a nascent research program, adherents of the Veblen–Ayres–(and sometimes)Foster tradition have not, again in my judgment, been able to develop an explicitly institutional model capable of showing policymakers how "good" *and* "workable" adjustments to the institutions structuring the utilization and remuneration of labor in the American economy might be effected.[17]

In a crude attempt to test the accuracy of these "judgments," I reviewed all issues of the *Journal of Economic Issues* (JEI) from 1972 to 1988. During that period, the JEI published some 795 articles, including papers presented at the annual meetings of the Association for Evolutionary Economics but not including review articles other than those dealing directly with theoretical interpretations of the labor market. Of the 795 articles reviewed, some 46 were focused on topics that more or less fall under the category of "labor economics." The majority of those 46 articles, at least 25, were to some degree "institutional" in spirit (as characterized below), yet their authors forwarded or employed no explicit and coherent alternative conceptualization (theory) of the processes underlying concrete patterns of labor utilization and remuneration. An additional six appeared to me actually to be neoclassical in spirit (as characterized below). Three forwarded the view (one that I attempt below to show is misguided) that institutional "insights" are compatible with the neoclassical interpretation of labor market behavior.[18] Two emphasized the importance of labor market "disequilibrium" and hence were in my view more post-Keynesian than institutional in spirit.[19] Six, *not a single one of which was substantively rooted in the mainstream institutional literature*, outlined or utilized the dual labor market theory.[20] One forwarded a "Veblenian" interpretation of the comparable worth issue but similarly provided no explicit model of the process(es) through which labor is remunerated.[21] In one, I attempted to assess the degree to which adherence to the institutional approach can be detected in the labor economics journal literature, but I provided only a perfunctory overview of the putatively institutional approach to which adherence was discerned and made no attempt to root the criteria employed in the mainstream institutionalist literature.[22] In another, I sought to show that Commons's "citizenship theory of labor" provides theoretical support for a revision of the nation's trade laws, but, although Common's framework was spelled out reasonably clearly, again I made no attempt to root it in *an* overarching institutional standpoint.[23] The final article attempted to show how the administered price concept can be applied to the market for corporate managers but, while pregnant with implications regarding *an* institutional conception of the labor market, it made no attempt to develop or examine those implications.[24]

All in all, then, it is impossible to infer from articles published in the JEI that mainstream institutional economists have produced a distinctive approach to the analysis or "modeling" of labor utilization and remuneration. Recent major works by mainstream institutional writers similarly fail to evince a distinctive institutional approach to the conceptualization of labor markets.[25] In short, the dual labor market theory—*a theory*, to repeat, *developed by individuals who reveal almost no familiarity with mainstream institutionalism and who accordingly have made no effort to root that theory in the broader institutional literature*—is apparently the single contender for the allegiance of present-day institutionalists interested in the microeconomics of labor utilization and pricing.[26]

Having shown that institutional economics currently provides no coherent alternative to the dual labor market theory, I now turn to the task of showing that the dual labor market theory does in fact manifest an institutional conception of economic processes. My method of doing so will be to develop first the general contours of the institutional standpoint regarding market outcomes and then to demonstrate that the dual labor market theory in fact reflects those general contours.

What is the Institutional Standpoint?

It has become customary to use either Thomas Kuhn's term "paradigm" or Imre Lakatos's term "scientific research program" in reference to the shared belief system and research agenda uniting a self-conscious" community of inquiry."[27] Unfortunately, neither of these concepts provides an appropriate way to organize the present discussion. For, in my view, *institutional economics*, as a term with historical meaning, *cannot* be reduced to a single paradigm or a research program manifesting a single hard core; indeed, as I have argued elsewhere,[28] institutional economics is properly understood as an umbrella term for a general standpoint or world view that has spawned two, and almost certainly several more, quite different theoretical orientations or research programs. This general standpoint incorporates some fundamental beliefs pertaining to 1) the nature of the abstraction "the economy" and 2) the nature of human action that, while imprecise, together condition the set of meanings through which economic phenomena are interpreted; perhaps it also includes a set of beliefs pertaining to 3) the manner in which valid knowledge about economic processes is produced and expressed. While a comprehensive examination of the relevant preconceptions cannot be attempted here, an overview will nonetheless prove indispensable to the task of showing that a putatively noninstitutional theory, the dual labor market hypothesis, *in fact* manifests the institutional standpoint.

The Institutionally Directed Economy

At the core of the institutional standpoint is a conception of the economy radically unlike the naturalistic conception reflected in mainstream economics. As Clarence Ayres once emphasized, '[R]ejection of the traditional conception of the economy is . . . the keynote of institutionalism. . . ."[29] Renouncing the view that the market organizes economic activity, that is, allocates resources and determines incomes, institutionalists pierce deeper and conclude that *institutions* actually perform that role. Ayres has articulated the institutionalist's position on this issue as directly and forcefully as possible:

> As I see it, the object of dissent [from orthodoxy] is the conception of the market as the guiding mechanism of the economy or more broadly, the conception of the economy as organized and guided by the market. It simply is not true that scarce resources are allocated among alternative uses by the market. The real determinant of whatever allocation occurs in any society is the organizational structure of that society—in short, its institutions. At most *the market only gives effect to prevailing institutions*. By focusing attention on the market mechanism, economists have ignored the real allocation mechanism.[30]

In supporting this position, institutional economists begin by noting that all—or almost all—individual participation in economic life takes place within a group context, whether the group be household, tribe, enterprise, union, cartel, or nation. Commons referred to such groups as "going concerns." Within each of the many concerns of which they become a member, individuals find themselves in a situation where their own objective interests (in appropriating for themselves more of the benefits and less of the burdens of their collective undertaking) conflicts with the objective interests of others (in appropriating for themselves more and less of the same things). If it is to remain ongoing in the face of such conflicts of interest, the group (going concern) must have a means of ensuring that members of the group interact with each other in an orderly manner; or to put it slightly differently, the concern must have a means of ensuring that each individual's actions are "correlated," that is, made mutually consistent, with the actions of others.[31]

Institutionalists reject the idea that order (correlated behavior) within the concern—and recall that the nation is but the largest "going concern"—obtains as the spontaneous product of voluntaristic, self-interested exchange; instead, they trace orderly (correlated) behavior to the existence *and enforcement by the group* of an intertwined web of both formal and informal rules patterning individual conduct within the concern's domain. The meaning attached by institutional economists to the word *institution* reflects this vision, namely: a prescriptive or proscriptive rule—whether a "micro rule" applicable, say, only to a specific family or business firm or a "macro rule" applicable to an entire industry, a nation, or even an historical epoch. In the mind of an institutional economist, then, institutions connotes the set of explicit and implicit rules (customs)[32] spelling out what individuals may, can, and must do or not do, *subject to sanctions*,[33] in each of their roles within the concern.[34] In other words, institutions are the intertwined set of enforced rules (web of rules) through which individual behavior consistent with the maintenance of order (correlated behavior) is obtained. Norm, standard practice, arrangement, usage, convention, law, regulation—all are subtypes of the basic category.[35]

As the institutionalist sees things, then, it is the *indispensable* function of an institution "... to set a pattern of behavior and fix a zone of tolerance for an activity or a complement of activities."[36] Or as Commons put it: "An institution [is] collective action in control of individual action."[37] It must not be overlooked that a central function of the controlling rules (institutions) is to allocate the burdens and benefits of their collective undertaking among the various members of a group (going concern). That is why, as Ayres so aptly put it in the passage cited earlier, "The real determinant of whatever allocation occurs in any society is the organizational structure of that society—in short, its institutions."

Institutions shape behavior in two ways. First is by direct control. By establishing rights with their correlative duties and liberties (privileges) with their correlative exposures (no rights),[38] the rules in effect prefigure, or "pattern," what individuals are observed to do within the concern. For to remain in good standing as members of the concern, individuals generally *must* limit their actions to those practices prescribed or authorized by the rules. In other words, unless they are willing to "exit" the concern[39]—and this option is simply not a viable one for most people insofar as the governing macro rules are concerned—individuals who are unhappy with the controlling rule structure have no real choice but to perform their roles within the concern "as if" (a play on words) their individual preferences correspond to the rules. More to the point, perhaps, it is confidence that the collectivity (going concern) will compel others to conform to the rule structure which enables individuals to acquire the security of expectations regarding future performance necessary for them willingly to enter into transactions with one another.[40]

Of equal or even greater importance than direct control is the indirect control effected by institutions (rules). As the forms of behavior ("roles" or "practices") allowed or mandated by the existing web of rules (institutions) are repeated, or observed to be repeated by others, individuals gradually come to "prefer," or deem "natural," many or all of those forms of behavior. In short, individuals, as "wills" or self-directing entities, tend to "become" the rules (patterns of activity, criteria for evaluation) governing their activities[41]; that is, through imitation and habituation, individuals generally come to *want* to do what is required of them as they carry out each of their roles.[42] Of course, members of diverse economic classes may to some degree develop dissimilar "habits of thought" due to the different economic roles they occupy.[43]

It is obvious that the institutional perspective regarding economic order (correlated behavior) sharply differentiates it from the "orthodox" tradition. Since Adam Smith, mainstream economists have premised their work on a belief that "the price mechanism," or, alternatively, "the market mechanism," is a "natural" feature of the social domain.[44] What other belief could legitimate the neoclassical theorist's evident presumption that its workings can be investigated and understood in isolation from a concrete setting or a specific set of instituted working rules? It is clear also that the "orthodox" perspective reflects a presumption that as long as a *fixed* set of "property rights" (always unspecified) are enforced, "the market mechanism" (spontaneous price movements in response to an imbalance between quantity demanded and quantity supplied) can be relied upon to harmonize "free" behavior (the actions of self-interested individuals undertaken pursuant to the terms of contracts entered into voluntarily). Why else the paeans to "economic freedom," and so on? Economic order (correlated behavior), in short, is perceived to be a natural consequence of free exchange, that is, to be the spontaneous product of "liberty."[45] In contrast, institutional economists perceive an inherent tendency for voluntaristic behavior to produce *disorder*, that is, discord and chaos. To the extent that order obtains, it is traced to the "coercive surveillance" of institutions,[46] that is, to the external (to the individual) structure of rules (institutions) regulating (patterning) the behavior of individuals within each of the concerns, including the nation, of which they are a "member." In short, institutionalists insist that, whether its exercise is explicit or implicit, coercion is central to the operation of a market system.[47]

It is clear, though, that in spite of the "coercive surveillance" they exercise over individuals, institutions (rule structures) do change over time. Due to factors related to personality or character, there are apparently always individuals who, to a greater or lesser degree, deviate from or reinterpret cultural instructions (rules). Moreover, as individuals, singly or collectively, struggle to find solutions to the problems that preoccupy them, that is, as they engage in "instrumental valuing," new types of know-how (technology) are developed and new practices are tried.[48] When a new practice is imitated by others and it becomes standard, that is, becomes a new institution, spontaneous institutional change (new rules/practices emerging without over-arching human design) has taken place.[49] However, the attempt to employ new types of know-how or to alter existing practices (spontaneous change) will often, if not generally, precipitate overt disputes between parties who have conflicting individual or class interests as to how the "burdens and benefits" of their collective undertaking are to be apportioned. At such times, authoritative figures within the concern—those who, if necessary, can call upon the state's power of violence to enforce decisions they have been authorized by the "sovereign" to make[50]—will, as guided by their own purposes, more or less rapidly modify the explicit rule structure (and hence the set of prescribed and proscribed practices) and thereby reestablish order (correlated behavior).

In short, institutional economists understand authoritative "institutional adjustment" (revision of rules/practices via authoritative determination) to be the true "balancing wheel" of economic life.[51] This explains why institutionalists have been preoccupied with the problem of power in economic life,[52] for clearly it is power that determines who adjusts the rules and in pursuit of what ends. As to the character of the new rules/practices, institutionalists reject completely the notion that there is a teleological end, such as "efficiency," automatically regulating the evolution of actual customs and working rules. As they see it, everything is a matter of, and nothing more than, instituted practices cumulatively wrought out of preceding practices through a process of instrumental valuing in which those with greater power dominate those with lesser power in deciding whether or not, and how, to alter past practices.[53]

It may be helpful at this juncture to spell out at greater length the conception of human action accompanying the foregoing interpretation of economic life. I will presently return to the task of outlining the institutional economist's conception of economic activity.

What Do Observed Choices Signify?

In an economy where most production and distribution ostensibly are organized through voluntary exchange, as they are in a modern market system, sought-after changes in the pattern of economic "outcomes" (real incomes) will occur only if individuals alter the choices they make. Accordingly, a theory of a market process must have at its core a conception of individual action. Implicit in that conception will be answers to such questions as: *How* do people decide what production and consumption activities to undertake? *Why* do people select the actions they are observed to undertake? and *What significance* should we attach to those actions? At the very root of systematic thinking about economic processes in a market society, in other words, must be a set of presumptions regarding the nature and meaning of human action.

It is well known that neoclassical economics embodies a conception of action emphasizing 1) hedonism (as evidenced by the emphasis on utility maximization), 2) rationality (as evidenced by models assuming constrained maximization), 3) atomistic motivation (as evidenced by models assuming independent utility functions), 4) unmalleability (as evidenced by models rigidly separating ends and means as, for example, in models assuming that utility or preference functions are path independent, that is, unaffected by actual choices), and 5) the priority of the individual to society (as reflected by the adherence to methodological individualism). The institutional standpoint reflects presumptions about human action that are inconsistent with *all* facets of this "theory of action."[54]

First is the matter of the appropriate "psychology" to be reflected in economic theory, that is, the matter of what constitutes an appropriate characterization of the mental proclivities of human beings as objects of nature. Institutional economists generally reject, although not always entirely,[55] the notion that hedonism provides an adequate psychological foundation for a theory of human behavior.[56] Indeed, Veblen argued that "the hedonistic conception of man" was incompatible with an evolutionary conception of economic processes.[57] Veblen himself attempted to substitute for hedonism an activist instinct theory of behavior, but few institutionalists have followed his lead in this regard. Despite some recent interest in the "hierarchy of needs" conception developed by Abraham Maslow,[58] institutionalists have usually adopted the standpoint that generalizations about human psychology should be obtained inductively through the study of actual behavior.[59]

A related issue pertains to how the process by which individuals reach their decisions is then to be characterized. While institutionalists do understand economic behavior (production and consumption) generally to be purposeful,[60] they do not perceive it to be "rational" if that term is taken to mean "maximizing" in either its procedural or substantive connotation. Indeed, Commons once went so far as to declare flatly, "[M]an is not a rational being . . . ; he is a being of stupidity, passion and ignorance."[61] Significantly, institutionalists do agree that the rationality that does exist is not due to "human nature" but is itself a consequence of living in a market (pecuniary) society.[62]

Unfortunately, it would be impossible to provide a tightly knit description of *the* institutionalist interpretation of how individuals decide in a specific context what action to take, for it is quite apparent that no consensus position exists.[63] In fact, significant questions of interpretation are encountered in determining the orientation of even an individual writer.[64] Still, it is clear that institutionalists presume that economic behavior often, if not usually, is nonreflective and habitual in nature.[65] Moreover, as already suggested, even conscious, deliberative choices are understood generally to be little more than reflexive expressions of 'habits of thought" (Veblen) or "habitual assumptions" (Commons) acquired through participation in group life.[66]

Another related issue pertains to the question of what it is that motivates the individual in his/her economic choice making.[67] In *The Theory of the Leisure Class*, Thorstein Veblen presented a theory of economic life in which the individual relentlessly endeavors, through the conspicuous display of wasteful uses of time and wealth, to obtain the esteem of others.[68] The underlying perception, one reflected in the work of all institutionalists, has been succinctly expressed by Karl Polanyi: "[M]an is not an economic, but a social being. He does not aim at safeguarding his individual interests in the acquisition of material possessions, but rather at ensuring social good will, social status, social assets. He values possessions primarily as a means to that end."[69]

This is not to say that institutionalists understand behavior to be *only* directed to the acquisition of social good will or the attainment of rank and status. Nevertheless, they do regard a concern with the expected reaction of others (approval/disapproval, envy/disdain, and so on) as central to individual choice making. Individuals are also understood to be preoccupied with the "fairness" of the manner in which the concern distributes the burdens and benefits of its collective undertaking; of course, given the preceding interpretation of the manner in which institutions control individual behavior, what is perceived as "fair" is in large part simply a matter of what is customary. In short, "other-related" concerns are treated not as an interesting complication but as the crux of choice making.[70]

In fact, institutionalists believe that economic behavior is so infused with other-directed motives as to invalidate completely the atomistic interpretations of behavior reflected in neoclassical economics. Indeed, it is not permissible from the institutional vantage point to presume without actual investigation that a specific action is undertaken because it objectively serves the interests of the acting individual.[71] Much economic behavior (production and consumption activities) is understood instead to be largely, and often predominantly, symbolic in nature ("ceremonial" behavior), that is, to be a means of communicating to others that one is a fit member of the group or where one fits into the group status hierarchy (via "invidious comparisons").[72]

Given the foregoing understanding institutional economists are unable to accept the view that individuals can be partitioned meaningfully into "economic man," "social man," "political man," and so forth, each with different motives and behavioral principles. Institutionalists instead maintain that what one observes is a single "whole man" whose actions appear to reflect the same underlying motives and the same mental processes across the behavioral spectrum.[73] And that whole man is one to whom his/her relationships (acceptance, status, equitable treatment, and so on) with other members of the going concerns to which he/she belongs are of primary interest. In short, institutional economics has at its core a sociological conception of the individual, that is, it is social man who is understood to populate the economy.[74]

Another issue pertains to the question of whether it makes sense to employ models in which the ends/values of individuals are treated as unaffected by the specific means used to advance them. Institutionalists have uniformly rejected this approach, arguing that means and ends are always interrelated.[75] I have already outlined how institutional theory presumes that individuals generally come to view the practices/procsses in which they participate as ethically "right." What that means, of course, is that individual values ("preferences") are inescapably path-dependent.

However, institutionalists do not presume that values, once internalized, are fixed and unchangeable. When individuals find that their behavior (means) is yielding unsatisfactory solutions to the problems (ends) they are individually or collectively trying to solve, they are understood by institutionalists to assess not only the appropriateness of the means employed but also of the ends being pursued, that is, *the values they embrace.* In other words, human problem-solving behavior, which is necessarily path-dependent, is understood to involve not only an adjustment of means but also an adjustment of ends themselves.[76] Decision making, in short, involves "instrumental valuing."[77] Since both the socialization processes that shape values and the process of instrumental valuing through which values are modified are understood to be path-dependent, institutionalists are not inclined in their analysis of concrete issues to treat ends as necessarily independent of the specific process under investigation, just as they cannot take "given ends" as necessarily a meaningful standpoint from which to assess the relative attractiveness of alternative institutional arrangements.[78]

All the foregoing considerations lead inescapably to the final major element of the institutional theory of action, namely, the relationship perceived to obtain between "society" and individual. Probably nothing is of greater importance to an understanding of the institutional perspective than its wholesale rejection of methodological individualism.[79] But rather than positing *either* than society is "prior" to the individual[80] *or* the individual to society, institutional writers perceive a process of *circular causation*.[81] When looking at individual behavior from this standpoint institutionalists begin with the fact that a "going concern" typically is already functioning so as to be "ongoing" prior to the individual's "admission" into membership (via birth, hiring, certification, initiation ceremony, and so on); hence they understand the individual to have no real choice but to accommodate his/her behavior to the set of rules (institutions) already in place. Accordingly, when they observe concrete behavior within a going concern, and recall that society or a nation is but the largest and most encompassing going concern. institutionalists consider institutions to be analytically prior to behaving individuals; that is, institutions are perceived as the fundamental "cause" of observed patterns of behavior. At the same time, as indicated earlier, it is to the "wills" of the individuals who have, at some earlier date, established (whether "spontaneously" or "authoritatively") the actual practices, of which society or culture or going concern is but the active expression, that the rules themselves are traced; that is, individual actions and purposes are perceived to be the "cause" of institutions (rules).[82]

What the institutional economist discerns, then, as Walton Hamilton put it, is a process in which "[t]he individual and society [are] remaking each other in an endless process of [cumulative] change."[83] But within this circular process, to repeat, institutionalists understand individual behavior *at a given moment in historical time* to be far more the expression of culture (behavioral rules) than an expression of individual personality.[84] To borrow again from Hamilton: "While 'interests' may be the forces impelling activity, the form of that activity is determined by the scheme of social conventions under which they must assert themselves. . . . *Differences [in behavior] are mere variations from a common response. . . .*"[85] Or as Ayres put it: "[H]uman nature . . . is an expression of institutions. . . . Social patterns are not the logical consequents of individual action; individuals, and all their actions, are the logical consequents of social patterns."[86]

When observing concrete behavioral events, then, institutional economists see economic agents first and foremost as socially conditioned beings, as members of groups who evince habits of mind and patterns of behavior reflecting the actual "web of rules" (both formal and informal) patterning group life within the concerns of which they are a member.[87] That is to say, institutional economists perceive an economy populated not by "economic man" but by "socio-cultural man."[88] It is to social psychology that the institutional economist accordingly turns for insights regarding behavioral principles. Indeed, Radhakamal Mukerjee went so far as to assert in his neglected classic, *The Institutional Theory of Economics*, that "[i]nstitutional economics . . . is a branch of social psychology."[89]

It bears emphasizing that while the institutional perspective is obviously determinist to a large extent, it does not eliminate entirely a role for free will since "variations from a common response" are acknowledged to occur and since institutions (rules) themselves are understood to originate in the wills, that is, in the purposeful action, of individuals.[90] Instrumental valuing, moreover, involves the extension of free will to the domain of values themselves (even if the adjustment of values is always culture-bound).[91] In spite of the fact that coercion clearly is understood to be an indispensable, if unseen, factor in all market behavior,[92] the institutional perspective similarly retains a role for the exercise of free choice in economic behavior. From the institutional standpoint, though, free choice is not perceived as a natural right or a natural (independent of human design) way to organize economic affairs as per the invisible hand metaphor. Rather, widening areas of discretion are established and revised through rule creation and modifications; that is, free choice, being authorized behavior and hence inherently limited to choices and inducements that law-makers are willing to sanction, is itself an expression of the principle of "collective action in control of individual action."[93] It should also not be forgotten that, from the institutional standpoint, nominally free choice within the authorized domain is still substantively determined insofar as it merely gives expression to culturally acquired "habits of thought" (Veblen) or "habitual assumptions" (Commons).

The foregoing explains why institutional economists attribute far less significance to free choice than do mainstream practitioners. For the institutionalist, free choice is not a *deux ex machina* through which an individual proceeds to select the "best" (utility maximizing) choices from among the feasible set of opportunities; instead, free choice is understood to engender "variations from a common response," that is, to entail mainly the selection of culturally prescribed or "functional" alternatives.[94]

To sum up, institutional economists discern an economic realm populated by individuals who tend to "become" (as self-directing entities guided by values and preferences) the norms, conventions, practices, and so on, patterning their production and consumption activities and who hence adhere voluntarily to the requirements of the going concerns and roles into which they have been thrust. Whether such action is "rational" in the means–end sense is of limited concern to institutionalists since they understand the means themselves to be largely implicit ("the common response") in the ends acquired through socialization. Still, institutionalists, by and large, do not apprehend human action as the expression of "rationality" (constrained maximization); rather, action is perceived to manifest, in a more or less "tropismatic" (unreflective) manner, the rule structure to which the actor has had to accommodate him/herself in order to participate peaceably and reputably in group life. To the extent that action *is* explicitly means–ends-oriented (purposeful), group dynamics and interpersonal considerations are understood to be of utmost importance to the individual trying to identify the best action he/she can make at a specific moment in the context of a specific set of circumstances.

More on the Institutional Conception of Market Activity

It should be apparent that different conceptions of a market and an economy, the central abstractions of economics regarding the *structures* through which production is organized and outputs distributed, as well as a different conception of competition, the central abstraction regarding the associated *process*, are implicit in the institutionalist perspective. In particular, given the foregoing interpretation, it makes no sense to conceptualize institutions (rules) as constraints ("frictions") that redirect or divert "forces" (demand and supply) rooted in the inherent qualities ("preferences") of *analytically prior* individuals; or alternatively, as constraints limiting the automatic transformation, via "competition" between self-seeking individuals, of "data"—technology, and the preferences, skills, and resource endowments of those individuals (sometimes acting collectively via organization)—into market-clearing "equilibrium" prices and quantities, that is, into "efficient" outcomes. In other words, institutionalists reject completely the conventional conceptualization of a market, as reflected in mainstream micro *and* macroeconomics, as a natural mechanism *imbedded* in inhibiting institutions, just as they reject the complementary notion of competition as a natural form of behavior (transcultural process) *constrained*, or even *thwarted*, by institutions. From the institutional perspective, a market *is*, and is nothing more than, a behavioral domain giving effect to a specific matrix of interrelated rules; competition, in turn, is the concrete pattern of behavior implicit in or allowed by those rules. In short, economic competition is understood to be an *instituted process*.[95]

Because neither price mechanism nor competition is perceived to have inherent content absent actual instituted rules, institutionalists reject completely the relevance of the Newtonian notional "frictionless world" in which market outcomes, prices, and quantities spontaneously gravitate toward natural or normal magnitudes *to which actual outcomes can meaningfully be compared*.[96] From the institutional standpoint, quantities produced, prices charged, incomes obtained, and so on, are understood to be most fundamentally consequences of the specific rules consecutively adopted or authorized by those empowered to do so in their efforts to correlate the activities of the various members of a going concern.[97] Of particular significance is the interpretation of prices to which this standpoint necessarily leads: since costs of production are perceived as simply the pecuniary consequence of adherence to the practices mandated or authorized by the extant set of rules, prices also are understood as socially constructed or instituted, not natural, phenomena.[98]

Once this standpoint is adopted, it becomes evident that the operation of a firm, a market, or an economy cannot be known *independent of a knowledge of the actual rules* (institutions), of which economic activity (working, pricing, selling, investing, and so on) is but the active expression,[99] *and their interrelations.* And just as there is in nature no one natural plant form, but rather an almost infinite array of remarkably different, yet successful, adaptations to specific environmental challenges, so institutionalists perceive that there is in the economic realm no ubiquitous natural form of market behavior (competition) but rather a variety of behaviors expressing an array of different rule structures reflecting a variety of successful adaptations of earlier rules and practices to a variety of specific environmental challenges (labor scarcity, unreliable supply of raw materials, threat of bankruptcy, and so on). For the institutional economist, in other words, there is no presumption that there exists a single logic applicable to questions across the economic landscape or that the rules (institutions) determined to explain behavior, and thus outcomes, within a specific productive enterprise (a firm), market, or group of markets (an economy) will reveal themselves elsewhere. If different enterprises or different markets give life to behavior patterned by nonhomogeneous rules, then, if the differences are significant, each will require its own unique explanatory structure (model).[100]

On Institutional Explanation

The foregoing should make it obvious that the central precepts of neoclassical price theory have no place in a *genuinely institutional* research program. For, clearly, institutional economics, with its rejection of methodological individualism, the atomistic constrained maximization conception of action, and the conception of a market or the economy as a self-equilibrating natural mechanism imbedded in a concrete institutional context, are premised on beliefs that nullify the hard core of neoclassical economics.

This reality is not always appreciated; endeavors to paper over the fundamental incompatibility between the two perspectives abound in the literature.[101] The following observation by Herbert Parnes in reference to the labor economics literature is a fairly typical example:

> To a considerable degree, the argument between the "institutionalists" and the [neoclassical] "theorists" has always struck me as being akin to the debate between the optimist and the pessimist as to whether the bottle is half-full or half-empty. The "theorist" has never believed that there are "perfectly competitive" labor markets, nor, to the best of my knowledge, have "institutionalists" argued that competitive forces are completely absent in the market place. The former have simply chosen to emphasize the tendencies and the latter the exceptions.[102]

What Parnes and other "synthesizers"[103] have not grasped is that the real question is actually not whether the bottle is half-full or half-empty but rather what is *in* the bottle. And with respect to that question—What is the essential nature of economic life (the hard core of a research program)?—the two perspectives are antithetical.[104] As indicated earlier, the neoclassical economist presumes that within the swirl of market activities there lies hidden a core process reflecting the operation of a universally applicable set of forces (as summarized by the competitive model) through which inherent "tendencies" can be discerned; accordingly, actual events are characterized in terms of their deviation ("exceptions") from that hidden "reality." The institutional economist, on the other hand, accepts what he/she encounters on its own terms and refrains from imposing an alien logic upon what he/she finds.[105] In other words, the institutionalist forswears the use of notional constructs, imposes no a priori logic (notional tendencies) on actual events, and hence discerns no deviations (notional exceptions) from that logic. In a word, Parnes's frame of reference itself—notional tendencies and exceptions—has no meaning for the institutional economist.[106]

Institutional economists also reject individualistic explanations of collective outcomes and refuse to treat the individual, with his/her unique "preference function," as the basic building block of economic theory. In their view, to get at the heart of behavior one must emphasize collective explanations of the patterns revealed in individual behavior.[107] To be sure, it is not denied that individuals have (often substantial) discretion within the limits established by institutions. Nonetheless, the institutional structure (the existing network of rules) is regarded as *analytically prior to the individual*[108]: norms, customs and formal rules, to repeat, all generally predate the entry of a specific individual into the group (going concern) and

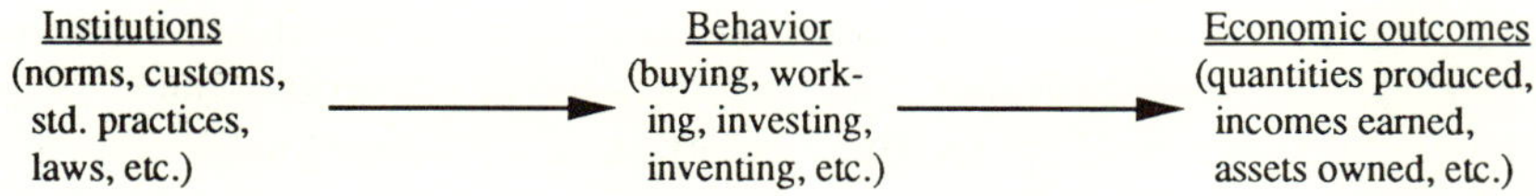

Figure 5-1. Structure of institutional explanation.

live on after his/her departure.[109] Since individual behavior is understood to be principally the objective expression of the underlying web of rules, that is, of the existing institutional structure, institutional economists maintain that if one is to trace events causally, one has to dig beyond individual behavior and explain it in terms of its more fundamental collective/social/cultural origins. As Ayres put it, "[F]or the [institutionalist] the objective [of economic theorizing] is the explanation of human nature (working, buying, consuming, investing, and so forth) *as an expression of the social order. . . .*"[110] The underlying perspective is summarized in Figure 5.1.

A *valid* explanation of economic behavior and its resultant outcomes or flow of outcomes, then, must show how it/they are linked to the actual rules (institutions) and the resultant practices through which they are produced. In short, from the institutional standpoint, to explain production and distribution outcomes is to delineate their connection to the institutional matrix (web of rules) through which they are effected. Actual behavior, to repeat, is itself understood to be the active expression of the underlying rule structure (institutions). Accordingly, for the institutionalist theorist the task is to construct sufficiently detailed explanations (models) showing how *specific* behaviors, and hence *specific* economic outcomes, are related to *actual* institutions (customary or obligatory rules and practices).

However, institutional theories adhering to this requirement will not take the same form as the theories produced by neoclassical economists. Since institutions include such things as laws, customs, mores, norms, habits of thought, and so on, it is obvious that they cannot easily, and often not even meaningfully, be expressed in quantitative terms.[111] As a result, institutional theories generally will not be reducible to formal structures summarizing the quantitative relationships between variables.[112] In a word, institutional models will never be rigorous.

Indeed, there are many who believe that institutions function as organic wholes in which the effect of any rule (institution) can be understood only in terms of its working interrelation with other rules (institutions).[113] If this is the case, institutional models of actual occurrences (outcomes) not only will not but *cannot* be reductionist in structure. Indeed, a holistic institutional theory or model cannot be anything more than a statement of the more important rules (institutions) influencing specific observed patterns of behavior in terms of their relative importance.[114] *Exactly* how those rules work in combination to give rise to that specific pattern—and hence how specific rule changes are likely to alter behavior—will be knowable to an investigator only as a gestalt perceived through an intuitive leap. In other words, causality can never be fully specified (formally modeled) or, perhaps, even adequately communicated to others[115]; to "explain" an event or action is simply to show its place in the broad pattern of events and factors that together have holistically occasioned it. In short, the institutional economist will tend to develop "pattern models" to convey his/her understanding of the way that specific market phenomena are effected.[116] As a result, probably the best that can be done with regard to higher level generalizations about the operation of markets, the development of a general theory with respect to its nature, is to develop summaries of the various types the investigator has discovered to exist, that is, to isolate and describe "arenas of competition (and cooperation)" within which the behavior of buyers and sellers manifests similar practices (institutions).

Abstract concepts and generalizations about different arenas of competition (and cooperation) within which the behavior of buyers and seller manifest similar practices (institutions) may emerge from an investigator's examination of actual economic structures/processes. But those abstractions, the holist's general theory, will tend to be little more than high-order summaries of the various types one can discern from the observation of actual economic activity (buying, investing, working, and so on).[117] As abstractions separated from a specific context, it cannot be expected that such summaries will be particularly helpful to the investigator attempting in the context of a *specific* problem to determine *exactly* what institutional adjustments to make in order to produce "better" outcomes. For, to repeat, such a determination necessarily requires holistic familiarity at a detailed level with the *unique* constellation of rules and customary practices (institutions) patterning the activities of individuals within the going concerns and markets producing outcomes the investigator (or his/her sponsor) desires to alter. At the least, it requires an accurate knowledge of the more important characteristics associated with the different types of concerns and individuals whose behavior must be changed. Still, once a typology (theory) is developed with sufficient clarity, it can become the basis for an explicit "research program" with a "positive heuristic" of showing how the typology, when coupled with a detailed knowledge of the specific rules involved, can be used to model an ever-expanding domain of market phenomena.[118]

It should be understood that nothing in the foregoing is intended to suggest that there is not a single legitimate presupposition or concept in the "analytical tool kit" of the neoclassical economist. Certainly, institutional economists accept, in the context of the present-day American setting, that many, and perhaps most, individuals and families are strongly motivated to increase their income levels; that rather fierce competition, in the rivalry sense, occurs among producers of certain products; that many firms strive ceaselessly to discover and institute practices (rules) that lower their costs of production; and so on. They similarly accept that concepts such as "product demand" and "derived demand" summarize important aggregate regularities evident in the choices actually made by productive enterprises. But to accept the validity of a presupposition or concept is not to accept the wider framework of meanings to which it ordinarily is tied—after all, Gary Becker has shown that the "law of demand" would be observed to hold even if individuals act aimlessly and make their purchases in a strictly random fashion.[119] For the institutional economist, laws or regularities summarized by such terms as *demand* and *supply*, if used, are tied to the framework of meaning outlined above and hence are always understood as institutionalized modes of behavior.[120]

Thus it may be that some of the familiar analytical tools of orthodox economics can be borrowed by institutional economists without undercutting their own agenda. What has no place in an institutional research program, to repeat, is the analytical centerpiece of neoclassical economics—the competitive model, with its theory of household behavior, firm behavior, and market equilibrium, the latter with its own "law of one price." A genuine institutional economist will never employ structures of explanation in which auxiliary assumptions about institutional factors *are added to* the competitive model.[121] Neither, in using the model to explain the existence of particular outcomes, will he/she reveal the "habits of thought" produced by the "doing" of neoclassical economics, particularly so the habits of 1) comprehending actual outcomes in terms of their deviation from the outcomes that would have obtained in the absence of "frictions" ("exceptions") in the operation of "perfect competition" ("tendencies") and 2) by referring to auxiliary assumptions *added to* the competitive model to explain why such deviations occur (as in efficiency wage theory). It is for this reason, in fact, that post-Keynesian analysis is often more orthodox than institutional in spirit: institutional economics is "economics *without* equilibrium."[122]

Significantly, nothing in the preceding has been intended to imply that there is one and only one form that an institutional theory of market phenomena can take. For as Walton Hamilton once put it, the significance of institutional doctrine "... lies in its being the only way *to the right sort of theory*."[123] There are in principle, surely, many fundamentally different ways to group institutions and thereby to construct higher level abstractions and typologies. All that the foregoing establishes is that one can judge a theory of market phenomena to be institutional in character, that is, to be "the right sort of theory," as long as: 1) it reflects a cultural or social (versus individualistic or atomistic) interpretation of individual behavior, that is, the view that individual behavior is most meaningfully explained by identifying the prevailing institutions (rules and customary practices) of which it is the active expression (not through reference to a process of constrained maximization rooted in individual preferences); 2) it reflects a particularistic (versus abstract) conception of individual markets, that is, the view that a specific economic outcomes can be explained only by pinpointing the actual, unique constellation of institutions (rules and customary practices) through which it has been produced (not through reference to an imaginary, idealized conception such as perfect competition); and 3) it reflects a Darwinian (versus Newtonian) conception of market adjustment, that is, the view that the maintenance or reestablishment of economic order (correlated behavior) must be explained by identifying the specific alteration of established practices (institutional adjustment) through which it was effected (not through reference to equilibrating price adjustments that only *reflect* such changes).[124]

Additional evidence would exist if: 4) a theory is articulated through a typology—a general theory—summarizing various distinct types of arrangements within the domain to which the theory is addressed; or 5) it is applied to the analysis of a specific context or issue via the pattern model.

These criteria are used over the following pages to assess whether the dual labor market theory is in fact a genuinely *institutional* theory of the utilization and pricing of labor. Before initiating that assessment, however, I first want to make note of an important implication of the foregoing discussion for institutional analysis in general.

A Digression on Institutional Linguistics

The foregoing discussion reveals clearly that institutional economics and neoclassical economics embody antithetical standpoints regarding the analysis of pricing and allocation processes in a market economy. However, the incompatibility of the two standpoints may not always be fully apparent to outsiders due to the penchant of institutional economists to utilize commonplace analytical terms—or, as Walter C. Neale has put it, "nouns"[125]—whose meaning may not be obvious when they are detached from the neoclassical framework.

Take, for example, the term *market*. When joined with the article *the*, it (*the market*) is a descriptive term referring to a *process* of decentralized exchange based on the motive of self-interest (as in, "let the market decide"); similarly, whenever one speaks of the market system, one is making reference to a system in which production and distribution are principally organized via decentralized, self-interested exchange (transactions).[126] When joined with the article *a*, it (*a market*) would appear to again be a descriptive term, but now connoting a *place* where individuals go to exchange particular types of items (as in *a fish market*, *a flea market*, and so on). However, *a market* connotes something entirely different to most economists.

The standard meaning of a market within the vernacular of academic economics reflects an orientation that can be traced back at least to Alfred Marshall: "Economists understand by the term *Market*, not any particular market place in which things are bought and sold, but the whole of any region in which buyers and sellers are in such free intercourse with one another that the prices of the same goods tend to equality easily and quickly."[127] By the 1930s, the implications of this interpretation were fully recognized: "A market in economic parlance is the area within which the forces of demand and supply converge to establish a single price."[128] This same usage remains conventional today: "[A market connotes] an area, however large or small, where buyers and sellers are in sufficiently close contact with each other to ensure that the price of a commodity tends to be the same in all parts of the market, allowances being made for transportation costs, tariff barriers, and other obstacles."[129] What is obvious is that a market is actually not an area at all but an invention of the mind,[130] that is, a notional construct circumscribing mentally the domain within which a notional *equilibrium price* is established.[131] But if this is so, is it not obvious that the institutional economist who is committed to an "economics without equilibrium" *must therefore reject the analytical utility of the concept market itself*! In short, the philosophical preconceptions of institutional economics nullify the concept of a market. From the institutional standpoint, in other words, it is a hindrance to clear thinking to conceive of the economy as a set of interrelated markets.

That a market has no established *analytical* meaning separable from the framework provided by neoclassical economics is a reality that has not, in my judgment, been fully grasped by institutional writers. Certainly, institutionalists have generally not revealed sufficient concern about how careful one must be in using the term *market* when communicating with the broader community of economists.[132] The mainstream economist understands the economy and the market system as an interrelated set of markets. As a result, by continuing to use market as a descriptive term, institutional speakers (writers) unwittingly allow the mainstream economist to remain within his/her own framework of meanings. Worse yet, when market is used as an analytical concept,[133] even institutional readers may find it difficult to comprehend the argument being made without utilizing the framework of meanings (neoclassical economics) they putatively reject.

While a careful demonstration is not possible here, I suspect that the borrowing of other terms central to the neoclassical framework poses a similar danger, perhaps even demand and supply. It is my view, accordingly, that institutional writers must devote much greater attention to the task of developing an appropriate language for articulating the logic of their theories/models if the truly radical nature of institutional analysis is to be conveyed to outsiders—and perhaps even to insiders themselves! This task is not without its dangers, as Commons learned only too well.[134] Still, to maintain the use of familiar terms with well-established meanings while trying to redefine[135] or broaden[136] them is likely to be an exercise in futility.

Regrettably, the task of creating a set of terms through which the pricing and allocation of human labor can be modeled in adherence to institutional preconceptions is far too difficult an undertaking to begin here.[137] Hence, in what follows, I will continue my adherence to established practice in referring to the dual labor *market* theory. The reader should understand, however, that in subsequent usages the term *market* refers only to a structured process of interaction between actual or potential buyers and sellers, not to a domain within which a single equilibrium price is presumed to emerge or exist.

Labor Economics and Institutional Analysis: The Background

It was not until the late 19th century that the study of labor problems, the forerunner of labor economics, first became a recognized subdivision of economics. Significantly, given that Richard T. Ely, Commons, and Robert F. Hoxie, a student of Veblen's, were among those who were most influential in its early development, the new field of labor problems developed more or less *pari passu* with institutional economics itself. The new labor specialists were most interested in, and generally also advocates of, unions and collective bargaining. Thus they accorded little attention to the economic analysis of wage and employment outcomes or to the task of developing an alternative conception of the processes and structures through which such outcomes are produced. The few that did attempt to develop an alternative theory—Commons, for example—had no success at all in making their ideas clear to others. As a consequence, no explicitly institutional conception of the labor market took root within labor economics during its formative years. Indeed, it came to be widely believed that the institutional movement was essentially nontheoretical, perhaps even antitheoretical.[138]

The flowering of "labor market analysis," as Paul J. McNulty has referred to it, began shortly after the conclusion of World War II.[139] During the postwar period, labor practitioners remained close students of unions and collective bargaining. What was new, however, was an intense interest in developing an adequate conceptualization of the processes through which labor services are actually allocated and priced.[140] Three quite distinct research programs, reflecting three distinct conceptions of the labor market—the neoclassical, the neoclassical-"plus", and, to borrow Clark Kerr's phrase, the "neorealist,"[141] are evident in the writings of labor economists working on these problems.[142]

None of the three 1950s labor economics research programs was rooted explicitly in the literature of institutional economics, and hence none was self-consciously institutional. Kerr, for example, has even suggested that he considers such a designation offensive.[143] All the same, in my judgment the "neorealist" program unambiguously manifests important elements of the institutional standpoint delineated above.[144] This is of considerable importance, for the neorealist program must also be understood to have provided the foundation upon which the dual labor market theory was constructed.

To establish the basis for this assertion, it will be helpful to summarize briefly the viewpoints reflected in the three labor economics research programs. Of central importance to the present line of thought is the approach each group took in attempting to characterize the market process(es) giving rise to actual pricing and allocation outcomes in markets for labor services.

Members of the neoclassical group were the intellectual forerunners of the present-day Chicago School in labor economics. Among this group may be included such figures as John R. Hicks,[145] George Stigler,[146] and Simon Rottenberg.[147] They maintained that neoclassical economics (price theory) provides the analyst with *the* set of concepts through which the operation of a labor market can be understood. The heart of this approach lies in the concepts of labor *demand*, derived from profit maximization coupled with diminishing marginal productivity, and labor *supply*, derived from individual (or household) utility maximization coupled with diminishing marginal utility (or diminishing marginal rates of substitution among "desired" things). A definite mental image of how the labor market works is coupled to this basic framework. As John T. Dunlop has emphasized repeatedly, each labor market is conceptualized as a "bourse" in which the forces of supply and demand drives the wage rate to its market-clearing level.[148] It is further maintained that competition among "rational" buyers and sellers ensures that the actual wage rate will be driven to its optimal level, that is, into conformity with *the* wage structure consistent with optimal allocation of the labor force among competing uses. The specific nature of this wage structures depends on 1) the demand for various products; 2) technology; 3) the availability, and hence the prices, of other productive resources; 4) initial household endowments; and 5) household preference functions regarding the intertemporal leisure-labor tradeoff.

In short, the textbook competitive model provided the neoclassical group with its image of *the* reality reflected in actual wage and employment outcomes. To the extent that institutions were incorporated into the analysis by neoclassical practitioners, it was always through abstract conceptions such as monopsony rather than as actual, concrete rule structures. Indeed, given that they already understood how a labor market works, members of the neoclassical group considered detailed knowledge of actual labor market practices to be superfluous to the production of valid conclusions about labor market outcomes.[149] It was not part of the neoclassical research program's "positive heuristic," accordingly, to accumulate knowledge about the actual institutions through which labor is allocated and priced.

Adherents of the neoclassical-plus approach accepted the general validity of the competitive model but considered the labor market to present special challenges requiring special tools of analysis.[150] Among the prominent economists who can be associated with this group are John T. Dunlop, Charles A. Myers, Albert Rees, and Melvin Reder.[151] In particular, they considered it inappropriate to treat each labor market as a bourse in which a single price is produced for each job. According to members of this group, labor market institutions diffuse or deflect the equilibrating process so that *an* equilibrium wage structure is not effected. The effects of competitive forces on specific labor market outcomes will not be discernable, therefore, unless the basic theory is supplemented with a detailed statement of the institutional factors *disguising its operation*. Accordingly, members of the neoclassical-plus group evinced a belief that in order to do satisfactory labor market analysis, that is, to develop valid explanations of concrete labor market outcomes, the economist must be well grounded in both economic theory (neoclassical price theory) *and* institutional detail. Thus the systematic gathering of information about existing rules and customary practices *was* a central element in the research program of this group. It was likewise an important element of the neoclassical-plus research program to produce concepts—for example, "wage contours"[152]—that could be *added* to the neoclassical tool kit whenever it was utilized for short-run analysis.[153] In spite of these concessions to realism, however, the neoclassical element remained at the core of this group's outlook, a reality evident in the following assertion by Dunlop:

> All wage theory is in a sense demand and supply analysis. A wage is a price, and the wage structure is a subsystem of prices. Prices and price systems are fruitfully to be interpreted in terms of demand and supply. There is no special or peculiar "demand and supply" theory of wages. The notion of a "political" theory of wages involves confusion.[154]

The third group, the neorealists, proceeded completely outside the framework provided by neoclassical price theory.[155] Clark Kerr, Arthur M. Ross, and Richard Lester must be included among the neorealists.[156] To characterize the perspective of this group properly, it is necessary to resort to the concepts of pattern model[157] and holistic general theory.[158] Based on their own detailed investigation of wage-setting and job-allocation processes, members of this group discerned a world in which workers are "satisficers" rather than "maximisers,"[159] in which interpersonal (sociological and political) rather than atomistic factors predominate, in which formal rules with only a tenuous relationship to cost minimization dominate wage-setting and job-allocation processes, in which "wage markets" (wage-setting) and "job markets" (job allocation) are typically independent of one another and, significantly, in which there is no single price for any specific type or grade of labor. The members of this group further failed to apprehend a competitive process common to the operation of all labor markets. Instead, they perceived a world in which different labor markets evince different sets of instituted rules, some of which are firm-, locality-, or industry-specific, others of which are nation-specific. Fundamentally different types of institutional configurations, that is, different types of labor markets, were seen to produce fundamentally different wage and employment outcomes.[160]

The dual labor market literature is replete with citations to the published work of *both* neoclassical-plus and neorealist labor economist.[161] Indeed, Peter Doeringer and Michael Piore's *Internal Labor Markets &*

Manpower Analysis—arguably the initial contribution to the genesis of the dual labor market theory literature[162]—reflects an uneasy tension due to the two authors' evident failure to recognize that in this work they were attempting to synthesize incompatible perspectives about the essential nature of labor markets. In particular, Doeringer and Piore failed to grasp that the neorealism group, toward which Piore later gravitated, had developed a de facto alternative to the neoclassical hard core, whereas the neoclassical-plus group, toward which Doeringer subsequently gravitated,[163] insisted only on supplementing it with a *market-specific* "protective belt" of institutions or, alternatively, with a broadened "positive heuristic" (discovering the various "plus" elements in different markets).[164] As the attempt to articulate more satisfactorily the theoretical underpinnings of the dual labor market conceptualization of labor market processes moved forward, with Piore quickly taking the lead, the perspective reflected in the work of the neorealist (institutional) writers increasingly came to be explicitly embraced. As a result, in my judgment, development of the dual labor market theory clearly constitutes a continuation of the institutional research program begun by members of the neorealist group.

The Institutional Character of the Dual Labor Market Theory

Overview

Before I proceed with the task of explaining why the dual labor market theory is properly understood to constitute an institutional conceptualization of labor market outcomes, it might be helpful first to recapitulate its central tenets.[165] Development of the dual labor market theory began with the insight, inferred from actual observation, that the labor market can fruitfully be segmented into two fundamentally dissimilar sectors (hence the *dual* labor market theory)—a primary sector and a secondary sector—in which "the behavior of the critical economic variables changes systematically as one moves across market segments."[166] In the primary sector, jobs provide relatively high wages, good working conditions, chances of advancement, equity and due process in the administration of work rules, and perhaps most important, stable employment. In the secondary sector, on the other hand, jobs provide low-wages, poor working conditions, little chance of advancement, a highly personalized relationship between workers and supervisors, harsh and capricious work discipline, unstable employment, and a high turnover among the labor force.

While the division into a primary and a secondary sector is basic to the

Characteristic	Primary Sector		Secondary Sector
	Lower Tier	Upper Tier	
Earnings & Status	Relatively High*	Highest*	Low
Job Security	Relatively High	Relatively High	Low
Working Conditions	Relatively Good	Good	Poor
Job Ladder	Intra-Firm	Intra- and/or Inter-Firm	None
Potential for Advancement	Good	Good	Poor
Workplace Control	Formal Rules	Internalized Code	Employer's Discretion
Turnover	Low	Moderately High	High

*Will increase with movement up a job ladder.

Figure 5-2. Job characteristics within labor market segments.

theory (fundamentally, as good jobs versus bad jobs), there are distinctions among primary jobs in many ways as important as the distinctions between the two sectors. Hence, as shown in Figure 5.2, the primary sector is itself segmented into two tiers. In the upper tier are professional and managerial jobs, as well as some craft jobs.[167] Higher pay and status and greater promotion opportunities distinguish these jobs from those in the lower tier. However, mobility and turnover patterns tend to resemble more closely those of the secondary sector—except that in the upper tier, unlike the secondary sector, mobility and turnover tend to be associated with advancement. Again, like those of the secondary sector, upper-tier jobs lack the elaborate set of work rules and formal administrative procedures characterizing lower-tier employments. But the personalized relationship between workers and supervisor which takes the place of such rules in the secondary sector are replaced in upper-tier employments by an internalized code of behavior. Finally, upper-tier work offers greater economic security and considerably more variety and room for individual creativity and initiative than is the case in the lower tier. What is common to both tiers, and hence what differentiates both from the secondary sector, is the existence of a career or job ladder along which a worker can advance toward higher-paying and higher-status jobs.

The division between a discrete set of upper-tier primary sector jobs separate from other jobs within the labor market inheres in the distinction between general and specific traits, where "trait" connotes a "behavioral pattern which will be reproduced in response to a given stimulus in a particular type of environment."[168] *General traits* are derived from rules which enable the individual, even in novel circumstances, to deduce from an environment and a stimulus what constitutes the appropriate response. General traits are acquired principally through formal education. *Specific traits*, on the other hand, occur as direct responses to stimuli offered by the environment. Unlike general traits, specific traits are acquired through automatic incidental learning, that is, automatically through exposure to, participation in, and repetition of a specific behavioral pattern (as in on-the-job training). Upper-tier jobs require the holder to display general traits, whereas jobs in the remainder of the labor market require only that the holder display specific traits. In other words, upper-tier jobs are ones in which the occupant must be able to deduce appropriate behaviors from a set of abstract general principles which are generally learned only through formal education, whereas lower-tier and secondary-sector jobs are ones in which the occupant must only be able to acquire and perform appropriate specific traits learned incidentally as a byproduct of actual workplace experience.

The existence of an upper-tier primary sector separate from the remainder of the labor market, then, inheres in the distinction between general and specific traits *and the realization that such traits are acquired through intrinsically different learning processes*. The labor market's further division into a lower-tier primary sector and a secondary sector finds its rationale in an entirely different distinction, this one centering on the existence of two fundamentally dissimilar techniques of production. According to the dual labor market theory, firms face a basic choice every time they must decide how to produce a particular output. One choice is to select a production process utilizing large amounts of capital equipment whose operation requires personnel with specific traits taking considerable periods of time to acquire. Because of the learning time involved in acquiring the more difficult traits, a job ladder will be established through which individuals can contribute to production at the same time they utilize free time to acquire more difficult traits. Since employees who have acquired appropriate traits are in effect valuable assets, firms have a strong incentive to make their jobs good ones in order to minimize employee turnover. That is, jobs requiring such traits will tend to be located in the primary sector as described above.

However, firms can make a fundamentally different choice by selecting a less capital-intensive production process, utilizing workers who possess only specific traits that are menial in nature or that can be learned quickly.[169] Such firms have no need to create a job ladder. Similarly, because their employees can be easily replaced, such firms suffer little economic loss from employee turnover and hence have no incentive to make jobs good ones. Jobs within such firms consequently tend to be located in the secondary sector.

In markets for a standardized product whose demand is stable and reasonably certain, participating firms generally can presume that they will be able to keep their capital equipment more or less fully employed. Such firms therefore will consider it unlikely that they will be thrust into a situation where they must continue making payments associated with the acquisition costs of their capital investment in the absence of an offsetting revenue flow. Hence these firms will tend to conclude that it makes sense to select the first type of production process and thereby create lower-tier primary-sector jobs. Firms who do not produce a standardized product or whose demand is unstable or uncertain, by analagous reasoning, will find it makes more sense to select the second type of production process; such firms accordingly will tend to create secondary-sector jobs. Of course, some firm might respond to their unique circumstances by establishing both lower-tier primary sector and secondary-sector jobs or by dividing the same function into primary and secondary-sector jobs.

The dual labor market theory, then, divides the labor market into *three* discrete segments ("types") reflecting jobs in which three fundamentally different modes of thought and understanding underlie three distinct behavioral patterns—"instrumental" behavior in the upper tier of the primary market,[170] "customary" behavior in the lower tier, and "commanded" (by the supervisor) behavior in the secondary sector.[171] As noted, this threefold division can be understood to be rooted in economic forces consequent to, first, the two fundamentally different learning processes through which productive traits required for successful performance in a job are acquired and, second, the two fundamentally different production processes within which a job will tend to be located.

Despite its economic aspect, job segmentation is not treated in the dual labor market theory as a phenomenon unto itself. Rather, jobs are seen in their relation to a broader *mobility chain*. That is, jobs are conceived of in the dual labor market theory as *stations* along more or less regularized channels of socioeconomic movement from family backgrounds and neighborhoods to schools to a limited set of employment situations. The phenomenon of labor market segmentation in the dual labor market theory, in other words, is understood to have at its root *distinct and largely separate* mobility chains through which discrete strata of a society or nation are delivered to discrete segments of the labor market. It may be this feature of the dual labor market theory that distinguishes it most sharply from other theories of the labor market developed by labor economists.

The dual labor market theory traces the emergence and perpetuation of separate mobility chains, first, to factors associated with *social class* and, second, to the tendency for different environments, such as home, school, and work, to evolve in convergent directions and therefore gradually to manifest the same characteristics. Unfortunately, one cannot do justice in a brief overview to the subtle manner in which social class and the process of convergent evolution interact in the dual labor market theory to generate and maintain separate mobility chains delivering discrete groups of workers to the three segments of the labor market.[172] Still, a few central points can be noted.

With respect to class, the dual labor market theory roots the three types of mobility chains in stations—family, neighborhood, school, church, and so on—related to social class. In particular, the theory posits that the mobility chains leading to *adult* confinement in the secondary sector are rooted in the lower-class subculture. The upper- and lower-tier primary-sector mobility chains are similarly rooted in middle-class and working-class subcultures. Significantly, the three mobility chains—the class-rooted sets of stations through which the three segments of the labor market are maintained—are understood to have been found rather than made by the capitalist system; that is, they are perceived as adaptations of class patterns predating their "new" uses.[173] In addition, the lower-class subculture is understood in the main to be a derivative of the working-class subculture, with the evolution of a different mobility chain in which lower-class groups fail to make the transition to routine working-class life-patterns being traced to the disruptions of family life engendered by migration, whether inter- or intranational, in combination with the limited opportunities for stable employment typically afforded migrants.[174]

In regard to convergent evolution, points of emphasis include the matter of how individuals obtain access to a specific initial station on a mobility chain not rooted in their own class subculture, the ways that extraneous characteristics (such as affective traits associated with class background) can block upward movement even if access to such a station is gained, the manner in which traits associated with such a station undergo change as individuals from new environments gain access in significant numbers, and, as soon as the now-altered traits associated with the affected station become incompatible with the requirements of higher stations, the manner in which that station detaches from its original mobility chain.

Formal education, first at the secondary and next at the university level, can be used to illustrate the manner in which convergent evolution influences the adjustment of mobility chains. Since upper-tier jobs emphasize general traits, individuals must be delivered into them via mobility chains that develop both a knowledge of the appropriate general principles and a minimal level of proficiency in their application. Successful performance in lower-tier jobs, however, depends only on the acquisition of appropriate specific traits—ones, moreover, that are normally acquired via on-the-job-training. But whereas advanced (secondary and university-level) formal education emphasizing abstract reasoning and intrinsic understanding is a genuine prerequisite for successful performance in upper-tier jobs, that is, constitutes a necessary station along upper-tier mobility chains, it is essentially unrelated to successful performance in lower-tier jobs where extrinsic understanding normally suffices. The logic of the dual labor market theory hence suggests that advanced formal education constitutes a necessary station only on upper-tier, or middle-class, mobility chains. Put slightly differently, the theory suggests that advanced formal education is *not* a necessary station on working-class or lower-class mobility chains. If evidence of advanced formal education (secondary and higher education) comes to be required of individuals on those mobility chains, convergent evolution would further suggest that one will observe a temporal process in which the character of the school experience afforded those individuals comes gradually to deviate in significant ways from the character of the experience provided individuals proceeding along an upper-tier mobility chain in that the former will come to emphasize activities requiring specific rather than general traits, that is, concrete rather than abstract learning processes.[175] Subsequent to the extension of advanced formal education to a wider segment of society, therefore, one world anticipate the development within high schools and higher education of separate stations for the different mobility chains, perhaps in the form of different curriculums, such as college preparatory versus vocational, or, alternatively, in the form of discrete sets of schools and universities. To a large extent, this is exactly what appears to have happened in the United States over the course of the 20th century.

A Preliminary Assessment

Even this brief overview should suffice to establish that there are solid grounds for associating the dual labor market theory with institutional economics. It is apparent, first of all, that the underlying conception of individual action is consistent with the institutional standpoint as summarized above. For, as Piore put it, "At the core of labor market segmentation are social groups and institutions"; the phenomena it seeks to understand, accordingly, are "social, as opposed to individual phenomena."[176] At the heart of the dual labor market theory is a presumption that individual behavior is based on and expresses attitudes and cognitive processes inseparable from one's mobility chain. *Society* and *individual*, in other words, are perceived to be indissolubly intertwined. In a word, it is sociocultural man who populates the world summarized by the dual labor market theory.

Second, it is also apparent that the dual labor market theory is holistic general theory of the purest form. As reported by its own progenitors, the dual labor market theory arose initially out of an attempt to summarize a series of disparate local labor market studies designed to understand the labor force problems of disadvantaged workers in urban areas.[177] As a theory, it summarizes neither functional relationships nor economic laws. Neither does it have a logic capable of representation through a formal language. The dual labor market theory, as characterized to this point, simply summarizes three fundamentally different types of labor markets, identifies some factors related to their emergence, and loosely links the three types of labor markets to three types of mobility chains along which specific jobs will be located. To repeat, if it is to be regarded as economic theory, the dual labor market theory is clearly holistic general theory.

As outlined to this point, the dual labor market theory provides no explanation of the way that wages are determined and workers are allocated among specific jobs in actual labor markets. It is to the dual labor market theory's modelling of actual labor market outcomes that I now turn.

Job Allocation and Wage Outcomes in the lower Tier of the Primary Labor Market

Economists are accustomed to using the concepts of demand and supply to structure their thinking about the processes through which allocation and pricing outcomes are generated. In a limited sense, the dual labor market theory can accommodate itself to this practice. What the theory asserts is that there are fundamentally three discrete types of employees whom firms seek out or demand (hence segmented markets), namely, those who can function effectively in upper-tier, lower-tier, and secondary-sector jobs. It is similarly the function of mobility chains to deliver a steady flow of workers—that is, a supply—to each labor market segment. However, despite the seeming ease with which its insights can be translated into demand and supply terminology, it is clear that the dual labor market theory cannot actually be synthesized with mainstream economics. For, as suggested above, in the dual labor market framework neither demand nor supply is conceived of as a functional relationship between quantity demanded or supplied and price (the wage rate). Indeed, at the core of the dual labor market theory is a presumption that, in general, prices are *not* determined by supply and demand,[178] that is, that the "price mechanism" is *not* the operative force in allocating jobs among competing workers or in determining the wages to be paid to individuals occupying those jobs.

How, then, does the dual labor market theory characterize the process(es) through which wages are determined and jobs allocated in each of the three segments of the labor market? The dual labor market theory's conception of the job-allocation and wage-setting processes in the lower tier of the primary sector has been spelled out carefully by Piore in a paper titled "Fragments of a 'Sociological' Theory of Wages."[179] A brief summary of that conception runs as follows.[180]

As already indicated, jobs in the lower tier of the primary sector require occupants to possess specific traits (job skills) which can only be acquired through lengthy on-the-job-training. To facilitate employee acquisition of required traits, job ladders are constructed that allow individuals to move to better jobs as they master new traits. Thus access into all but the entry-level job on the job ladder is restricted to individuals who are already occupying a rung. In short, lower-tier jobs are found principally within internal labor markets sheltering those who are already on the job ladder from the potential competition of workers who are not.

Since on-the-job-training in these protected enclaves necessarily occurs within social groups, it can be understood in terms of socialization, that is, in terms of a coercive structure[181] compelling individual adherence to the standard practices, norms, and role patterns of the group. Indeed, since they involve tasks that cannot be performed in the absence of cooperation by others, many skills cannot even be distinguished independently of the concrete social setting in which they are performed. What this means, to repeat, is that trait (skill) acquisition cannot occur unless an individual conforms to the prevailing customs, norms, roles, and so on, of the workplace—that is, to workplace institutions. As the patterns associated with conformity to existing institutions are repeated again and again, an individual will quickly become committed to them "for their own sake . . . independent of their effect upon the ends presumed in conventional analysis."[182]

Among the principal customs (institutions) of the workplace are those pertaining to the relationship between wages on different jobs. Thus the development of a commitment to the existing structure of wage differentials is itself inherent in the process through which the internal labor market supply of labor is generated. This commitment, in fact, is so strong that workers generally come to view wage relativities, both within and outside the work group of which they are a part, as moral or ethical absolutes.[183] Workplace dynamics, therefore, eviscerate "competitive pressures" capable of undermining the internal wage structure as well as, in large part, those within *interfirm* "orbits of coercive comparisons."[184] As Piore put it: "[The idea, 'internal labor market,'] is basically an assertion that in large territories of the labor market, job allocation and pricing are governed by institutional rules and customs which are only tenuously linked to rational, instrumental behavior or to competitive market forces, if they are so linked at all."[185]

"[B]y hinging upon nonwage factors as determinants of the allocation of labor, [models of labor market stratification incorporating the 'sociological' theory of wages] free the wage from its traditional role in economic theory and open the way for noneconomic determinants."[186] Indeed, the "reservation wage" at which a worker would be willing to labor at a specific rung on the job ladder is itself a product of workplace socialization. The socialization process similarly ". . . affect[s] job preferences in such a way as to make preferences for different jobs consistent with the requisite movement between them."[187] Labor supply within the internal labor market (the ability and willingness of individuals on the job ladder to perform a given task at a particular wage rate), in other words, is fundamentally a *consequence of* socialization within the workplace. That is, insofar as they affect the supply of labor within the internal labor market, to put it into orthodox parlance, job preferences are endogenous.[188]

Given its presumption that socialization, rather than optimizing adjustments of behavior in response to changing price differentials, constitutes the core process through which workers are delivered as required within internal markets, the sociological theory of wages clearly lies outside the neoclassical domain. More to the point, it unquestionably reflects the institutional perspective.

First of all, it is clear that the distinction between socialization and institutions is semantic rather than substantive. For, in drawing attention to the similarity between the sociological theory of wages and "institutional models of wage determination developed by labor economists in the 1940s and 1950s," Piore acknowledges that "'sociological' and 'institutional' forces are closely related; at root, perhaps, they are the same thing."[189] It is equally clear, moreover, that, in order to be in conformity with the sociological theory of wages, models of specific allocation and wage outcomes must be constructed so that institutions, not individuals with their atomistic "preferences," are the basic unit of explanation. Piore has been quite explicit on this matter:

> [W]e found that by starting from the premise of groupings that are institutionally defined, we could analyze individual behavior as the response to rules and incentives that develop in different segments of society. . . . The result is that individuals' choices, attitudes, and behaviors vary across the segments of society. Indeed, *if we start from institutions*, only a minimal set of assumptions about individuals is required: that the persons found in any particular social and economic universe have at least those predispositions and capabilities that make it possible for them to function there.[190]

It is, of course, the function of previous stations on individual mobility chains—family, neighborhood, school, and so on—to ensure that an individual in fact possesses the "predispositions and capabilities" to which Piore here makes reference.

Nowhere in Piore's writings are atomistic preferences assigned a role of any kind in explaining the division of the labor force into its various segments. What is emphasized instead is the adaptation of the individual to the established norms and patterns of the group from which he/she must obtain acceptance (cooperation and assistance).[191] Clearly, voluntary individual supply behavior within the lower tier of the primary sector is perceived as essentially nothing more than the active expression of workplace institutions.[192] In short, the sociological theory of wages reflects an institutional structure of explanation.

Second, it is equally evident that wages in this conceptualization are assigned meaning through an institutional lens. For Piore clearly does *not* understand wage adjustments to be the means through which imbalances in the internal labor market are resolved. Instead, revisions of the controlling rules—*institutional adjustment*—is perceived to perform that role.[193] It should also be noted that Piore's understanding of enterprise price determination is wholly outside the neoclassical framework. In particular, he endorses the pricing rules approach in which fixed percentage markups predominate.[194] The key point is that price structures (including wages), not individual prices, are the unit of analysis in this conceptualization. This also is wholly consistent with the conception of prices associated earlier with the institutional standpoint.

Third, it is significant that Piore discerns that the lower tier of the primary sector is populated with workers who are in large part "other-oriented" with respect to their economic decisions rather than "individualistically-oriented wealth seekers" as per "economic man"; this is revealed in their asserted attachment to the maintenance of existing wage relativities. Moreover, the asserted behavior of those same workers arises only from the fact that they are treated, first and foremost, as members of social groups for whom acceptance by others in the group is a necessary preoccupation. It is also evident that in this conceptualization Piore understands lower-tier workers to be "cultural" creatures, that is, beings whose wants and desires are consequences of their participation in (work) group life. In short, the sociological theory of wages reflects the sociocultural conception of man shown above to lie at the heart of the institutional standpoint.

Fourth, it is also significant that Piore explicitly repudiates the utility of comparing a "customary wage structure" (internal labor market wage structure) with "the structure which would prevail in a perfectly competitive economic system:". . . "The assertion is . . . that[, given the *necessity* of 'socialization' within the work place,] there cannot *be* a perfectly competitive labor market in the sense that it is generally envisaged in theory" (as a "market" giving effect to fixed, atomistic individual preferences).[195] This belief, of course, is also a central component of the institutional standpoint as outlined above.

Fifth, Piore clearly indicates his belief that in order to develop a valid model of a specific internal labor market it is necessary to first obtain a knowledge of the specific rules/customs patterning behavior within its ambit. Since the operation of each distinct internal labor market is likely to reflect the interaction of its own unique constellation of rules, this means that a multiplicity of possibly fundamentally different models, will have to be developed in order to understand how economic pressures or public policy will impact on the lower tier of the primary sector as a whole.[196] This is another presupposition earlier associated with the institutional standpoint. Unfortunately, for the economist who desires to understand how public policy will affect lower-tier wages and employment, the need for a multiplicity of models is an intimidating reality: "The understanding of the detailed customary relationships required to administer [policy in] such a system may turn out to be too much to expect from ordinary men."[197]

Finally, even though the sociological theory of wages does not dismiss out of hand the possibility that competitive pressures (market forces) can affect the evolution of workplace customs or rules, such pressures are not judged by Piore to be of great significance. Indeed, he asserts that at a conscious level they are not even generally perceived: "For most price and wage setters the structure embodied in their rules *is* reality: nothing in their experience leads them to be aware of the deeper market structure that economists postulate. . . . From the agent's perspective the traditional rules of price and wage setting represent the *best* construction they can make of economic reality: they don't see any higher, more basic set of forces from which those rules derive."[198] Existing workplace customs, whether informal or institutionalized via collective bargaining agreements, are to be understood, therefore, not in terms of how they reflect the "coercive surveillance" of economic forces but simply as adaptations or outgrowths of past customs and practices.[199] This also is a presupposition associated with the institutional standpoint.

The foregoing analysis would appear to establish conclusively that the dual labor market theory embodies an institutional conception of the structures (processes) through which jobs are allocated and wages established in the lower tier of the primary labor market. But Piore makes it clear that the sociological theory of wages applies *only* to that stratum of the labor market.[200] Can the same conclusion, therefore, be reached regarding the theory's conceptualization of job allocation and wage determination in the other two strata? It is to the matter of how the theory explains job allocation and wage determination in the secondary labor market that I turn next.

Job Allocation and Wage Determination in the Secondary Labor Market

It will be recalled that central to the institutional standpoint is a belief that there is no reason to presume that a single core process reveals itself in different types of markets. Since secondary labor markets are characterized by high turnover, one would expect an absence of cohesive social groups at the workplace and, consequently, a more individualistic orientation to work. Given these realities, it should come as no surprise to discover that, with respect to the operation of secondary labor markets, Piore has advanced a conception of job allocation and wage determination at first glance quite different with respect to the controlling principles from that outlined above for the lower tier of the primary labor market.

Piore's conception of the secondary labor market's workings, significantly,[201] resulted *from* the actual study of two dissimilar low-wage labor markets.[202] First was the low-wage labor market in Boston, for which systematic information was available for an eight-year period as the by-product of a larger effort to study Puerto Rican migration into that city. Throughout the period for which information was available, Boston's was a "labor shortage economy" in which wages at the bottom of the scale were consistently above the statutory minimum. Piore found that Boston's secondary labor market needed to be further separated into two more or less distinct subsectors, one in which wages are tied to the lower tier of the primary sector and one in which they are not.

The first grouping consisted of unionized low-wage jobs that were generally in firms employing a sharply differentiated work force—either highly skilled or extremely low-skilled. In firms with this type of "bimodal" work force, a union typically was observed to negotiate a single wage structure covering both components of the work force, with maintenance of wage relativities between skilled and unskilled workers—clearly an institution as that term was developed above—providing the principal determinant of wage rates for the unskilled segment of a firm's work force. Unionization, however, did not appear to affect the nonwage characteristics of jobs held by low-wages workers. Hence, in spite of unionization, these jobs were judged by Piore as actually being situated in the secondary sector of the labor market.

The remaining jobs in Boston's secondary labor market were in nonunionized firms located in highly competitive product markets. Even here, though, Piore was unable to discern a wage-determination process more or less in conformity with the mainstream competitive model. What he did find was that wages were seldom altered in response to variations in labor market conditions. Indeed, Piore determined that most wage rates in this sector generally changed only under the impetus of legislated changes in the statutory minimum. This discovery led Piore to adopt the term *stagnation* (as opposed to *competition*) to characterize the forces underlying wage determination in the low-wage sector of the labor market.

Piore traced this stagnation to two realities of the secondary labor market. First, he discovered that individuals seeking to sell their labor services in this sector are mostly "target earners" working to accumulate a fixed amount of money (versus individuals marginally adjusting leisure and goods in response to changing relative prices). Since employers therefore face a "supply curve" of labor that is "backward bending," they have come to associate an increase in the wage rate with a reduction in the amount of labor they are able to obtain. Accordingly, they are *not inclined* to raise wages when they experience a labor shortage. Second, given the sometimes extreme economic marginality of most firms seeking to purchase labor services in the secondary sector and the fact that wage payments are usually a very large component of total costs of production, secondary sector employers feel *unable* to raise wages even if a labor shortage persists. Piore discovered that whenever there were shortages in the total secondary labor supply in the Boston area, an increase in the available work force was usually secured via an intensified recruiting effort in the rural areas of Puerto Rico. As a result, over long periods of time the supply of low-wage workers in the Boston area actually was perceived by employers to be more or less perfectly elastic at the existing stagnant wage.

What Piore found to be the case even in the nonunion Boston low-wage labor market, in summary, is that wages do *not* perform the roles assigned them in mainstream theory of, first, allocating workers among competing uses and, second, "balancing" the quantity of labor services demanded with the quantity being offered. An intensified recruitment effort is instead the customary way to obtain additional workers; that is, the *institutional adjustment* of altering recruitment practices is revealed to be the true balancing wheel in Boston's low-wage labor market. Then what of the wage rate itself? As noted, it was found to move only in response to an alteration of the statutory minimum. The actual wage paid in low-wage markets, in other words, was found to bear a more or less fixed relationship to the statutory minimum wage. Piore concluded that the wage paid actually is a "social minimum" in keeping with an established moral standard, that is, in keeping with a social norm or *institution*. Again, in a word, we find that Piore has explained the existence of a specific wage rate by asserting that it is essentially the objectification of an institution. Similarly, it is a pattern model through which Piore has identified the factors impinging on the process of wage determination in the Boston area low-wage labor market.

The second low-wage labor market studied by Piore was in south-western Louisiana, where shrimp-packing and sugar cane are the principal industries. There is a special federal wage statute establishing minimum wages for various occupations in the sugar cane industry,[203] and the sugar cane minimum is set substantially above the federal minimum for industry (surprisingly, at approximately the level of the social minimum in Boston). In the shrimp-packing industry, however, it was standard practice to pay the federal minimum.

It was Piore's contention that this second low-wage labor market was in fact "qualitatively different" from Boston's in that the current practices reflected in wage-determination are an adaptation of the practices prevailing on the plantation prior to enactment of a federal minimum wage law for the sugar cane industry. Sugar plantations were organized so that all lines of authority were vertical, with workers developing no allegiance to each other or even an interest in what others were earning. It became the custom for each plantation owner to set as the minimum wage on his plantation what he individually conceived to be "subsistence," with various "extras" added to that base for his faithful retainers. Social pressure served as the mechanism keeping subsistence on different plantations at more or less the same level (including in-kind payments). Against this background, Piore interpreted the federal minimum wage scale for the sugar industry as simply substituting state control for the control of the individual patron. He further observed that labor relations in the shrimp packing industry evolved so as to more or less duplicate those on the plantation. The lower wage paid in shrimp packing was accordingly accepted by workers as a matter strictly within the "patron's" (the employer's) discretion. At the same time, Piore noted that *social pressure* from other local employers coerces individual employers into paying only the prescribed minimum even if they want and are able to pay workers more.[204] At the same time, Piore noted that many, if not most, suppliers of labor services in southwestern Louisiana, as in Boston, are target earners and that shrimp-packing firms are similarly too marginal to absorb wage increases in the absence of a general industry-wide increase.

Given these realities, Piore discerned in southwestern Louisiana a secondary labor market in which the competing buyers (employers) are not inclined, even in the event of an imbalance at the present wage between their individual labor requirements (quantity demanded) and the amount they individually are able to obtain (quantity supplied), to deviate from the minimum wage. In Piore's view, what is found in Louisiana is a market in which the minimum wage structure "appears to substitute for a subsistence wage in a very traditional and paternalistic industrial relations system."[205] In the model implicit in this conception of the Louisiana low-wage labor market, the wages paid in different types of jobs are discerned, pure and simple, as the objectification of institutions, namely, the controlling minimum wage statutes. Significantly, those controlling institutions (minimum wage statutes) are clearly *not* understood by Piore as having been overlaid onto, and thereby masking the operation of, a labor market with a core process adhering to the standard competitive model. In the interpretation forwarded by Piore, what the present-day wage-determination process (minimum wage statutes) instead masks is the modification, yet essential continuity, of a wage-determination process in which custom (the patron's paternalistic, yet class-regulated, conception of subsistence) was *wholly* the factor explaining the wage structure.

In short, it is clear that, with respect to the principles reflected in the operation of the southwestern Louisiana low-wage labor market, Piore, has again forwarded what must be understood to constitute an institutional conception of wage determination. It is equally clear that it is a pattern model that Piore has forwarded to juxtapose the factors influencing the operation of the Louisiana low-wage market.

A Summing Up

In an article titled "Labor Market Segmentation: To What Paradigm Does It Belong?,"[206] Piore explains carefully why the dual labor market theory must be considered as an *alternative* to the conventional theory of labor market behavior. This is because:

> ... [a]t the core of labor market segmentation are social groups and institutions. The processes governing allocation and pricing within internal labor markets are *social*, opposed either to competitive processes or to instrumental calculation. The marginal labor force commitment of the groups which creates the potential for a viable secondary sector of a dual labor market is social. The structures which distinguish professional and managerial workers from other members of the labor force and provide their distinctive education and training are also social. To understand these phenomena, one therefore needs a paradigm which recognizes and encompasses social, as opposed to individual phenomena.[207]

Then what label should we employ in reference to this alternative conception of economic processes? The "structuralist" paradigm, Piore declares.[208]

What has been shown over the preceding pages is that as an overarching conception of labor market segmentation, the dual labor market theory evinces a conception of economic (producing, pricing, exchanging) behavior wholly in harmony with the philosophical preconceptions constituting the institutional standpoint. The accompanying models of wage determination and labor allocation in individual labor markets also have been shown to be consistent with those preconceptions. In short, Piore's self-labeled structuralist paradigm has been shown to consistently and comprehensively manifest the philosophical preconceptions of institutional economics. The dual labor market theory, in other words, is clearly the right sort of theory, that is, *a type of institutional theory*.[209]

Given that the dual labor market theory's development was not influenced in any discernable manner by the literature of mainstream institutional economics, it represents, as noted at the outset of this chapter, a striking example of the "compulsive shift toward institutional analysis" evident in 20th century economic thought.[210] Indeed, I am personally convinced that the dual labor market theory developed by Piore and his collaborators actually represents the most successful undertaking to date (in this case, unconsciously so) to develop explicit models of *actual present-day market processes* in conformity with the declared philosophical beliefs of mainstream institutional economists.[211] In other words, it is my judgment that the dual labor market hypothesis represents the most successful institutional research program directed to the problem of institutional impact analysis in contemporary economics.

To say this is not to ignore the incomplete development of the theoretical framework. For example, no carefully articulated analysis of upper-tier primary sector labor markets has yet been forwarded by a proponent of the structuralist paradigm.[212] Neither, insofar as the lower tier of the primary sector is concerned, has an explanation for the wage level (as opposed to the wage structure) been forwarded. It also should not be forgotten that neither the task of fully translating the dual labor theory into a language free of neoclassical concepts nor the task of systematically integrating it into a more comprehensive institutional general theory of the market system has yet to be undertaken. But to acknowledge that much work remains in no way negates the significance of what already has been achieved in constructing an institutional conceptualization of wage determination and job allocation in the contemporary American setting.[213]

Concluding Observation

In the introductory section of this chapter, I advanced the view that mainstream institutionalists have been reasonably successful in developing various general theories identifying the types of institutions through which behavior is patterned in the modern-day, machine-based market system. I also observed that they have not shown nearly so much progress in forwarding exemplars of uniquely institutional pattern models capable of being used for institutional impact analysis. As regards the first end-in-view, the dual labor market theory provides another notable example of what can be achieved, for it clearly is holistic general theory of the highest form.[214] As regards the second, it should not be overlooked that Piore has frequently utilized the dual labor market theory to assess (predict) the likely impact of proposed labor market policies with respect to the public purposes of high levels of employment and price stability.[215] Thus the dual labor market theory would appear to have met the test for theory forwarded by Wesley Clair Mitchell in the opening sentence of this article.

At the same time, it is apparent that in Piore's hands the dual labor market theory has been employed as a tool for institutional impact analysis almost entirely in regard to macro-economic phenomena, that is, with respect to outcomes reflecting the aggregate of many individual markets or industries. The preoccupation with aggregate phenomena is not accidental, for the dual labor market theory illustrates perfectly the quandary facing institutional economists who seek to do "applied institutional *micro*-economics" *within* the subdisciplines of economics (industrial organization, labor economics, public finance, and so on).

For what the foregoing analysis makes evident is that acceptance of the institutional standpoint necessitates an abandonment of the notion that there is a generalizable microeconomic logic (price theory) upon which one can build an adequate model of price formation (wage determination) or resource allocation (job allocation). Acceptance of the institutional standpoint, in other words, means that the economist can have no hope of assembling an analytical tool kit that can be taken with him/her when shifting attention from the study of one industry or market to the study of another. In fact, since pattern models must be continually adjusted to match the structure of an ever-evolving reality, the development and maintenance of a truly valid pattern model pertaining to a specific domain of microeconomic phenomena probably require that the microeconomist spend his/her entire career focused on a single industry or market, or at most a few.[216]

Particularly troubling is the fact that only someone who has similarly devoted enormous energy to the analysis of the same industry or market will be fit to judge whether an articulated microeconomic pattern model is in fact valid. One has to wonder if such a reality is compatible with the maintenance, as a going concern, of a university-based, professionalized discipline.[217] It may soon be that institutional microeconomists capable of participating in microeconomic institutional impact analysis will be found only outside academe. Given current realities, they are certain to be located outside of economics departments.

Notes

1. The author would like to thank Marc Tool and Ric McIntyre for helpful comments on an earlier draft. He also wants to thank Benjamin Ward for the guidance and encouragement without which the foundation for this chapter would never have been laid.

2. This dictum was passed on to me by one of Mitchell's students, a man who was in many ways the inspiration for my own "dissent" from mainstream economics, the late labor economist and historian, Charles A. Gulick.

3. The term *market economy*, or alternatively the *market system*, is used here to connote an economic system in which the production and distribution of needed or wanted things is effected, in the main, through voluntary exchanges (contracts) between self-interested, gain-seeking parties or their agents.

4. Throughout this essay the term *theory* is used to connote a coherent group of general propositions used as a principle of explanation for a class of phenomena. The term *model* is used in reference to a simplified representation of the structure/process through which a system produces specific observed phenomena. I am borrowing the term *institutional impact analysis* from A. Allan Schmid, who in turn attributes it, along with a companion term, *institutional development analysis*, to a dichotomy forwarded by Frederic C. Pryor. See A. Allan Schmid, *Property, Power & Public Choice: An Inquiry into Law and Economics*, 2nd ed. (New York: Praeger, 1987), p. xv. note 1.

5. For various overviews of the intellectual orientation reflected in dissident labor economics, see Bruce E. Kaufman, "The Postwar View of Labor Markets and Wage Determination," in *How Labor Markets Work: Reflections on Theory and Practice by John Dunlop, Clark Kerr, Richard Lester, and Lloyd Reynolds* edited by Bruce E. Kaufman (Lexington,

MA: DC Heath and Company, 1988), pp. 145–203; Clark Kerr, *Labor Markets and Wage Determination: The Balkanization of Labor Markets and Other Essays* (Berkeley and Los Angeles: University of California Press, 1977); Paul J. McNulty, *The Origins and Development of Labor Economics: A Chapter in the History of Social Thought* (Cambridge: The MIT Press, 1980); and Martin Segal, "Post-Institutionalism in Labor Economics: The Forties and Fifties Revisited," *Industrial and Labor Relations Review* 39 (April 1986): 388–403.

6. By "labor economist" I refer to a practitioner whose research is directed to the explanation of wage and employment outcomes.

7. This is not to deny the existence of isolated individuals who adhere to "institutional" precepts in explaining wage and employment outcomes. For an example, see Clair Brown, "Income Distribution in an Institutional World," in Garth Mangum and Peter Phillips, eds., *Three Worlds of Labor Economics* (Armonk, NY: M.E. Sharpe, 1988), pp. 51–63.

8. In this essay, the term *institutional economics* refers only to the "traditional" or "old" type of institutional economics; contributions to the "new" institutional economics—see Richard N. Langlois, "The New Institutional Economics: An Introductory Essay," in Richard N. Langlois, ed., *Economics as a Process: Essays in the New Institutional Economics* (Cambridge: Cambridge University Press, 1986), pp. 1–25, for an overview—are thus excluded. See the various contributions to the *Journal of Economic Issues*, Volume 21, Numbers 3 and 4 (September and December 1987), for a collection of excellent essays pertaining to the character and practice of the old type of institutional economics. By "mainstream" institutional economists, I refer to 1) those who regularly publish in contemporary institutional journals, especially the *Journal of Economic Issues*, and who regularly attend the annual meeting of institutionalist associations such as the Association for Evolutionary Economics and the Association for Institutional Thought and 2) those to whom numerous members of the first group trace their intellectual antecedents, such as, for example, Thorstein Veblen, John R. Commons, Clarence Ayres, Karl Polanyi, and J. Fagg Foster. All subsequent references to institutional economists refer to these individuals, just as all subsequent references to institutional economics refer to their published writings.

9. Marc R. Tool, "The Compulsive Shift to Institutional Analysis," *Journal of Economic Issues* 15 (September 1981): 569–592.

10. C. Brown, "Income Distribution in an Institutional World," is a partial exception.

11. The meaning being attached to the term *general theory* will be developed below.

12. For various attempts to characterize the central features of the institutional approach, see the sources cited in Yngve Ramstad, "'Reasonable Value' Versus 'Instrumental Value:' Competing Paradigms in Institutional Economics," *Journal of Economic Issues* 23 (September 1989): 761–777.

13. Clarence E. Ayres, *The Theory of Economic Progress*, 2nd ed. (New York: Schocken Books, 1962), p. xii; Allan G. Gruchy, *The Reconstruction of Economics: An Analysis of the Fundamentals of Institutional Economics* (Westport, CT: Greenwood Press, 1987), ch. 1.

14. Again, the reference here is to theory useful for institutional impact analysis.

15. See Yngve Ramstad, "The Institutionalism of John R. Commons: Theoretical Foundations of a Volitional Economics," in Warren J. Samuels, ed., *Research in the History of Economic Thought and Methodology*, Vol. 8 (Greenwich: JAI Press, Inc., 1990), pp. 53–104, for an overview of Commons's "volitional" conception of economic activity; and Yngve Ramstad, "Free Trade versus Fair Trade: Import Barriers as a Problem of Reasonable Value," *Journal of Economic Issues* 21 (March 1987): 5–32, for an overview of Commons's "citizenship theory of labor." For complementary explanations as to why Commons had such a difficult time communicating his views to others, see Jeff Biddle, "The Ideas of the Past as Tools for the Present: The Instrumental Presentism of John R. Commons," in JoAnne Brown

and David van Keuren, eds., *The Estate of Social Knowledge* (Baltimore: Johns Hopkins University Press, 1991), pp. 84–105; and Yngve Ramstad, "A Pragmatist's Quest for Holistic Knowledge: The Scientific Methodology of John R. Commons," *Journal of Economic Issues* 20 (December 1986): 1067–1105.

16. See, for example, the general neglect of Commons's substantive theoretical propositions in the "Foundations of Institutional Thought" volume published by the *Journal of Economic Issues* in September 1987 (Vol. 21, No. 3). It ought perhaps to be noted that the same point can be made regarding the contributions of Walton Hamilton, who also deserves to be classified as a "founder" of institutional economics. See in particular Walton Hamilton and Stacy May, *The Control of Wages*, reprint edition (New York: Augustus M. Kelley, Publishers, 1968), where an institutional theory of wages is articulated.

17. The important partial exception is the scattered theoretical insights of William Dugger; Ramstad, "Free Trade versus Fair Trade," might also be considered an exception. For various perspectives on "instrumental valuing," see Wendell Gordon, *Institutional Economics: The Changing System* (Austin and London: University of Texas Press, 1980); Wendell Gordon and John Adams, *Economics as Social Science: An Evolutionary Approach* (Riverdale, MD: The Riverdale Company, 1989); and Walter C. Neale, "Language and Economics," *Journal of Economic Issues* 16 (June 1982): 355–369; and "Institutions," *Journal of Economic Issues* 21 (September 1987): 1177–1206. Excellent discussions of "instrumental value theory" are provided in Paul D. Bush, "An Exploration of the Structural Characteristics of a Veblen–Ayres–Foster Defined Institutional Domain," *Journal of Economic Issues* 17 (March 1983): 35–66; and "The Theory of Institutional Change," *Journal of Economic Issues* 21 (September 1987): 1075–1116; Steven Hickerson, "Instrumental Valuation: The Normative Compass of Institutional Economics," *Journal of Economic Issues* (September 1987): 1117–1143; Marc R. Tool, *Essays in Social Value Theory: A Neoinstitutionalist Contribution* (Armonk, NY: M.E. Sharpe, 1986); and William T. Waller, Jr., "The Evolution of the Veblenian Dichotomy: Veblen, Hamilton, Ayres and Foster," *Journal of Economic Issues* 16 (September 1982): 757–771. I should perhaps make explicit my own belief that no valid inferences can be made about aggregate phenomena in the absence of an accurate conception of "micro-economic" processes.

18. Peter Gottschalk, "A Synthesis of Contour and Flexible Wage Hypotheses," *Journal of Economic Issues* 15 (September 1981): 629–640; Irvin Sobel, "Human Capital and Institutional Theories of the Labor Market: Rivals or Complements?" *Journal of Economic Issues* 16 (March 1982): 255–272; and Stephen A. Woodbury, "Power in the Labor Market," *Journal of Economic Issues* 21 (December 1987): 1781–1807.

19. Marvin E. Rozen, "Segmented Work and Divided Workers: A Review Article," *Journal of Economic Issues* 17 (March 1983): 215–224; and "Labor Markets, Wage Policy, and Macroeconomic Equilibrium: A Review of Annable's *The Price of Industrial Labor*," *Journal of Economic Issues* 19 (March 1985): 153–174.

20. Bennett Harrison and Andrew Sun, "The Theory of 'Dual' or Segmented Labor Markets," *Journal of Economic Issues* 13 (September 1979): 687–706; Stephen A. Woodbury, "Methodological Controversies in Labor Economics," *Journal of Economic Issues* 13 (December 1979): 933–955; Gregory C. Weeks, "Labor Markets, Class Interests, and the Technology of Production," *Journal of Economic Issues* 14 (June 1980): 553–556; Robert N. Horn, "A Case Study of the Dual Labor Market Hypothesis," *Journal of Economic Issues* 14 (June 1980): 615–630; Robert Cherry, "What Is So Natural about the Natural Rate of Unemployment?" *Journal of Economic Issues* 15 (September 1981): 729–743; and Michael J. Carter, "Competition and Segmentation in Internal Labor Markets," *Journal of Economic Issues* 16 (December 1982): 1063–1077.

21 Daphne Greenwood, "Determining Comparable Worth," *Journal of Economic Issues* 18 (June 1984): 457–464.

22. Yngve Ramstad, "Institutional Economics: How Prevalent in the Labor Literature?" *Journal of Economic Issues* 15 (June 1981): 339–350.

23. Ramstad, "Free Trade versus Fair Trade."

24. William M. Dugger, "The Administered Labor Market: An Institutionalist Analysis," *Journal of Economic Issues* 15 (June 1981): 397–407.

25. *Cf.* William M. Dugger, *An Alternative to Economic Retrenchment* (New York and Princeton: Petrocelli Books, 1984); W. Gordon, *Institutional Economics*; Gruchy, *The Reconstruction of Economics*; Wallace C. Peterson, *Our Overloaded Economy: Inflation, Unemployment, and the Crisis in American Capitalism* (Armonk, NY: M.E. Sharpe, 1982); J. Ron Stanfield, *Economic Thought and Social Change* (Carbondale and Edwardsville, IL: Southern Illinois University Press, 1979); and Marc R. Tool, *The Discretionary Economy: A Normative Theory of Political Economy* (Santa Monica, CA: Goodyear Publishing Company, 1979).

26. A review of articles published during the 1980s in the *American Journal of Economics and Sociology*, another outlet for institutional writers, produced results that only reinforce this conclusion. A review of articles published during the 1980s in *Industrial Relations*, which among the labor journals is perhaps most receptive to a diversity of views regarding the nature of labor markets, similarly failed to provide evidence that mainstream institutional economics has produced a coherent alternative conception of the labor market. However, see Martin Brown and Peter Phillips, "The Decline of Piece Rates in California Canneries: 1890–1960," *Industrial Relations* 25 (Winter 1986): 81–91, for a recent article in *Industrial Relations* by nonmainstream labor economists in which an explicitly institutional model of labor market processes is employed.

27. Thomas Kuhn, *The Structure of Scientific Revolutions*, 2nd ed. (Chicago: University of Chicago Press, 1970); Imre Lakatos, "Falsification and the Methodology of Scientific Research Programmes," in Imre Lakatos and Alan Musgrave, eds., *Criticism and the Growth of Knowledge* (New York: Cambridge University Press, 1970), pp. 91–196. For an overview of Lakatos's framework, see Mark Blaug, *The Methodology of Economics* (New York: Cambridge University Press, 1980), pp. 34–44; or Bruce Caldwell, *Beyond Positivism: Economic Methodology in the Twentieth Century* (London: George Allen & Unwin, 1982), pp. 85–89.

28. Ramstad, "'Reasonable Value' versus 'Instrumental Value.'"

29. Clarence E. Ayres, "The Legacy of Thorstein Veblen," in *Institutional Economics: Veblen, Commons and Mitchell Reconsidered* (Berkeley and Los Angeles: University of California Press, 1964), p. 55.

30. Clarence E. Ayres, "A New Look at Institutionalism—Comment," *American Economic Review, Proceedings* 41 (May 1957): 26, emphasis added.

31. J. Fagg Foster, "The Relation Between the Theory of Value and Economic Analysis," *Journal of Economic Issues* 15 (December 1981): 900.

32. Institutionalists have long noted that written rules often make formal implicit rules of long standing. For example, in an extremely interesting and meticulously documented study, Benjamin M. Selekman and Sylvia K. Selekman, "Productivity—And Labor Relations," *Harvard Business Review* 27 (May 1949): 373–392, demonstrate conclusively that "featherbedding" has a long history, predating "restrictive union work rules" by centuries.

33. Sanctions are of three fundamental types: 1) the moral sanction of disapproval from those whose approval is desired, 2) the economic sanction of poverty or bankruptcy, and 3) the physical sanction of violence. See John R. Commons, *Institutional Economics*, reprint edition (Madison: The University of Wisconsin Press, 1961), pp. 77–78.

34. *Social role* is a principal organizing concept in the sociological theory of symbolic interaction developed by George Herbert Mead. Within Mead's framework, a "role" is a distinctive way of behaving associated with a specific status or position. For an extended discussion, see Robert A. Nisbet, *The Social Bond: An Introduction to the Study of Society* (New York: Alfred A. Knopf, 1970), especially pp. 148–156.

35. For an excellent overview, see Neale, "Institutions." The classic discussion is Walton Hamilton, "Institution," in *Encyclopaedia of the Social Sciences*, vol. 8, edited by Edwin R. A. Seligman (New York: The Macmillan Company), pp. 84–89. Benjamin Ward, "Institutions and Economic Analysis," in Roy Krupp, ed., *The Structure of Economic Science* (Englewood Cliffs, NJ: Prentice-Hall, Inc., 1966), pp. 184–200, also provides an interesting overview. It should perhaps be noted that critics of institutional economics have repeatedly argued that when used as an analytical category, the meaning of institution is very difficult to tie down. See, for example, E.H. Burns, "Does Institutionalism Complement or Compete with 'Orthodox' Economics?" *American Economic Review* 21 (March 1931): 86; Abram L. Harris, "Types of Institutionalism," *Journal of Political Economy* 40 (December 1932): 732; Talcott Parsons, "Sociological Elements in Economic Thought," in Harry Elmer Barnes et al., eds., *Contemporary Social Theory* (New York: D. Appleton-Century Company, 1940), p. 643; and Louis Schneider, *The Freudian Psychology and Veblen's Social Theory* (New York: King's Crown Press, 1948), pp. 81–85. Certainly, it cannot be denied that institution has been defined by self-avowed institutionalists in a number of ways. Whatever the specific definition, however, careful examination will reveal it to embody the same meaning: rules revealed in conduct.

36. W. Hamilton, "Institution," p. 84.

37. Commons, *Institutional Economics*, p. 69.

38. I am here using Commons's framework to organize the discussion. See *ibid.*, pp. 77ff.

39. Albert O. Hirschman, *Exit, Voice and Loyalty: Responses to Decline in Firms, Organizations, and States* (Cambridge: Harvard University Press, 1970).

40. Commons, *Institutional Economics*, p. 226.

41. See Commons, *Institutional Economics*, p. 703. Also *cf.* W. Hamilton, "Institution," and David Hamilton, *Evolutionary Economics: A Study of Change in Economic Thought* (Albuquerque: University of New Mexico Press, 1970), ch. 3.

42. Radhakamal Mukerjee, *The Institutional Theory of Economics* (London: Macmillan & Co., Ltd., 1940), pp. 15, 199–200.

43. Commons, *Institutional Economics*, p. 699.

44. Kenneth E. Boulding, "Toward the Development of a Cultural Economics," in Louis Schneider and Charles Bonjean, eds., *The Idea of Culture in the Social Sciences* (New York: Cambridge University Press), p. 47; Charles M.A. Clark, "Equilibrium for What? Reflections on Social Order in Economics," *Journal of Economic Issues* 23 (June 1989): 599ff; Maurice Dobb, *Theories of Value and Distribution Since Adam Smith: Ideology and Economic Theory* (Cambridge: Cambridge University Press, 1973), p. 38.

45. Economists have generally forgotten that the "invisible hand" was Adam Smith's way of bringing a deistic natural law into economics. On this point, see Charles M.A. Clark, "Adam Smith and Natural Law," paper presented to the History of Economics Society (June 1988). While the deistic overtones have long since been stripped from the concept, the natural law implications have not. See Neale, "Language and Economics," pp. 355–356, or Kurt Dopfer, "Causality and Consciousness in Economics: Concepts of Change in Orthodox and Heterodox Economics," *Journal of Economic Issues* 20 (June 1986): 509–523.

46. W. Hamilton, "Institution," pp. 84–89. The term *coercive surveillance* was used by Veblen in a critical swipe at the putative influence of natural law over the course of economic

events. See Thorstein Veblen, *The Place of Science in Modern Civilization and Other Essays* (New York: B.W. Heubsch, 1919), p. 61.

47. Warren J. Samuels, "On the Nature and Existence of Economic Coercion: The Correspondence of Robert Lee Hale and Thomas Nixon Carver," *Journal of Economic Issues* 18 (December 1984): 1027–1048. Also see John S. Gambs, *Beyond Supply and Demand: A Reappraisal of Institutional Economics* (Morningside Heights, NY: Columbia University Press, 1946), p. 11; and John R. Commons, *A Sociological View of Sovereignty*, reprint edition (New York: Augustus M. Kelley Publishers, 1964), p. 62.

48. Neale, "Language and Economics" and "Institutions."

49. For an excellent overview of "spontaneous" institutional change, see Robert Sugden, "Spontaneous Order," *Journal of Economic Perspectives* 3 (Fall 1989): 85–97. In his analysis, Sugden emphasizes that, since individual values evolve *pari passu* with new practices, it will generally be the case that others will *not* imitate deviant individuals, especially in those cases where established practices have an important bearing on individual real income attainments. It is of course a central insight of the instrumental value theory school of institutional economists that ceremonial institutions are generally what inhibit the adoption of new practices. See Bush, "The Theory of Institutional Change."

50. Commons always traced the development of market institutions in the Anglo-American experience back to the year 1066 and the conquest of William the Conqueror. It was one of Commons's central points that within the Anglo-American tradition all individual rights and empowerments were, in the formal sense, rights and powers *taken from* the king. In other words, from Commons's point of view, "Property is sovereignty taken from the king" (John R. Commons, *Legal Foundations of Capitalism* [New York: The Macmillan Company, 1924], p. 221).

51. See Ramstad, "The Institutionalism of John R. Commons," for a more extended discussion of this issue. It should not be forgotten that a corporation is a legal entity created by the state in which the "owner(s)" is authorized to determine intra-concern rules except as proscribed by law (as, for example, with respect to health and safety). For reasons already indicated, it should be apparent that in determining what rules to adopt, authoritative figures ("owners") generally act in ways that are consistent with the "habitual assumptions" ("institutions") through which their mental impulses obtain content.

52. Philip A. Klein, "Power and Economic Performance: The Institutionalist View," *Journal of Economic Issues* 21 (September 1987): 1341–1377; Marc R. Tool and Warren J. Samuels, eds., *The Economy as a System of Power*, 2nd rev. ed. (New Brunswick: Transaction Books, 1988).

53. In using the term *instrumental valuing*, I am adopting the usage forwarded by Walter N. Neale, namely, "the proposition that valuing emerges in the process of trying to solve problems, in contrast to such other putative sources as intuition (conscience), revelation, or unanalyzable tastes" (Neale, "Institutions," p. 1197). It should be added that there is at present considerable debate among institutionalists as to whether the evolution of economic institutions manifests an inherent dynamic toward "instrumentally warranted" (nonsubjectively legitimated) values. For the strongest argument that there is, see Tool, *Essays in Social Value Theory*. For an opposing view, see Warren J. Samuels, "The Self-Referentiability of Thorstein Veblen's Theory of the Preconceptions of Economic Science," *Journal of Economic Issues* 24 (September 1990): 695–718.

54. For various views of institutional economists regarding the nature of human action, see Thorstein Veblen, "Why Is Economics Not An Evolutionary Science?" *Quarterly Journal of Economics* 12 (July 1898): 373–397; Wesley C. Mitchell, "The Rationality of Economic Activity, I," *Journal of Political Economy* 18 (February 1910): 97–113; and "Human Behavior

and Economics: A Survey of Recent Literature," *Quarterly Journal of Economics* (November 1914): 1–47; John Maurice Clark, "Economics and Modern Psychology," *Journal of Political Economy* 26 (January, February 1918): 1–30, 136–166; Walton Hamilton, "The Institutional Approach to Economic Theory," *American Economic Review* 9 (Supplement 1919): 309–318; Commons, *Institutional Economics*; Clarence E. Ayres, "Fifty Years' Developments in Ideas of Human Nature and Motivation," *American Economic Review* 26 (Supplement 1936): 224–236; Karl Polanyi, in George Dalton, ed., *Primitive, Archaic and Modern Economies* (Boston: Beacon Press, 1968); Tool, *The Discretionary Economy*; W. Gordon, *Institutional Economics*; and Geoffrey M. Hodgson, *Economics and Institutions: A Manifesto for a Modern Institutional Economics* (Philadelphia: University of Pennsylvania Press, 1988).

55. See, for example, Commons, *Institutional Economics*, p. 725, on marginal utility.

56. Whether hedonism, as a psychological thesis, is in fact implicit in the neoclassical framework is a disputed point. For example, see James Griffen and Derek Parfit, "Hedonism," in John Eatwell, Murray Milgate, and Peter Newman, eds., *The New Palgrave: A Dictionary of Economics*, Vol. 2 (London, New York, and Tokyo: The Macmillan Press, Limited, 1987), pp. 634–635. Whether it is or not makes little difference to the themes I am developing.

57. Veblen, "Why Is Economics Not An Evolutionary Science?"

58. Cf. Hodgson, *Economics and Institutions*, ch. 11.

59. See, for example, Commons, *Institutional Economics*, p. 97; Clarence E. Ayres, "The Co-ordinates of Institutionalism," *American Economic Review, Proceedings* 41 (June 1951): 44–49. Also *cf.* Gambs, *Beyond Supply and Demand*, ch. 2; D. Hamilton, *Evolutionary Economics*, ch. 3; W. Hamilton, "The Institutional Approach to Economic Theory," p. 316; and K.W. Kapp, "In Defense of Institutional Economics," *Swedish Journal of Economics* 70 (1968): 2.

60. Cf. Gambs, *Beyond Supply and Demand*, p. 49; W. Gordon, *Institutional Economics*, p. 104; and Robert F. Hoxie, *Trade Unionism in the United States* (New York: D. Appleton and Company, 1917), p. 369.

61. Commons, *Institutional Economics*, p. 682.

62. Cf. Veblen, *The Place of Science*, pp. 239–240; Mitchell, "The Rationality of Economic Activity," pp. 210–212; Polanyi, *Primitive, Archaic and Modern Economies*, pp. 63–64.

63. See Hans Jensen, "The [Institutional] Theory of Human Nature," *Journal of Economic Issues* 21 (September 1987): 1039–1073, for an illustration of the impossibility of circumscribing *the* institutional interpretation.

64. For example, see Veblen, *The Place of Science*, pp. 73, 239, versus Veblen *ibid.*, p. 156.

65. Cf. W. Gordon, *Institutional Economics*, p. 19; Allan G. Gruchy, *Modern Economic Thought: The American Contribution* (New York: Prentice-Hall, 1947), pp. 56, 564. Neoclassical economists will no doubt acknowledge that much behavior is habitual. However, given the neoclassical concept of man, such behavior is interpreted to be just another rational adjustment to constraints, that is, to be the product of a "rational" endeavor to economize in the use of one's limited decision-making capabilities (A.P. Barten, "Trends in the Analysis of Consumer Demand," in T.J. Kastelein et al., eds., *25 Years of Economic Theory* (Leider, The Netherlands: H.E. Steufert Kroese, 1976), p. 17). Institutionalists clearly cast the role of habit in a fundamentally different mold.

66. For an excellent discussion of the social roots of individual perception and "preferences," see Geoffrey M. Hodgson, "The Rationalist Conception of Action," *Journal of Economic Issues* 19 (December 1985): 825–851. Also see Mukerjee, *The Institutional Theory of Economics*, ch. 6.

67. See Neale, "Institutions," p. 1188, for the argument that institutional theory can actually dispense with the issue of what it is that motivates individual economic actors.

68. Thorstein Veblen, *The Theory of the Leisure Class: An Economic Study of Institutions* (New York: B.W. Huebsch, 1899).

69. Polanyi, *Primitive, Archaic and Modern Economies*, p. 65.

70. Edyth S. Miller, "Institutional Economics: Philosophy, Methodology and Theory," *Social Science Journal* 15 (January 1978): 15. In addition to Veblen, Ayres, *The Theory of Economic Progress*, ch. 8, and Mukerjee, *The Institutional Theory*, ch. 6, have emphasized the other-directed nature of human motivation. David Hamilton, *The Consumer in Our Economy* (New York: Hougton Mifflin, 1962), has developed an explicitly other-oriented theory of consumption behavior. Even though Commons never focused on this dimension of individual behavior, he did state explicitly that he agreed with Veblen's critique of "the faulty conception of human nature embraced by the Austrian economists." See Commons, *Institutional Economics*, p. 656.

71. For a careful analysis, from a noninstitutional standpoint, showing that economic behavior is infused with "irrational" behavior (behavior that does not advance the objective interests of the actor), see Jon Elster, "Social Norms and Economic Theory," *Journal of Economic Perspectives* 3 (Fall 1989): 99–117.

72. Mukerjee, *The Institutional Theory*, p. 159; Milton Lower, "The Evolution of the Institutionalist Theory of Consumption," in John Adams, ed., *Institutional Economics: Essays in Honor of Allan G. Gruchy* (Boston: Martin Nihjoff Publishing, 1980).

73. Veblen, *The Place of Science*, p. 77; Neale, "Institutions," p. 1187.

74. Mukerjee, *The Institutional Theory*, ch. 6.

75. See, in particular, Tool, *Essays in Social Value Theory*, pp. 58–60. See Philip Mirowski, *Against Mechanism: Protecting Economics from Science* (Totowa, NJ: Rowman & Littlefield, Publishers, 1988), ch. 2, for the argument that it was the infelicitous transfer to economics of the energetics framework developed by 18th century physicists that necessitated this assumption, just as it did the assumptions of perfect competition.

76. Wendell Gordon, *Institutional Economics*, p. 43, has referred to this as a process of "self-correcting value judgment."

77. For a discussion of instrumental valuing, see Anne Mayhew, "The Beginnings of Institutionalism," *Journal of Economic Issues* 21 (September 1987): 977–978; Neale, "Language and Economics," pp. 364–336; Neale, "Institutions," pp. 1197–1198; or Gordon and Adams, *Economics as Social Science*, pp. 87–89.

78. For an attempt to transcend the whole problem of subjectivity in identifying "good" ends/values, see Tool, *Essays in Social Value Theory*, chs. 2 and 3.

79. *Cf.* J.M. Clark, "Economic Theory in an Era of Readjustment," *American Economic Review* 9 (Supplement 1919): 289; Commons, *Institutional Economics*, pp. 697–719, especially pp. 702 and 703; John R. Commons, *The Economics of Collective Action* (New York: The Macmillan Company, 1950), pp. 150–153; Mukerjee, *The Institutional Theory*, pp. 8, 58, 80, 125, 155, 455; and Veblen, *The Place of Science*, pp. 242–243; also see Gambs, *Beyond Supply and Demand*, p. 38; Gruchy, *Modern Economic Thought*, pp. 3, 19; D. Hamilton, *Evolutionary Economics*, p. 54; Kapp, "In Defense of Institutional Economics," p. 3; Miller, "Institutional Economics," p. 15; K.P. Saxena, "Views of the Institutional Economists on the Nature and Scope of Economics," *Indian Economic Journal* 15 (1968): 625; and Edwin E. Witte, "Institutional Economics as Seen by an Institutional Economist," *Southern Economic Journal* 21 (October 1954): 136.

80. This orientation is often labeled "holist." *Cf.* D.C. Phillips, *Holistic Thought in Social Science* (Stanford: Stanford University Press, 1976), or W.H. Dray, "Holism and Individualism in History and Social Science," in Paul Edwards, ed., *The Encyclopedia of Philosophy*, Vol. 4 (New York: The Macmillan Company and The Free Press, 1967). The term "holism"

has taken on a somewhat different meaning in the institutionalist literature; *cf.* Charles K. Wilber and Robert S. Harrison, "The Methodological Basis of Institutional Economics: Pattern Model, Storytelling, and Holism," *Journal of Economic Issues* 12 (March 1978): 61–90; Ramstad, "A Pragmatist's Quest for Holistic Knowledge;" F. Gregory Hayden, "Social Fabric Matrix: From Perspective to Analytical Tool," *Journal of Economic Issues* 16 (September 1982): 637–662; and F. Gregory Hayden, "Integration of Social Indicators into Holistic Geobased Models," *Journal of Economic Issues* 17 (June 1983): 325–334.

81. Gunnar Myrdal, *An American Dilemma: The Negro Problem and Modern Democracy*, 2 vols. (New York: Pantheon Books, 1944), Appendix 5; also *cf.* Paul D. Bush, "'Radical Individualism' vs. Institutionalism, II," *American Journal of Economics and Sociology* 40 (July 1981): 289–291; Dopfer, "Causality and Consciousness in Economics;" Robert A. Gordon, "Institutional Elements in Contemporary Economics," in *Institutional Economics: Veblen, Commons and Mitchell Reconsidered* (Berkeley and Los Angeles: University of California Press, 1964), p. 124; D. Hamilton, *Evolutionary Economics*, p. 56; Kapp, "In Defense of Institutional Economics," p. 8; Philip A. Klein, "Demand Theory and the Economist's Propensity to Assume," *Journal of Economic Issues* 7 (June 1973): 213; Miller, "Institutional Economics," p. 15; and Tool, *The Discretionary Economy*, p. 52.

82. Malcolm Rutherford, "Introduction to the Transaction Edition," in John R. Commons, *Institutional Economics: Its Place in Political Economy*, reprint edition (New Brunswick: Transaction Books, 1990), p. xxii, has suggested that "institutional individualism," a term coined by Joseph Agassi, properly characterizes Common's conception of individual action. Since Commons's conception of individual action is fully consistent with the schema under discussion, the term would appear equally apt with respect to the institutional standpoint in general.

83. Walton Hamilton, "Charles Horton Cooley," *Social Forces* 8 (December 1929): 185.

84. Mayhew, "The Beginnings of Institutionalism," pp. 973ff.

85. Walton Hamilton, *Industrial Policy and Institutionalism*, reprint edition (New York: Augustus M. Kelley Publishers, 1974), pp. 8–9.

86. Ayres, "Fifty Years' Developments," p. 235; Clarence E. Ayres, "The Co-ordinates of Institutionalism," *American Economic Review, Proceedings* 41 (June 1951): 49.

87. Tool, *The Discretionary Economy*, pp. 41, 52–53. To so maintain, to repeat, is not to deny that individuals and groups engage in "instrumental valuing," that is, assess whether or not the means selected have in fact facilitated the ends pursued or even whether, once attained, the ends are worth pursuing.

88. Jensen, "The Theory of Human Nature," p. 1069; also *cf.* Gruchy, *The Reconstruction of Economics*, p. 3.

89. Mukerjee, *The Institutional Theory*, p. 151. For his full discussion of this issue, see Mukerjee, *The Institutional Theory*, Chap. 6. Also see Gruchy, *Modern Economic Thought*, p. 19, and Hodgson, "The Rationalist Conception of Action." Some writers—see, for example, Ayres, "The Co-ordinates of Institutional Economics," and D. Hamilton, *Evolutionary Economics*—use the word "behaviorism" rather than "social psychology" in reference to the fact that consciousness and individual "will" are essentially socially produced and hence that "human nature" is malleable. Given the analysis developed below, it should perhaps be added that the social origins of individual consciousness and aspirations are also emphasized in modern cognitive theory. For sources, see the bibliography in Hodgson, "The Rationalist Conception of Action."

90. "What is the [institutionalist's] response to the question of 'free will versus determinism?' 'I'll take a little of both, thank you'" (Bush, "'Radical Individualism' vs. Institutionalism," p. 289).

91. Philosophers have noted that the assumption of utility maximization in the context of fixed tastes in effect removes free will—the power to not maximize or to alter one's "preferences"—from the neoclassical "theory of action." See Brian J. Loasby, *Choice, Complexity and Ignorance: An Enquiry into Economic Theory and Practice of Decision Making* (Cambridge: Cambridge University Press, 1976), p. 5.

92. See Samuels, "On the Nature and Existence of Economic Coercion."

93. Ramstad, "The Institutionalism of John R. Commons."

94. Functional here refers to the fact that individuals, as wills, come to internalize attitudes appropriate to their particular place (role or "function") in a culture. See Ayres, "The Co-ordinates of Institutional Economics," and Gambs, *Beyond Supply and Demand*, ch. 2.

95. George Dalton, "Introduction," in George Dalton, ed., *Primitive, Archaic, and Modern Economies: Essays of Karl Polanyi* (Boston: Beacon Press, 1968), p. xxxi.

96. This was the practice that led Veblen to classify orthodox economic analysis as being "taxonomic" in nature, a practice he vigorously rejected as "unscientific" (Veblen, "Why Is Economics Not An Evolutionary Science?"). On the refusal of institutionalists to grant relevance to the notional world implicit in the neoclassical approach, see D. Hamilton, *Evolutionary Economics*, ch. 2. It should also be noted that absent a commitment to methodological individualism, "allocative efficiency"—the equality of market prices with their "natural" or "normal" configuration—is stripped completely of significance as a normative criterion. On this point, see Frank H. Knight, "The Ethics of Competition," in Frank H. Knight, *The Ethics of Competition and Other Essays* (New York: Harper & Brothers, 1932), pp. 49–51.

97. For an outstanding explication of the almost infinite number of ways in which both costs of production and income shares in a "market system" are dependent on the rules selected, see Schmid, *Property, Power, & Public Choice*. Also see P.S. Attiya, *The Sale of Goods*, 4th ed. (London: Pitman Publishing, 1971), and Daniel W. Bromley, *Economic Interests & Institutions: The Conceptual Foundations of Public Policy* (New York: Basil Blackwell Inc., 1989), for discussions that make clear how basic rules are to the market mechanism.

98. For more on this often-neglected point, see Robert Brady, *Organization, Automation, and Society: The Scientific Revolution in Industry* (Berkeley and Los Angeles: University of California Press, 1961), pp. 21ff. That costs of production are not natural phenomena, but the consequence of policy decisions regarding accounting practices, was established by John Maurice Clark, *Studies in the Economics of Overhead Costs* (Chicago: University of Chicago Press, 1923), in his analysis of *overhead cost*, a category that is much broader than usually recognized. This would equally appear to be the case respecting *direct costs* (that is, marginal costs) in the multiproduct firm.

99. "An *institution* is identified by three characteristics. First, there are a number of *people doing*. Second, there are *rules* giving the activities repetition, stability, predictable order. Third, there are *folkviews* . . . explaining or justifying the activities and the rules" (Neale, "Institutions," p. 1182).

100. This is a very important point, for a central element of the orthodox mindset is a belief in the possibility, indeed, the necessity, of developing *a* theory whose logic ("principles") can be applied across the economic landscape. By requiring of institutional economics that it also must provide such a theory in order to be considered as a viable alternative to neoclassical economics, mainstream economists in effect already have settled the issue of which theory is "superior" without considering a single substantive issue. This is exactly the approach Paul Samuelson, "Economic Theory and Wages," in David McCord Wright, ed., *The Impact of the Union* (New York: Kelly & Millman, 1951), p. 323, took in asserting, "In economics it takes a theory to kill a theory; facts can only dent the theorist's hide." For a similar defense of neoclassical economics, see Mark Blaug, *Economic Theory in Retrospect*, 3rd ed. (London: Heinemann, 1978), pp. 710–713.

101. Surprisingly, prominent mainstream institutionalists themselves have not always been

free of the misconception that institutional economics "complements" orthodoxy. See, in particular, Commons, *Institutional Economics*, p. 5, and *Economics of Collective Action*, p. 117; and Gruchy, *Modern Economic Thought*, p. 612, and *The Reconstruction of Economics* p. 23. But also see Gruchy, *The Reconstruction of Economics*, p. 36.

102. H.S. Parnes, "Labor Force Participation and Labor Mobility," in *A Review of Industrial Relations Research* (Madison, WI: Industrial Relations Research Association, 1970), p. 66.

103. The classic statement of the synthesis viewpoint is Fritz Karl Mann, "Institutionalism and American Economic Theory: A Case of Interpenetration," in Ingrid H. Rima, ed., *Readings in the History of Economic Theory* (New York: Holt, Rinehart and Winston, 1970). For recent examples, see Woodbury, "Power in the Labor Market," and Stephen L. Mangum, "Comparable Worth: The Institutional Economist's Approach," in *Three Worlds of Labor Economics*.

104. "Institutionalism represents—to institutionalists, at least—a revolutionary way of observing economic phenomena. It is not complementary to [neo]classical economics, merely completing the sociological aspects of an otherwise logically tight system. Nor does institutionalism present a body of maxims such as all the varieties of classical economics have done. Institutionalism and classicism stem from different backgrounds and have different antecedents; they are products of antithetical ways of thinking about economic behavior. Where classicism was developed out of eighteenth-century Newtonianism, institutionalism is a product of the Darwinian revolution of the nineteenth century" (D. Hamilton, *Evolutionary Economics*, p. 4).

105. This orientation explains the frequent assertion that institutionalists advocate the inductive approach to theory construction.

106. For an interesting discussion regarding the source of the misunderstanding, see Karl Pribham, "Prolegomena to a History of Economic Reasoning," *Quarterly Journal of Economics* 65 (February 1951): 1–37.

107. Cf. Gambs, *Beyond Supply and Demand*, p. 55; Gruchy, *Modern Economic Thought*, p. 3; and D. Hamilton, *Evolutionary Economics*, p. 55.

108. Recall the underlying presumption of *circular* causation. Group to individual causation is viewed as the more important relationship, but not as the only one.

109. Commons, *Legal Foundations of Capitalism*, p. 135.

110. Ayres, "Fifty Years' Developments," p. 233, emphasis added. Ayres juxtaposed this observation against the claim that for the orthodox theorist "the objective is not, as it has always been, the explanation of social order (price equilibrium) as an expression of human nature (wants and satisfaction) . . ." (*ibid.*, p. 235).

111. Nicholas Georgescu-Roegen, *The Entropy Law and the Economic Process* (Cambridge: Harvard University Press, 1971), pp. 14–15 and ch. 2.

112. Paul Diesing, *Patterns of Discovery in the Social Sciences* (Chicago: Aldine-Atherton, 1971), p. 224.

113. See Wilber and Harrison, "The Methodological Basis of Institutional Economics." With respect to Commons only, see Ramstad, "A Pragmatist's Quest for Holistic Knowledge."

114. For a creative and highly promising research program with a "positive heuristic" of developing "pattern models" in conformity with this institutional conception of explanation, see Hayden, "Social Fabric Matrix"; "Integration of Social Indicators"; "Defining and Articulating Social Change Through the Social Fabric Matrix and System Digraph," *Journal of Economic Issues* 20 (June 1986): 383–392; and "Values, Belief, and Attitudes in a Sociotechnical Setting," *Journal of Economic Issues* 22 (June 1988): 415–426.

115. Yngve Ramstad, "Institutional Existentialism: More on Why John R. Commons Has So Few Followers," *Journal of Economic Issues* 21 (June 1987): 661–671.

116. "A pattern model explains human behavior by carefully placing it in its institutional

and cultural context" (William M. Dugger, "Methodological Differences between Institutional and Neoclassical Economics," *Journal of Economic Issues* 13 [December 1979]: 900). Also see Wilber and Harrison, "The Methodological Basis of Institutional Economics."

117. Galbraith's "market system" versus "planning system" constitutes such a typology. See John K. Galbraith, *Economics and the Public Purpose* (Boston: Houghton Mifflin, 1973).

118. Perhaps the outstanding example of such a research program in institutional economics is the "instrumental value theory" developed out of Veblen's ceremonial–technological dichotomy. For by far the best explication of the logic of this approach, see Bush, "An Exploration of the Structural Characteristics" and "The Theory of Institutional Change."

119. Gary S. Becker, "Irrational Behavior and Economic Theory," *Journal of Political Economy* 70 (February 1962): 1–13.

120. *Cf.*, for example, Lower, "Evolution of the Institutionalist Theory of Consumption," p. 84; Mukerjee, *The Institutional Theory*, p. 155.

121. This would appear to be the approach taken by Mangum, "Comparable Worth."

122. On this point, see W. Gordon, *Institutional Economics*, pp. 99ff. The phrase, "economics without equilibrium" is actually Nicholas Kaldor's; see Kaldor, *Economics without Equilibrium* (Armonk, NY: M.E. Sharpe, 1985). While the phrase is felicitous, Kaldor's reference was not to institutional economics. In fact, Kaldor's work has never been associated with mainstream institutionalism (see note 8 above), and certainly one will not learn anything about the institutional approach from his writings. For a devastating technical critique of the manner in which the concept of equilibrium has been employed in economics, see Philip Mirowski, "The Rise and Fall of the Concept of Equilibrium in Economic Analysis," *Recherches Economiques de Louvain* 55 (December 1989): 447–468. For an interesting argument in support of the self-conscious development of a "nonequilibrium" approach, see C. Clark, "Equilibrium for What?"

123. W. Hamilton, "The Institutional Approach to Economic Theory," p. 309, emphasis added.

124. I am *not* considering in this essay the structure that institutional theories directed at the process of economic evolution itself must take. See Bush, "The Theory of Institutional Change," and Ramstad, "The Institutionalism of John R. Commons," for extended discussion of two quite different models of that process, both of which are clearly institutional according to the criteria developed here.

125. Neale, "Language and Economics."

126. David W. Pearce, ed., *The Dictionary of Modern Economics* (Cambridge: The MIT Press, 1983), p. 272.

127. Alfred Marshall, *Principles of Economics*, 8th ed. (London: Macmillan and Company, 1920), p. 270.

128. Charles O. Hardy, "Market," in Edwin R.A. Seligman, ed., *Encyclopaedia of the Social Sciences*, vol. 10 (New York: The Macmillan Company, 1933), p. 131.

129. Alan Gilpin, *Dictionary of Economic Terms* (London: Butterworths, 1973), p. 136. Surprisingly, *The New Palgrave: A Dictionary of Economics*, 4 vols., edited by John Eatwell, Murray Milgate, and Peter Newman (London, New York, and Tokyo: The Macmillan Press, Limited, 1987), contains no entry under the title "Market."

130. See, for example, Marshall's discussion of this problem. Or, for amusement, see the attempt to define a market in the typical introductory textbook.

131. For an extremely insightful and interesting discussion of the philosophical standpoint through which this conception of a market is legitimated, and why it cannot be accepted as legitimate by institutionalists, see Pribham, "Prolegomena."

132. Take, for example, Ayres's ringing challenge to orthodoxy on p. 179 above.

133. For examples, see William M. Dugger, "A Research Agenda For Institutional Economics," *Journal of Economic Issues* 22 (December 1988): 983–1002; Anne Mayhew, "The Sherman Act As Protective Reaction," *Journal of Economic Issues* 24 (June 1990): 389–396; and James A. Swaney, "Trading Water: Market Extension, Social Improvement, or What?" *Journal of Economic Issues* 22 (March 1988): 33–47.

134. Commons acknowledged that "comments and criticism by readers and students of both my *Legal Foundations of Capitalism* and the various mimeographed copies and revisions of [*Institutional Economics*]" revealed that they "could not understand my theories nor what I was driving at" (Commons, *Institutional Economics*, p. 1).

135. See, for example, Hodgson, *Economics and Institutions*, pp. 172–179.

136. See, for example, Bromley, *Economic Interests & Institutions.*

137. See Bush, "An Exploration of the Structural Characteristics" and "The Theory of Institutional Change," for dramatic evidence that this process has been admirably achieved with respect to the development of the instrumental value paradigm.

138. Cf. Eric Roll, *A History of Economic Thought*, 3rd ed. (Englewood Cliffs, NJ: Prentice Hall, 1953), p. 454; Joseph Schumpeter, *History of Economic Analysis* (New York: Oxford University Press, 1954), p. 954; and Benjamin Ward, "Organization and Comparative Economics: Some Approaches," in Alexander Eckstein ed., *Comparisons of Economic Systems: Theoretical and Methodological Approaches* (Berkeley and Los Angeles: University of California Press, 1971), pp. 105–106.

139. Paul J. McNulty, "Labor Market Analysis and the Development of Labor Economics," *Industrial and Labor Relations Review* 19 (July 1966): 538–548.

140. Kerr, *Labor Markets and Wage Determination*, p. 1.

141. Clark Kerr, "The Intellectual Role of the Neorealists in Labor Economics," *Industrial Relations* 22 (Spring 1983): 298.

142. For a systematic defense of this tripartite partitioning of postwar American labor economics, see Yngve Ramstad, "'Neoclassical Revisionism' or 'Neoinstitutionalism'? A Further Look at Labor Economics in the 1950s," Unpublished manuscript.

143. Clark Kerr, "The Neoclassical Revisionists in Labor Economics (1940–1960)—R.I.P.," in Kaufman, *How Labor Markets Work*, p. 13.

144. Ramstad, "'Neoclassical Revisionism' or 'Neoinstitutionalism'."

145. See John R. Hicks, *The Theory of Wages* (London: Macmillan and Company, 1932). Hicks later repudiated his early perspective and characterized *The Theory of Wages* as "a juvenile work" and "a thoroughly bad book." See John R. Hicks, *The Theory of Wages*, 2nd ed. (London: Macmillan and Company, 1963), pp. 310–311.

146. See George J. Stigler, "The Economics of Minimum Wage Legislation," *American Economic Review* (June 1946): 358–365.

147. See Simon Rottenberg, "On Choice in Labor Markets," *Industrial and Labor Relations Review* 9 (January 1956): 183–199.

148. John T. Dunlop, "Labor Markets and Wage Determination: Then and Now," in Kaufman, *How Labor Markets Work*, p. 49.

149. Cf. Rottenberg, "On Choice in Labor Markets."

150. John Corina, *Labour Market Economics: A Short Survey of Recent Theory* (London: Heinemann Educational Books, 1972), pp. 4–5.

151. See John T. Dunlop, "The Task of Contemporary Wage Theory," in John T. Dunlop, ed., *The Theory of Wage Determination* (London: Macmillan & Co., Ltd., 1957), pp. 3–27; Charles A. Myers, "Labour Market Theory and Empirical Research," in Dunlop, *The Theory of Wage Determination*, pp. 317–326; Albert Rees, "The Economic Impact of Collective Bargaining in the Steel and Coal Industries During the Postwar Period," in *Proceedings*

(Industrial Relations Research Association, 1950), pp. 203–212; and Melvin W. Reder, "Wage Determination in Theory and Practice," in Neil W. Chamberlain, ed., *A Decade of Industrial Relations Research* (New York: Harper and Brothers Publishers, 1958), pp. 64–97.

152. Dunlop, "The Task of Contemporary Wage Theory."

153. Reder, "Wage Determination in Theory and Practice." It should be noted that "wage contours," as a concept, is fully separable from the neoclassical framework; that is, its meaning remains the same when removed from the neoclassical-plus context in which it was first presented.

154. Dunlop, "The Task of Contemporary Wage Theory," p. 14. The reference to a political theory of wages is a pointed rejection of the theory forwarded by Arthur M. Ross, a prominent member of the neorealist group to be discussed next.

155. This is true whether or not, as Clark Kerr has insisted, members of this group were in "dialogue" with conventional theorists. See Kerr, "The Neoclassical Revisionists in Labor Economics," p. 13.

156. See Kerr, *Labor Markets and Wage Determination*; Arthur M. Ross, *Trade Union Wage Policy* (Berkeley and Los Angeles: University of California Press, 1948); Arthur M. Ross, "The State of Wage Theory—Discussion," in *Proceedings* (Industrial Relations Research Association, 1953), pp. 266–269; Richard A. Lester, "Shortcomings of Marginal Analysis for Wage-Employment Problems," *American Economic Review* 36 (March 1946): 63–82; Richard A. Lester, "The State of Wage Theory—Discussion," in *Proceedings* (Industrial Relations Research Association, 1953), 269–272.

157. Cf. Ross, *Trade Union Wage Policy*.

158. Cf. Clark Kerr, "Labor Markets: Their Character and Consequences," *American Economic Review, Supplement* 40 (May 1950): 278–291.

159. "Satisficers" are individuals who evaluate multidimensional alternatives solely on the basis of whether or not they are satisfactory along all dimensions without in any way attempting to "maximize," that is, optimally trade off more of this for less of that, with respect to any criterion. In particular, the search for additional information will end as soon as a "satisfactory" alternative has been identified. See Flemming Hansen, *Consumer Choice Behavior: A Cognitive Theory* (New York: The Free Press, 1972), p. 452.

160. See Kerr, *Labor Markets and Wage Determination*, for a collection of essays reflective of this standpoint.

161. See the selections in Michael J. Piore, ed., *Unemployment & Inflation: Institutionalist and Structuralist Views* (White Plains, NY: M.E. Sharpe, 1979).

162. Peter B. Doeringer and Michael J. Piore, *Internal Labor Markets and Manpower Analysis* (Lexington, MA: D.C. Heath and Company, 1971). This landmark work must be understood as an attempt to develop in much more careful fashion generalizations about labor markets originally outlined many years earlier by Clark Kerr in his landmark essay, "The Balkanization of Labor Markets" (included in Kerr, *Labor Markets and Wage Determination*). Significantly, Kerr is in my judgment the prototype neorealist (that is, institutional researcher). See Ramstad, "'Neoclassical Revisionist' or 'Neoinstitutionalist.'"

163. See, for example, Peter B. Doeringer, Phillip I. Moss, and David G. Terkla, "Capitalism and Kinship: Do Institutions Matter in the Labor Market," *Industrial and Labor Relations Review* 40 (October 1986): 48–60.

164. Doeringer and Piore were John T. Dunlop's students and did this work under his guidance. In "'Neoclassical Revisionist' or 'Neoinstitutionalist,'" I have, with some misgivings, associated Dunlop's work with the neoclassical-plus orientation. Certainly, Professors Dunlop and Rees would represent the opposite ends of the spectrum within this grouping.

165. My characterization of the dual labor market theory follows closely, indeed is but a

condensation of, that provided in Michael J. Piore, "Notes for a Theory of Labor Market Stratification," in Richard C. Edwards, Michael Reich, and David M. Gordon, eds., *Labor Market Segmentation* (Lexington, MA: D.C. Heath and Company, 1975), pp. 125–150. The reader familiar with the logic of the dual labor market theory may want to skip to the next section.

166. Michael J. Piore, "Introduction," in Piore, *Unemployment & Inflation*, p. xiii.

167. Since the not insignificant problems involved in integrating craft jobs into the dual labor market theory have no bearing on the present analysis, the existence of a separate category, "crafts," is ignored in the ensuing discussion. For an extended discussion of this matter, see Piore, "Notes."

168. *Ibid.*, p. 130.

169. They can also involve general tasks requiring obvious but nonroutine judgment. In other words, such firms may also have a need for trained craft workers or professionals. However, lacking intermediate positions, such upper-tier jobs will not be stations on an intrafirm career ladder. Rather, they will be stations on an upper-tier mobility chain with a single station located within a given firm.

170. Piore uses the term *instrumental* to connote decision-making where "decisions involve the selection of the most efficient means for the achievement of given ends" (Piore, "Introduction," p. xiii). Whereas orthodox economists assume all behavior is instrumental within this meaning, Piore "assumes [it] is true, *if at all*, only for professional and managerial workers" (*ibid.*, p. xiii, emphasis added). It must be remembered, however, that within mainstream institutional economics, the term *instrumental* is widely employed in reference to actions that are rooted in standards of judgment tied to the logic of "efficient cause." See Bush, "The Theory of Institutional Change," p. 1080.

171. Piore, "Introduction," p. xiii.

172. Again, see Piore, "Notes," for an overview.

173. *Cf.* Suzanne Berger and Michael J. Piore, *Dualism and Discontinuity in Industrial Societies* (New York: Cambridge University Press, 1980), p. 49.

174. *Cf.* Michael J. Piore, "Upward Mobility, Job Monotony, and Labor Market Structure," in James O'Toole, ed., *Work and the Quality of Life* (Cambridge: The MIT Press, 1974), p. 86.

175. There is obviously much more to the dual labor market theory treatment of the learning process than what is conveyed in this short paragraph. For a more complete treatment, see Piore, "Notes."

176. Michael J. Piore, "Labor Market Segmentation: To What Paradigm Does It Belong?" *American Economic Review*, Papers and Proceedings 73 (May 1983): 252.

177. David M. Gordon, *Theories of Poverty and Unemployment: Orthodox, Radical, and Dual Labor Market Perspectives* (Lexington, MA: D.C. Heath and Company, 1972), p. 43; Piore, "Notes," p. 125.

178. Cf. Michael J. Piore, "Pricing Rules," in Piore, *Unemployment & Inflation*, p. 144. Contrast this to the position articulated by Piore's mentor, John Dunlop, on p. 199 above.

179. Michael J. Piore, "Fragments of a 'Sociological' Theory of Wages," in Piore, *Unemployment & Inflation*, pp. 144–149.

180. The general form of this summary is inferred from Piore, "Fragments." I will include citations only when fleshing out the argument with details from Piore's other works.

181. Cf. Michael J. Piore, "Wage Determination in Low-Wage Labor Markets and the Role of Minimum Wage Legislation," in Piore, *Unemployment & Inflation*, p. 198.

182. Piore, "Introduction," p. xiii.

183. Piore, "Introduction," p. xiii; "Pricing Rules," p. 146.

184. Arthur Ross coined the phrase "orbits of coercive comparisons." See Ross *Trade Union Wage Policy*, p. 53. Ross similarly utilized the phrase "process of equitable comparison" in reference to the tendency for interfirm wage structures to remain more or less in place despite destabilizing "market pressures." It is worth noting that Ross's analysis is included in Piore, *Unemployment & Inflation*, and is explicitly cited to support Piore's own assertions about the intrafirm wage structures (cf. Piore, "Fragments," n. 2).

185. Piore, "Labor Market Segmentation," p. 251.

186. Piore, "Fragments," p. 134.

187. *Ibid.*, p. 139.

188. In contemporary parlance, job preferences, insofar as they affect the supply of labor within the internal labor market, are endogenous.

189. Piore, "Fragments," p. 135. The reader is reminded that the "labor economists in the 1940s and 1950s" were themselves unfamiliar with the ontological and epistemological beliefs, or "preconceptions," reflected in the writings of mainstream institutional economists.

190. Berger and Piore, *Dualism and Discontinuity*, p. 3, emphasis added.

191. *Cf.* Piore, "Fragments," p. 136.

192. *Ibid.*, p. 137.

193. *Cf.* Piore, "Pricing Rules," p. 148.

194. *Ibid.*, pp. 144–145.

195. Piore, "Fragments," p. 138.

196. The latter objective was earlier referred to as "institutional impact analysis."

197. Piore, "Fragments," p. 143.

198. Piore, "Pricing Rules," p. 147.

199. Cf. Piore, "Fragments," p. 136.

200. *Ibid.*, p. 141.

201. See p. 189 above.

202. See Piore, "Wage Determination in Low-Wage Labor Markets." The next several paragraphs are taken entirely from this article.

203. Piore, "Pricing Rules," p. 203.

204. Piore, "Wage Determination in Low-Wage Labor Markets," p. 201.

205. *Ibid.*, p. 206.

206. Piore, "Labor Market Segmentation."

207. *Ibid.*, p. 252. One is reminded here of Mukerjee's assertion that "Institutional economics . . . is a branch of social psychology." See p. 186 above.

208. *Ibid.*, p. 253. Thus the subtitle of *Unemployment & Inflation*—namely, *Institutionalist and Structuralist Views*, where the term *institutionalist views* emcompasses both of the views of the postwar labor economists I referred to above as neoclassical plus and neorealist.

209. See pp. 193–194 above. The reader will recall that the present analysis is premised on a belief that there exist in principle many possible theories, perhaps even incompatible ones (see Ramstad, "'Reasonable Value' versus 'Instrumental Value'"), that would be consistent with the institutional standpoint delineated above.

210. *Cf.* Tool, "The Compulsive Shift to Institutional Analysis."

211. Needless to say, no single institutional writer has "explicitly embraced" all of the elements reflected in the present attempt to articulate a synthetic institutional standpoint.

212. See Dugger, "The Administered Labor Market," for a promising start, even if it is not self-consciously articulated in the lexicon of the dual labor market theory, toward the construction of an explicitly institutional theory of wage-determination in the upper tier.

213. Actually, Piore has proposed that dualism is in fact a transnational phenomenon

(Berger and Piore, *Dualism and Discontinuity*, p. xx). Thus the significance of the theory transcends its applicability to the American setting.

214. *Cf.* Berger and Piore, *Dualism and Discontinuity*, Part I.

215. *Cf.* Michael J. Piore, "Unemployment and Inflation: An Alternative View," in Piore, *Unemployment & Inflation*, pp. 3–16.

216. The career of John Blair probably best exemplifies what I am talking about here. See John Blair, *The Control of Oil* (New York: Pantheon Books, 1976), for the "pattern model" resulting from his endeavors.

217. Benjamin Ward of the University of California, Berkeley, who supervised my unpublished PhD dissertation (Yngve Ramstad, "The Analytical and Methodological Orientations of Institutional Economists: Inferences from the Case of Labor Economics" [University of California, Berkeley, 1981]), told me on more than one occasion that it was his belief that the transformation of Berkeley's economics department during the 1950s, from one including a large number with institutional leanings in the late 1940s to one in which nearly all were of the neoclassical persuasion by the early 1960s, was facilitated enormously by the fact that the institutionalists within the department could never agree as to which of the institutional applicants for an opening was actually doing good work. Serious disputes were avoided by settling on a neoclassical applicant whose facility at employing that framework could be ascertained much more objectively.

Commentary by Stephen L. Mangum and Frank Borgers

Yngve Ramstad has made a valuable contribution in his chapter "Institutional Economics and the Dual Labor Market Theory." If he errs, it is in trying to do too much, which is much less damning than succeeding at doing too little. We have learned from this chapter, we have questioned it, and we have reflected as a result of it. For all of this, it has contributed to our understanding and, we assume, to that of others.

The chapter is composed of three major sections: 1) a discussion of the characteristics that an institutionalist theory of labor pattern and reward must possess; 2) a classification and discussion of three primary labor economics research programs—neoclassical, neoclassical plus, and neorealist; 3) a discussion of how dual labor market theory meets the criteria of an institutional theory of labor allocation and reward.

We believe that Ramstad's chapter has two major weak points: 1) the prescriptions for "proper" institutional economics lack conceptual clarity; and 2) the taxonomy developed to define and divide up the institutional approach appears to be a rather awkward construction. We will address these concerns as we comment on each of the chapter's three sections in turn.

Characteristics of an Institutional Theory of the Labor Market

The first section poses the question, Has mainstream institutional economics produced a theory of the labor market? and then describes the institutional "standpoint." It contains a fascinating array of institutionalist viewpoints on, and references to, the nature of economic processes and their outcomes. In content this section is as good as any description that we have read of the basic principles of mainstream institutional economic thought. However, the discussion wanders, addressing a number of interesting but fairly minor points while almost losing the main points in the process. These survive via a couple of well-placed, excellent summaries. Further more, although Ramstad's attention is on labor issues, the conditions for a theory to be "institutional in character" are stated at a general level rather than expressed in terms of how work effort is patterned and rewarded.

Ramstad lacks clarity with regard to three conceptual issues. First, his discussion of the role of generalizability and, consequently, the way in which policy relevant theory and knowledge is generated are unclear. Ramstad describes institutional theory as rejecting individualistic explanations of collective outcomes, as rejecting atomistic constrained maximization, and as rejecting the notion of markets as self-equilibriating mechanisms imbedded within a "concrete" institutional context. Institutions (prescriptive or proscriptive rules) are analytically prior to individuals, yet rules are the product of the actions of historically preceding individuals interacting with the environmental and social phenomena of their day.

Individual actions are the logical consequents of established social patterns or rules. Markets give effect to the prevailing institutions or rules, but the institutions allocate resources and determine income. Therefore, the only way to understand economic phenomena is to have knowledge of the rules and their interactions. Yet there is no natural form to which these processes and outcomes gravitate. Specific behaviors and specific economic outcomes are related to actual institutions. Behaviors and outcomes have no life, no meaning, beyond the set of rules in which they occurred. There is no a priori logic and hence no deviation from that logic. There is only an array of different rule structures. Each is an adaptation to previous rules and phenomena. Each requires its own explanation (model).

Says Ramstad, "[E]xactly how these rules work in combination to give rise to that specific pattern—and hence how specific rule changes are likely to alter behavior—will be knowable to an investigator only as a gestalt perceived through an "intuitive leap". He suggests that institutionalists develop "pattern models" or summaries of the various types that have been discovered but that these summaries separated from the specific context "cannot be . . . particularly helpful . . . in the context of a specific problem to determine exactly what institutional adjustments to make in order to produce 'better' outcomes". Yet he also says that "once a typology (theory) is developed with sufficient clarity, it can become the basis for an explicit research program with a positive heuristic of showing how a typology, when coupled with a detailed knowledge of the specific rules involved, can be used to model an ever expanding domain of market phenomena". Left unaddressed is any distinction between generalization and predictability. Do theory building and modeling serve the purposes of prediction and prescription as well as of description in Ramstad's view?

Second, Ramstad's discussion of "politically correct" institutionalist terminology lacks clarity. Ramstad warns institutionalists to be leery of using value-laden neoclassical analytical terms and cautions noninstitutionalists against interpreting institutional writers within the reader's context. He suggest that "some of the familiar analytical tools of orthodox economics can be borrowed by institutional economists without undercutting their own agenda". What are these transferable tools? Conversely, there must be some analytical tools whose use would undercut the agenda. What are these tools and why are they so dangerous? Ramstad identifies some of them in saying that "the competitive model with its theory of household behavior, firm behavior and market equilibrium—the latter with its 'law of one price'" has no place in an institutional research program. He searches for an institutionally correct definition of market, settling on a "structured process of interaction between actual or potential buyers and sellers, not to a domain within which a single equilibrium price is presumed to emerge or exist". While we understand Ramstad's concerns with the competitive model and market equilibrium, we suspect that many economists, and particularly labor economists, would likely be comfortable with Ramstad's market definition.

Lastly, Ramstad's discussion is unclear as to whether he sees institutional systems as gravitating toward a state of equilibrium. Ramstad describes institutional economics as "economics without equilibrium". Is it disequilibrium economics? Probably not; movement in the direction of equilibrium until additional changes intervene is generally implied by most disequilibrium theories. But distinctions in the definition of "equilibrium" and Ramstad's notion of "patterns" needs further exploration. To the extent that equilibrium is viewed as a consistency of process and outcome as opposed to an absence of process and a uniformity of outcomes, the distinctions may diminish.

Worth pondering is whether the neoclassical model can itself be described as a pattern model or a positive heuristic, though admittedly a pattern model lacking institutional detail. Cannot the neoclassical model be used to "model an ever-expanding domain of market phenomena"?

Perhaps neoclassical economics could be termed a theory of "know nothingism." Knowing little about the world, application of its assumptions frequently yields a useful (but incomplete) understanding of economic processes and outcomes. Its insights provide a beginning. The goals of theory: description, prediction, and prescription so as to "make this world a better place in which to live" and to explain "human nature as an expression of the social order" are approachable, not by supplementing the neoclassical pattern model with institutional reality but by gradually replacing its starkness with the rich detail of institutional patterns that develop with exposure to real-world institutions. In this view, the neoclassical framework is far from useless; rather, it is the (often necessary) first cut.

Yes, orthodox economists tend to overstate the applicability of the framework. The framework seems at times to take on a life of its own. Many become so wedded to it that they believe it provides finite answers and that it mutes any need for information on institutional patterns. These individuals are just as misguided as those who would deny any value to the tools of neoclassical economic analysis.

Ramstad relies heavily on a carefully constructed taxonomy to define who is and who is not a "true" institutionalist. Ramstad concludes this first section of his chapter by stating the criteria by which one can judge "a theory of market phenomena to be 'institutional' in character, that is, to be 'the right sort of theory'". Theory is institutional in character if it: 1) reflects a cultural/social versus individualistic/atomistic interpretation of individual behavior; 2) reflects particularistic conceptions of markets in that specific outcomes are explained only by pinpointing the unique constellation of institutional rules and customary practices through which those outcomes are produced; 3) reflects the Darwinian concept of market adjustment—evolution of institutional adjustments—rather than the Newtonian concept of equilibriating price adjustments; and 4) is constructed by pattern modeling.

It is our belief that his taxonomy may be a little too rigid and a little too tightly constructed to capture the ambiguities generated by the individual evolutions of real-life economists and their intellectual collaborations. Ironically, this rigidity may stem from Ramstad's admirably cogent and reasoned analysis of what institutionalism should be about. However, his prescription should not be confused with the actual beliefs and practices of those who have considered themselves to be institutionalists.

Neoclassical Plus and Neorealists

Ramstad indicates that the early study of "the labor problem" developed side by side with the development of institutional economics and that labor market analysis began to blossom only after World War II. Looking to the postwar period, he identifies the roots of three distinct research programs and labels them as neoclassical, neoclassical plus, and neorealist. The first, Ramstad associates with individuals such as Sir John Hicks, George Stigler, Simon Rottenberg, and eventually Greg Lewis. It is built on microeconomic price theory with profit maximization underpinning labor demand, utility maximization underlying labor supply, and the price mechanism functioning as a bourse. The neoclassical-plus program he identifies with John Dunlop, Charles Myers, Al Rees, and Melvin Reder. Ramstad perceives this group as accepting the validity of neoclassical theory but arguing that labor markets are different from other markets. Information gathering on rules and customary practice is seen by this group as vital to an understanding of labor market functioning. The third program, neorealist, is identified with Clark Kerr, Arthur Ross, and Richard Lester. Ramstad views this research program as progressing completely outside the framework of neoclassical price theory and as involving detailed investigation of wage practices and job allocation processes. The outcome is one where different labor markets are characterized by very different sets of institutionalized rules. Ramstad states that although none of these research programs is rooted in institutional economics, the neorealist program manifests many of the key criteria of institutional theory established in the first section of the chapter.

This comparison and contrast of the three research programs is instructive and enlightening. However, in our view, Ramstad's discussion has two potential flaws. First, Ramstad overstates the distinctions between the neoclassical-plus and neorealist groups. We doubt if any of the Kerr, Ross, or Lester group would have differentiated themselves from Dunlop with whom, after all, they were constantly coauthoring. For example, after the publication of *Industrialism and Industrial Man*, Kerr and Dunlop, along with Myers and Harbison, were frequently referred to as the "four horsemen." That this affinity was more than publishing-based is vividly demonstrated in recent pieces by Clark Kerr in which he refers to Dunlop, himself, and others as "neoclassical revisionists." Kerr perceives the revisionists to have been united in belief and practice:

> [They] were interested, first of all, in markets, and they recognized the great role of market forces. At the same time, they were concerned with the social forces that limit the role and affect the influence of competition—with markets in the embrace of custom, of concepts of justice, of rules and regulations, of combined power. . . . The members of this group wanted to look at things as they really are, to render the precise details of relationships. They also wanted to connect faithfully theory to practice, since they rejected efforts to present complex relations in an abstract or idealized form. The effort to connect theory (whether neoclassical at the microlevel or Keynesian at the macrolevel) with practice constituted the essence of the efforts of this core group.[1]

Second, Ramstad's claim that Kerr and his fellow neorealists operated completely outside neoclassical theory must be rejected on the basis of Kerr's characterization of the revisionists' beliefs:

> The neoclassical revisionists were . . . eclectics. We got our theory from the neoclassicists, our history from Commons and the Webbs, our contact with ideology from Marx on one side and Simons and Hayek on the other, our appreciation of unions from Commons and Perlman and the Webbs and our understanding of the workplace separately from Slichter and Mayo. . . .
>
> Members of the revisionist group had been trained in the theory of the thirties . . . [but] were more descendants of Smith, Marshall, and Pigou than of Commons and Perlman. They did not reject theory as did the institutionalists, whose work "was not meant to complement economic analysis as it had always been understood, but to replace it" (Blaug 1978: 713); rather, they respected theory and wanted to make it more useful in understanding practice. . . . The labor economist revisionists, it is true, stood between the orthodox neoclassical absolutists and the abolitionist institutionalists, but far from either of these extremes. They were, instead, incorporationists, and as such, much closer to the neoclassical side of the argument.[2]

In summary, we believe that Ramstad's differentiation between the neoclassical-plus and neorealist groups is overstated. We believe that a more relevant differentiation within the institutionalist school is between those who have acted as social critics and those who have acted as practitioners. The former stream is associated with Thorstein Veblen, Clarence Ayres, and John Dewey, and the latter stream has its source in John R. Commons.

Neither stream is necessarily more theoretical than the other, but for one school theory is more ideology and for the other, more a tool. In that sense, institutionalists of the social critic orientation are like some neoclassicists: defenders of the faith. Ramstad's comment that he is unaware of anyone influenced by Commons who has produced "a coherent alternative to the neoclassical theory of labor utilization and pricing" implies that doing so is the goal of institutionalist thought. It denies legitimacy for the practitioner orientation.

When theory is viewed as a tool, effectiveness is determined by the task to which it is applied and no theory is inherently better than another. All theories are to be examined and utilized if they aid in accomplishment of the task at hand. On the other hand, when theory is viewed as ideology, one must adhere or risk excommunication. Thus, from the ideological vantage point there cannot be two streams of institutionalism; rather, there is only a true path and an apostate one. Admittedly we overstate the distinction here but do so to raise an important distinction. Theory creation and tool creation are interactive processes. One need not become reliant on a single theoretical framework, however. Our view is that no one framework is complete for all tasks to which theory is put.

Clark Kerr implicitly recognizes the distinction between theory as tool versus theory as ideology. In comparing the neoclassical revisionists to the neoclassicists and the institutionalists, he states:

> In any event, we, the revisionist labor economists, ended up as little foxes knowing many things, not as hedgehogs committed to one all-embracing theory. We looked for small truths, not the one overwhelming truth; or, at least, for the small truths that amended the big truth. We became pluralistic foxes, not monistic hedgehogs. The "fox knows many things", as the ancient Greek adage goes, and for a very good reason: there are many things to know. . . . [M]any in the intellectual world want simplicity and certainty—the "one big thing" that the hedgehog knows—to guide their thoughts, a central vision that gives coherence to their many perceptions; a single explanation that makes sense out of the many events. There is an eternal tension between those who follow the pluralistic path and those who follow the monistic path.[3]

A tracing of the evolution of the practitioner stream reveals further weaknesses in Ramstad's neoclassical-plus versus neorealist differentiation. Tracing the practitioner stream also allows one to place Michael Piore's work within its proper intellectual context.

John R. Commons was heavily involved in practical reform both in Wisconsin and in Washington, DC. Sumner Slichter, Selig Perlman, Phil Taft, Bill Haber, Ed Witte, Wight Bakke, many of them Commons students and all sharing the same hands-on practical reform bias, began their writings in the 1930s, mostly in collective bargaining and all viewing the union as an engine of reform.

Emerging from graduate schools just before the war were John Dunlop, George Taylor, George Hildebrand, Richard Lester, Charles Myers, Clark Kerr, Charles Killingsworth, Fred Harbison, and Arthur Ross. Most served as functionaries of the War Labor Board and were thrust into the settlement of real labor disputes and into practical wage setting. All of them had economics backgrounds, but there were others such as Bob Livernash and Jim Healy whose training was in industrial relations and Willard Wirtz and Ben Aaron in law, but whose work experience was similar. Several became the first generation of arbitrators and mediators, carrying the War Labor Board experience into private relationships.

Individuals such as George Schultz, Lloyd Reynolds, Lloyd Ulman, Herb Northrup, Herb Parnes, and Mel Reder did their undergraduate work before the war and their graduate study after military service. Another generation did their military service first and both their undergraduate and graduate work later. Among these individuals are Ray Marshall, Al Rees, Arnold Weber, Garth Mangum, Martin Segal, Gerald Somers, Morris Horowitz, and Melvin Rothbaum.

Several in these lists staffed the Wage Stabilization Board during the

Korean War and served on emergency board and various governmental commissions such as the Presidential Railroad Labor Board and the Livernash study of the causes of the 1959 steel strike. All turned out people in their own image with a heavy practitioner bias. They introduced them to Washington policymakers and to union and management labor relations people. Dunlop, Schultz, and Marshall subsequently served as secretaries of labor; Ulman and others served as labor economists on the staff of the Council of Economic Advisors. Practitioners created practitioners.

Michael Piore is a member of the next generation of "practitioner institutionalists" which came to the scene at a time when collective bargaining and unionization were no longer the central activities. Piore's kin include Peter Doeringer, Daniel Quinn Mills, Richard Freeman, Vernon Briggs, and Chris King. Manpower programs and poverty alleviation were where the action was. Attention was increasingly turned to understanding the internal rules governing human resource management (though that term had not yet emerged) and how human resource decisions could be influenced by public policy. It was within this context that Piore's work on dual labor market theory occurred.

Dual Labor Market Theory and Ramstad's Institutionalist Criteria

The dual labor market notion emerged while exploring the ineffectiveness of Boston antipoverty programs. The basic policy conclusion was that manpower programs were too supply-side-oriented and would not be effective unless they addressed the demand side as well. It was born from investigation, the product of pattern modeling, and motivated by multiple observations that appeared inconsistent with the expectations of the standard competitive economic framework. Dual labor market theory emerged as a device to describe and explain what was observed.

Ramstad provides an excellent summary of the tenets of dual labor market theory and its perspectives on wage determination and job allocation. Although we agree with Ramstad's discussion of the differences in the "sociological approach" as compared to the neoclassical treatment of these processes, he may overstate the differences and understate the usefulness of the neoclassical view as a "first cut."

A couple of specific examples of overstating the differences and one example of understating the usefulness of the first cut might be appropriate. First, Piore in his early work, recognized the operation of market forces in the economy and the usefulness of orthodox economics:

> [I]n the course of my own research, I have had a lot of discussions with workers and managers about labor market decisions, and the conventional view does seem to be a fairly accurate, albeit incomplete, picture of what emerges from their comments.[4]

Second, he describes wage-setting and job allocation decisions as reflecting the nature of the training process and the

> . . . adaptation of the individual to the norms and role patterns of the work group. It is literally socialization in that a good deal of what is required to perform effectively on-the-job and is involved in the improvement of productivity during the "training period" is the understanding of the norms of the group. . . . Such norms appear to be essentially what economists and industrial relations specialists have generally referred to as custom.[5]

But interestingly, he does not see custom as resting outside mainstream orthodox economic thought.

> Although custom has never achieved a place in the formal analytical apparatus of economics, its role in wage determinations has been recognized by virtually every student of the labor market from Adam Smith to J.R. Hicks.[6]

Third, while Piore's later writings clearly evince a "structural" or "cognitive-linguistic" orientation,[7] quite distinct from the neoclassical view, the above statements reveal Piore's early reliance on neoclassical tenets as a starting point for investigation and explanation.

Conclusion

Ramstad has made a significant contribution with his chapter in this book. Hopefully it will be fruitful ground for further discussion and further investigation. We recognize the importance of Piore's work on dual labor market theory. Along with Ramstad, we applaud the theory and its policy implications. Clearly these meet the Wesley Clair Mitchell test for "the study of economic theory": "to make this world a better place in which to live".

We agree that Piore's dual labor market theory does significantly correspond to the criteria of institutional theory as Ramstad states them. However, it is not clear whether this list simply reflects an ex ante construction around Ramstad's interpretation of Piore or whether it is a truly general list that can be applied across all institutionalists. What of the myriad of other "segmented labor market" theories? To what extent do they or don't they also meet the criteria?

Showing that Piore fits into an abstract category deemed institutionalist may be a less interesting question than some others. For instance, of additional interest would be a systematic tracing of Piore's influencers and mentors, a detailed evaluation of the compatability of dual labor market theory and general neoclassical economics, and a critique and extension of Piore's work as an alternative framework. Only in exploring these types of questions will it become clear why we should care whether Piore's work is or is not "institutional."

Finally, there are important, unresolved issues regarding theory: its definition, its construction, its usefulness, its evaluation. Ramstad concludes his essay with the fascinating statement that "acceptance of the institutional standpoint necessitates an abandonment of the notion that there is a generalizable 'microeconomic' logic", and that "the economist can have no hope of assembling an analytical tool kit that can be taken with him/her when shifting attention from the study of one industry or market to the study of another". We have heard "scientific discipline" defined as the ability to *categorize*, *analyze*, and *generalize*. If Ramstad's statement is true and if this definition of scientific discipline is accurate, then is institutionalism disciplinary anarchism? This we refuse to believe.

Acknowledgments

The authors recognize the comments of Garth Mangum and Howard Stanger. These individuals are absolved of any responsibility for what appears here.

Notes

1. Clark Kerr, "The Neoclassical Revisionists in Labor Economics (1940–1960)—R.I.P.," in Bruce E. Kaufman, ed., *How Labor Markets Work: Reflections on Theory and Practice* (Lexington, MA: Lexington Books, 1988), p. 14.
2. *Ibid.*, pp. 12–13.
3. *Ibid.*, p. 9.
4. Michael Piore, "Fragments of a 'Sociological' Theory of Wages," in Michael Piore, ed., *Unemployment and Inflation: Institutionalist and Structuralist Views* (New York: M.E. Sharpe, 1979, p. 134).
5. *Ibid.*, p. 135.
6. *Ibid.*, p. 136.
7. Michael Piore, "Labor Market Segmentation: To What Paradigm Does It Belong?" *The American Economic Review: Papers and Proceedings* 73 (May 1983): 249–253.

6 INSTITUTIONS AND ECONOMIC DEVELOPMENT: STRUCTURE, PROCESS, AND INCENTIVE

John Adams

Institutional economists have made important contributions to the study of economic development. At the same time, many development economists have stressed the importance of institutions in shaping national rates of growth and profiles of development. This affinity has meant that, in the field of development economics, many of the divisions that exist between institutionalists and orthodox economists are muted or absent. This chapter discusses the origins of economic development as a subject, arguing that its emergence grew from acceptance of the proposition that institutional differences are fundamental in explaining national development paths.

The chief contribution of this chapter is to explicate three alternative but complementary ways of looking at the role of institutions: as structure, process, and incentive. Early anthropologists emphasized the first viewpoint, which many critics found too static and confining. Bringing acquisitive, achievement-oriented individuals into the picture, along with time, creates a basis for studying social processes and social change. Lastly, an institutional pattern comprises a set of incentives and disincentives that configure how individuals and groups act. The chapter concludes with a review of institutional contributions to the analysis of Latin America and South Asia.

Institutions and the Economics of Development

The field of economic development or development economics emerged distinctively only after the end of World War II. In the beginning its legitimacy within the economics profession was challenged on several grounds; and, down to the present, controversy over its status and distinguishing features has never subsided. Some early critics said that concern with growth had been an important interest of economists since Adam Smith, so that nothing novel was being done.[1] Others remarked that the concepts and tools used by development economists were no different than those of general economics. There was thus no singular body of theory. If there were novelty, it came only from using the standard constructs of economics in exotic locales. Even in such venues, it was declared, the utility of those ideas remained more or less the same. Familiar thought packages, such as those surrounding supply-and-demand relations, competitive markets, savings and capital formation, and tax and expenditure evaluation, would yield good analysis and good policy regardless of the settings in which they were applied.

On these multiple grounds there was resistance to offering the field of economic development as a separate subject in graduate programs. This hesitancy was usually broken through by the concerted efforts of committed faculty members and interested graduate students, many of whom came from overseas and perceived that the standard theory and the institutional framework in which it was purported to operate did not jibe with realities at home. During the 1960s, specialized textbooks and journals codified and deepened the field.[2]

The challenges to the field of development economics met a multipronged response. Notwithstanding the fertile legacy of Smith, Mill, and Marx, economists of the first half of the 20th century had not expended much energy examining problems of growth, particularly in very low-income economies, so it was evident that much was not known. Many neophyte practitioners in the first waves of vagabonding experts found that their conventional mental utensils did not work very well amidst the conditions in underdeveloped nations. Market behavior was absent or weak, especially in rural areas. Capital markets were frequently entirely absent, and only a small portion of the work force labored for wages or contracted for hire in the market. Manipulation of public spending, the money supply, and interest rates had little effect on chronic underemployment or cost-based inflation. The economic systems of less-developed countries were, it was discovered, dissimilar to those of the economically advanced part of the world. Poor economies were dualistic; the effects of trade and foreign investment were infructuous or negative; there were few entrepreneurs; farmers responded unevenly to price and innovation incentives; and attitudes and reward arrays were inconsistent with attaining efficiency, high savings rates, and innovation. Concerns with getting growth going and sustaining momentum led to much deeper attention to investment decision making, education and human resources, and trade policies.[3]

The conflicts inherent in the crossfire between those who advocate the uniqueness of development economics and those who dispute it are by no means resolved.[4] Many of these entail matters of theoretical abstruseness, fundamental assertions about human nature, or sharp and ingrained differences in policy tastes, about which little more can usefully be said. There has, however, been one constant touchstone in all the back-and-forthing about whether economic development is a valid and distinct field of study. This is the portrayal of institutions. For the moment it is sufficient to define an institution as a learned, habitual pattern of behavior, supported by ingrained attitudes, values, and ways of thinking. Illustrations are marriage customs, the dispersion of irrigation water across village fields, the technique of curing a baby's fever, or the ceremonies and distributions that accompany the annual harvest. Each of these four activities has separable meanings for economists, political scientists, and sociologists because they involve welfare, security, wealth, production, property, power, authority, social rank, and religion, in greater or lesser degree.

Regardless of one's disciplinary persuasion, it is apparent that institutional practices are more or less shared in a particular society and that institutions diverge, sometimes dramatically, across societies. Differences in the way people behave in two contrasting societies amount to differences in institutions, which are the components of a society. Since institutions have economic content, it follows that economic behavior will deviate. A large or small dowry, or none at all, may come with the bride; or the groom may transfer a bridewealth. Irrigation water may be sold, controlled by a village elite, or taken first-come, first-served. One mother buys aspirin, another burns incense in front of a god-statue, and a third wraps the feverish baby in warm herbal towels. A portion of the harvest bounty is given to the landlord, or sold to the farmer's cooperative, or donated to a temple.

If institutions matter, in the sense of shaping economic comportment in dissimilar social systems, then there are forceful implications for the debate over the legitimacy of development economics. Some part of market-based economic theory cannot apply in contexts where economic agents do not behave according to standard postulates and markets are absent or only poorly formed. New thinking has to be fashioned to cope with the simultaneous existence of survival and profit motives, subsistence and commercial households, and imperfect factor and product markets that generate inappropriate price signals. Because institutions have material, social, religious, and political aspects, understanding economic behavior must lead to expanding the range of relevant variables in an analysis—holding fewer things constant, in the usual idiom. Making an economy grow would entail, if institutions matter, effecting simultaneous changes in social arrangements. The persistence and mutability of institutions would need prior examination, as would the social concomitants and consequences of economic change. Furthermore, if institutions matter, then cultural differences would be important in shaping variations in economic performance even in rich societies. It would be artificial and inconsistent to maintain a rigid dichotomy between two classes of countries, in one of which institutions mattered and another in which they did not, in determining levels and rates of growth and development. For all of these reasons, development economics has from its infancy embraced the study of institutions and its validity as a field must rest on the proposition that institutions matter.

The linking of economic development with the study of institutional arrangements would not surprise one of the founders of the field, Sir W. Arthur Lewis. Early on, in an analysis yet to be surpassed, he identified three proximate causes of growth. These were: economizing on resources, increasing levels of knowledge, and raising the amount of capital in use per head. He continued:

> The second stage in the analysis takes us behind these proximate causes to ask why it is that they are found strongly operating in some societies but not in others, or at some stages of history but less so in others. . . . First, we must enquire which kinds of institutions are favorable to growth, and which are inimical to effort, to innovation, or to investment. Then we must move into the realm of beliefs . . . valuations . . . ideas of the right way to live. . . .
>
> How do beliefs and institutions change? Why do they change in ways favorable to or hostile to growth?[5]

Generally speaking, the original contributors to the field of development economics made their marks either by recognizing the unsuitability of indigenous institutions for modern economic growth or by itemizing conditions under which markets and market agents would not yield the best social outcomes. The prerequisite of institutional reform appeared to mandate a considerable role for a modernizing elite, operating with or without democratic sanction, in setting an agenda for social improvement. Likewise the attestation of pervasive market failure led to the advocacy of a large governmental mission in correcting and bettering the market structure. There is no need to provide an exhaustive roster here, but among the most prominent early development theorists were Albert Hirschman writing on unbalanced growth and rigidities in decision making, Harvey Leibenstein on the low-level equilibrium trap, Hla Myint on export typologies, John C.H. Fei and Gustav Ranis on surplus labor economies, Gunnar Myrdal on backwash and spread effects, and Ragnar Nurkse on problems of capital formation.[6] The institutional elements featured in this early literature mostly had to do with the paucity of public and private decision makers or entrepreneurs in a typical organizational context, perverse demographic behavior, and ineffectual or absent political and regulatory processes. The forms of market failure that were usually identified sprang from the pervasiveness of positive externalities and divergences of social and private benefits and costs.

To meet the challenges of many of the critics of development economics it was not sufficient to argue that institutions matter—many were willing to concede that they might matter a little, in the odd instance of cultural rigidity or political immaturity. What was needed to allay skepticism among those willing to be convinced, was convincing quantitative evidence of *how much* institutions mattered. The response came in a courageous and creative book that applied a relatively unknown quantitative technique, factor analysis, to the previously unmeasurable: the weight of complexes of institutional factors in influencing levels of per capita income across a spectrum of countries. In 1967, Irma Adelman and Cynthia Taft Morris presented, in *Society, Politics, and Economic Development: A Quantitative Approach*, a detailed exploration of the role of institutions at different levels of development.[7] They devised scales to register the salience of social and political features in each of 74 less-developed countries. Values for variables such as the importance of the middle class, extent of social mobility, modernization of outlook, degree of administrative efficiency, and political strength of the traditional elite were generated.

The Adelman and Morris method established that differences in levels of development were connected systematically to variations in noneconomic variables. In their most aggregative framework the factor analytic method affirmed that 69.9 percent of the variation in the per capita incomes of the 74 sample countries in 1961 could be attributed to four factor components that combined 24 social and political variables. They wrote, "The results of the analysis show that a remarkably high percentage of intercountry variations in the levels of economic development (70 percent) is associated with differences in noneconomic characteristics. Thus it would appear that it is just as reasonable to look at underdevelopment as a social and political phenomenon as it is to analyze it in terms of intercountry differences in economic structure."[8]

Structure: What Are Institutions?

Development economics has carved out a place for itself by establishing that institutions do matter in Third World contexts and has used that toehold as a means to establish the crucial role of noneconomic factors and market failures in explaining underdevelopment. In the American tradition of evolutionary institutional economics the premise that "institutions matter" is fundamental to the analysis of the economy and its place in society. American institutionalists have tackled the different and larger task of explicating the role of institutions in all contexts; that is, in rich and poor countries alike. This means not only showing how economic behavior always and everywhere depends on the cultural contexts and historical backgrounds within which people operate, but also delving into the manifold political and social attributes that derive from institutions, such as power and greed, antagonism to technological and scientific advance, and human perverseness in the face of ostensible opportunity. The embeddedness of the production and exchange relations in social relationships, and the effects of industrialism and the market system on that embeddedness, were the subject of Karl Polanyi's life work.[9]

The initial orientation of the institutionalists had one important bearing on their relationship with development economists. Institutionalists had no difficulty, as a rule, in allying themselves with specialists in development economics in the study of Third World problems. Many institutionalists found a fertile domain for their talents in this expanding new subfield of economics, and they made important conceptual and empirical contributions to it. A special forte was the broad study of a particular national economy, and many valuable case studies were written. Despite much agreement and interaction, an important division remained between institutional economists and development economists: the former stressed the importance of institutions and the dysfunctions of a market capitalist system, in all settings, while the latter generally held to the tenet that institutions mattered and markets were meaningfully flaw-ridden only in relatively underdeveloped areas.

Economists in the American evolutionary institutionalist tradition who have been attracted to the study of developing economies have drawn upon a rich legacy that stretches from Thorstein Veblen and John R. Commons, through the immediate postwar era, and down to the present.[10] Those who are comfortable with institutionalism have little or no difficulty employing the ideas of Hirschman, Lewis, Myint, and Nurkse. Myrdal explicitly placed himself in the institutional camp. John Kenneth Galbraith possessed an early interest in problems of global development that was particularly manifest during his stint as ambassador to India.[11] Many institutionalists have embraced the analysis of economic change provided by Clarence Ayres as the most useful overarching conceptual framework. This partiality in no way detracts from the serviceability of the work of Commons or others because there is such a considerable overlap, but Ayres's work stands out in that it makes economic change central.

In Ayres's most influential book, *The Theory of Economic Progress, A Study of the Fundamentals of Economic Development and Cultural Change*, which appeared in 1944, he distills Veblenian ideas into a general theory of evolutionary economic progress.[12] Although Ayres influenced many students working on developing areas, the book—and his classroom lectures—contained few explicit comments about them. *The Theory of Economic Progress* begins with a scathing critique of orthodox equilibrium theory, but its constructive chapters are devoted to the elaboration of a theory that explains how economic systems change over time. The simplicity and lucidity of Ayres's central principle are matched by its power and generality. It is that human history pivots on two opposing cultural forces: past-binding ceremonialism and forward-pushing technology. When the former predominates, there is stagnation; when the latter prevails, there is progress.

Almost all of Ayres's illustrations of his principle are taken from European economic history. It is only in the preface to the 1962 edition of the book that he mentions the applicability of the theory to Third World cases. He puts his own special meanings on terms such as "big push" and "sustained growth," which had sprung from the writings of the early developmentalists. As always, he recognized how precarious the balance was between restrictive and progressive forces in populations engaged in the struggle to advance. He writes, with characteristic vigor:

> No doubt Hindu priests and Mohammaden mullahs will resist the enlightenment of their people with all the wiles at their command, just as the Christian Church resisted the translation of the Bible. . . . According to their lights, they will be right in doing so; for—we must face it—technological revolution brings its own values to fruition, to the detriment of all local and tribal value systems. . . . [T]he arbitrary authority and irrational values of pre-scientific, pre-industrial cultures are doomed. . . . The only [effective response] is that of intelligent, voluntary acceptance of the industrial way of life and all the values that go with it.[13]

In the work of Ayres and his affiliated American institutionalists there are clear answers to the two questions: What are institutions? How do they shape the rate and course of economic growth, development, and progress?

For evolutionary social scientists the demarcation of institutions is a means of reducing the incredible complexity of a society to mentally manageable proportions: a means of setting out its characteristic features and differentiating it from other societies.[14] Institutions mediate between a society-at-large and the everyday actions of the persons who are members of that society. It is easy to see that French society and Indian society are different and that French people do not behave like Indian people behave. They do not speak the same languages, worship in the same manner, wear the same clothes, farm in the same fashion, make shoes (or sandals) with the same tools or manual skills, or drive automobiles on the same side of the road. To describe how the French conduct themselves it is necessary to break down French society into components or arrays of behavior; and this must also be done with the Indian. The result of this mental exercise is institutions: families, churches, governments, enterprises, venues of work, traffic rules; and in the Indian case, particularly castes, villages, and joint families. Institutions are identified by affiliated rules of conduct, and associated values, words, emotions, and physical objects, such as crosses, plows, buildings, or automobiles, these latter objects being the material culture of the people.

Institutions are structural, meaning that they are organized and form a unit of regulated social space, that people operate within them, and that there are links and overlays with the domains of other institutions. There are vertical elements of command, power, and enforcement. This combination of regularity and hierarchy combines in the mind into a perception of structure. If this were all that could be said, institutional arrangements would be fixed, static, and sterile; the world would be unchanging, and human beings would be little more than socially programmed robots, acting exactly as their forebears had done. In fact, there are always unsettled relations within and between institutions: in expansive terms one can draw upon European history to cite tensions in the feudal hierarchy between kings and nobles; or, latitudinally, between church and state or town and farm. Because of everchanging climatic, demographic, resource, or technological circumstances, institutional evolution is always in train. Exploration, migration, expansion, warfare, trade, and the commingling of populations open pathways to crosscultural exchanges and conflict.

In Ayres's language, institutions are organization structures or segments of society.[15] Tensions arise because any act of behavior, and hence any rule-component of an institution, involves a ceremonial aspect and a technological aspect. The ceremonial dimension suppresses change, which can be thought of as deviant or experimental behavior, because conventional ways of doing things are supported by ingrained values, social sanctions, and the powers of authorities. Most deviant behavior is legitimately viewed as a threat to the social and economic order and is properly resisted, controlled, or isolated, as by exile. In many cases, however, such as trying a new crop rotation or devising a creative way to rig a ship's sails to gain speed, the innovation merits retention and dispersion. The creative or technological element is progressive because it represents the expression of people's unremitting quest for better ways of doing things such as binding couples, families, and clans together via marriage, fairly and efficaciously dividing irrigation waters, curing feverish babies, or harvesting wheat. Technology is also cumulative; as its mass grows the opportunities for new combinations rise exponentially. The quest for efficacious behaviors is intrinsic to the human species, whose hallmark is conscious problem solving in the face of changing material and social conditions.

Following Veblen, Ayres uses the term *institutional* as a synonym for ceremonial, thus giving it a second denotation. Institutional resistance works against technological change. It does not help immediate understanding of his logic that technology, to Ayres, does not mean simply material tools, but rather embraces the sum total of human problem-solving capacities: ideas, procedures, science, words, and all knowledge about how to do things. Instrumental means the same thing as technological, so that the instrumental–institutional dichotomy is equivalent to the technological–ceremonial dichotomy. What is particularly hard to grasp is that any institution (organization structure) and any act of behavior it sanctions have at once an instrumental (technological) and an institutional (ceremonial) dimension. All behavior is dichotomistic but not dualistic. Even physical tools and tool-using behavior have both characteristics. A gold-inlaid sword with a jewel-encrusted haft will kill effectually even as it emblemizes rank. A modern automobile is an excellent instrument for going from one place to another, but it also makes a powerful statement about one's social status. A rhythmic chant may thank the local Earth Goddess for the bountiful harvest, while at the same time easing and coordinating the work of a team of sickle-wielding stalk-cutters.

Process: What Do Institutions Do?

There are three elements in Ayres's theory that make it helpful in examining the prospects of developing economies over the long term, Change is inevitable but difficult, is the first; a potent corollary being that social evolution is fitful—at times very slow, at times brisk. Change will entail outbursts of conflict between progressive and contrary forces, is the second.

In recognizing the inevitability of forms of friction, Ayres had in mind not only arid controversies between competing academies or ideologies about proper ethics or policies, but the street riots and guerilla warfare that accompany protest and revolution. This observation is a useful reminder that more is involved in economic development than getting the prices right. There is finally Ayres's insistence that the inevitable forward movement of instrumental evolution amounts to progress; that is, that improvement and enlightenment are manifest in human history.[16]

The notion of institutions-as-structures has given rise to several misunderstandings, of which two are pervasive.[17] The first is that when a social structure is reified into component institutions, it appears rigid. This sense is aggravated when, as is commonly the case, an institution such as the feudal manor or the Indian caste system is outlined as an ideal type for descriptive or comparative purposes. Such a construction has a changeless and timeless appearance, and introducing and then explaining historical metamorphosis require developing a causal theory. In actuality, human action takes place through time, in a sequence of connected behaviors. Thus, it is as valid to envisage social relations as a process as it is to characterize them as a structure. When thinking about the economic constituents of social action, the same distinction applies. For some purposes, many find it helpful to regard the market economy as a static equilibrium system. This is emphatically not a good way to commence when the challenge is to illuminate the nature of economic growth and change over time.

A second limitation of the structural viewpoint is the absence of individual human actors from the stage. An abstract description of the set of institutions that distinguish a particular society leaves little, if any, room for individuals—neither the ordinary folk going about their everyday routines nor the great leaders of armies, flotillas, kingdoms, and industrial empires. Since orthodox economics is based on the premise that society is composed of hedonistic individuals pursuing utility and gain, then reconciling that position with the structural-institutional one would appear difficult. As much as anything, this methodological polarity of institutions and individuals has separated conventional economics from mainstream social and historical science, including evolutionary institutional economics. One way of stating the difference is to reduce it to a double question: Do institutions make people? Or: Do people make institutions? Of course, the correct answer to both questions is "yes," but this has not stopped generations of structuralists and individualists from misunderstanding each other's ideas or taking extreme positions.

In order to move beyond a bare structuralist conception of society as a complex of inflexible and timeless institutions it is necessary to energize social relations by injecting artful and wily human actors into the scene. Each action is unique in that it occurs at a point of time and in a particular social space; and, it cannot be repeated because of the irreversibility of time. The persistent regularities in those actions over time make it possible to identify institutionalized behavior—as customs, habits, rules, or mores, and as expressions of values, attitudes, or motives. People act as individuals or as members of families, groups, coalitions, corporations, governments; this is to say that human action is individual and collective at the same time. The juxtaposition of established institutional modus operandi and the spontaneous daily conduct of thousands or millions of actors is what gives rise to social process. These actors work within and upon the institutional pattern and that pattern, in turn, configures their conduct.

Orthodox economists have recently begun to think anew about institutions and their capacity to shape individual conduct and channel processes of change and development.[18] Consistent with their predilections, they have placed great emphasis on the rational individual as prime mover. One consequence of this proclivity is that institutions are perceived exclusively to be constraints on behavior. Douglass North writes, "Institutions are the humanly devised constraints that structure political, economic, and social interaction."[19] It is not entirely wrong to say this, but the proposition is one-sided, for institutions not only limit choice but also offer alternatives for action. They are at once restrictive and suggestive. Their principal worth is to provide an immediate and sanctioned method, or several methods, that enable a person or group to achieve what is desired: curing a baby or planting wheat.

The shelf of available practices offers a readily applicable index to behaviors that have been efficacious in the past. Accepted conduct provides information; it carries forward a people's wisdom and culture. It is when thinking of social interaction as process that the artificial and ultimately self-defeating distinction between institutional structure and individual animation vanishes. Necessary, too, is the realization that no human calculation or action takes place in a vacuum. Contrary to the ab initio premise of the rational chooser favored by conventional economists, each decision anyone makes is predicated on the knowledge transmitted forward in the culture—in one's memory or obtainable by conversation or reading. In Ayres's dichotomy, ceremonial resistance to change stems from the conservatism inherent in human ratiocination and activity. Ways that are tried-and-true have safety, comfort, and approbation in their favor, but they also have the merit of having working in the past. The need for change arises when circumstances change and new potentials must be discovered and added to the roster of practical conduct.

Prior to the resurgence of interest in the interplay of institutions and individuals on the part of orthodox economists, anthropologists had become embroiled in a debate over the role of the individual in social analysis. A group who became known as the formalists protested the absence of the individual from what they charged were overly structural accounts of community life. Drawing upon the tenets of formal economic theory (hence their appellation), they argued that even in tradition-bound rural societies people acted as selfish, rational maximizers. Many formalists made neophytic errors in the use of economic theory; and, since most of economic theory is nonoperational, there was difficulty in defining, much less observing and measuring, what was being maximized, especially in premodern economies lacking money, prices, and accountancy. As Mayhew has pointed out, there arose much confusion and brickbatting within the ranks of anthropologists, and between them and the economists who became implicated in the debate.[20] The controversy was not entirely sterile since it grew out of highly practical concerns. Because anthropologists applied their craft almost entirely in non-Western cultures, and many were immersed in assessing the effects of development projects at the village level, their disputation had important implications for development theorizing.

However poorly they understood fundamental economics, the formalists had an undeniable point: economic anthropology had failed to incorporate individual agency into the structuralist scheme. Work in the field demonstrated that every culture had persons who were slick, sharp, aggressive, acquisitive, boundary-breaking, and entrepreneurial, and these creatures had plenty of what economists have sometimes called animal spirits. Crafty manipulators were found in niches in every social and economic system and sometimes amassed wealth, power, and status, particularly when market and monetary forces were injected into formerly isolated communities following contact with the West. What anthropologists saw, living day to day with the people they were investigating, was that such cultural sharpies consciously used and abused the rules of the game in their quest for gain in one form or the other.[21] By the mid-1970s, field anthropologists had shifted from codifying institutional regularities to portraying the interplay of actors and rules, often declaring that they were testing one or the other of the formalist or structuralist positions, or perhaps reconciling the two. Exhaustion has vitiated the controversy, but in total, it helped anthropologists and at least some developmental economists elevate awareness of individuals as manipulators of the institutional systems in which they reside and as agents of change.

In the broad area of rural development and agricultural economics, a parallel debate raged over the issue of whether the Third World's traditional farmers responded in predictable fashion to price and profit incentives, or whether they were so inculcated with customary habits that they would ignore price and profit signals. The issue was again a highly practical one in development policy. If farmers were responsive, then conventional supply-demand analysis could be used to set price policies that would determine the levels and mix of crops being grown. Also, by juggling output and input prices, and hence profitability, farmers could be induced to adopt higher-yielding packages of technology, thereby triggering innovation and diffusion. The larger implication was that conventional agricultural economics could be used to design effective policies for rural development anywhere in the world.

In its most simplistic form, the rational-peasant proposition obviated the requirement to consider local institutions in designing production and innovation policy. Theodore Schultz's influential book, *Transforming Traditional Agriculture*, simultaneously liberated agricultural economists from having to worry about differentiating their advice in various cultural settings and empowered them to proffer one-size-fits-all counsel.[22] On close inspection, Schultze's argument is only one other misapplication of the culture-free maximization approach and suffers the same weaknesses as the others.[23] Despite scores of econometric studies designed to check for supply responsiveness in agricultural regimes through history and around the globe, the evidence for or against rationality remained ambiguous.[24] Many studies established that education, infrastructure, extension practices, and other nonprice variables played key roles in supply and innovation outcomes. Recognizing the insufficiency of the rational peasant thesis as an explanation for agricultural innovation, Y. Hayami and V. Ruttan developed a theory of induced innovation in which political pressures on government led to research and extension responses, suited to local conditions. Although it was by no means a fully satisfactory effort, this formulation had the merit of bringing institutions, politics, and culture back into the picture, albeit from a conventional neoclassical base.

These parallel debates over the proper way to reconcile the structural and individualistic methods have cut across economics, anthropology, and agricultural economics. At root in each case is the mystery of how best to reconcile institutional structure with individual action. To do so properly requires examining the place of economies in societies. Economic activity embraces three forms of behavior: production, exchange, and consumption. Although it is fashionable to think of these as steps in a linear transformation of matter into value and benefit, in fact consumption is requisite for production and the connection is fully circular.[25] A society's institutions mold its economy and, as each society is different, so is each economy. The French and the Indians, again, do not produce the same goods in the same way, exchange products and services in the same way, or consume equal mixtures and amounts of goods and services. In the process of economic development societies experience modifications of their production, exchange, and consumption arrangements. Indeed, this is called economic change and is the sine qua non of growth and development.

From the early Middle Ages on, first Europe and now the world, have been experiencing an economic transformation that may be depicted succinctly as a shift from nonmarket to market modes of transacting. The colonial and postcolonial experience of the Third World, and recent dramatic events in the former Second World, illustrate the magnitude and acceleration of these forces. The erosion and collapse of alternative traditional or state-command modes of economic organization have led to heightened awareness of the political and legal context of economic activity. In all countries, First as well as Second and Third-World, renewed attention is being given to institutional arrangements as the fount and matrix of economic growth. Furthermore, it is indubitably true that, with judgment and care, frictions and burdens, including those associated with rapidly changing distributions of wealth and income, can be reduced by attention to rules governing access to and use of economic resources.

Institutional rules shape and coordinate the sequence of economic activities—this is what is meant by process. When the time dimension is joined with the structural characterization of institutions, the result is process, flow, and sequence. A farmer plows and harrows a field, manuring leads to the planting of seedlings, which is followed by irrigation doses and weeding, and so on. Parts arrive at the factory assembly line in the proper order and at the right times and are converted into automobiles. The extreme example is the just-in-time inventory system created by the Japanese. Resistance to adoption occurred in the United States because institutional changes, in such things as habits of work and union-directed job descriptions, had to be made and were resisted. All productive activity is arranged by institutionalized, time-responsive sequencing. Goods and services get made, moved through the social framework, and consumed according to progressions that are built into the operations of institutions by use of calendars, clocks, phases of the moon, angles of the sun, and other technologies of chronicity.

Incentives: Institutions, Individuals, and Development

In understanding economic development, the structural and processual views of institutions and their connection to growth and change are helpful but insufficient. What is missing are the links that reinforce conduct or discourage it. Among the earlier institutional writers, Commons is the most structured in his treatment of social supervision of bilateral or multilateral transactions. When people interact, they do so under the watchful eye of authorities or peers. Using such practices as force, beatings, jail, expulsion, ridicule, reasoning with, or cajoling, these socially interested parties attempt to regulate deviant or unjustified behaviors and bring them into line with conformity. Killing someone else's sheep or violating a commercial contract brings into play enforcement or remedial measures. People's consciences are not always sufficient to ensure appropriate behavior so that sanction, adjudication, and remedy are necessary to preserve social contours.

In general, measures that conserve social stability are desirable, but as Ayres pointed out, this historic bias in societies, without which they could not exist, militates against constructive technological progress and social revamping. The record of human history chronicles the tension between past-binding institutions and forward-pushing innovations. Sanction is, of course, not only negative, nor is repression always successful, so that progress does occur. Nonetheless, societies are primarily, but not exclusively, structured to reward those who harmonize their conduct with operative social values, offering wealth, rank, and power to the most compliant and to those at the apex of the social realm who safeguard obedience by use of force, religion, legal codes, or suasion and example. In early societies, technological innovation was more often resisted than not; but, a fundamental change occurred in Europe from about the 14th or 15th century on. Past this point the balance of reward shifts increasingly in favor of those who are innovative in their practices of enterprise management and in their application of inanimate power and workplace experiment to their productive and exchange deportment. This sea change marks the cleavage between economies that were essentially static and those that are dynamic. The difference may be reduced to the prevailing balance of incentive and disincentive. Innovators are increasingly rewarded with status, profit, and power, rather than ridiculed, excommunicated, or burned at the stake. Social support for innovation and changes in economic relations leads to the amassment of more capital per worker, rapid broadening of the technological portfolio, and enhanced skills in the work force.

The interpreter of the rise of capitalism who exhibits the deepest understanding of the interaction of incentives, rewards, and social attitudes is Joseph Schumpeter. He grasped that the central mechanism, and defining characteristic, of capitalism was its unique treatment of innovative individuals, whom he called entrepreneurs.[26] Schumpeter's consideration of the dynamics of capitalism is in accord with Ayres's principles of economic progress. Schumpeter succeeds brilliantly in dissecting the relationship between capitalist institutions and technological change. A capitalist society lavishes wealth on entrepreneurs who put a new process or commodity into productive play in the market economy. This profoundly disturbing event unleashes competitive forces, elevates output, carves out new market spaces, and brings a rush of monopoly profit to the innovator-founder. Social approbation is reluctantly given, however, by the existing social elites, and by intellectuals and the professoriate, who ultimately quench the entrepreneurial spirit and convert free enterprise capitalism into state-and-corporate capitalism.

The relevance of Schumpeter's doctrines for the development of the world's laggard economies is immeasurably profound. The lesson is that, to foment development, the social, political, and economic system must reward those agents who succeed in devising and implementing new technical and organizational devices. Contrary to much belief, this does not necessarily imply the exact mimicking of the institutions of 19th century laissez-faire capitalism, but that state socialism or any other elected form of economic organization must enshrine incentives and rewards for innovations that conduce rising productivity and incomes. This principle can apply to small farmers, health workers, managers of the state railways, oil-field drillers, environmentalists, and corporate executives. The rewards need not always be in the form of monetary profits or even material gains, but can be promotions, approbation, or promotion in the ranks of the dominant political party.

Applications of Institutional Development Economics

The institutional organization of societies has three aspects: structure, process, and incentive. The delineation of structure helps social scientists characterize and differentiate social systems for historical and comparative study. The recognition of process injects individual aspirations and motion into the social system. It also acknowledges the importance of time, which in turn prompts attention to the sequencing of behavior and permits the analysis of the unfolding of social, political, and economic evolution. Sequencing and coordinating are especially vital to the performance of the economy, where savings, investment, producing, distributing, sharing, growing, and consuming (one does not eat dinner before breakfast) are time-framed processes. Ayres would certainly agree that the discovery of time ranks among the most notable of technological advances. Lastly, incentives and disincentives provide means of social control so that individual conduct is regulated. For economic growth to occur, on a base of expanding economic resources and physical structures, in tandem with continuing technological improvement, rewards must be pitched in favor of innovators who play a lead role in the process.

Institutional economists have applied these ideas to many problems and cases in the field of development economics. It is not possible to include all of these studies in a brief synopsis; attention will be given here to two clusters of writings. One consists of a collection of scholarship on Latin America; the second comprises work on South Asia.

The nations of Latin America are a laboratory case of the effects of inhibitory and inappropriate institutions on technological and economic progress. Despite a favorable resource base, Latin American development has been stop-and-go, repeatedly punctuated by economic crises and political turmoil. Applications of the ideas of Veblen, Commons, Ayres, and Mitchell—via Simon Kuznets—have yielded important insights into the retardation of Latin American growth, as James Street has said.[27] The paramountcy of technological absorption and generation is recognized: "Institutionalist analysts question whether, without sustained and accelerated effort to implant an indigenous scientific and technological strategy to cope with the region's retarded technical evolution, the widening technological gap can be overcome."[28] Institutionalists such as Dilmus D. James have usually rejected extreme forms of the dependency school, criticizing their excessive reliance on class struggle analysis, overly negative view of international economic connections, fatalism, and rejection of internal policy reform.[29] Institutionalists have argued that programmed national strategies, predicated on institutional reforms, can overcome barriers to development. These reforms would affect such structures as land tenures, by breaking up the latifundia system and distribution, and dividing land more widely. Trade policies also need examination, as does the alliance among extractive bureaucracies, industrialists, and labor unions, which enjoy the protection of the state. These elite matrices are often involved with multinational corporations in ways that do not yield the best results for national development. Nonetheless, there are positive dimensions to corporations' activities in the Third World, and institutionalists are well placed to explicate their role and mission in stimulating development.[30]

Two early and extremely important delineations of the role of institutions in Latin American development took the form of book-length treatments. William Glade wrote a detailed and illuminating study of the region's institutional arrangements and their effects of development.[31] W.C. Gordon's *The Political Economy of Latin America* is a somewhat earlier study that remains a classical specification of the origins of the continent's institutions and their deleterious impact on personal initiative and collective development programming.[32] Selecting a passage more or less at random demonstrates the continuing relevance of his insights:

> In a very basic sense, Latin American governments exercise "control of entry" in connection with the establishment of new firms. . . . [T]he power to permit or prohibit operation has been the tool the low-level administrative official or policeman has been able to use to obtain bribes from the small merchant or tradesman, or stall holder in the market. . . . If the businessman is strong enough, he intimidates the official. If he is weak, he is intimidated by the official. But in either case, the formalizing of the relationship results in a fantastic amount of paper work.[33]

This remarkable passage merits comparison with the now-touted book of Hernando de Soto on the informal sector. De Soto's *The Other Path*, an account of his work and experience at the Institute for Liberty and Democracy in Peru, has galvanized informal political movements and policy responses, including foreign donor involvement.[34] There are strong institutional elements in his work, which is largely anti-Marxist, and he might be placed at the crest of a neostructuralist Latin American wave. His emphasis on individual action would to some degree differentiate de Soto's approach from than of the institutionalists, but both share a view of an activist and redistributive state that is more responsive to nonelite needs and pressures than previous governments.

The American institutionalist tradition and the structuralist school in Latin America share some common threads, and this has led to interpretative, comparative assessments. Street writes, "The structuralists showed that, given the peculiar cultural background of Latin America, reliance on market forces often contributed in exaggerated ways to conspicuous and wasteful consumption, as well as to speculative and superficial investment decisions inconsistent with the requirements of orderly growth."[35] Structuralism had its origins in a critique of orthodox theories for failing to explain Latin America's laggardness, given the region's heavy involvement in international trade and investment flows in the late 19th and early 20th centuries. The concern was that ". . . the orthodox recommendation to rely on market forces only can reinforce and widen Latin America's development lag."[36] Street discussed the parallels between institutionalism and structuralism in terms of convergence. The primary concern of the structuralists was with bottlenecks and obstacles to factor mobility and technological diffusion. In a long-running feud with monetarists, they argued that the unusually high inflation rates in the Latin American economies were attributable to supply and cost factors rather than to monetary expansion or excess demand. Institutionalists agreed with these points in the main, but contended that more attention should be devoted to progressive social reforms and technology.[37]

Institutionalist writing on Latin America has not been confined to examining the connections between institutional economics and the Latin American structuralists and dependency theorists, or to cultural and institutional patterns at the continental level. Considerable notice has been conferred on specific topics. James Peach and Kenneth Nowotny, among others, have looked at the *maguiladoras* in the Rio Grande Valley. Dietz has written on Puerto Rico's struggle to define a coherent and independent pathway to development. The Caribbean basin has attracted the interest of Glen W. Atkinson. W. Paul Strassman has devoted much inquiry to problems of housing in the Third World, including those of squatter settlements in Lima.[38]

South Asia has attracted considerable attention from scholars working in the institutional tradition. The panoply of non-Western institutions—caste, the jajmani system, the joint family, the village community, factions, tenurial arrangements, and higher political structures—offers a fruitful arena for analysis. The region offers a good test of the premise that economies and economic agents are "the same" the world over, in the conventional economists' sense. It require a feat of dazzling sightlessness to maintain this investigative stance if one has set foot in an Indian village or read detailed accounts of the villagers' production and exchange patterns. Walter C. Neale has studied land tenures and reform in northern India in the pre- and post-Independence period.[39] In a series of papers on village economies and the effects of development policies on rural life, he has argued that the meshing of reforms and traditional institutions yields a mix of positive and negative outcomes that are often unforseen.[40] Neale and I have traced the path of India's post-independence development, emphasizing the role of democratic planning in setting priorities and policies.[41] Sabiha Iqbal and I examined Pakistan's international trade in a political economy framework, arguing that commercial policies grow out of domestic politics, not from abstract theoretical debates.[42]

In the past few years Asia and North Africa have attracted the attention of several scholars who have sought to apply collective action and new institutional economic theory to economic development questions. Representative of the current tendency is the work of Robert Wade on village life in southern India. He studies determinants of collective action and public good provision. He finds differences across villages that depend upon their ecological circumstances, including whether they have dry or irrigated lands. His careful study suggests strongly that all behavior cannot be accounted for with a purely individualistic explanation, but includes a pervasive sense of obligation and sanction.[43] At the national level, a study of Tunisia's economy and its institutional framework has been orchestrated by N.K. Nabli and Jeffrey Nugent. A compendium of contributions by Nugent, Nabli, and others applies collective action and new institutional economics language to a number of sectoral topics.[44] In spirit and analysis, these interpretations differ little from those of the old institutionalism, although their language may be more acceptable to dedicated orthodoxophiles.

Conclusion

It is prudent to conclude this survey of the contributions of the institutional tradition to the study of development by reiterating a few elements of the argument. The claim of development economics to be a differentiable field in the discipline must rest on the premise that "institutions matter." They matter, as I have argued, in three ways. Institutional analyses is fundamental in explaining how societies and economies differ across time and from each other. This claim denies that economic principles transcend the institutional arrangements that define a particular culture, in which people behave in accord with conventional and continuing practices, always with the allowance that individuals have the capacity to manipulate and transform those arrangements. The concept of process introduces time, sequence, and order into the study of economic systems. Different institutions breed different processes and thus societies have clearly distinguishable rates of capital accumulation, export growth, consumption, or capacity utilization. The role of individuals is particularly salient in a dynamic context where the balance of reward and restraint tilts in favor of innovation in all its forms: technological, legal, political, and social, an insight brilliantly realized by Joseph Schumpeter.

I will end by remarking once again that a great deal of the work done by orthodox economists in the field of development economics is institutional and coincides to a large degree with that of institutionalists. This implies that there is a wide avenue for common dialogue and comprehension that is sometimes lacking in other subfields of our discipline. To go beyond this point, which has been valid since the pioneers of the field began to mark out its boundaries after World War II, I will further assert that development economics is now, in the early 1990s, having an incredibly profound influence on standard theorizing and empirical work. The worry in the West about laggard growth, most apparent in the United States in the 1980s, has led to greatly enlarged interest in technology, innovation, economic policy, and national programs for development (but never call these "planning"). There is recognition that savings rates depend upon more than interest rates; that the quantity and quality of the work effort of the labor force rests on attitudinal factors, and even upon social interactions in such forms as quality-control teams; that probing the motives and rate of progress of scientists and engineers requires looking deeply into cultures and psyches; that schooling and workplace education—the transmission of ideas—is fundamental to progress.

The fear is no longer that development economics will be dismissed as a field of legitimate inquiry and brought back underneath conventional macroeconomics and microeconomics. Many of the ideas that originated in development economics, of the institutional type or of the slightly renegade conventional type, are finding new value in debates over the best means to reinvigorate growth in developed economies.[45] The emphases on infrastructure, linkages, and externalities are now realized as heavily relevant in all economies regardless of their level of income. The effects of trade on economies cannot always be taken as positive and, therefore, a national trade policy appears imperative—immiseration by foreign trade is as threatening to the United States as it ever was to Brazil or Kenya. The proper role of the state in guiding the economy, and the appropriate sphere of the market, remain enigmatic and subject to experiment and redefinition. The extraordinarily sudden demise of the Eastern Bloc has reopened a host of questions about the legal foundations of economic activity, property rights, tenures, and the contractual necessities for commerce and industrial organizations.

Institutionalists are well placed to enter into these exciting debates affecting most fields of modern economics. We have nothing to lose but our self-imposed chains that have limited dialogue for too long.

Notes

1. The best set of essays on classical development economics remains Bert F. Hoselitz, ed., *Theories of Economic Growth* (New York: The Free Press, 1960). Joseph J. Spengler's essay on John Stuart Mill is a true gem that has high pertinence. He says, "Mill believed that noneconomic factors played an important role in human affairs, which involved economic progress. Among these factors he included beliefs, habits of thought, customs, and institutions" (pp. 118–119).

2. The first true textbook to survey and synthesize development economics was Benjamin Higgins, *Economic Development* (New York: W.W. Norton, 1959). Higgins drew heavily on standard ideas from classical and neoclassical economics, including public finance, in which he had a background. The text surveyed in a mostly sympathetic fashion the then recent

contributions of the early development economists. He provided chapter-length case studies of several countries, including Indonesia and Libya. Although he insisted on the global relevance of standard economics, he recognized country differences and incorporated the role of social and cultural factors in development.

Among the first journals in the field was *Economic Development and Cultural Change*, which took a broad multidisciplinary view of the subject, as its title suggests.

3. Economists' changing views of economic development are well described in H.W. Arndt, *Economic Development, The History of an Idea* (Chicago: University of Chicago Press, 1989). The cross-currents are much more complex than suggested by the simple pro and con polarity I have used.

4. Two recent compendia that review the dimensions of development economics are: Gustav Ranis and T. Paul Schultz, eds., *The State of Development Economics, Progress and Perspectives* (Oxford: Basil Blackwell, 1988); Hollis Chenery and T.N. Srinivasan, eds., *Handbook of Development Economics*, Volumes I and II (Amsterdam: North Holland, 1989).

5. W. Arthur Lewis, *The Theory of Economic Growth* (London: George Allen & Unwin, 1955), pp. 11–12.

6. The conventional references are: A.O. Hirschman, *The Strategy of Economic Development* (New Haven: Yale University Press, 1958); Harvey Leibenstein, *Economic Backwardness and Economic Growth* (New York: John Wiley & Sons, 1957); Hla Myint, *Economics of the Developing Countries* (New York: Praeger, 1965); John C.H. Fei and Gustav Ranis, *Development of the Labor Surplus Economy* (Homewood, IL: Richard D. Irwin, 1964); Gunnar Myrdal, *Economic Theory and the Under-developed Regions* (London: Gerald Duckworth, 1957); Ragnar Nurkse, *Problems of Capital Formation in Underdeveloped Countries* (New York: Oxford University Press, 1953).

7. Irma Adelman and Cynthia Taft Morris, *Society, Politics, and Economic Development: A Quantitative Approach* (Baltimore: The Johns Hopkins University Press, 1967). Their second book, *Comparative Patterns of Economic Development, 1850–1914* (Baltimore: The Johns Hopkins University Press, 1988), investigates the influence of institutional patterns on national growth during the period of the global spread of industrialization.

8. Adelman and Morris (1967), p. 150.

9. The substantiation of universal modes of premarket exchange—reciprocity, redistribution, and householding—is the subject of Karl Polanyi, Conrad M. Arensberg, and Harry W. Pearson, eds., *Trade and Market in the Early Empires* (Glencoe, IL: The Free Press, 1957). The emergence in the economy of a separate sphere of monetary, price-guided production and exchange is interpreted in Karl Polanyi, *The Great Transformation, The Political and Economic Origins of Our Time* (Boston: Beacon Press, 1957; c. 1944).

10. Perhaps the most directly linked and tangible representation of the institutionalist tradition is the Land Tenure Center at the University of Wisconsin, where scholars in the Commons tradition, such as Kenneth Parsons and Donald Kanel, have worked on a variety of development problems.

11. John Adams, "Galbraith on Economic Development," *Journal of Post-Keynesian Economics* 7 (Fall 1984): 91–102. Galbraith wrote a short textbook on development economics and, in India, gave many talks on the subject. He recalls that it was at his initiative, taken in response to expressions of student interest, that Harvard initiated graduate courses in development economics.

12. Clarence E. Ayres, *The Theory of Economic Progress*, 2nd ed. (New York: Schocken Books, 1962); 1st ed. (Chapel Hill, University of North Carolina Press, 1944).

13. Ayres, pp. xxiv–xxv.

14. No social science tradition has a patent on the use of institutional analysis to study

social systems. Although one may favor one standpoint or another, a particularly lucid exposition is still Bronislaw Malinowski, *A Scientific Theory of Culture and Other Essays* (New York: Oxford University Press, 1960; c.1944). The bridges between Malinowski's sociological representation and the American institutionalists may be found in Walter C. Neale, "Institutions," in Marc R. Tool, ed., *Evolutionary Economics, Volume I, Foundations of Institutional Thought* (Armonk, NY: M.E. Sharpe, 1988), pp. 227–256.

15. Ayres, p. 182.

16. Ayres's position on progress, and that of institutionalists, derives from the instrumental theory of value of pragmatic philosophy. There are many treatments on instrumentalism; for a recent example, see Philip Mirowski, "The Philosophical Bases of Institutional Economics," in Tool, *Evolutionary Economics*, I, pp. 51–88. A longer discourse is Wendell C. Gordon and John Adams, *Economics as Social Science, An Evolutionary Approach* (Riverdale, MD: The Riverdale Company, 1989), especially chs. 1–8.

17. Another weakness of a purely structural formulation is that it unduly favors the formal or high culture of a civilization because it is the apex elites who leave behind the extant law codes, religious and ethical writings, and massive architectural remains. The people of the mass, folk, or low culture did not have the means to depict and pass down the patterns of their lives. This skewedness needs correction; it is now widely recognized and has created many avenues for revisionist history.

A related criticism of overly formal social history is made by the French historians of the *Annales* School. Many dimensions to their contributions have much in common with the work of Karl Polanyi and the substantivist historians and with American institutionalists. Among these touchstones are the importance of everyday working and exchange patterns, the material culture, and the importance of institutions. Initial references are Carole Fink, *Marc Bloch: A Life in History* (New York: Cambridge University Press, 1989), which has an excellent list of Bloch's writings, and the works of Fernand Braudel—for example, *The Identity of France, Volume I, History and Environment* (New York, Harper & Row, translated by Sian Reynolds, 1988; published in French in 1986).

18. An excellent thoughtful essay is R.C.O. Matthews, "The Economics of Institutions and the Sources of Growth," *The Economic Journal* 96 (December 1986): 903–918. Matthews welcomes the renewal of interest but does not agree with the extreme position of many neoclassical economists that relative costs, prices, and incentives, including unrealized gains of exchange, will prompt institutional change in directions favorable to market transactions. He writes, "Recapitulating, then, I have suggested a number of reasons why institutional change is not likely to be merely a matter of Pareto-improving innovations and adaptations: the involvement of the state, non-voluntary interactions (externalities), and inertia and complexity, with their tendency to produce a random walk" (p. 915).

19. Douglass C. North, "Institutions," *Journal of Economic Perspectives* 5 (Winter 1991): 97–112. This article is a curious mixture of error and wisdom, sometimes hard to distinguish because of an incredible clumsiness of language.

20. A good assessment of the formalist battles is Anne Mayhew, "Atomistic and Cultural Analyses in Economic Anthropology, An Old Argument Repeated," in John Adams, ed., *Institutional Economics, Contributions to the Development of Holistic Economics, Essays in Honor of Allan G. Gruchy* (Boston and The Hague: Martinus Nijhoff Publishing, 1980), pp. 72–81.

Although I have characterized the debate as formalist versus structuralist, it was more complicated than that. In addition to throwing rocks at the functional structuralist tradition in anthropology, the formalists attacked the substantivist work of Karl Polanyi in economic history; this battle line became known as the substantivist–formalist controversy.

21. The phrase "cultural sharpy" I first heard from Murray Leaf, an anthropologist who has done considerable field work in Indian Punjab. Long discussions among myself, him, Anne Mayhew, and Walter C. Neale helped me—and the others—sort out exactly what was at stake in the formalist individualist challenge.

22. Schulze provided little or no evidence in support of his thesis that peasant farmers were everywhere rational. He resorted to truncating a key passage in a field report on an Indian village, in a manner that reversed its meaning, in order to furnish a compelling example. In turn, this passage was quoted repeatedly by others who did not take the time to read the original text from which it was excised.

23. Kusum Nair got the strongest blows in, in her now classic ripostes. See, for example, Kusum Nair, *In Defense of the Irrational Peasant: Indian Agriculture after the Green Revolution* (Chicago: University of Chicago Press, 1979).

24. In departments of agricultural economics, the burgeoning of the estimation of farm supply functions appeared to grow out of the need to find dissertation topics for the scores of foreign students who had arrived to study the American agricultural miracle. Rather than see how local institutions affected agricultural practices, the motif was rather to demonstrate, using whatever measure of arcane econometrics it took, that farmers were the same the world over. This practice had the effect of maintaining the value-added of a doctorate in farm economics, whatever it did for understanding or effectiveness once the candidate returned home.

These points are further developed in: John Adams, "The Analysis of Rural Indian Economy: Economics and Anthropology," *Man in India* 52 (January–March 1972): 1–20; *idem*, "The Emptiness of Peasant 'Rationality': Demirationality as an Alternative," *Journal of Economic Issues* 16 (September 1982): 663–672.

25. The failure to think in terms of this closed circle, and of the connections between this circle and natural cycles in the physical world, has been responsible for the belated recognition in industrial societies of the environmental and waste disposal predicaments that arise from the linear view of resource processing.

26. Joseph A. Schumpeter, *The Theory of Economic Development, An Inquiry into Profits, Capital, Credit, Interest, and the Business Cycle*, translated by Redvers Opie (New York: Oxford University Press, 1961; published by Harvard University, 1934; first German edition, 1911). Also, *Capitalism, Socialism, and Democracy*, 3rd ed. (New York: Harper & Row, 1962; first published in 1942).

27. James H. Street, "The Institutionalist Theory of Economic Development," in Marc R. Tool, ed., *Evolutionary Economics, Volume II, Institutional Theory and Policy* (Armonk, NY: M.E. Sharpe, 1988), pp. 443–469. Also, James H. Street and Dilmus D. James, "Institutionalism, Structuralism, and Dependency in Latin America," *Journal of Economic Issues* 16 (September 1982): 673–689.

28. *Ibid.*, p. 463.

29. Richard Bath and Dilmus D. James, "Dependency Analysis of Latin America: Some Criticisms, Some Suggestions," *Latin American Research Review* 11 (Fall 1976): 3–54.

30. William P. Glade, "Multinationals and the Third World," in Tool, *Evolutionary Economics*, II, pp. 471–502.

31. William P. Glade, *The Latin American Economies: A Study of Their Institutional Evolution* (New York: Van Nostrand, Reinhold, 1969).

32. Wendell C. Gordon, *The Economy of Latin America* (New York: Columbia University Press, 1950).

At the University of Texas, Austin, a number of theses and dissertations applied institutional theory to Latin American development. A notable example is Milton D. Lower's doctoral dissertation, "The Institutional Bases of Economic Stagnation in Chile," University of Texas, Austin, 1970.

33. Gordon, *op. cit.*, p. 39.

34. Hernando de Soto, *The Other Path, The Invisible Revolution in the Third World*, translated by June Abbott (New York: Harper & Row, 1989).

35. James H. Street, "A Holistic Approach to Underdevelopment," in Adams, ed., *Institutional Economics*, p. 241.

36. James L. Dietz and James H. Street, "Latin America's Economic Development," in Dietz and Street, eds., *Latin America's Economic Development: Institutionalist and Structuralist Perspectives* (Boulder, CO: Lynne Rienner Publishers, 1987), p. 10.

37. James H. Street, "The Latin American Structuralists and the Institutionalists: Convergence in Development Theory," in Dietz and Street, eds., *Latin America's Economic Development*, pp. 101–114.

38. These four studies form a symposium in the *Journal of Economic Issues* 16 (June 1982): 489–523. Strassman's writings include *The Transformation of Urban Housing* (Baltimore: The Johns Hopkins University Press for the World Bank, 1982).

39. Walter C. Neale, *Economic Change in Rural India: Land Tenure and Reform in Uttar Pradesh, 1800–1955* (New Haven: Yale University Press, 1962).

40. Walter C. Neale, *Developing Rural India: Policies, Politics, and Progress* (New Delhi: Allied Publishers; Riverdale, MD: The Riverdale Company, 1990).

41. Walter C. Neale and John Adams, *India: The Search for Unity, Democracy, and Progress*, 2nd ed. (Princeton: D. Van Nostrand & Co., 1976).

42. John Adams and Sabiha Iqbal, *Exports, Politics, and Economic Development, The Case of Pakistan, 1970–1982* (Boulder, CO: Westview Press, 1983; Lahore: Vanguard Books, 1987).

43. Robert Wade, *Village Republics, Economic Conditions for Collective Action in South India* (New York: Cambridge University Press, 1988).

44. N.K. Nabli and J.B. Nugent, *The New Institutional Economics and Development, Theory and Applications to Tunisia* (Amsterdam: North-Holland, 1989).

45. Discussions with Shahid Alam, my colleague in the Department of Economics, Northeastern University, have sharpened my awareness of this reversal of fortune now being enjoyed by development economics.

Commentary by James L. Dietz

The Crisis in Development Economics

As John Adams notes in the introduction to his chapter, development economics has suffered an almost constant crisis of identity since its inception. This is because development economists have insisted that an understanding of the lag in living standards between the advanced nations and the greater part of the world's people and nations requires ways of thinking, seeing, and analyzing beyond the body of mainstream economic theory, be it neoclassical or Keynesian. This was, and remains, a conviction that has encountered considerable resistance within the mainstream of the economics profession.[1]

Adams identifies the crux of the disagreement this way: "[D]evelopment economics has from its infancy embraced the study of institutions, and its validity as a field must rest on the proposition that institutions matter." It is not simply that a society's institutions act as additional constraints on the maximizing behavior of individual economic agents, be they households (consumers) or firms (including peasants and other farmers, small businesses, etc.), a point that neoclassicals concede can affect behavior, though in fairly predictable ways.[2] It is rather that the institutions of any particular society "matter" in that they can engender modes of behavior—both thinking and acting—that are fundamentally distinct from, and often quite alien to, the utility and profit-maximizing assumptions that underlie mainstream analysis.

Without the assumed neoclassical behavioral anchor of maximization to provide determinate solutions, the regularity and predictability of action as responses to profit and pleasure signals by individuals in their multiple roles as consumers and producers are relinquished. The motivations for individual behavior, then, must be investigated and discovered, and not simply assumed, within the particular institutional structure that conditions and molds that behavior.

The critical issue to development economics is, then, according to Adams, not whether institutions matter,[3] but whether they matter to the extent that distinct motivations for the behavior of economic actors can be posited in societies with different institutional structures. For example, neoclassicists assert, given the a priori acceptance of an underlying (profit- or utility-) maximizing calculus animating the producer, that peasant farmers in Mexico do not choose to increase their production of corn when demand increases *because they rationally, in the neoclassical sense, choose not to, as it will not increase their expected profits or utility*. The existence of thin credit markets for working capital, or government price ceilings that ultimately discourage such action, or ill-defined property rights, may account for this inaction. This lack of output response is, however, the *predicted* outcome of profit-maximizing behavior given the specific institutional constraints: peasant/capitalists would like to produce more, but they are unable to do so because of the institutional barriers they confront.

Contrast this way of telling the story to that of a development economist who might analyze the behavioral response of the peasant farmer within a noncapitalist and nonutility- and nonprofit-maximizing paradigm, if that seems from observation to be the pertinent frame of analysis. The absence of supply response by the peasant farmer to increased demand might then be understood as the consequence of *satisficing* behavior in the context of a complex of limited desires in consumption that condition economic actors in noncapitalist environments.[4] In this view, higher demand and higher prices do not impart a "signal" to the peasant to produce more, as the neoclassical maximizing assumption posits, but rather to its opposite. This is peasant "rationality" of quite a different order from the neoclassical variety, but such rationally acting peasant farmers, as Adams suggests, cannot simply be assumed away as the neoclassicals do.

The difference in policy implications between the two perspectives is profound. In the neoclassical view, an improvement in credit markets, the reduction of government interference with the mechanisms of the market, and a clearer definition of property rights will call forth the predicted increase in output to increased demand and higher prices as profit-maximizing peasant capitalists are permitted to pursue the ever-higher standard of living that fundamentally motivates them. In the alternative view, peasant farmers are not assumed to be profit or even utility maximizers. They are satisficers whose current standard of living has a finite ceiling prescribed and bounded by traditional values about what is socially necessary. Thus even with the most smoothly functioning credit markets and the least invasive government imaginable, higher prices still may fail to elicit the expected supply response: a key "institution" that remains unaltered is precisely the peasant farmer's (perverse, to the neoclassical) behavioral response to higher prices.[5] Institutions in the development view are more than simply constraints on immutable behavioral motivations across nations and cultures. Institutions create different motivations while, at the same time, these behavioral norms are themselves institutions.

The neoclassical view of development begins with the premise of the maximizing, capitalist economic agent; the development perspective alternatively posits institutional economic actors whose motivation is not a priori knowable but rather must be determined. In the development view all life is "institutionalized." We all live, work, and play in institutional structures with rules, norms, and expectations that not only constrain and condition behavior but that are also functional, to greater or lesser degrees, in defining what we actually desire to do as economic, social, and political agents.

The Institutionalist Dissent

The contemporary crisis in development economics is the consequence of the current dominance in practice of the neoclassical perspective. The escape from backwardness—in both the former Third and Second Worlds—is, the neoclassicals argue, to be found in the expansion of the institutions of the market and in a redirection—and radical shrinking—of government intervention in the economic and other spheres. Economic agents are presumed to be rational maximizers whose energies have been thwarted by the "wrong" institutional, especially governmental, structures. With the release of the constraints on individual fulfillment that the extension of market institutions will unleash, ever-higher levels of output and living standards will be generated, from Moscow to Montevideo. Market systems, in this view, are virtually synonymous with, and seemingly automatically generative of, economic development.

For the institutionalist economist, this perspective is seriously deficient.[6] It is not markets per se that bring in their wake economic development.[7] In fact, as Adams notes, there are reservations among institutionalists about the contributions and value of the unfettered operation of markets wherever they operate. More profoundly, the neoclassical focus on markets misses the fundamental founts of economic progress: technology and an appropriately educated population.

In his chapter, which tends to focus more on institutions and their variation across nations and cultures, Adams does not elevate these two forces to the level of importance they deserve in thinking about the development process. Institutions are but one facet of a symbiotic unity of institutions (ceremonialism) and technology intersecting and interacting in all societies. At the core of the institutional understanding of the process of economic development is the constant dualistic tension existing between the underlying, forward-reaching push of the worldwide pool of technological knowledge and the prevailing ceremonial/institutional structure of society, a structure, that by nature of being institutionalized, tends to impede the flow and hence the fruits of technological change.[8]

Technology in the institutional analysis of development—meaning not only the entire accumulated complex of scientific and machine-tool knowledge and the tools themselves but also the human understanding, skills education, and training essential for making use of such knowledge and tools—is the indispensable source of greater productivity, expanded output, and higher income. The more rapidly that technology is able to advance, the more rapid will be the pace of economic growth. Slower technological progress means slower economic growth and reduced possibilities for augmenting or creating the social mechanisms that promote greater equity. In some societies, the existing institutional structure is conducive to a more rapid pace of technological advance than in others. This is why institutions ultimately matter to the institutionalist. It is not only because different institutional structures engender dissimilar patterns of behavior that render simple prediction difficult if not impossible; it is rather more fundamentally that different institutional structures, and the ways of doing, thinking, and acting they produce, have quite disparate repercussions on the potential for technological change in any society, and it is the pace of technological advance that decisively determines the level of economic development of a nation.[9]

Technological change is the consequence of scientific discovery, experiment, and innovation. The successful introduction of ever higher levels of technology into the domestic production process of any country—what can be called domestic innovation—requires a domestic scientific establishment capable, first, of adopting and adapting foreign-produced technological knowledge (including machines and tools) to local conditions and, later, of conducting its own research, designing its own experiments, and recognizing the potential and periodic dangers of its own discoveries when applied to the domestic economy. Ronald Dore usefully refers to these two capacities as ITLC and ITCC—"independent technology *learning* capacity" and "independent technology *creating* capacity."[10]

The creation of an ITLC implies the acquisition over time of technological autonomy. Creating an ITLC, and not the market system, has been the essential first step toward greater technological self-sufficiency and toward progress on the road to economic and social development. It has been an ITLC that has undergirded the Japanese, Korean, and Taiwanese so-called development miracles in the post-World War II period; the successful export regime so often identified as the reason for the achievements of the countries would have failed in the absence of augmented technological autonomy.[11] An ITCC comes later, with the further maturation and deepening of the ITLC process that logically precedes it. An ITLC is essential if a country is to make headway on the path to development; an ITCC may be necessary to continue that development over the longer term, after the gains from the ITLC strategy become more difficult to sustain, as Japan would appear to be learning now.[12]

The creation of an indigenous technological capacity, supported by a technologically supportive cultural milieu, is absolutely necessary since the preconditions for development cannot be borrowed.[13] Technology, properly conceptualized, cannot be imported off-the-shelf as a bundle of things since, it must be emphasized again, "technological progress can be understood only by recognizing that human skills and the tools by and on which they are exercised are logically inseparable."[14] It is thus not possible to effectively borrow the *manifestations of technology*—physical capital, tools, and implements that are the usual focus of the technology transfer literature—and expect to "become" developed if the human skills and the culture required to make effective use of this fragment of technology are absent or poorly formed within the borrowing country. This embedding of human skills and knowledge *within* the concept of technology is one of the fundamental insights of institutional theory that separates it from other analyses on the sources of development, be they neoclassical or among more heterodox development economists.

It is the human resource dimension of technology that makes an indigenous technological capacity so important to any successful process of development and that returns our attention to the nature of society's prevailing institutions and their functions. Technology is more than tools, blueprints, and machines; it is a complex, value-laden social process that becomes imbedded in key institutions of society from the family to the religious sphere to the schools to the state that, in the case of successful developers, inculcates an unconscious but deeply formed *technological culture* as an integral aspect of society's ideology and canon. This culture must exist, or be in substantial formation, if there is to be any hope for meaningful technological borrowing and adaptation, let alone to have technological progress that is at least partly internally generated and then applied to domestic production processes.

The importance of technology and particularly the enrichment of the human resource component of technology, often imprecisely termed "human capital" accumulation, have been widely identified as contributors to economic growth.[15] But it is within institutional development analysis that the overwhelming significance of *indigenous* technological knowledge and of education have been thrust forward as empirically verified, theoretical constructs of paramount importance to successful development. At the same time, any society's particular institutions, which are both structures and evolving processes for doing, thinking, and acting, will have a notable impact on the rapidity with which the unfolding world store of technological knowledge will be able to be domesticated in the service of economic and social development. And this complex, evolving, and vibrant interaction of a society's institutional structure and the forces of technological change decides the pace of a nation's economic development.

Where I would augment Adams, then, is in a more profound insistence not just on institutional variations among nations that result in alternative behavioral motivations and drives besides those of the neoclassical assumption of profit and utility maximization. For the institutionalist development economist, a consideration of institutions is guided by, and in fact necessitated by, a parallel and reciprocal need to understand what is happening in terms of the spread of technological knowledge and its application in production. What is essential is to grasp how any society's institutions affect the prospects and pace of domestic technological absorption and of the creation of a capacity for technological autonomy (an ITLC).

The institutionalist is thus interested in institutions for different reasons than are neoclassicals, or even most heterodox development economists. Institutions either, on balance, thwart or contribute to technological autonomy and progress. The focus of the institutionalist development economists is on this "two-legged" essence of economic development: technology (and the education to achieve higher levels of such progress) and society's institutions. In particular, the institutional development economist is concerned to determine the possible means for encouraging the institutions and structures that are likely to be most efficacious for the promotion of expanded technological autonomy in nations where technological change, and hence economic and social development, are being held back.

New Directions

The previous section insists on the importance not just of technology to the social and economic development of a nation but of technological *autonomy*.[16] This emphasis was always implicit in institutionalist analysis, but the broad literature on the possible gains from technology transfer from the developed to the underdeveloped world has tended to obscure the need for an ITLC, even among some institutionalists. Meaningful technology transfer by multinational corporations via the learning effects from their location in less-developed nations has been vastly overstated. Multinational corporations have too much invested in their proprietary knowledge to freely permit its acquisition, and the evolving structure of such corporations into spatially segmented, vertically integrated international entities since the 1960s has severely limited the potential gains from learning via the mode of technology transfer.[17]

Research by development economists on the bases for the successes of the East Asian economies of South Korea, Taiwan, and Japan compared, particularly, to the continued weaknesses apparent in the Latin American economies since the late 1970s has confirmed the importance of domesticated technology, that is, of technological autonomy, and of an appropriately educated population able to make use of this technology. This literature also has stressed not only the need for technological autonomy but for the imperative dominant role of domestic capitalists/entrepreneurs in all successful processes that eventually lead to economic and social development. Multinational corporations are not vehicles of economic development. Economic development proceeds from a growing and linked network of indigenous and local sources of finance, production, capital, innovation, and knowledge. Research on the bases for the success of the East Asian economies after the 1960s and for the weakness of the Latin American economies has suggested, too, the significance of "good" state policy in creating an environment that permits the international pool of technological knowledge to contribute to higher levels of economic development.[18]

In particular, the East Asian experience strongly suggests that a "developmentalist" state can accelerate the pace of economic growth. It is not unfettered markets that foster economic and social development, as the current neoclassical obsession suggests, but rather a developmentalist state with a vision of the future and the power to implement that vision. The developmentalist state not only can correct for market failure, an area of government intervention that many neoclassicals recognize as legitimate, but actually can improve upon the outcome of an efficiently operating market system.[19] The successful East Asian states thus have been able to make policy decisions that actually result in overall performance that is superior to what would have been the market-determined outcome.

The more successful East Asian experience can be attributed then, to a significant degree, to the state's "getting policies right," rather than to simply "getting prices right" and letting the economy respond to the impersonal signals emanating from the world market, as neoclassical proponents insist. The "getting policies right" strategy at times implied, paradoxically perhaps, finding the correct "wrong" prices (including the exchange rate) that could most effectively raise production and income.

The right policies and effective price interference by a developmentalist state actually *bend* the allocation of resources, especially of investment goods and of education, in favor of rapid economic growth and productivity gains that help to bring a country, or at least key sectors, up to world levels of competitiveness by creating an institutional environment (including, especially, an appropriately educated populace) propitious for more rapid technological change. The state is not a barrier to development nor simply a handmaiden in this process; the state is as much an axis of the developmental project as the market and those private entrepreneurs who are enabled to prosper within the favorable parameters shaped by the state and its policies. The East Asian achievements and the Latin American failures in development thus reinforce the institutionalist analysis: nations that succeed in creating institutional structures—including (perhaps especially for less-developed nations) the state—that accelerate the pace of indigenous technological adaptation, that utilize the new technology to empower local producers, and that make ever-increasing use of local sources of finance, capital, and knowledge, will develop more quickly than nations that fail to do so.

Conclusions

In John Adams's chapter, the focus of the analysis tends to be more on institutions than on technology, though discussion of the latter is not absent. In fact, in any appraisal, these two legs of institutional development economics are of one body and hence are inseparable. I would simply put more emphasis on the empirical relevance of technology as the primary progressive force for social and economic development and the potentially constraining capacity of those institutions found to be inappropriate to further progress. Furthermore, recent research on the sources of successful development efforts confirms the significance of local ownership of production and of sources of financial capital, of local control over the technological process and the ability of local entrepreneurs and producers to domesticate the world pool of knowledge for domestic purposes, and of a visionary state with the means and power to pursue a developmentalist agenda without undue interference from local vested interests. These aspects, too, deserve to become part of the institutional development paradigm.

Economic and ultimately social development is not about markets; markets may be a means to facilitate economic development, but they are not the primary agent of such a transformation. Development results from the progressive and continuous application of new technology in production within an institutional environment supportive and conducive to such change. Where more substantial work in institutional development economics is warranted is in understanding how inappropriate institutions might begin to be transformed when powerful vested interests are resistant to such change.

Notes

1. For a forthright statement by a contemporary dissenter to the need for a separate "development economics," see Bauer (1984). One needs to be cautious, however, to not assume that those like Lord Bauer, who do not accept that there is a field of study called development economics with tools distinct from those of mainstream economic theory, are not aware of the *limitations in use of* those tools in specific situations.

> There are no special economic theories or methods of analysis fashioned uniquely for the study of the under-developed world. But while the tools of analysis are of wide relevance, in a study of under-developed countries the situations to which they must be applied vary greatly.... The results of an analysis which is appropriate to an economy in which the subsistence sector is negligible may have to be modified materially when applied to an economy in which exchange is peripheral or not pervasive [Bauer and Yamey, 1957, pp. 8–9].

This extract makes clear, as does Lord Bauer's writing of an entire text on underdeveloped countries, that the neoclassical dissenters to an economics of development do not gainsay the significance of the particularities of any country or situation in modifying the application of the mainstream economic toolbox. That toolbox, however, retains its relevance as a predictor and as an explanatory paradigm.

2. In fact, a growing number of neoclassical economists identify themselves as institutionalists, in the sense that they do think that institutions matter. However, such economists, like the economic historian Douglass North or the industrial organization economist Oliver Williamson, remain convinced that the neoclassical maximizing assumptions as they apply to individual motivation retain their predictive applicability. Institutions thus act as constraints on fixed behavior modes without determining such behavioral norms. However, as the quote from Lord Bauer in note 1 above suggests, the awareness by such new institutionalists as to the conditioning affect of different institutions is one with a long pedigree among neoclassicals. "New" institutionalism should not be confused with institutionalist, or evolutionary, economics as discussed further in this chapter. For a spirited critique of the new institutionalists, see Dugger (1983, 1990).

3. Adams's definition of an "institution as a learned, habitual pattern of behavior, supported by ingrained attitudes, values, and ways of thinking" is succinct and adequate. The variety of examples of such institutions he provides in the chapter is extremely rich. Also see Walter Neale (1987) for a more detailed discussion of the institutionalist conception of institutions.

4. Higher prices for output mean that it is now easier to reach the desired (finite) level of consumption with the same, or even less, output. One might try to force this outcome into the neoclassical backward-bending labor supply curve framework, but then it is unclear why the same analysis would not apply to other "firms" in other circumstances, and not just to peasant farmers.

5. In Latin America, this debate over the response of producers has revolved around the elasticity of supply for agricultural products, especially food products. After 40 years of debate and research, the evidence remains controversial.

6. For an overview of institutionalist development economics, with a focus on Latin America, see Street (1987). Most development economists are not institutionalist economists. Institutionalist development economists have their greatest disagreements with neoclassicals, but there are also substantial and noteworthy differences between institutionalists and development economists. Nevertheless, the latter differences are perhaps more likely to be able to be bridged given the greater openness to heterodox analysis characteristic of development economics thinking, at least of the pre-1980s variety.

7. Not answered to this point is precisely what is meant by "development"? How does one determine if a particular country is developed, underdeveloped, developing, or perhaps even undeveloping? Though often used as a proxy indicator, development is not simply about growth over time in the real per capita level of gross national product (GNP) or gross domestic product (GDP). Development has economic and social dimensions, not all of which are even capable of precise measurement. Economic and social development is inherently multidimensional and complex; it is a matrix of goals, themselves subject to change over time as the level of development changes.

Development as such is a process of a particular type of change over time; it is not a thing or a definable final goal. And while economic growth may contribute to economic and social development under certain circumstances, there is no unambiguous or dependable link assuring that it will. Success along the vector of economic growth is no guarantee of economic and social development, and it is less likely to so contribute the lower the current level of per capita income, especially in the absence of a visionary state, as discussed below.

A list of the factors constituting economic and social development could be extended and refined nearly ad infinitum, but the following broad categories are sufficient to illustrate the fundamental constituent elements: 1) a higher real average standard of living (which is not necessarily the same as higher real per capital GNP or GDP); 2) expanded employment opportunities for an ever-larger proportion of the population of working age, particularly the most disadvantaged; 3) a tendency toward greater equality, along with a reduction in the numbers of absolute poor; 4) production and distribution of public services (including a safe environment) to reach those most in need of them; and 5) greater participation in economic, political, and social life of an ever-larger share of the population (Streeten, 1979; also see the helpful overview in Meier, 1989, pp. 5–9). An improvement in more than one of these categories without deterioration in any of the others is required if one is to be assured that economic and social development is truly occurring.

8. Ayres (1978, Foreword).

9. To return to our nonmaximizing peasant farmer in Mexico, an institutionalist economist might argue along the following lines: the lack of output response to higher demand and higher prices of the peasant farmer, even when the institutional barriers the neoclassical economist noted are removed, can be understood as an institutionalized resistance of the farmer to change. In such circumstances, new technologies, which are fundamentally necessary to raise living standards, are unlikely to be able to be introduced, as traditional means dominate in production. In effect, the "institution" of the nonmaximizing and tradition-bound peasant farmer leads to a lack of progress, that is, to a very low level of productivity and technological advance, and this is one of the institutional barriers that must be overcome (most likely through expanded education).

10. Dore (1984, pp. 65–68).

11. See Dietz (1992) and the references cited there.

12. ITLC involves both "know-*how*" and increasing progress on the path of "know-*why*," or deep technological learning, to use Lall's distinction (Lall, 1984, pp. 116–117).

13. Street (1987, pp. 1878, 1881); also see Reséndiz (1987–1988).

14. Ayres (1978, p. xv).

15. Denison (1967, pp. 299, 315) was one of the earliest investigators, noting that these factors were responsible for over 40 percent of growth in the United States and the United Kingdom

16. For a more detailed discussion of these issues, see Dietz and James (1990, especially chs. 8–11).

17. See Dietz (1982) and the sources he cited, for a fuller analysis of the spatially segmented, vertically integrated international corporation.

18. The complementary components noted in the text also are confirmed by the economic history of the already developed nations. See Dietz (1992) for further discussion.

19. See Wade (1990).

References

Ayres, C.E. *The Theory of Economic Progress*, 3rd ed. (Kalamazoo, MI: New Issues Press, 1978; originally 1944).

Bauer, P.T. "Remembrance of Studies Past: Retracing First Steps," In Gerald M. Meir and Dudley Seers, eds., *Pioneers in Development* (New York: Oxford University Press, 1984).

Bauer, P.T. and Basil S. Yamey, *The Economics of Under-developed Countries* (Chicago: University of Chicago Press, 1957).

Denison, Edward. *Why Growth Rates Differ: Postwar Experience in Nine Western Countries* (Washington, DC: The Brookings Institution, 1967).

Dietz, James L. "Export-Enclave Economies, International Corporations and Development." *Journal of Economic Issues* 19 (June 1985): 513–522.

Dietz, James L. "Overcoming Underdevelopment: What Has Been Learned from the East Asian and Latin American Experiences?" *Journal of Economic Issues* 26 (June 1992): 373–383.

Dietz, James L. and Dilmus, D. James, eds. *Progress Toward Development in Latin America: From Prebisch to Technological Autonomy*. (Boulder, CO and London: Lynne Rienner Pubs., 1990).

Dore, Ronald. "Technological Self-Reliance: Sturdy Ideal or Self-serving Rhetoric." In Martin Fransman and Kenneth King, eds., *Technological Capability in the Third World* (Hampshire, England: Macmillan, 1984).

Dugger, William A. "The Transactional Cost Analysis of Oliver E. Williamson." *Journal of Economic Issues* 17 (March 1983): 95–114.

Dugger, William A. "The New Institutionalism: New but not Institutionalist." *Journal of Economic Issues* 24 (June 1990): 423–431.

Lall, Sanjaya, ed. Special issue on "Exports of Technology to Newly-Industrializing Countries." *World Development* 12 (May–June 1984).

Meier, Gerald M., ed. *Leading Issues in Economic Development*, 5th ed. (New York and Oxford: Oxford University Press, 1989).

Neale, Walter. "Institutions." *Journal of Economic Issues* 21 (September 1987): 1177–1206.
Reséndiz Nuñez, Daniel. "Science and Technology in Mexico: Looking Forward." *Voices of Mexico* 6 (December–February 1987–1988): 38–45.
Street, James H. "The Institutionalist Theory of Economic Development." *Journal of Economic Issues* 21 (December 1987): 1861–1888.
Streeten, Paul. "From Growth to Basic Needs" *Finance and Development* 16 (September 1979).
Wade, Robert. 1990. *Governing the Market: Economic Theory and the Role of Government in East Asian Industrialization* (Princeton: Princeton University Press, 1990).

7 INSTITUTIONALIST POLICYMAKING

F. Gregory Hayden

The history of institutionalist thought is a history of concern for policy, both with reference to the influence of policy on the sociotechnical system and to instrumental evaluation to determine good policy. Karl Polanyi stated that the substantive approach to economics leads inevitably to policy.[1] John Dewey foresaw the marriage of the social sciences and policymaking when he wrote that "the tools of social inquiry will be clumsy as long as they are forged in places and under conditions remote from contemporary events."[2] Policymakers have forged institutionalist thought into solutions for social problems. Thus, as Gilman Ostrander has stated, "every new era of twentieth-century American thought has derived new stimulation from Thorstein Veblen's writing."[3] Rexford Tugwell was one of those who derived new policy from Veblen's thought. Russell Long once stated, "[A] great deal that now goes on . . . in the way of decent land use, soil conservation, the rehabilitation of tenants, a recognition of the rights of labor, consumer protection, and a valiant clear realism derive directly from Tugwell."[4] Consistent with a concern for policy, Martin Gellen explained that institutionalists have been successful in structuring and implementing planning. "The intellectual roots and theory of national economic planning as we know it in the United States today can be traced back to Institutionalist Economics."[5]

The purpose here is to extend the institutionalist concern for policy more explicitly in the realm of public policymaking. It should be called metapolicymaking because the concern is about institutionalist policymaking regarding policymaking. Recent volumes on policymaking indicate that the advice of Polanyi, Veblen, and Dewey has been heeded. There has been a progressively tighter interlocking of social science research and public policymaking.[6] The premises of this chapter are, first, that for the interlock to become more effective, institutionalist insights are needed, and second, that institutionalists should become more effectively interlocked with all aspects of policymaking. The policy science and policymaking literature has exploded since the 1960s, yet that literature continues to practically cry out for what the institutionalists have to offer—an integrated transdisciplinary approach to the social and policy sciences.

This is an opportune time for a more complete development of the institutionalist policymaking paradigm. Much of the activity at the national level in the United States in the 1980s has been to dismantle the institutionalist policy legacy from past decades. Because of that dismantling, problems of crisis proportions are developing in numerous areas: environmental degradation, homelessness, collapse in major financial sectors, deprivation of medical care, to mention a few. This means institutionalists will have an opportunity to take a prominent leadership role in policymaking in the 1990s as people demand that public bodies solve the problems that were caused or exacerbated as neoclassicalist ideals have been operationalized.

Figure 7-1 is offered to provide an overall view of policymaking. It is not intended as a model, or a linear sequence, or even a complete taxonomy. It is offered to outline the most relevant phases and levels of policymaking. Across the top of Figure 7-1 are the phases of policymaking, and from the top down are the levels. The levels are policy, strategy, and tactics as indicated on the lefthand side of Figure 7-1, with their respective sciences indicated on the righthand side. The lines connecting the boxes are there to indicate that for policymaking to be effective, all phases and levels must be consistent and integrated—not to indicate a mechanistic lock-step operation. Institutionalists need to fill the 30 boxes contained in Figure 7-1 with tools and integrate them in a complete policymaking process. No one scholar, or policymaker, can be an expert in all the areas; each box is an area of study and expertise.

The more northwesterly area of Figure 7-1 is where most academic institutionalists work; toward the southeast corner policy is finalized and implemented. For effective planning and policymaking, all corners need to be mastered and tied together through the integration of all areas in between the corners. If an institutionalist laboriously cultivates the knowledge vineyard in the northwest quarter without the means to integrate the knowledge created, the work will not bear fruit in the policy field. In order to avoid such frustration, institutionalists must continue to close the gap between science and tactics—between theory and operations. In addition to the production of science and philosophy, there is need to produce strategies and tactics, or stated differently, to produce institutionalist politicians, lawyers, planners, lobbyists, economists, accountants, budget analysts, and the like.

The purpose of Figure 7-2 is to indicate three serious and prominent policymaking problems that occur when the message of Figure 7-1 is not heeded. Figure 7-2A is labeled the "Bureaucratic Approach" to policymaking. In this approach tactical and administrative personnel make policy or conduct their activities without respect to the knowledge base, philosophy, problem research, belief system, or policy strategies. This approach is usually guided by techniques acquired by experts without inspecting the techniques to determine their appropriateness. "If the expert is to be useful at all he must be integrated into a general scheme and led by a generalist who is sensitive to the interplay of all the parts."[7]

The second approach demonstrated in Figure 7-2B is the "Pseudo-strategic Approach" in which strategists: 1) lack the technical expertise of the accountants, psychologists, computer scientists, fiscal analysts, and so forth, 2) do not have the knowledge base of the policy scientists, and 3) are seldom trained in strategic sciences. They usually consider themselves too experienced to be concerned with the findings of scientists or the details of tactical expertise, thus generating great frustration for all those who are attempting instrumental policymaking.

The "Scholarly-King Approach," indicated in Figure 7-2C, leads to wasted efforts and resources rather than bad policy because the advice from such an approach is seldom heeded. Scholars who devote themselves to general theoretical and philosophical research sometimes direct abstract solutions (often with no more than a page or two of explanation) to operation and implementation personnel although their "solutions" are not grounded in case studies of the problem area and have not been legitimized and approved through the advocacy process. This kind of suggestion cannot be utilized; thus it usually engenders no more than a polite reply that often frustrates the scholar.

Technology

Before beginning to discuss the particular phases and levels in Figure 7-1, to which most of this article will be devoted, this section will address the

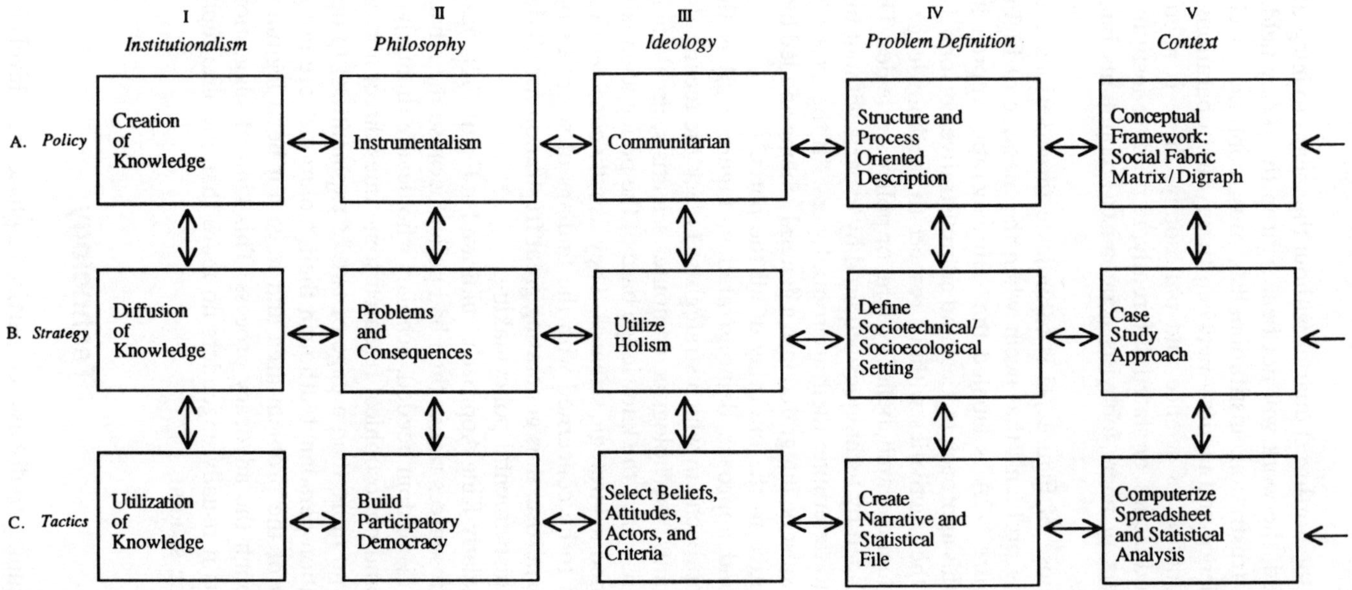
I
Institutionalism
II
Philosophy
III
Ideology
IV
Problem Definition
V
Context
A. Policy
Creation of Knowledge
Instrumentalism
Communitarian
Structure and Process Oriented Description
Conceptual Framework: Social Fabric Matrix / Digraph
B. Strategy
Diffusion of Knowledge
Problems and Consequences
Utilize Holism
Define Sociotechnical/ Socioecological Setting
Case Study Approach
C. Tactics
Utilization of Knowledge
Build Participatory Democracy
Select Beliefs, Attitudes, Actors, and Criteria
Create Narrative and Statistical File
Computerize Spreadsheet and Statistical Analysis

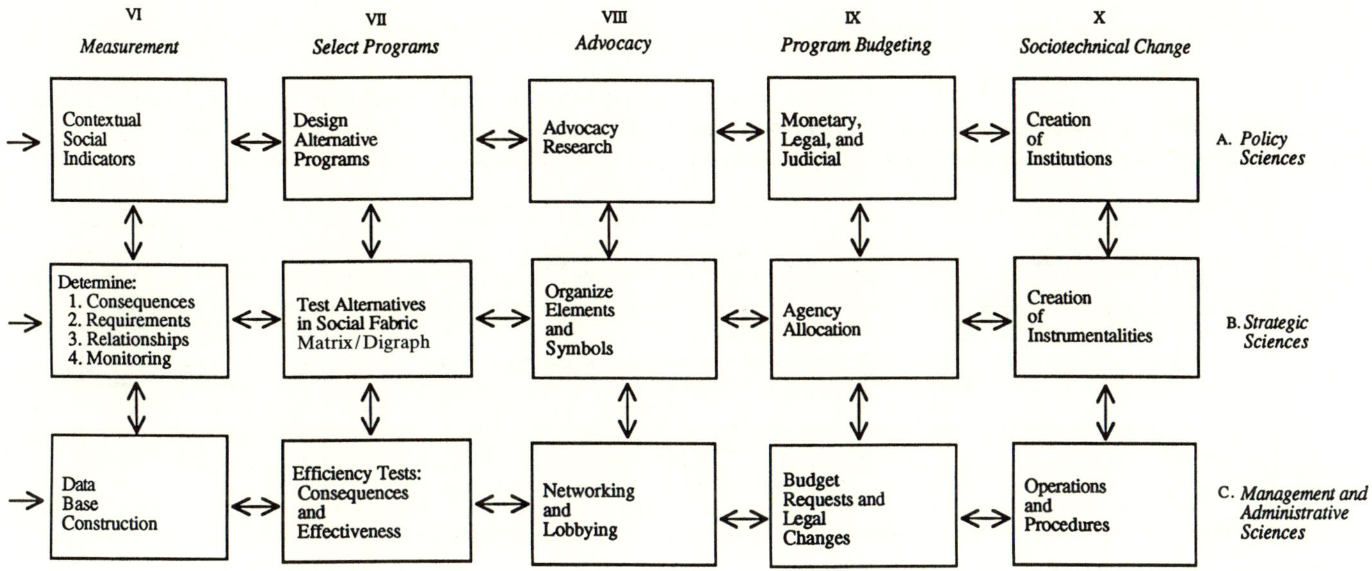

Figure 7-1. Phases and levels of institutionalist metapolicymaking.

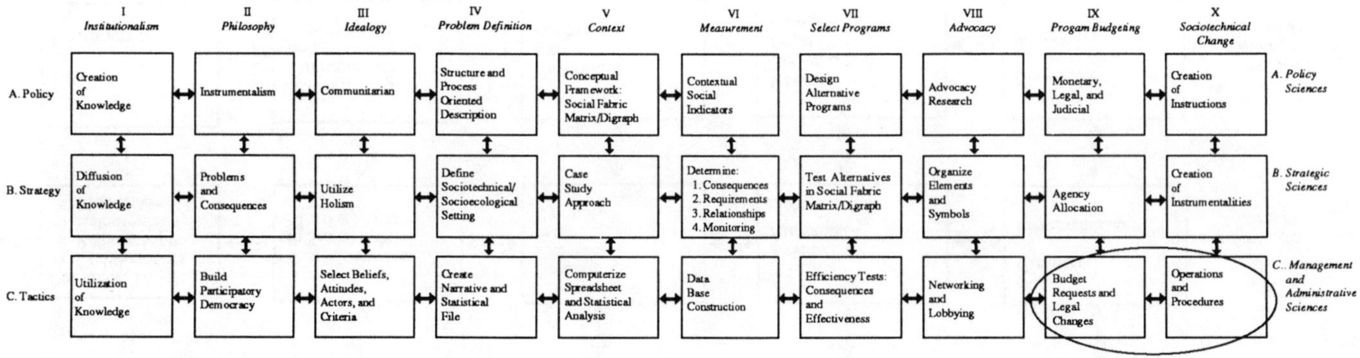

Figure 7-2A. Bureaucratic approach: A "practical" approach concerned only with operations in the implementation phases. Directs tactics and operations in the implementation phases without concern for higher level beliefs and basic research, and without concern for policy strategies. Leads to bureaucratic rigidity.

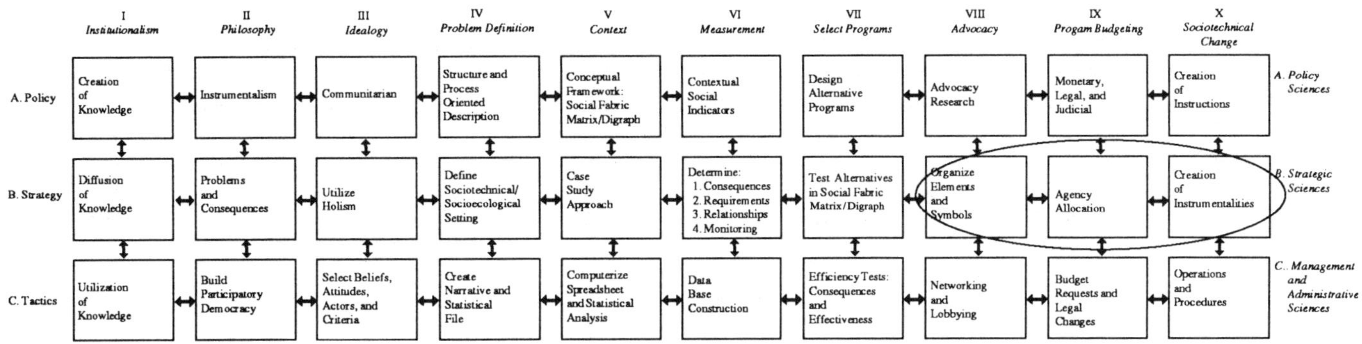

Figure 7-2B. Pseudostrategic approach. Concerned with designing strategies without being concerned with whether strategies have either a research base or operational feasibility. Practiced by "political" types who are too "experienced" to be concerned with ideology or research. They listen to the latest charlatan and follow fads. Regularly promote new strategies. If pseudostrategists get a government appointment, they create great bureaucratic scar tissue which must be overcome by serious strategists.

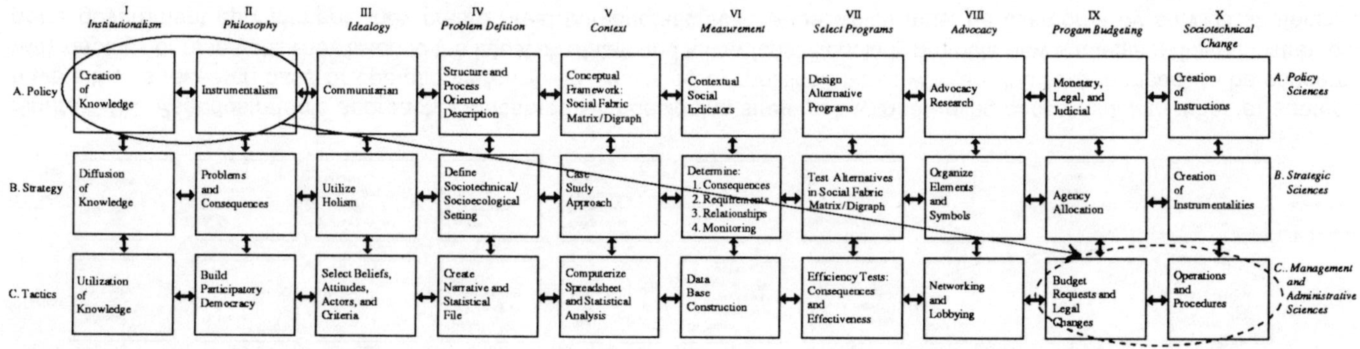

Figure 7-2C. Scholarly-king approach. Main concern is with the research level of the knowledge and philosophy phases, and with suggesting abstract "solutions" to implementation personnel. Not concerned in a constructive way with other phases and levels and not integrated into the policy process. Often communicates suggestions with one- or two-page statements that are ignored.

issue of technology. It is important to emphasize that the study of any phase-level conjunction in Figure 7-1 should focus on technology. Probably the primary reason for the failure of modern society to solve its problems is the failure of policymakers and policy scientists to direct their focus in this way. The aspect of policymaking most ignored in the policy science literature and most emphasized in the institutionalist literature is technology; thus the integration of the two literatures is essential for theoretical advances in policymaking.

Technology is indeed the tail that wags the societal dog. Its great power comes from its important role in defining and determining social relationships. Therefore, the first ingredient we should consider in any problem is technology. The way we live, the way we relate to each other, the way we communicate, or whether we do, are all heavily influenced by technology. Technology is defined as the combination of tools, skills, and knowledge which are organized as the industrial arts of a society. Its change stimulates creation of new social relationships and thus a new society.

Institutionalists have long understood technology's impact on well-being and its impact on the structure and process of society. "The institutionalists saw technological innovation as the preeminent factor which determines the institutional superstructure of modern society."[8] While technology has been recognized as offering great potential for human welfare and scientific advancement, institutionalists have demonstrated that inhibiting institutions often prevent this potential from being realized.

For institutionalists, technology is not the consequence of some benign natural evolution. The tools, knowledge base, and skills are deliberate acquisitions that are usually "ceremonially encapsulated," to use Paul D. Bush's term,[9] by the social forces that have the power and policy means to direct and guide the development and use of technology. Polanyi believed the strength of the policy-technology connection was such that policy, *not process*, determines alternative technology as well as alternative ways of instituting technology.[10] Veblen was pessimistic about the possibility of technology being directed for the good of the social whole because of the encapsulated hold that the corporate business world had on technology. Reminiscent of Veblen, Dewey stated, "[T]he simple fact is that technological industry has not operated with any degree of freedom. It has been confined and deflected at every point; it has never taken its own course. The engineer has worked in subordination to the business manager whose primary concern is not with wealth but with the interest of property. . . ."[11] The ability of corporations to guide, control, and suppress technology has received considerable attention recently.[12]

From a policy analysis perspective, real technological advancement or progress, when subjected to a serious holistic technological assessment, is much more infrequent than usually assumed. To be sure, there is a vast explosion and proliferation of new knowledge, skills, and innovations in the form of new gadgetry, new molecular combinations, engineered genetic mutations, and artificial intelligence. And these are sometimes combined to provide for human, social, economic, and general biophysical enhancement. Yet too often, the combination is not enhancing but rather deteriorating. Knowledge, intelligence, and inquiry—what we usually call research—are powerful weapons in the determination of the kind and structure of technology that will be instituted and of the enhancing or deteriorating uses to which it will be put. For this reason the research universities and think tanks have become a fierce battleground in the struggle to direct and control research and technology.

The established centers of corporate power have learned the lesson that technology structures society as well as the product mix in the economy, and that it influences the degree of centralization in the decision processes as well as the condition of ecosystems. They have arrived at the conclusion that social and physical technology can be controlled to a great extent by controlling the research centers. By influencing the selection of researchers and professors, and guiding the funding for research, they can also influence and guide the kind of technology, society, decision processes, and ecosystems that will emerge. With this realization, business corporations, along with other power centers with a similar interest and ideology, have invaded the universities.

The power structure and conditions of life are at stake; thus universities have become combat zones for their determination. The battle has been fierce but to date very one-sided. The people are losing; the corporate power centers are winning.

One example is the success regulated industries have had in promoting the theoretically bankrupt techniques of neoclassical cost-benefit analysis. David Bollier and Joan Claybrook explain this success as follows:

> The success of regulated industries in winning respectability for cost-benefit analysis is symptomatic of an important political fact: industry dominance of regulatory knowledge and debate. By funding public policy institutes, trade associations, research projects, and university chairs, regulated industries have helped underwrite scholarship stressing the costs and constraints imposed by regulation.
>
> The void in knowledge about health and safety regulation can be traced to the superior resources that industries command in generating regulator knowledge and disseminating it. ... Victims of corporate misconduct ... lack the

> financial means and political organization to give greater intellectual dimension or currency to the beneficial freedoms that regulation can secure for them.[13]

Those economic power systems that stand in opposition to the development and use of technology to enhance human life and the ecosystem have their act together—from theory to bureaucratic appointments, from ideology to computer data systems, from rhetoric to power bases, from the provision of research funds to the sponsorship of scientific journals, from the takeover of universities to the destruction of regulations. They are organized and they are delivering. They are effectively wielding complete paradigms, from philosophy and theory to advocacy and operations.

Technology, which is one of the most important ingredients of human welfare, has become a foul word in the minds of many people because it is so regularly associated with hazardous spills, unemployment, cancer, community disruption, consumer victimization, ozone depletion, and so forth. If technology is to advance in the sense of enhancing progress for human and ecosystem welfare, the people's legislative bodies must explicitly and directly take back control of the research functions of their public universities.

The concept of technological change without progress is not new to institutionalism. John Dewey recognized that in a holistic sense, advancement is infrequent[14] because the expanded ability to capture energy, increase speed, and process information often is not matched by the ability of human governing bodies to analyze and control themselves and their technology. But Dewey held "steadfast to his faith in science, in collective intelligence, and in a machine age that . . . will be a means of life and not its despotic master."[15] For Dewey "the evils in our system, . . . call for knowledge and scientific insight to surmount difficulties and eliminate sources of defect and ill; they call for a renewal of spirit, for moral development, and for a remaking and redirection of social forces and conditions."[16] None of these relates to the call now being imposed on research universities by corporate donors.

Institutionalists have always been concerned with determining, through technological assessment, which direction is forward. But there is no implication in institutionalism "that something ought to be done simply because it can be done, scientifically and technologically. We do not intend the intrusion of any kind of technological determinism."[17] To use Marc Tool's much-quoted statement. "[T]he direction is forward which provides for *the continuity of human life and the noninvidious re-creation of community through the instrumental use of knowledge.*"[18] Consistent with Tool's overarching criterion, Fagg Foster and James Swaney have developed additional criteria for technological assessment. Foster's criteria apply in the case of institutional adjustment due to the application of new technology. His criteria are technological determinum, recognized interdependence, and minimal dislocation.[19] Swaney states that Foster's criteria "may be used to facilitate adjustment of the institutional structure, and are particularly useful when technologically induced problems arise in the social structure."[20] Swaney adds the criterion of coevolutionary sustainability which means that development paths or applications of knowledge that pose serious threats to continued compatibility of sociosystem and ecosystem evolution should be avoided."[21] Had the advice of Tool, Foster, and Swaney been an integral part of Secretary of Agriculture Clayton Yeutter's policy judgment criteria, he would not have written to the Europeans with regard to the banning of beef treated with hormones to say: "We just cannot and should not, stop technological progress in this world."[22]

Institutionalist Metapolicymaking

The remainder of the chapter will be devoted to a detailed consideration of the phases and levels of Figure 7-1. The three levels—policy, strategy, and tactics—for each phase will be discussed beginning with *Phase I: Institutionalism* and continuing through *Phase X: Sociotechnical Change*.

Phase I: Institutionalism

Creation of Knowledge (Policy)

The titles for the levels in this phase (Figure 7-1, lefthand column) are taken from the title of the journal, *Knowledge: Creation, Diffusion, and Utilization*. The concept of the "creation of knowledge" is particularly germane to the inquiry and discovery process of institutional analysis and to the creation of theories and warranted assertions. This concept recognizes that science and knowledge creation are completed by humans, through discretionary action within their social processes. Knowledge is not "out there' waiting to be discovered. It is created. Albert Einstein and Gunnar Myrdal clarified this point: Einstein said that findings in physics are determined by the frame chosen by the investigator. Myrdal said that there is an inescapable a priori element in all scientific work. This means the frame of reference is not given for economists; it is created by them.

As will be explained later, the a priori assumptions and frame of reference for knowledge creation need to be consistent with the context of the problem to be solved; otherwise the resulting theories and warranted assertions will not be relevant to policymaking. Milton Lower explained that this is why Veblen cautioned against the "given and immutable" frame of economists in the classical tradition. Veblen said of that tradition, it "limits their inquiry in a particular and decisive way. It shuts off the inquiry at the point where the modern scientific interest sets in."[23]

Therefore, when the neoclassicalists insist on the market system ideology as their a priori element and market models as their frame of reference, the findings of their inquiry are usually irrelevant to policymaking. What was left of the neoclassical model of the market system was swept away around the globe in the 1930s. In the United States, institutionalists played a major role in structuring the New Deal which designed and implemented the welfare state, consistent with the work of Veblen and Commons. Notable institutionalists such as Rexford Tugwell and Adolf Berle were major advisors to President Roosevelt. Well beyond those notables, however, many policymaking agencies at the federal, state, and local levels were strongly influenced by institutionalists. Veblen, after his death, had far more influence on policymaking than while he was alive. Ostrander wrote in 1971 that "Veblen's economic ideas gained currency during the New Deal era . . ." while his sociological critique of the industrial structure influenced scholars in the 1960s as never before.[24] The thrust and direction of the New Deal continued in the 1970s as well, especially in the ecological and membership rights areas.

The "alphabet soup" of the SEC (Security and Exchange Commission), FDIC (Federal Deposit Insurance Commission), FDA (Food and Drug Administration), EPA (Environmental Protection Agency), OTA (Office of Technology Assessment), ASCS (Agricultural Stabilization and Conservation Service), and SCS (Soil Conservation Service), begun in the New Deal or added since, is a core which guides our lives and regulates the economy in the United States today. It is a world consistent with the institutionalist approach; it is a world inconsistent with the neoclassical market approach; and it is a world that the Reagan Administration set about to dismantle. Jerry Petr wrote that the Reagan revolution would fail, because it was an attempt to roll back the policies and programs that evolved with the modern technological society. To revert to processes controlled by the market system would require that sociotechnical processes revert back to those before the modern technological society. As Petr demonstrated, that could not happen; the Reagan revolution was doomed to failure.[25] Unfortunately on its inevitable march to ignobility, numerous casualties were suffered along the way.

The Reagan Administration, reflecting this prior neoclassical idea and the market model frame of reference, undertook policies to reestablish the market approach to policy, with unsatisfactory results. For example, the Secretary of Interior under Reagan decided to assess corporations for their ecosystem damage from hazardous waste spills according to the market value of the damage. Of course, the character, structure, and subtleties of ecosystems cannot be defined and valued by market processes nor do many of the natural elements ever enter the production process. That fact did not deter neoclassicalists from providing techniques for market valuation so that corporations could be assessed for damages far less than the cost of restoration. Congress rejected the neoclassical approach and called for restoration costs plus use values as the appropriate assessment base. The U.S. Court of Appeals agreed with the nonmarket concept of efficiency chosen by Congress. The court opinion stated that "efficiency, standing alone, simply means that the chosen policy will dictate the result that achieves the greatest value to society. Whether a particular choice is efficient depends on *how the various alternatives are valued*."[26] Does this not have the ring of Myrdal and Einstein? The court also stated that "restoration is the proper remedy for injury to property where measurement of damages by some other method will fail to compensate for the injury."[27] This is a simple example of the divergence between the neoclassical market approach and the instrumentalist approach. Congress can clearly see that to restore the value of an ecosystem, restoration is necessary; thus, restoration costs are the relevant frame of reference. That is why the continued development of the institutionalist policymaking paradigm is so important. Its theoretical frame can be utilized in real-world settings where deliberative bodies attempt to solve real-world problems.

Assuming the market system to be the institution to which everything else is to be compared is not the only immutable belief in the neoclassical paradigm. Equally immutable is utility analysis. However, in the real world, there is no such entity as utility, nor utils, nor utility functions. This has been explained by institutionalists since Veblen. (The demise of the idea of utility in the other social sciences will be explained below.) Most neoclassical theoreticians now admit that utility does not exist, or, as Varian put it, "a utility function should not be given a psychological interpretation."[28] Herbert Simon explained in his Nobel Prize recipient lecture that on the basis of numerous studies, the idea that people behaved so as to maximize subjective expected utility (SEU) was false.

> The refutation of the theory has to do with the *substance* of the decisions, and not just the process by which they are reached. It is not that people do not go through the calculations that would be required to reach the SEU decision—neoclassical thought has never claimed that they did. What has been shown is

> that they do not even behave *as if* they had carried out those calculations; and that result is a direct refutation of the neoclassical assumptions.[29]

Yet utility maximization is the criterion for neoclassical policy analysis in such techniques as cost-benefit analysis and contingent valuation. However, since utility does not exist, alternative value criteria are needed. Institutionalists turn to the belief criteria of society: they recommend those that inquiry finds contribute to solving the problem; they recommend against those that contribute to the problem.

Another reason the "Creation of Knowledge" designation is germane is because, as Marc Tool explained, all communities require constant re-creation. Human life is feasible only in the context of community; we are members one of another "in a community in which institutions pattern (prescribe and proscribe) our lives. Re-creating community means reconstituting the structural fabric of that social order, . . . the task is to re-create."[30] Institutionalist inquiry, like all science, is a social process that needs to be continually re-created. The way the social processes function will determine the kind of science created. The competency and rate with which institutionalism creates relevant policy science depend on the adequacy of research funds and the adequacy of the scientific environment in which institutionalists work.

With regard to funded research, historically institutionalists have had an advantage in the pursuit of foundation and governmental research grants because of the problem orientation of institutionalist research. This has not been true, however, with regard to federal government funds during the Reagan Administration. Moreover, resources to support research from within the universities have become as inadequate for institutionalists as has their working environment. If institutionalists are to create knowledge at a rate consistent with problem creation in the technological society, policies will be needed to prevent the harassment of institutionalists by those promoting neoclassicalism. The problem is not just one of sharing resources. It extends to denial of research assistants, exclusion from administrative positions, and refusal to hire. It includes the refusal to allow institutionalism to be taught and the hazing of graduate students who declare an interest in institutionalism. As Wassily Leontief explained, the prevailing practices of economics departments in the United States is a situation where "tenured members of leading economics departments continue to exercise tight control over the training, promotion and research activities of their younger faculty members and by means of peer review, of the senior members as well. The methods used to maintain intellectual disciplines in this country's most influential economics departments can occasionally remind one of those employed by the Marines to maintain discipline on Parris Island."[31] Thus, if the policymaking benefits of institutionalism are to be reaped in any proportion close to the harvest needed, it will probably be necessary for policymakers to intervene more directly to bring academic freedom, freedom of inquiry, and diversity of thought into economics departments.

Diffusion of Knowledge (Strategy)

Although the production and creation of institutionalist knowledge is adequate, and for most areas excellent, its diffusion is still done largely as our ancestors did 200 years ago. The main strategy for diffusion is to publish articles, pamphlets, and books, and to deliver class lectures. Notable exceptions of persons who make use of modern diffusion technologies, of course, exist. John Kenneth Galbraith's television series, "Age of Uncertainty," comes to mind as do Harry Trebing's yearly institutes on public utility issues for state and local government personnel. The "Hunger for Profit" video documentaries on agribusiness and world hunger included a number of institutionalists. Michael Sheehan is in the courtroom on a regular basis carrying research results into the fray of judicial proceedings, and many institutionalists explain their findings at legislative hearings. Modern diffusion technologies include the printed and electronic media, computers, phone networks, desktop publishing, electronic text, and so forth, but institutionalists are not effectively using them at this time. While the physical, natural, and medical scientists regularly place printed media releases on the wire services and make videotapes for use by television stations, institutionalists do not usually so diffuse their new findings. How are people to know about this knowledge if it is not carried in modern diffusion channels?

In a *New York Times Magazine* article, Pat Choate is referred to as the most influential institutionalist on the policy scene today. Dr. Choate said that the telephone and his rolodex are his most important policymaking tools. It is through the phone that he communicates daily with editors and others across the nation.[32] My own policy experience confirms Choate's advice, but it is necessary to reach far beyond that technology. Institutionalists should be using and accessing a whole array of sources. For example, we should be regularly downloading our computers to the computers of federal, state, and local policymakers. Electronic text networks are used regularly by strategists in the field and tacticians in the bureaucracies.

To quote Arne Leemans, "information processes are part of a policymaking process. Information is one of the main bases for power and influence."[33] Some even depict "professionals as dominating the policy process through professional issue networks in and out of government that have replaced the old, special-interest pressure groups."[34] Yet institutionalists have not really developed a strategic science for the diffusion of policymaking knowledge, although William Melody's writings on information will serve well as the base for such studies and transfer activities. Melody has explained how information flows and communication technologies are central to policymaking as well as how the control of these by powerful interests can determine the kind and flow of decisions. "A major challenge for public policy will be to find methods to insure that developments in the information and communication sector do not exacerbate class divisions in society and that its benefits are spread across all classes."[35] Due to the dynamic changes in knowledge transfer technologies, "opportunities are appearing for institutionalists to develop their research so as to inform public policy decisions. Now they have an opportunity to do more than just interpret the world. In the Commons tradition, they can participate in changing it!"[36]

Utilization of Knowledge (Tactics)

A well-developed scientific base with regard to the utilization of knowledge now exists. The conclusions gleaned from that work are consistent with institutionalism.

First, for institutionalism to play its full role in policymaking, institutionalist findings need to be utilized in disciplines beyond economics. This means multidiscipline interfacing is necessary on a regular basis with disciplines such as political science, anthropology, policy science, communications, systems sciences, law, engineering, sociology, finance, accounting, medicine, and all the other applied sciences.

Second, it is necessary to stay involved in the application process of scientific findings if those findings are not to be corrupted. Recent research has shown that "information is processed in wondrous ways, few of which are replicative of the original information."[37] Information is a weapon—a rather powerful weapon—in the policymaking process; thus it is abused and misused. Scientists need to regularly correct misinterpretations of their work and to convey through the policymaking process, which includes the media in a democracy, when their findings are being utilized to achieve misdirected policy.

Third, applied research needs to provide for the dovetailing of research information and the information needed by planners and policymakers. The results of policy science research, if they are to be adopted, need to be translated into numerous formats and modes for utilization by those not familiar with the original scientific knowledge. The policy tools discovered will need to be written up for the media; data must be transferred to agency computers; new software must often be developed for use in the public policy research agencies; and training manuals will be needed to train operational personnel on the use of the new technology. Much of the literature regarding the innovation of basic scientific ideas into commercialized products applies here. Policy science utilization must deal with the same kind of technology transfer problems as other products.

The fourth conclusion deals with the concept of information lead. The concept is in agreement with Melody's ideas presented above: "in order to have power and influence, an actor should build up an information lead over the other actors, or, on the other hand, reduce his information arrear."[38] Or, stated differently, excellent research is of little use if it is not timely.

The need for control in the policymaking process is obvious at the strategic and practical levels when observing Figure 7-1. There is also need for standardization and control at the policy research level. When verification of theories or social research techniques is sufficient to give them warrant, they are standardized.

> There can be no intelligent objection to standardizing instrumental equipment, theoretical and practical. Standardization is necessary for efficiency and precision in control. But there is fundamental cause for intelligent objection when control over the standardized equipment is substituted for control in the solution of an actual problem which the use of the standardized equipment can give. When such substitution is made, the use of the equipment, instead of enriching experience and helping its growth, stunts and distorts it.[39]

The latter is what has happened to neoclassical economics; it has been disconnected from solving real-world problems. The theories and other standardized equipment which were developed originally for and from the market system have been chiseled in granite to be rigidly preserved for rigorous indoctrination of all young economists and for further manipulation when reaching their postdoctorate positions—manipulation without respect to social consequences. The problem is the market system has been replaced by the welfare state and the market-based theoretical equipment is not relevant to solving social problems. This means the taxes taken from citizens, which include more and more low-income and poor families, for supporting graduate education in economics in public universities is being spent without hope for return. Although massive resources are used to support and educate economists, many such economists occupying positions in government bureaucracies are not capable of conducting relevant policy research. Many times, in fact, their neoclassically based policy and program recommendations do serious damage. The connection between theory and social well-being was explained by Joseph Ratner in his explanation of instrumentalism. He wrote, "[W]hen the practical and theoretical activities are separated from each other, we have the kind of 'advance' exhibited in the tragic history of modern society."[40]

Phase II: Philosophy

Instrumentalism (Policy)

The philosophy, or "welfare economics" of institutionalism, is instrumentalism, as John Dewey named it. Its literature is so broad, rich, and well known that it is not necessary to summarize it here. It may, however, be worthwhile to recall that instrumentalism is a philosophy that is inherently concerned with policy. "For those who believe it is the philosopher's task to juggle the universe on the point of an argument, Dewey is a complete disappointment. The world he starts out with and also ends with is the common world we all live in and experience every day of our lives."[41] As James Street explained, "instrumental valuation was concerned with the intellectual selection of future alternative actions,"[42] or, as William James stated, the instrumentalist method "is to try to interpret each notion by tracing its respective practical consequences."[43]

Problems and Consequences (Strategy)

An orientation toward problems and consequences is the instrumentalist strategy. It is also an effectiveness strategy. Great effort can be saved during research, deliberations, discussions, and lobbying if the focus is maintained on the problem at hand and the need to look at consequences. Alternative agendas can be turned aside if institutionalists continue to bring discussions back to the problem. If they continue to emphasize the consequences of a problem—how many children are dying, how much venture capital is needed, the extent of soil erosion—attention will be directed to policy research for achieving altered consequences. People *are* concerned with problems and consequences. As policy advisors, institutionalists do not distract by bringing alternative ideologies and personalities into the discussion. They bring the knowledge base to bear and tenaciously maintain, in very clinical language, the focus on the problems and consequences. There is power in the problem and consequences strategy—power well beyond political portfolio. As policy scientists, the institutionalists' basis of legitimacy is research competence. They cannot appeal to a political base; they are brought into the policymaking process to recommend answers to problems.

When institutionalist give testimony, irrelevant questions may well be posed. It is wise, for the purposes of informing, to turn every question toward the relevant research base of the problem at hand and to use the time to explain the research. This is true whether in open testimony or back room discussions. Precious clock time available should not be used to explain why the question is irrelevant. The opposition is under the same pressure of clock time so they will probably not want the session to end without making their own points. Only if the opposition severely attacks for not answering the question (now they look like bullies) does one explain why the question as directed is irrelevant. Explanations should be offered with politeness (still in clinical language) and thoroughness (now they look like irrelevant bullies). It is important for the legislators, the press, the bureaucracy, and lobbyists to deal with the problem and consequences as defined by the research. Only with that kind of intense focus will its strengths, weaknesses, and meaning become understood.

Institutionalists are not elected officials. They should not undermine their legitimacy and credibility by making the conjectures that are rightly expected of politicians. They should not become advocates of a view for a politician without a verified research base. If institutionalists act like politicians, they will divert attention from problems and consequences. If an institutionalist wants to assume the role of a politician, he or she should run for election.

The institutionalist researcher's strategy should be to focus attention constantly on the set bounded by the problem and its consequences, and the incremental changes needed to transform the first set into the latter set.

Build Participatory Democracy (Tactics)

None of the policy considerations and strategies discussed above will be possible without a democracy that provides for and ensures freedom of inquiry, open hearings, problem-solving processes, public research universities, the diffusion and utilization of information and knowledge, and so forth. Government intervention to sustain such conditions through democratic processes must be relevant and continuous.

Democracy is the tactical necessity and operational expression of instrumentalism. It is also a weapon—the most powerful weapon institutionalists have. In all aspects of policymaking, institutionalists must constantly strengthen democracy and its operation. The assistance of political scientists and public administration scholars must be enlisted to help find better ways to make a democracy function at the operational level. Our research, philosophy, norms, and legislation can all be lost if the operational tactics are not consistent with the democratic ideal. How agencies should be structured, or procedures routed, or monitoring conducted, or bureaucrats disciplined, or task force membership determined, or administrators selected, or research and development R&D contracts structured—are all issues to be considered at the tactical level in order to strengthen democracy.

The right-wing ideologues such as Milton Friedman and James Buchanan understand that democracy is the enemy of the unfettered market system, or of any other dogmatic ideology that is intended to structure the economy in a manner to make humans and their institutions subservient to it in an immutable manner. They have both called for changes in our system of Western democracy to stop democratic processes from intervening through the government to solve social problems. In Polanyi's terms, they want a system in which the economy and financial institutions dominate, structure, and direct society.

Polanyi demonstrated that to have a "free" market system requires a market society in which people do not have a right to form new institutions that elevate human life above being a labor commodity or to form institutions that protect the environment.[44] Under the unfettered market system, humans were bought and sold as commodities and thereby were deprived of cultural roots or community protection. Many societies have had markets, but those markets were not integrated into a system over which societal processes had no control. The era of the full-fledged free market system is often dated from approximately the 1830s to the 1930s. As Polanyi documented, it took that long for the countermovement to this market system to overcome the strong liberal government that planned and enforced the institutions of the market system. With the spread of democratic enfranchisement, people intervened to destroy the free market system. Democracy and free market systems are incompatible.

Does this mean that institutionalists cannot complete policy research or offer relevant advice in nondemocratic societies? No, it means that institutionalist policymaking can never be as effective as under conditions of democracy. It also means that institutionalists should use every opportunity to complete research and offer advice that is consistent with building and strengthening democratic institutions. Thus the instrumentalist tactics are to approach all the phases and levels in Figure 7-1 in a manner consistent with democracy. Progress in that direction is more possible in some cases than in others.

Phase III: Ideology

Communitarian (Policy)

Institutionalism is an ideology. Institutionalists have beliefs: a broad base of beliefs about knowledge, philosophy, ceremony, technology, government, and political theory—beliefs that are organized in a systematic and congruent manner. An ideology is the integration and systematization of congruent beliefs. The institutionalist ideology is certainly a different kind of ideology than most, but it does fit the definition of an ideology. It differs in kind from neoclassicalism and Marxism in that they prescribe immutable structures and behavior patterns predetermined for societies and humans, respectively. For the neoclassicalist there must be a free market system and humans must maximize utility. Institutionalism has no predetermined socioeconomic structure to dictate to people.

Institutionalism is an approach to science, evaluation, and policymaking—an approach that arrives at beliefs through scientific inquiry. Institutionalist beliefs regarding policymaking were outlined by Jerry Petr. He stated: "[T]he institutionalist's approach to economic policy is (1) values driven, (2) process-oriented, (3) instrumental, (4) evolutionary, (5) activist, (6) fact-based, (7) technologically focused, (8) holistic, (9) non-dogmatic, and (10) democratic."[45] These are beliefs, which are systemic and integrated, beliefs about the most effective way to approach policy.

Generally, the institutionalist ideology could, borrowing George Lodge's term, be categorized as communitarian; meaning it is believed that people's lives are organized and their welfare determined by a community's organic social process. The community, which is more than the sum of its parts, has special ongoing needs. If those needs are not regularly met, whether it be factory, neighborhood, city, or world community, the people in the community will be alienated, frustrated, and without means to satisfy basic needs. The promise of policymaking can be fulfilled if there is a sense of societal purpose, "an end of fragmentation and individualism, a coming together around the need for more equitable distribution of wealth and power among all. . . ."[46] This includes the community's explicit provision of membership rights for goods and services such as education, credit, housing, health care, and so forth. For a well-designed community that can coordinate the resources necessary to provide the goods and services (without the bads and disservices such as degradation of the natural environment and community disintegration) necessary to fulfill membership rights, government planning is required. Institutionalists "acknowledge that government has the responsibility and should have the capacity to perform the task of community analysis and planning, as well as of determining priorities and allocating resources accordingly."[47] Such determinations and allocations must, as noted above, be and remain democratically accountable.

Utilize Holism (Strategy)

The ideological strategy of communitarianism is to practice holism, to take a holistic approach to all aspects of policymaking whether it is in conducting research, lobbying, building statistical bases, or writing a legislative bill.

Holism is a modeling approach and perception of reality that integrates real-world elements and components into wholes which are comprehensive systems. Holism rejects the atomistic and reductionist approach of neoclassical economics. It has been found that reality is organized so that transactional, rather than interaction or self-actional, wholes guide and determine the behavior of the parts of a system. This should be heeded throughout the policymaking process. For example, many data bases have been compiled from a reductionist point of view. They cannot be recycled into holistic models. Sloppy science, as stated above, harms people and environments. "The scientist cannot be left to devise our undoing, however unwittingly."[48] Neither can the planner or policymaker. "The old idea of scientific specialization has given way to a new conscientiousness of the interrelatedness of all things. Spaceship earth, the limits of growth, the fragility of our life-supporting biosphere have all dramatized the ecological and philosophical truth that everything is related to everything else."[49] It is going to be necessary to educate large numbers of experts in holistic science and planning tools. Without a large cadre of competent holists, we will continue to throw resources down reductionist holes; billions will be provided for large-scale programs that make life less bearable.

Select Beliefs, Attitudes, Actors, and Criteria (Tactics)

One of the reasons that governments continue to spend billions without constructive or progressive results is that there has not been a detailed concern to make tactics consistent with strategy.

At the tactical level, it is necessary to select specific beliefs and attitudes consistent with the communitarian ideology and to implement them through the selection of relevant criteria and actors. It is especially necessary to select the correct actors at the level where policy, strategy, and tactics are conducted. This cannot be done without personnel who are not only competent in their area of expertise but who also have the appropriate beliefs, attitudes, and ideology. If the minds of operation personnel are not in sympathy with the beliefs about what is to be accomplished, it is unlikely that much will be accomplished. A potpourri of beliefs and ideologies among cabinet officers and ministers, and among directors in the bureaucracies, will lead to a potpourri of defacto policies and programs that will at best be in conflict with each other, and worse, move policy in the wrong direction.

Phase IV: Problem Definition

Structure and Process-Oriented Description (Policy)

As stated earlier, the problem orientation is the only reliable way that instrumentalists have found to organize scientific research and policymaking. Since solving social problems always requires changing institutions, and in many cases technology, the problem should be described in terms of the structure and process that are delivering the problem. With most studies, Joseph Coates has stated, "[T]he examination of the problem is all too often neglected and not continually repeated throughout the course of the study. Thus the result is that many fine efforts are directed at a problem which is not at the heart of the matter."[50] Social problems, from the delivery of carcinogens to the delivery of low incomes, are generated through the process of the social structure. Polanyi found policy and process to be inseparable. For Veblen the goal was to define the sequence of events in a process. Thus, problem definition should be a structure and process description.

Define Sociotechnical and Socioecological Setting (Strategy)

The context of any research is important. If the context is not relevant to the problem to be solved, the structure and process that need to be impacted by policy will not be the appropriate ones. Therefore, the problem definition should be embedded in the sociotechnical setting in order to know the institutions and technologies that need to be changed. This means a great deal of the research should be done in the field as well as in the library, standard-operating-procedure manuals, and court records.

Create Narrative and Statistical File (Tactics)

Coates, as noted, has been concerned that the problem is too often neglected in policy research. The author's experience has found the same to be true at the tactical level. Managers, administrators, and fiscal analysts seldom are aware of the research that initiated programs, how the problem was defined, or the context of the problem. Thus the definitions, findings, including notes from field observations and surveys, should be brought on line in the computer system for ready access in the bureaucracies. The problem definition should be readily available to tacticians in all phases so they are constantly reminded of what problems they are attempting to solve.

Phase V: Context

Conceptual Framework: Social Fabric Matrix and Digraph (Policy)

Harold Lasswell, whose work is often credited with creating an area recognized as policy science, emphasized, consistent with what has been explained above, that the approach of policy scientists is problem-oriented and contextual. A framework is needed to insure that the context is holistic and transactional. Most policy scientists agree that the main deficiency in the policy sciences is the lack of an integrated framework to carry the theory and research into the policy arena in an organized and effective manner. Yngve Ramstad has stated, institutional theory "will be meaningful (instrumental) only if it permits one to *act* correctly, that is to show how institutions can be altered *in a specific context* so as to actually effect the intended consequences."[51] He also stated that the social fabric matrix and digraph approach, hereafter explained, is the holistic framework best suited for such an instrumental endeavor; it is moreover, very consistent with the path laid by John R. Commons for policymaking.[52]

The social fabric matrix (SFM),[53] developed by the author, is a technical framework based on the convergence of theoretical and technical developments in numerous areas, including institutionalism, systems analysis, boolean algebra, and ecology. The purpose of the SFM is to provide an analytical tool that will integrate diverse scientific literature and diverse kinds of data bases. In this way it is possible to describe a system and identity knowledge gaps in the system for future research; evaluate policies, opportunities, and crises within the system; and create a data base for future monitoring. The SFM is also used to organize policy research. With the SFM, diverse technical expertise can be harnessed into a unified system to strengthen evaluation and decision making. Thus, the character and structure of the SFM is consistent with its use as an instrumental tool for organizing policy analysis for complex systems.

Components of the Social Fabric Matrix (Strategy)

Drawing on work from anthropology, social psychology, institutional economics, and ecology, seven major components have been identified to be integrated in the SFM.[54] They are as follows: 1) cultural values, 2) societal beliefs, 3) personal attitudes, 4) personal tastes, 5) natural environment, 6) technology, and 7) social institutions. Although, in the majority of applied cases, cultural values can be represented by social beliefs which apply to the particular problem, the values are defined here along with the other components.

Cultural Values. Values are a subset of culture. A culture is a collective systemic mental construct which contains a group's abstract ideas, ideals, and values from the superorganic and supernatural world and is found in legends, mythology, supernatural visions, folklore, literature, elaborated superstitions, and sagas. Culture is provided by tradition and not by the human agent or social institutions. Culture, although a powerful directive and prescriptive influence on society, is cerebral, while society is the set of sociotechnical relationships that direct behavior patterns. Society changes regularly but culture does not. Values are cultural *criteria* or evaluative standards for judgment with regard to what is ideal. They are the ultimate criteria in the sense that they are above institutions and people.

Some Western values that have been the same for centuries include 1) strong domination of nature by humans, 2) atomistic conceptualization, 3) extensive hierarchical relationships, 4) flowing time, 5) dualistic thought, and 6) dynamic expansiveness. They are found in our legends, songs, religions, myths, and literature, and are acted out in our social arrangements. Although powerful and transcendental, cultural values are not deterministic because numerous alternative beliefs and institutional arrangements can satisfy a set of criteria. They limit and exclude but do not determine. Thus, if we have a culture with a strong emphasis on dominating nature, we cannot solve environmental problems by designing programs to live in harmony with nature. Instead we should design programs that allow us to dominate without adverse repercussions. For example, there are ways to cultivate the soil that cause high rates of soil erosion, and there are ways to cultivate it that result in building the soil. Both allow for humans to express the domination trait; however, the latter does it in a manner that serves civilization.

Social Beliefs. Whereas cultural values are transcendental, social beliefs are activity- and institution-specific. The connection between values and beliefs provides the bridge between culture and society. Society is a set of relationships, not people, or bronze, or horses. The relationships are determined by institutions, which are patterns of activity that prescribe the roles for the elements (humans, animals, machines, trees) as well as the emotional commitments for the human element.

As Walter Neale stated in his recent explanation of social institutions, an institution is identified by three characteristics: 1) there are patterns of activities; 2) there are rules giving the activities repetition, stability, and order; and 3) there are folkviews explaining or justifying the activities and the rules.[55] The latter are the social beliefs. The answers to the questions about *why* "reflect the beliefs of the participants about how and why the activities are carried on or beliefs about what justifies or ought to justify the activities."[56]

Since institutionally prescribed behaviors are accepted as normal behavior, the belief criteria are the social criteria for what is good and bad, correct or incorrect, and are, in a stable nonalienated society, in conformity with cultural values. Each institution and activity will have a cluster of beliefs that is specific to that institution. An ideology, as stated above, is the systemization of congruent societal beliefs. Therefore, in analyzing a social or economic problem, ideological analysis is very important.

To determine system efficiency, it is necessary to consider whether institutions and economic processes fulfill cultural values and societal beliefs. In a modern society, beliefs are usually expressed through codification in statutes, court decisions, and legal opinions; and legal criteria are established for judging everything from university hiring procedures to water quality. The statutes, agency rules, regulations, and operation procedures are the operationalized social belief criteria.

Social beliefs and institutions establish roles for the elements. For each institutional situation there are obligations, permissions, and prohibitions for the elements. The human element is socialized to respond to signs and symbols in order to fulfill the responsibilities and duties of a situation. These responses are referred to as attitudes. Beliefs and institutions regulate people's attitudes toward signs and symbols and thereby regulate behavior.

Attitudes as Human Responses. Attitudes, which are held by specific people, represent several social beliefs focused on a specific object or situation. It is through attitude responses that the machines are minded, the children get fed, the flags are saluted, and the trees cut. It is through attitude theory that the human actor and human action are brought into institutionalist modeling.

After hedonism and instinct theory fell into scientific disrepute, inner drives and motives were postulated as the mechanisms from within the human that arouse, direct, and sustain activity. *The Dictionary of Behavioral Science* defines a motive as "a state within an organism which energizes and directs him toward a particular goal."[57] Reductionists assumed that attitudes come from the actor's motives. Time and time again, attempts to study attitudes through introspection were lacking in verification.[58] The reductionist approach has also been denied by the historical tide. The claims of utility calculation and hedonism "when tested in the crucible of social policy, proved inadequate."[59] The scientific reliability of motives was soon questioned even for studying hunger, thirst, and the sex drive.

With the development of social psychology, the idea that motives were operative continued to lose credibility. *The Encyclopedic Dictionary of Psychology* states that in the early days of behavioral science, "motivation was envisaged in terms of the drive that was necessary for the manifestation of behavior: sexual behavior was due to the sex drive, eating to the hunger drive, etc. This is no longer a prevalent view and it is generally recognized that it is not necessary to account for behavior in terms of motive force."[60] Today the concern is with attitudes and the role of social institutions in determining attitudes. "Attitudes are individual mental processes which determine both the actual and potential responses of each person in the social world."[61] Some, especially those in psychology, are more interested in the mental processes. Economists are more interested in the responses and their origin in the social system. What are the responses to price changes? Safety devices in the meat packing plants? Innovations? The attitudes originate from outside the individual, not from motives, or hedonistic urges, or utility. Social psychologist William J. McGuire, in the latest *Handbook of Social Psychology*, stated that "institutional structures have intended or unintended impacts on attitudes by determining the stimulus situations to which the person is exposed, the response options available, the level and type of motivation, and the scheduling of reinforcements."[62] "Or put another way, the objects and situation we encounter have meaning for us not only because of the attitudes they activate within us but also because they are perceived to be instrumental to realization (or to stand in the way of realization) of one or more social beliefs."[63]

It is fortunate for policymaking and social planning that attitudes can be changed without serious disruption of the social system. "Attitudes, while important and generally resistant to change, nevertheless are of less connective importance to society and easier to change than central beliefs."[64] Basic social beliefs are very difficult to change, while cultural values are unchangeable for policy purposes. The more transcendental the concept, the more social entities there are for expressing, reinforcing, and maintaining it, and thus the greater the connective importance.

Tastes as Inconsequential Attitudes. Commodity tastes are treated here as a special category of attitudes because they are related to the institution of demand. Although tastes have been given a lofty status in the classical tradition of economics, they are the least important of the attitude categories. This does not mean that tastes cannot have a profound effect. For example, food tastes can have a deleterious effect on human health. The point is that those tastes can be changed without a deleterious effect on the social structure or belief system.

Natural Environment. The natural environment is probably the most difficult category to conceptualize and define as a separate component because humans, their society, and their economy are so dependent on the environment. In addition, both the society and environment are in a common coevolutionary process. The natural environment is a whole system process. This has been understood since the famous philosopher, Alfred Whitehead, used the environment as a vehicle for explaining holistic philosophy.

Technology. Technology was defined above as tools, skills, and knowledge. Technology in a system structure has a pronounced effect on production requirements, social relationships, and the environment. A change in the tool base requires a change in institutional relationships and thus a change in beliefs. Those changes in turn change the inputs from and outputs to the natural environment.

Social Institutions. Social institutions were defined above in the section on beliefs. To summarize, they are repetitive patterns of activity that contain the roles of the elements, provide for the structure of societal relations, and direct the flow of societal substance. The prescribed and proscribed institutional roles of the elements of society are based on rules of prohibition, obligation, and permission. These rules are the norms and beliefs that evolve from and are enforced by the social process.

Integration of Components. To integrate the seven components in the SFM, two principles are emphasized. One principle is that *flow levels* are needed to fully describe societal and environmental processes. The flows of goods, services, information, and people through the network both structure and maintain community relationships. For example, the flow of investment to particular kinds of cultivation technology will determine the level of organic matter in the soil.

The other principle being emphasized for the SFM integration is that real-world systems depend on *delivery* among the component parts. Systems deliver bads and disservices as well as goods and services. Natural environments deliver nitrogen-fixing bacteria as well as floods. Factories deliver output as well as pollution. The continuity of a system depends on delivery among components according to social rules and natural principles. For example, income must be delivered to households for the continuance of the economic system, and organic residue and amino acids must be delivered to ammonia-producing bacteria for the continuance of the nitrogen cycle. Problems are created in systems when the delivery among the components is inconsistent with the maintenance of the system.

Thus, the SFM is based upon the concept of the social components receiving from and delivering to each other. (This broadens the analytical possibilities beyond what is found with input–output, cross-interaction, and cross-impact matrices.) A process is ongoing and a system has no end.

Kind of Matrix. The SFM is an integrated process matrix designed to express the attributes of the parts as well as the integrated process of the whole. The initial objective in employing the matrix is to organize the scientific knowledge base to serve as a thinking tool, and to discover components and delivery linkages not yet recognized. Thus research begins, whether it is conducted by a research team or an individual researcher, by the posing of a question or the articulation of a problem followed by the accumulation of a broad scientific knowledge base, to include field observations of the problem being studied. The first step after researching the problem is to construct a list of the main components and elements of the components that make up the real world. What one immediately finds with any problem is that many of the separately listed components affect each other. Therefore, the same list of components is listed for the matrix rows as arranged across the columns (see Figure 7-3). In this way, a row component can be followed across the matrix to discover the columns to which it makes direct deliveries based on the research evidence available. Some of the deliveries will be qualitative and some quantitative; the deliveries will include criteria, court rulings, pollution emissions, goods production, services, and so forth.

Delivering Components \ Receiving Components		A Cultural Values A1 Dominance Over Nature 1	A2 Dynamic Expansiveness 2	A3 Bimodal Duality 3	A4 Egalitarianism 4	B Societal Beliefs (Norms) B1 Work Ethic 5	B2 Property Rights 6	B3 Affirmative Action 7	B4 Allure of Bigness 8	C Personal Attitudes C1 Soil Conservation 9	C2 Gun Procurement 10	C3 Racism 11	C4 Commodity Tastes 12	D Environment D1 Forest 13	D2 Land 14	D3 Animal 15	D4 Water 16	E Technology E1 Tool & Skill I 17	E2 Tool & Skill II 18	F Institutitions F1 Kinship 19	F2 Courts 20	F3 Government 21	F4 Industry I 22	F5 Industry II 23
A Cultural Values A1 Dominance Over Nature	1					X	X	X	X															
A2 Dynamic Expansiveness	2																							
A3 Bimodal Duality	3																							
A4 Egalitarianism	4																							
B Societal Beliefs (Norms) B1 Work Ethic	5																							
B2 Property Rights	6																							
B3 Affirmative Action	7																							
B4 Allure of Bigness	8																							
C Personal Attitudes C1 Soil Conservation	9																							
C2 Gun Procurement	10																							
C3 Racism	11																							
C4 Commodity Tastes	12																							
D Environment D1 Forest	13																						X	
D2 Land	14																							
D3 Animal	15																							
D4 Water	16																							
E Technology E1 Tool & Skill I	17																						X	
E2 Tool & Skill II	18																							
F Institutitions F1 Kinship	19																							
F2 Courts	20																							
F3 Government	21																			X			X	X
F4 Industry I	22																X			X			X	X
F5 Industry II	23													X									X	X

Cellular Information

Deliveries	Amount
Location	Time

Figure 7-3. Hypothetical social fabric matrix.

At this point the SFM itself becomes an instrumental tool to aid thinking. As the researchers are forced to deal with each cell across the row on a cell-by-cell basis, linkages among elements will be discovered that otherwise would have been overlooked. This process helps in the discovery of research gaps, as indicated by particular matrix cells that need to be researched. Also, the process of filling the matrix will jog the researcher's memories of new component elements to be added to the original list. They can quickly be inserted and their deliveries noted.

The SFM is a noncommon-denominator matrix without common flow properties; for example, it can handle energy, pollution, and dollars as well as water, steel, and belief criteria. It will be necessary to develop many different kinds of numerical modalities in order to capture the essence of the various flows and relationships. This means that standard matrix algebra is not appropriate to the matrix, and that all the information in the rows and columns are not summative (as in an input–output matrix). The number and kind of entries in the matrix will depend on the problem being studied and the policymaker's interests. For example, if the problem is the economic structure and operation of the fertilizer industry, a few broad natural environmental categories are sufficient. However, if the problem is the impact of commercial fertilizer on nitrogen cycles, numerous refined environmental entires will be needed to understand the relationships of the nitrates to the micro-organisms, and so forth.

The concepts of equilibrium, harmony, or wants being satisfied are not forced into the SFM system if they are not relevant. Toxic waste lagoons can be delivering pollution to the water aquifer, police can be delivering arrests to individuals, and industrial processes can be delivering cancer to workers. None of them is harmonious or want satisfying, although all are part of the system.

Cellular Information. The hypothetical SFM is Figure 7-3 will be utilized to demonstrate some cellular information. The elements in Figure 7-3 are generally defined too broadly to be of more than demonstrative use. The cells are given a designation of (*i*, *j*), which means the *i*th row and the *j*th column. Explanatory comments on particular cells are as follows:

(22, 22), (22, 23), (23, 22), and (23, 23). These cells are laid out as the standard industrial input–output (I/O) matrix. Although the layout is the same, several differences exist. First, it is apparent that interindustry transactions are a minor part of the total process. As will be demonstrated next, other entities outside the I/O table must be delivered. Training must be provided from the government to the families for the delivery of skills before factories can operate (21, 19). (21, 22) and (21, 23). To structure industry, the government must provide the legislation.

(13, 22) and (23, 13). The forest will provide lumber as industry delivers the harvesting process to the forest.

(17, 22). Technology delivers criteria and requirements to structure the production process.

(22, 16). Industry delivers pollution to the water.

(1, 5), (1, 6), (1, 7), and (1, 8). Value criteria are delivered to beliefs.

It becomes evident that no cell is an island. Numerous cells in a sequence are processing in order to deliver a tractor to the field,health care to the public, or nutrients to wildlife. That sequence has stability and dependability because of the instituted process that can be expressed in

	1	2	3	4	5	6	7	8	9	10	11	12	13	14	15
1	1	0	0	0	0	0	0	0	0	0	0	0	0	0	0
2	0	1	0	0	0	0	0	0	0	0	0	0	0	0	0
3	1	1	1	1	1	0	0	1	1	0	0	0	0	0	0
4	1	1	0	1	1	0	0	0	1	0	0	0	0	0	0
5	0	1	0	0	1	0	0	0	0	0	0	0	0	0	0
6	0	1	0	0	0	1	0	0	0	0	0	0	0	0	0
7	1	1	1	1	1	0	0	1	1	0	0	0	0	0	0
8	1	1	1	1	1	0	0	1	1	0	0	0	0	0	0
9	1	1	0	1	1	0	0	0	1	0	0	0	0	0	0
10	0	1	0	0	1	1	0	0	0	1	0	0	0	0	0
11	1	1	1	1	1	0	1	1	1	0	1	0	0	0	0
12	1	1	1	1	1	0	1	1	1	0	0	0	0	0	0
13	1	1	0	1	1	0	0	0	1	0	0	0	1	0	0
14	0	1	0	0	1	1	0	0	0	1	0	0	0	1	0
15	0	1	0	0	1	1	0	0	0	1	0	0	0	0	0

Figure 7-4. Boolean adjacency matrix. *Source*: John N. Warfield, *Societal Systems: Planning, Policy, and Complexity* (New York: John Wiley & Sons, 1976).

the SFM. Understanding the organization of a system requires understanding how much, how, when, and where particular ordering relationships are imposed.

System Sequence: Boolean Matrix and Digraph. After the completion of the information in the cells, the matrix can be used to define the system sequence, as called for by Veblen, through boolean algebra manipulations. To convert the matrix to a sequence digraph, each SFM cell in the matrix in which there is a delivery is labeled as 1 and each cell with no transaction is labeled as 0. This conversion of the SFM can be treated as a boolean adjancency matrix, a hypothetical example of which is displayed in Figure 7-4.

The adjancency matrix can then be converted to a boolean digraph (directed graph) such as represented by the simple digraphs in Figure

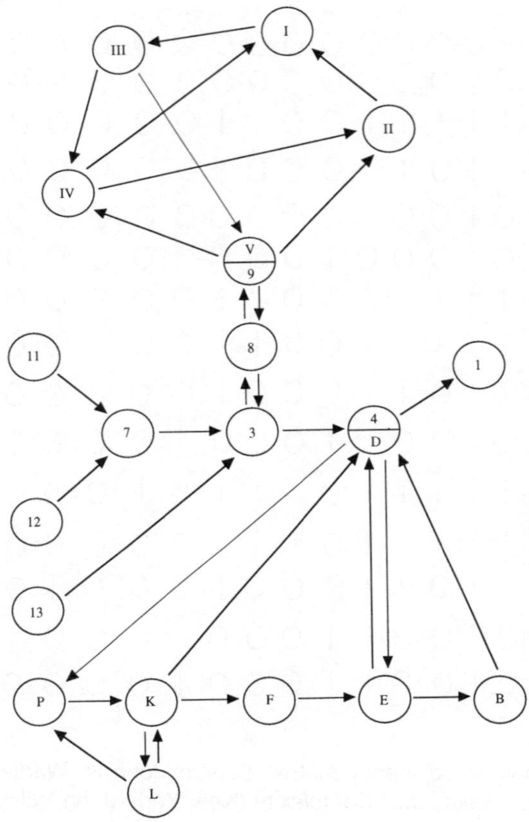

Figure 7-5. Convergence of balanced, unidirectional, and centralized system.

7-5. Each node (circle) in the digraph represents a row entry in the matrix, and each edge (line) represents a cell delivery. The digraph shows the sequential process of the system.

A simple hypothetical digraph is constructed in Figure 7-6. The digraph can be used to organize further research and to collect data. Different parts of the system require different kinds of expertise, such as soil scientists, chemists, economists, water quality engineers, and so forth. The experts will not see themselves as specialists whose work is disconnected from others. Each researcher will know with whom to coordinate and the kind of information that must be provided to other researchers. The data from the digraph can be stored in a common relational data-management spreadsheet system. Because of the importance of deliveries to a system,

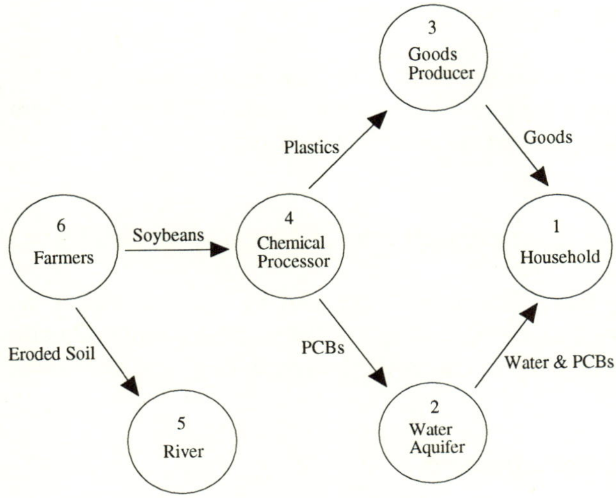

Figure 7-6. Hypothetical digraph.

Table 7-1. *Data management spread sheet.*

Years	*Soybeans* 6 ⟶ 4	*Eroded Soils* 6 ⟶ 5	*Plastics* 4 ⟶ 3	*PCBs* 4 ⟶ 2	*Goods* 3 ⟶ 1	*Water & PCBs* 2 ⟶ 1

the delivery from component to component serves as the columnar headings in such data systems, as in Table 7-1. The headings in Table 7-1 are taken from Figure 7-6.

The relationships among the various deliveries can, through this kind of research process, be discovered and built into the spreadsheets so that if a policy change is made in one part of the system, the impacts on other deliveries would be indicated. In this way, indirect impacts from policies can be identified along with the direct ones as alternative policy scenarios are developed. For budgeting purposes, it also allows the determination of results per dollar spent on programs. The columns of the spreadsheet can be added for different programs and those totals compared to the budgets of the different programs.

Case Study Approach (Strategy)

As is evident from the description above, the context strategy of institutional policymaking is case-by-case studies that are problem-oriented in the holistic social fabric matrix framework.

Computerize Spreadsheets and Statistical Analysis (Tactics)

The social fabric matrix research can be operationalized at the tactical level, by computerizing the digraph spreadsheet explained above. It can be utilized for agency monitoring, data updating, and statistical analysis.

Phase VI: Measurement

Contextual Social Indicators (Policy)

The social indicator movement that began in the 1960s is no longer a movement. Now it is understood that all useful measures are social. It is now broadly understood that price is not *the* measure of either programs or benefits, nor is there any other measure that can be a common denominator. Various interests have promoted various elixirs that were to serve the common denominator function; economists had exchange ratios, energy engineers had BTUs, some environmentalists had protein ratios in the food chain, anthropologists had leisure time, and so forth. There is no such easy solution to measurement. Indicators must be developed consistent with the problem, the context, and the ideological criteria. "There is the recognition that all observation, all measurement, all experience is necessarily subjective. Neither the measurer, the measure, nor the measured is absolute."[65]

Elsewhere I have provided a summary of Dewey's advice regarding social indicators, that reads as follows:

> (1) They must be consistent with the needs of the social problem being pursued. Social data should not be recycled data collected for other purposes. (2) They are not all in numerical form. (3) Mere separation of discrete objects is not to the basis of numerical identity. Quantification should be designed to express a system. (4) Aggregation of discrete objects is not a case of measuring but mere counting. Until a system is defined, quantification leads to indeterminate aggregates. (5) Social measurement must be relative and limiting; relative to the system and expressing the limits required by all systems. (6) Systems principles

of arrangement and order should guide numerical expression. Thus the data system should be designed to articulate patterns, sequences, ordering, and linkages. (7) It is important to remember that in reality systems are not disintegrated. Environmental conditions, institutions and organisms exist only as a synthetic whole. (8) System specification must include physical laws and their interactions along with technology. (9) It must also include conditions like soil, sea, mountains, and climate; the environment in general. Thus, a social indicator system should be a geobased data system.[66]

Determine Consequences, Requirements, Relationships, and Monitoring Indicators (Strategy)

Following Dewey's advice, the strategy with regard to social indicators for policymaking is to derive the indicators and data base needed to complete the contextual analysis with the social fabric matrix and to monitor policy. For policymaking, it is necessary to develop indicators that demonstrate the following[67]: 1) *consequence*, or impact indicators, which are designed to measure the results of policies, or ongoing system processes; 2) *requirement* indicators, which measure the contributions to the system of the required system elements or components as defined by the working rules of going concerns or social processes; 3) *relationship*, or linkage, indicators, which measure the relationships and congruency among system elements and components; 4) *monitoring* indicators, which are selected to provide information on some part of a system, especially after policy initiatives.

All of these are defined and available in the social fabric matrix and digraph.

Construction of Data Base (Tactics)

These measurement indicators should be established in the governmental computer mainframe and made readily accessible as a data base for agencies, lobbyists, and citizens. As tacticians from those groups insist on data that are useful in making policy decisions, we can overcome one of the lingering criticisms of social indicators. Possibly the most striking error of commission for which the societal accounting movement can be faulted has been the lack of decision-relevance of its products.

The irony of the so-called Information Age is that information is less and less available for two reasons. First, although there is more and more concern with the latest hardware and software, there is less and less concern about the theoretical and conceptual base for what is useful and what is useless information. The volume of data could be drastically cut if the data were meaningfully organized. It is not so organized; therefore, many users have great volumes of data but little useful information. Second, many people can no longer access the information sources. In the past, printed copy was available to almost everyone through public and university libraries. Now that more and more of our data bases and text are available only via computer access, most of our citizens and many of our small businesses can no longer access the information base necessary for democratic deliberations and control, or for business information and technological innovations.

The SFM and measurement approach explained above provide a conceptual framework for meaningful information and knowledge. The tactical responsibility is to provide computer systems so that all agencies can access each other's data bases and provide computer access to citizens as well.

Phase VII: Select Programs

Design Alternative Program (Policy)

There is no training or framework with which the author is acquainted that guarantees that policy scientists can arrive at creative program alternatives. They cannot succeed if they try to make the world fit into a neoclassical mold: for example, by suggesting price or free market solutions where regulations and institutional changes are needed.

It is my contention that the policy scientist will be in a much better position to be insightful and design viable alternative programs if he or she has been immersed in Phases I through VI. Of course, neither should a bit of experience at the strategy or tactical levels in Phases VII through X hinder (although it sometimes does). A mixture of scientific research, field work, policy experience, and a review of solutions utilized in other societies are usually helpful but not always sufficient to design creative policy alternatives.

Test Alternatives in the Social Fabric Matrix and Digraph (Strategy)

The strategy for program development is to test alternative programs with the social fabric matrix to determine direct and indirect consequences. The

SFM articulates and describes the structure, process, and deliveries of the problem area. Programs designed to solve the problem can be tested in the SFM by adding the contemplated program as a new row and column or number of new rows and columns. Then the task is to determine the deliveries in the old and new columns of each new row, and the deliveries of former rows in the new columns. In this way a new matrix and digraph can be developed for each of the alternative programs. After that is completed for each new program, the total deliveries in all the matrix can be aggregated. Selection criteria provided by instrumental theory can be applied in order to determine if the program created has improved or deteriorated the situation. Because indirect effects are included, the new program might have made the condition worse.

Efficiency Tests: Consequences and Effectiveness (Tactics)

The tactical task is to judge the myriad consequences that any program manifests and to select the best program. Because there is no common denominator, policymakers have the opportunity to judge the different mixes of results projected for the different programs.

Effectiveness can be determined for the different programs by comparing the total consequences of each program with the budgetary requirements of each program. Therefore, it provides an alternative to neoclassical cost-benefit analysis.

Phase VIII: Advocacy

Advocacy Research (Policy)

Policy advocacy is a matter of doing the research, getting organized, and working your network. Sound easy? It is not. It is the most difficult, with the least probability of success (although often the most fun), of all the phases. All the resistance to change, to include ceremonial lag as well as established power, taught to us by Veblen, Ayres, and Commons, comes into play. Advocacy research integrates, combines, and repackages basic research in order to persuade. One of the best procedures for pursuing advocacy research is the use of a citizen task force if the task force is provided with an adequate and competent staff that can utilize the scientific research base already completed.

Because advocacy research builds on basic policy research, there sometimes is a communication problem. First, as stated earlier, a tremendous knowledge gap exists in the transfer process due to the lack of attention to the diffusion and utilization of knowledge. Advocates may not be able to understand the basic research, and the scientists may have no contact with the advocates. Second, the interest of advocates is to pursue the interest of their group and therefore they have a tendency to be less concerned than they should be about the quality of the basic research that they utilize to support those interests. The third and most severe problem is that there is a paucity of research being conducted that provides adequate understanding of modern problems. Before basic research can be utilized, it must already have been completed. President Lyndon Johnson, when asked what is the most important ingredient to policy success, is purported to have said, "Seize the moment! Seize the [expletive deleted] moment!" Relevant basic research needs to be on the shelf when the opportunity for its use presents itself or it will not be possible for advocates to seize the moment to pursue problem resolution through policy initiatives.

This chapter is not about politics; it is not a handbook on how to run a political campaign. Advocacy, however, comes close to political campaigning, and shares some of the same goals and techniques. This means that a special effort must be made not to allow institutional policymaking to be subverted by politics. However, a couple of caveats concerning any presumed neat separation of advocacy and politics are in order, unless we think we can become sanitized from politics. First, a policy or idea entrepreneur without some political savvy is just another promoter. Second, let's remember how John R. Commons explained the commonality between politicians and others involved in concerted effort. He wrote, "[P]olitical parties, like all concerted action, . . . have the very practical purpose of getting and keeping control of the officials who formulate the will of the state."[68] In the same way, those engaged in policy or advocacy research cannot ignore politics. Neither should advocates ignore that they are in a power struggle. As Commons said, concerted action is "designed to get and keep control of the concern and its participants."[69] Nor should we be surprised when opponents who are in that struggle flex their muscle or kick below the belt. Be assured they do. This is why progress is slow at best, and extremely difficult in the usual case. As Pat Choate has said, "[T]here will be maybe 11,000 bills introduced in this Congress. Maybe 600 or 650 will be passed, and out of those, 400 to 500 are standard reauthorization bills. So what we are really taking about is a salmon run of policy and ideas. You've got to have persistence. When you're working ideas, you've got to be prepared to hang in there."[70] Choate counsels for persistence. I would add organization.

Organize Elements and Symbols (Strategy)

The strategy for advocacy is organization, organization, and more organization. The computer is now key to that organization. It is no longer possible to match the opposition without computer-aided organization. Policy and program advocacy is where task force reports, corporate jets, favors, lobbyists, scientific testimony, media manipulation, special interests, direct mail pieces, and computers are mixed—hopefully in a fine-tuned manner—and usually fail, especially in the short term. Every aspect of the advocacy process has to be organized: the corporation jets to take advocates to Washington, DC, Austin, or Paris; the production and mailing of the four-page direct-mail piece; the identification and briefing of those who will give public testimony; the letters-to-the-editor campaign; the schedules and volunteers; the free media effort; the paid media effort; the areas to be canvased door to door; money for the canvassers. They all need to be organized. On and on organization grows.

Strategy studies for organizing policy advocacy have received little attention from institutionalists or from academics in general, although *advocacy is an important linkage between policy research and the adoption and implementation of new programs*. Even though institutional theory has dealt little with these organizational techniques, it does clarify what must be organized and what must be included in the network and lobbying effort. Institutionalist research defines and explains the elements, beliefs, and ceremonial symbols central to organizing advocacy efforts.

Networking and Lobbying (Tactics)

The job of the tacticians and operations personnel is twofold. First, it is to use symbolic means to achieve instrumental results, to use symbols to acquire substance. It is the job of the lobbying and networking process to close the gap between symbols and substance by making the consequences wanted into the symbols that others want. Second, it is to create new symbols when necessary. Although institutionalists have not devoted much effort to the study of lobbying, they have had numerous successful mentors—John R. Commons was one, Rexford Tugwell was another, but "Doctor Bob" Montgomery of the University of Texas surely must be the patron saint and most shining example. Institutionalists and instrumentalists, at least since Charles Peirce have explained the importance of mental habits, the power of symbols, and the relevance of both in patterning social institutions for both instrumental and deleterious purposes.

The life process, to include policymaking, takes place in a social and cultural milieu in which symbols are essential for organization and communication. The anthropologist, Raymond Firth, has stated that "man does not live by symbols alone, but man orders and interprets his reality by his symbols, and even reconstructs it."[71] Thus, as Charles Elder and Roger Cobb explain, "[P]ublic policymaking tends to be a highly stylized and ritualized process. It is replete with symbolism that conveys reassurances and serves to rationalize the product, whatever it may be."[72] Policy innovations need social and cultural moorings.

A social symbol is a human invention: "people invent them, acquire them by learning, adapt them, use them for their own purposes."[73] New symbols are "likely to occur in the face of dramatic events or major changes in the natural, social, or political environment."[74] Symbols may "emerge as a consequence of their deliberate advocacy by political leaders or issue entrepreneurs."[75] In some cases, a new policy may be so different from traditional institutional norms that new symbols will need to be generated to adequately represent the new policy. "New symbols can be created and old ones redefined (or discredited) so as to create a climate conducive to a significant policy innovation."[76]

A significant difference needs to be noted between traditional lobbying and the standard for institutionalists. Traditional lobbying has too often appealed to, and thereby reinforced, any symbol, whether or not the symbol and the institutions it represented was deleterious. Consistent with Dewey, means determine ends, so if deleterious symbol manipulation is used, it will encourage a deleterious result. Events must be exploited through effective symbol management. The instrumentalist standard, however, is that symbols should not be utilized that will reinforce deleterious consequences or institutions. Symbols must be utilized to generate human responses. Lobbying, to be consistent with instrumentalist thought, requires that social symbols and institutions to which the lobbying effort is appealing be instrumental. In this way, lobbying for a new program is also reinforcing social and mental habits that have been found to be instrumental.

In addition, an education and propaganda process will need to be developed in order to convince people of new symbols and social patterns needed to make the program a success.

Lobbying is referred to as the fifth estate of government, although not necessarily the fifth in power. There is more than the vast inequality in access to lobbying funds that is fueling the growth in lobbying. The more technology grows, and consequently, the more society becomes differentiated and complex, the more the lobbying component will and must grow. Lobbying will grow, and lobbyists, who are becoming much more technically competent about their subject matter, are crucial to policymaking. It is no compliment to most universities that they have master's of business administration (MBA) programs but not the equivalent for educating lobbyists.

Institutional research is ready-made for lobbying and organizing networks. It contains both the skeleton and the flesh. As Commons explained, "[A]lthough the concerted action of politics within a concern is founded on passion, stupidity, inequality and mass action, yet it can be investigated scientifically. . . ."[77] That is what institutional research does. It identifies power bases, deliveries, losers, winners, social groups, key social actors, institutions, beliefs, inequalities, government agencies, corporate interlocks, and so forth. Before an effective lobbying effort can be mounted, the actors, institutions, technologies, and financial flows must be identified.

One last concern about lobbying applies to a topic of discussion that has taken place at institutionalists' meetings in recent years. It has to do with whether institutionalists should align ourselves or form alliances with other ideologies such as Marxism or neoclassicalism, or whether they should choose a particular patron such as labor unions. Sometimes this concern has been stated in terms of whether principles and theories from other ideologies should be used. These are misquestions. Institutional analysis is problem oriented; thus it turns to the analysis needed to analyze the problem. As problems change, different methods, principles, data, and statistical techniques are needed. As problems change, different alliances are needed for policymaking. The analysis of the problem tells us with whom the lobbying effort should seek alliances. It will be bankers in some cases, the GI Forum in others, and the Sierra Club in others; and all three together in other cases. As the problem changes, the alliances change. Lobbyists are familiar with this. This is why civility and honesty are important among policy enemies. Today's enemy is tomorrow's friend in policymaking.

Phase IX: Program Budgeting

Monetary, Legal, and Judicial Budgeting (Policy)

Budgeting for programs is the process of allocating resources to continue old programs and create new ones. It includes: 1) the allocation of money flows; 2) making statutory changes; 3) making administrative changes; and 4) bringing about new judicial rulings in order to create new institutions, new technologies, and new human behavior patterns. Budgeting is not just a matter of allocating money. Probably far more resources are allocated and institutions changed through statutory, administrative, regulatory, and judicial means than through monetary allocation. Taxation, bond indebtedness, and monetary allocation theories are well developed. What needs research attention is the design of budgeting systems that reflect budgeting beyond the allocation of money.

Agency Allocation (Strategy)

The program budgeting strategy is to allocate and coordinate the monetary, statutory, administrative, and judicial changes across the agencies in a manner to allow for the creation of new instrumentalities necessary for delivering social beliefs and social programs to the correct clients.

Budget Requests and Legal Changes (Tactics)

The accountants, auditors, and fiscal analysts need to have skills and knowledge from an array of scientific disciplines to carry out the budget requests and performance audits. That has been understood by many budget agencies who have hired multidisciplinary staffs. However, the multidisciplinary personnel many times continue to be forced into the mold of neoclassical models and dualistic double-entry accounting systems. As was stated earlier, these are the actors most likely to become divorced from the original values, beliefs, and intent of programs. The tactical recommendation for all the phases has been designed, in part, to try to overcome this problem.

Phase X: Sociotechnical Change

Creation of Institutions (Policy)

The final phase to be briefly discussed is the building of new institutions consistent with programs and budgets. At the policy science level the main research activity is the design of institutions, the definition of roles to make the institutions effective, and the forecasting of behavior-effective models.

Creation of Instrumentalities (Strategy)

The strategic level of sociotechnical change is concerned with the creation of instrumentalities. The emphasis is on specific programs that need to be accomplished and strategies to make them a reality. These are usually applied systems that are manifest mainly in social and technological innovations: new airport systems, new disease prevention systems, new weapon systems, new industry regulation systems, new environmental protection systems, and so forth.

Operations and Procedures (Tactics)

At the tactical level are the technicians, clerks, word processors, labor unions, tractors, knowledge bases, water supplies, and so forth, that are to be managed and administered in efficient systems. This level actually puts the system variables in the right place each day to deliver the results of the policymaking process. Institutionalist theory with regard to the rigidity of mental habits is very relevant here. Old-line managers and bureaucrats with skills, knowledge, tools, and ideology from an undergraduate or graduate program of the distant past are often unable to understand the connection between belief systems and their own operations. Many times those who have worked their way up through the bureaucracy have learned "the system," and the last thing they want to do is endanger their position with a new mode of operation. It is important to realize that if operations and procedures in the active bureaucracy are inconsistent with the theory, intent, and strategy of policymaking, then pushing progressive bills through legislative bodies or achieving instrumental court decisions will be of little value. Likewise, to design policy research or programs, without considering the viability of tactical operations to finalize the research findings and programs, limits the value of the research no matter how intellectually pleasing or elegant it may be. Beginning with Veblen, "the Institutionalists saw planning and administrative 'control' as essential ingredients of economic organization whether in the public or the private spheres."[78]

Summary

In summary, the emphasis has been to extend and broaden the tool kit of institutional policymaking to include research and expertise on all the phase-level conjunctions of Figure 7-1. Without this extended base the delivery of instrumental policy can break down. Policy science, based on institutionalist research, cannot be delivered without effective principles from the strategic, management, and administrative sciences that have been grounded in a similar intellectual tradition. Likewise, managers and administrators are doing nothing more than carrying out procedures if they are not operating consistent with the philosophy, ideology, and research from the policy level, as was indicated in Figure 7-2. Relevant policymaking research on any complex social problem will require expertise in all phases of policy research. Significant policymaking will require concerted efforts to coordinate policy research with all phases of strategy and tactics.

Notes

1. Karl Polanyi, "The Economy as Instituted Process," in Karl Polanyi et al., eds., *Trade and Markets in Early Empires* (Glencoe: The Free Press, 1957).

2. John Dewey, *The Public and Its Problems,* 2nd ed. (Chicago: The Swallow Press, 1954), p. 135.

3. Gilman M. Ostrander, "Thorstein Veblen," in Gitman M. Ostrander, ed., *Ideas of the Progressive Era* (Clio, MI: Marston Press, 1971), p. 24.

4. Russell Long, *The Wallace of Iowa* (Boston: Houghton Mifflin, 1947), p. 73.

5. Martin Gellen, "Institutionalist Economics and the Intellectual Origins of National Planning in the United States," *Journal of Planning, Education and Research* 4 (December 1984): 75–85.

6. See Martin Bulmer, *The Uses of Social Research: Social Investigation in Public Policy-Making* (London: George Allen S. Unwin, 1982; Yehezkel, Dror); *Policymaking Under Adversity* (Oxford: Transaction Books, 1986); D.B.P., Kallen, G.B. Kosse, et al., eds., *Social Science Research and Public Policy-Making: A Reappraisal.* (Atlantic Highlands, NJ: Humanities Press Inc., 1982); Robert F. Rich, *Social Science Information and Public Policy Making* (San Francisco: Jossey-Bass Publishers, 1981); and Paul Whiteley, *Political Control of the Macroeconomy: The Political Economy of Public Policy Making* (London: SAGE Publications Ltd., 1986).

7. George C. Lodge, *The New American Ideology* (New York: Alfred A. Knopf, 1980), p. 319.

8. Gellen, "Institutional Economics . . . ," p. 78.

9. Paul D. Bush, 1986. "On the Concept of Ceremonial Encapsulation." *Review of Institutional Thought* 3 (December 1986): 25–45; idem, "The Theory of Institutional Change," *Journal Economic Issues* 21 (September 1987): 1075–1116.

10. Polanyi, "The Economy as Instituted Process," p. 249.

11. Dewey, *The Public and its Problems*, p. 108.

12. See Richard Dunford, "The Suppression of Technology As a Strategy for Controlling Resource Dependence," *Administrative Science Quarterly* 32 (December 1987): 512–525; and Wassily Leontief, "The Choice of Technology," *Scientific American* 252 (June 1985): 37–45.

13. David Bollier and Joan Claybrook, *Freedom from Harm: The Civilizing Influence of Health, Safety and Environmental Regulation* (Washington, DC: Public Citizen and Democracy Project, 1986), p. 203.

14. John Dewey, *Reconstruction in Philosophy* (Boston: Beacon Press, 1948), p. xxx.

15. Samuel M. Levin, "John Dewey's Evaluation of Technology," *American Journal of Economics and Sociology* 15 (January 1954): 123–136.

16. *Ibid*., p. 134.

17. Marc R. Tool, *The Discretionary Economy: A Normative Theory of Political Economy* (Santa Monica, CA: Goodyear Publishing Company, 1979), p. 296.

18. *Ibid.*, p. 293.

19. See J. Fagg Foster, "Syllabus for Problems of Modern Society: The Theory of Institutional Adjustment," *Journal of Economic Issues* 15 (December 1981): 929–935.

20. James A. Swaney, "Elements of a Neoinstitutional Environmental Economics" In Marc R. Tool, ed., *Evolutionary Economics: Volume II, Institutional Theory and Policy* (New York: M.E. Sharpe, 1988).

21. *Ibid.*, p. 332.

22. Clayton Yeutter, Letter to the Honorable Ray MacSharry, Member, Commission of the European Communities, Rue de la Loi 200, 1049 Brussels, Belgium. (July 1989) Washington, DC: Office of the Secretary.

23. Quoted in: Milton D. Lower, "The Concept of Technology Within the Institutional Perspective," *Journal of Economic Issues* 21 (September 1987): 1147–1176.

24. Ostrander, "Thorstein Veblen," p. 23.

25. Jerry Petr, "Economic Evolution and Economic Policy: Is Reaganomics a Sustainable Force?" *Journal of Economics Issues* 16 (December 1982): 1005–1012.

26. *State of Ohio v. U.S. Department of the Interior*, 880 F. 2d 432. (D.C. Cir. 1989), p. 456.

27. *Ibid.*, pp. 456–457.

28. Hal R. Varian, *Microeconomic Analysis* (New York: W.W. Norton and Company, 1984), p. 112.

29. Herbert Simon, "Rational Decision Making in Business Organizations," *American Economic Review* 69 (September 1979): 493–513.

30. Tool, *The Discretionary Economy*, p. 294.

31. Wassily Leontief, "Foreward," in Alfred S. Eichner, ed., *Why Economics Is Not Yet a Science* (New York: M.E. Sharpe, 1983).

32. Randall Rothenberg, "The Idea Merchant: Pat Choate Sells Economic Policies," *The New York Times Magazine* (May 3, 1987): 44.

33. Arne Leemans, "Information as a Factor of Power and Influence," *Knowledge: Creation, Diffusion, Utilization* 7 (September 1986): 39–58.

34. *Ibid.*, p. 45.

35. William Melody, "Information: An Emerging Dimension of Institutional Analysis," *Journal of Economic Issues* 21 (September 1987): 1313–1339.

36. *Ibid.*, p. 1337.

37. Bulmer, *The Uses of Social Research*, p. 35.

38. Leemans. "Information as a Factor of Power and Influence," p. 54.

39. John Dewey, "The Supremacy of Method," in Milton R. Kinvitz and Gail Kennedy, eds., *The American Pragmatists* (New York: Meridian Books, 1960), p. 190.

40. Joseph Ratner, "Introduction to John Dewey's Philosophy." In Rollo Handy and E.C. Harwood, eds., *Useful Procedures of Inquiry* (Great Barrington, MA: Behavioral Research Council, 1973).

41. *Ibid.*, p. 23.

42. James Street, "The Institutionalist Theory of Economic Development," *Journal of Economic Issues* 21 (December 1987): 1861–1887.

43. William James, *Pragmatism: A New Name for Some Old Ways of Thinking* (New York: Longmans, Green and Co., 1907), pp. 43–81.

44. Karl Polanyi, *The Great Transformation: The Political and Economic Analysis of Our Time* (Boston: Beacon Press, 1944).

45. Jerry Petr, "Fundamentals of an Institutionalist Perspective on Economic Policy," *Journal of Economic Issues* 18 (March 1984): 1–15.

46. George C. Lodge, *The New American Ideology* (New York: Alfred A. Knopf., 1974), p. 39.

47. *Ibid.*, p. 297.

48. *Ibid.*, p. 95.

49. *Ibid.*, p. 20.

50. Joseph F. Coates, "The Role of Formal Models in Technology Assessment," *Technological Forecasting and Social Change* 9 (1976): 139–190.

51. Yngve Ramstad, "A Pragmatist's Quest for Holistic Knowledge: The Scientific Methodology of John R. Commons," *Journal of Economic Issues* 20 (December 1986): 1067–1105.

52. *Ibid.*, p. 1097.

53. F. Gregory Hayden, "Social Fabric Matrix: From Perspective to Analytical Tool," *Journal of Economic Issues* 16 (September 1982): 637–662.

54. This section draws heavily from F. Gregory Hayden, "Values, Beliefs, and Attitudes in a Sociotechnical Setting," *Journal of Economic Issues* 22 (June 1988): 415–426.

55. Walter C. Neale, "Institutions," *Journal of Economic Issues* 21 (September 1987): 1177–1206.

56. *Ibid.*, p. 1183.

57. Benjamin B. Wolfman, ed., *Dictionary of Behavioral Sciences* (New York: Van Nostrand Reinhold, 1973).

58. Gordon W. Allport, "The Historical Background of Social Psychology," in Gardner Lindzey and Elliot Aronson, eds., *Handbook of Social Psychology, Volume I: Theory and Method* (New York: Random House, 1985).

59. *Ibid.*

60. Ram Harre and Roger Lamb, eds., *The Encyclopedia Dictionary of Psychology* (Cambridge: MIT Press, 1983).

61. Allport, "The Historical Background of Social Psychology."

62. William J. McGuire, 1985. "Attitudes and Attitude Change," in Gardner Lindzey and Elliot Aronson, eds., *Handbook of Social Psychology, Volume II: Special Fields and Applications* (New York: Random House, 1985), pp. 233–346.

63. Milton Rokeach, *Beliefs, Attitudes and Values: A Theory of Organization and Change* (San Francisco: Jossey-Bass, 1968), p. 43.

64. *Ibid.*, p. 45.

65. Lodge, *The New American Ideology*, p. 329.

66. See John Dewey, *Logic: The Theory of Inquiry* (New York: Henry Holt and Company, 1938), pp. 33–34, 205–211, and 492–499.

67. See F. Gregory Hayden, "Integration of Social Indicators into Holistic Geobased Models," *Journal of Economic Issues* 17 (June 1983): 325–334.

68. John R. Commons, *Institutional Economics: Its Place in Political Economy* (Madison, WI: University of Wisconsin Press, 1934), p. 752.

69. *Ibid.*, p. 749.

70. Rothenberg, "The Idea Merchant . . . ," p. 44.

71. Raymond Firth, *Symbols: Public and Private* (Ithica: Cornell University Press, 1973), p. 20.

72. Charles D. Elder, and Roger W. Cobb, *The Political Use of Symbols* (New York: Longman, 1983), p. 21.

73. Firth, *Symbols: Public and Private*, p. 427.

74. Elder and Cobb, *The Political Use of Symbols*, p. 30.

75. *Ibid.*, p. 30.
76. *Ibid.*, p. 110.
77. Commons, *Institutional Economics*, p. 748.
78. Gellen, "Institutionalist Economics," p. 78.

Commentary by Milton D. Lower

Greg Hayden's chapter is perhaps the most comprehensive effort yet made to define a specifically institutionalist approach to policymaking. This may be said even though, as Hayden notes in his opening sentence, "The history of institutionalist thought is a history of concern for policy". Hayden's chapter illuminates this implicit distinction between *policy* as collective action and the rather more conflictive process of *policymaking* that underlies it.

In contrast with the mainstream of economic thought, institutionalism is inherently policy-oriented, given its philosophical basis in pragmatism and instrumentalism, its substantive conception of the social economy, and its consequent rejection of economistic theories of self-adjustment. More to Hayden's historical point, most institutionalists whose names have become known to a broader public—John R. Commons and his "progressive" colleagues, New Deal "braintrusters" like Rex Tugwell and Adolph Berle, John Kenneth Galbraith, and now, perhaps, a rising policy entrepreneur such as Pat Choate—are indeed known largely for their policy positions and involvement. Thorstein Veblen is the looming exception who proves the rule, by his continuing influence on all who profess, more openly than he was usually inclined to do, their policy interest.

Yet, as Hayden also notes, the historic institutionalist concern for policy has not in recent years ensured vigorous linkage or cross-pollination of ideas between institutionalist thought as expressed, for example, in the *Journal of Economic Issues* and the burgeoning "policy science and policymaking literature." Still less has the institutionalists' continuing focus on substantive policy issues produced strong new demands for their heterodox expertise at the centers of power. Rather, as Hayden says: "Much of the activity at the national level in the United States in the 1980s has been to dismantle the institutionalist policy legacy from past decades".

Thus, Hayden's effort "to extend the institutionalist concern for policy more explicitly in the realm of policymaking" is timely and important not only for institutionalists but for any and all who may be concerned about the recent character and direction of policymaking in America. For, even as the policymaking process has become increasingly professionalized, with policy debate fully attuned to expert "information" provided by natural and social scientists, the *results* of policy, especially its measurable economic results, are increasingly difficult to square with any public interest conception of the *purposes* of the whole exercise.

These warped outcomes of public policymaking do not occur by chance, as Hayden explains. While the institutionalist and the policy science literatures that Hayden seeks to join (or re-join) have been going their separate ways, special interests having neither the institutionalists' societal problem-solving impetus nor the policy scientists' faith in open process have learned how to turn the policymaking machinery to account. As Hayden puts it so well:

> Those economic power systems that stand in opposition to the development and use of technology to enhance human life and the ecosystem have their act together—from theory to bureaucratic appointments, from ideology to computer data systems, from rhetoric to power bases, from the provision of research funds to the sponsorship of scientific journals, from the takeover of universities to the destruction of regulations. They are organized and they are delivering.

An overarching theme of Greg Hayden's chapter is that the policymaking process must be reclaimed from these special interests who have mastered the techniques of control at the numerous phases and levels he delineates. In this sense, Hayden's detailed specification of the phases and levels of policymaking—which constitutes the main body of his chapter—should be seen as an effort to provide a "roadmap" for institutionalists and others willing to coalesce in a public interest movement to reclaim this machinery of control.

Hayden's chapter will prove valuable in many ways to academic institutionalists who must, as he advises, do more "to close the gap between science and tactics—between theory and operations". One might add, in the spirit of what Hayden is saying, "between policy and policymaking." And to an institutionalist like the present reviewer, who has alternated between academic and Washington policy careers, Greg Hayden's roadmap to the phases and levels of policymaking—and perhaps especially to the hazards along the way—seems accurate almost to the last pothole, unmarked curve, and dangerous detour. I shall return to this experiential assessment later.

But Hayden is not addressing himself only to institutional economists, academic or otherwise, in this chapter. His deeper concern is that whoever becomes involved in the ever more specialized science and practice of policymaking should have the benefit of those generalist insights that informed social and economic policy when it once "worked." His plea is not for a new institutionalist "braintrust" but for broader recognition within the policy science and policymaking literature of the societal perspective that allowed that earlier generation of institutionalists to conceive and construct a machinery of control in the public interest.

Hayden spells out many of the core theoretical ideas and policy perspectives of institutionalism in the course of his chapter. Early on, in a separate section, he gives special attention to one defining concept of the institutionalist perspective which he says is most crucial for policy professionals to come to terms with if the policymaking process is to be returned to a societal problem-solving basis:

> The aspect of policymaking that is most ignored in the policy science literature and most emphasized in the institutionalist literature is technology; thus the integration of the two literatures is essential for theoretical advances in policymaking.

Hayden's discussion of the critical relationship between technology and the policymaking process here is first rate. I would urge readers—especially noninstitutionalist readers—to visit and revisit these comments as they work their way through the detailed discussion of the phases and levels of policymaking. Only by doing so might it become clear to a reader imbued with the all-too-common conception of technology as discrete "gadgetry" what Hayden means when he says ". . . the study of any phase-level conjunction [in his Figure 7-1] should focus on technology." Or that ". . . the primary reason for the failure of modern society to solve its problems is the failure of policymakers and policy scientists to so direct their focus".

My own favorite summary statement of the policy-technology connection within the institutionalist perspective is from Clarence Ayres, who wrote:

> The problem of general economic and social policy is that of making the most of our tools, of their potentialities as well as their present efficiency, by whatever institutional adjustments may prove necessary and possible [Ayres, 1953, p. 287].

Ayres was hardly intending to say that good policy maximizes gadgetry. Rather, public policy must ensure the greatest public good from our evolving "technology," defined as Hayden also defines it: "the combination of tools, skills, and knowledge that are organized as the industrial arts of a society". Ayres *did* mean to say that the realization of this technological potential by and for the population at large broadly defines the aims as well as the principal issues of policy in a modern society. Significantly, he went on to say: "The complexity and difficulty of the task is axiomatic" [Ayres, 1953, p. 287].

Solutions to this generic policy problem have, indeed, become increasingly complex and difficult as specific technologies of every kind have proliferated, as self-conscious efforts to gain control of the community's technological inheritance for private ends have increased, and as market-driven production and consumption have palpably begun to encroach upon the most basic environmental and public investment needs of the population.

An earlier generation of policy reformers could focus on what Veblen had called the "sabotage" of the economic system, or "conscientious withdrawal of efficiency" through the withholding of technological advances that would have benefited the mass of the population but failed the test of profitability to the large business interests sitting astride the price system. The "alphabet soup" of regulatory agencies created by Veblen's heirs in the New Deal was mainly concerned with freeing up the technological potential of the economy from the financial fetters, gross abuses of power, and macroeconomic instability arising from the unregulated market.

Increasingly, however, as Hayden's discussion makes clear, the policy problem has shifted focus. Even as the "present efficiency" of our tools has increased, and new production technologies have become the object of at least a "business-as-usual" process of corporate research and development, the societal potentialities of our technological knowledge have become more problematic. Policy must become—and to a remarkable degree has become, in name at least—oriented to the prior assessment of technologies, not merely in terms of their production potential but in terms of their broader societal and environmental impacts.

Today, every important policy issue at the national level, and most at other levels, in fact turns upon the assessed consequences of using or introducing specific technologies or combinations thereof—technologies of production, transportation, communications, or energy, of environmental control, consumer health and safety, medical treatment, information storage, retrieval, or transmission, and so on. Hayden's discussion of the policy-making process is replete with examples of these issues at every phase and level—but also of the too-frequent shortcomings of the process by which societal consequences are assessed and policy decisions are made.

In the "technology" section of his chapter—and again most notably in his discussion of the "creation of knowledge" phase and level of policy-making—Hayden shows us how the assessment of technologies can go wrong. *Because* such assessments are seldom informed by a broad conception of the role of technology in society—and because private interests assiduously cultivate the narrow view at every phase and level of the policymaking process—the assessment of consequences may be highly selective, biased, or misdirected, thereby yielding erroneous policy prescriptions. Hayden singles out for special (and well-deserved) contempt the "theoretically bankrupt techniques of neoclassical cost-benefit analysis".

In the first place, as should be obvious to any serious observer, cost-benefit analysis does not even attempt to "assess technologies." It seeks, as Hayden argues, to assess "utility" insofar as that nonoperational concept of "value" is presumed to underlie the monetary (market) measures that can be made of the "costs" and "benefits" of a course of action.

The defects of this approach are well known, even as a measure of monetary costs, and especially of any monetized "benefits," which are incurred largely outside of the market valuation process and largely at some time in the future. Hayden cites David Bollier and Joan Claybrook as to why this analytical technique has nonetheless gained a certain respectability in the assessment of complex technological issues. This success, the authors say, ". . . is symptomatic of an important political fact: industry dominance of regulatory knowledge and debate".

This reviewer happens to have been the staff economist of the House Subcommittee on Consumer Protection and Finance when hearings were held in the late 1970s on legislation, supported by Joan Claybrook as then-administrator of the National Highway Traffic Safety Administration (NHTSA), to require installation of passive restraints (airbags or passive belts) on new automobiles manufactured in the United States. The legislation—which more precisely would have authorized NHTSA to issue life-saving "performance standards," leaving choice of technology to manufacturers—failed to pass [U.S. Congress, 1977].

Legislation failed then and later for the reason Bollier and Claybrook indicate above, though I am pleased to say that NHTSA's analysis, and my own, of the life-saving potential of airbags was convincing to the subcommittee and many members of Congress—despite the unfavorable cost-benefit ratio (and despite test evidence later shown to be falsified) that industry "experts" were able to adduce. Happily, as we may judge from the Chrysler Corporation's TV ads today, the unfavorable ratio has in the fullness of time been reversed, since even Chrysler's vans will now be equipped with driver's side airbags to save the lives of selected occupants in a crash.

I seem now to have entered into my promised experiential assessment of the accuracy of Greg Hayden's roadmap. I can hardly hope to make this assessment for every one of his phases and levels of the policymaking process (columns and rows of Table 7-1, and accompanying discussions). So before moving on to the few additional hazards and points of interest that there will be space to discuss, let me be sure to endorse a second important point that Hayden makes about cost-benefit and other market-based schema for valuing the outcomes of policy. These pseudo-scientific modes of assessing complex sociotechnical events don't always "sell." This is especially so when they are confronted directly in the policymaking process with broader, explicitly instrumentalist criteria and common sense.

Hayden cites an instance in which Congress and the courts rejected market valuation of ecosystem damage in favor of "restoration costs plus use values as the appropriate assessment base". This, he says, shows why continued development and injection of instrumentalist perspectives and critique into real-world deliberative processes is so important. Decision makers eventually tire of the make-believe certainty offered by "hired-gun" experts, and sign on to statements such as the following, which appears in a 1980 Congressional Report, based on extensive hearings and drafted by David Nelson, a former student of mine:

> The idea that the costs and benefits of alternative rules can be quantified and then the most cost-effective alternative can be adopted is a simple and appealing concept. This Subcommittee submits that it is, indeed, simplistic . . . and dangerously wrong-headed. . . . Furthermore, in its investigation of the relationship between regulatory agencies and consulting firms which perform analyses for both those agencies and the regulated industry, the Subcommittee has found strong indications that the actual use of cost-benefit analysis is even worse in practice than in theory [U.S. Congress, 1980, p. 1].

Moving on, Hayden's roadmap to policymaking includes a specific list of routes to be avoided. The "three inadequate approaches to policymaking" he presents in Figure 7-2 identify very real behavioral types who appear at the designated phases and levels of policymaking. As his analysis suggests, "scholar-kings" are scarcely seen at the national level, having been screened out at earlier stages. Regarding his second type, Hayden says: "If pseudostrategists get a government appointment they create great bureaucratic scar tissue that must be overcome by serious strategists" (Figure 7-2). Fortunately, not many do get appointments in Washington, though pseudostrategists often clutter the witness lists of unwary hearings staff. The "bureaucrats" we shall always have with us.

One of Hayden's keenest insights in this chapter, from my own experience with the policy process, is in this injunction:

> The institutionalist researcher's strategy should be constantly to focus attention on the set bounded by the *problem* and its consequences, the set bounded by the *policy* and its consequences, and the incremental changes needed to transform the first set into the latter set [emphasis added].

This statement appears under the heading of "Problems and Consequences" where Hayden is discussing the "strategic" level in the "philosophy" phase. It applies, in my view, at many phases and levels. In any event,

Hayden's injunction models to perfection the strategy taken by the House Subcommittee on Oversight and Investigations, its staff, and its Chairman, Bob Eckhardt of Texas, in "The Case of the Billion Dollar Stripper."

It is perhaps worth noting that this subcommittee, where I had the bulk of my Washington experience, is concerned, as its name implies, with overseeing existing legislation and policy, rather than proposing new legislation. However, its jurisdiction is exceedingly broad—coextensive with the legislative mandate of the House Committee on Energy and Commerce (from 1789 to 1980, the Committee on Interstate and Foreign Commerce). The committee and the subcommittee legislate and oversee, among other things, U.S. energy policy.

The "case of the billion dollar stripper," as Eckhardt himself dubbed it, involved direct violations of federal law and policy, which at the time staff uncovered them had bilked consumers of approximately $1 billion in illegal charges for crude oil whose price was regulated under the Energy Policy and Conservation Act of 1975. The immediate "problem and its consequences" were uncommonly clear in this instance. Indeed, as senior economist I defined these in a single graph and table based on official Department of Energy (DOE) data. Two data series showed that in the course of 1979, reported "refinery receipts" of a price-deregulated category of crude known as "stripper oil" had exceeded reported *production* of this oil by some 75 million barrels.

Since these excess receipts obviously were *not* stripper oil qualifying for the market price, they were price-regulated barrels that had been "miscertified" (mainly by crude oil resellers) to refiners. Refiners could pass on to consumers certified crude-oil costs they incurred. In the course of the OPEC (Organization of Petroleum Exporting Countries, community) crisis of 1979, the per barrel gain from fraudulently certifying controlled oil as stripper had risen from as little as $2 to about $30. The rising tide of "unproduced" stripper oil, at rising prices, implied a consumer ripoff of $1 billion in 1979, but foretold that much again by mid-1980, as the subcommittee called the DOE before it in an April 1980 hearing.

Ignoring further details of the crime, the point of this story is the resistance met by the subcommittee in getting what Hayden calls "incremental changes needed to transform" the set bounded by the problem and its consequences, into "the set bounded by the [existing] policy and its [lawful] consequences."

The hearing, in which the administrator of the DOE's Economic Regulatory Administration was confronted with the gross facts above, yielded the clearest example imaginable of what Hayden means by "bureaucratic rigidity." Faced with a huge graph showing refinery receipts that had risen from zero to 257,000 barrels per day in excess of production, the administrator said:

> We are pleased, Mr. Chairman, ... to have an opportunity to discuss these two data series which are, frankly, not a part of our enforcement effort.... The [production] data that you have used, as well as the [refinery receipts] were developed at different times in the Department of Energy.... They support distinct programs.... These two different forms were never designed to track various categories of crude oil from the first purchaser to the refiner [U.S. Congress, April 1980, p. 5].

Only the most tenacious insistence over several months by the chairman and subcommittee staff that, in Hayden's words, "the focus [be] maintained on the problem at hand and the need to look at consequences" sufficed to break through DOE's resistance to the obvious facts and the equally obvious need to restructure its enforcement effort. In the hearing itself, where interrogation of the administrator produced a spirited defense of the *production* data and their adequacy—which had not been called into question—Chairman Eckhardt in his inimitable way explained how the *policy* set related to the *problem* set through the differing consequences:

> When we drafted the act, we did not merely intend it to limit the price that producers get for oil.... If we do not control the question of price beyond the producer, all we succeed in doing is denying the producer that money which at least conceivably could encourage production, and at the same time we lay a heavy inflationary load on the consumer. Now that is what we are trying to get at here—whether or not after production and after adequate controls have been administered in what you call a highly disciplined system, whether that discipline extends to the point where the consumer enjoys the lower price as a result of our regulations [U.S. Congress, April 1980, p. 8].

Persistence does pay off. Even though Bob Eckhardt was defeated for re-election later that same year by the largest war chest the oil industry has ever mounted against a candidate, this investigation and others continued by the subcommittee under Chairman John Dingell established a pattern of violations that were still yielding court-ordered payments from oil companies to consumers (through the states) a decade later.

There is linkage here to another of Hayden's strongest sections—his discussion of the "advocacy" phase of policymaking, at all three levels. The events above unfolded in the context of an "energy inflation crisis," more severe than the OPEC crisis of 1973–1974 that gave rise to the oil price control legislation under which stripper oil and other fraud developed [U.S. Congress, December 1980].

Matters (including DOE attitudes toward enforcement) were complicated further by the fact that the Carter administration's "accelerated decontrol" of oil, pursuant to the same Energy Policy and Conservation Act, had already begun—and was, as the subcommittee had shown in other hearings, responsible for much of the *legal* increase in oil prices and in the escalating U.S. inflation during 1979–1980.

It would be difficult to imagine an issue that has given rise to more activity by advocacy groups on every side than energy policy in the midst of the 1979–1980 crisis. Hayden's extremely perceptive discussion of advocacy at the policy, strategy, and tactical levels is on the mark with respect to how it works—and what does *not* work. Regarding the latter, my introduction as a congressional staffer to the complexities of energy policy was to be "networked" by a friendly public interest coalition with a "fact sheet" on pending legislation supported by my chairman (and by me). The fact sheet presented our shared position on the issue in a self-contradicting mish-mash of verbal symbols and "numbers" drawn indiscriminately from price-theoretical and sociological models of reality. This incoherence "in the friendly camp" defined clearly my policy research challenge for the next two years.

I cannot conclude without mentioning Greg Hayden's presentation here, under the policymaking phase he calls "context," of his social fabric matrix, which is in general familiar to readers of the *Journal of Economic Issues*. Many will see more clearly than before, perhaps—in *this* context of the overall policymaking process—the necessity of this kind of modeling, which is essentially input—output without a common denominator. As such, it models real flows and deliveries without committing the fallacies to which the earlier discussion of cost-benefit and market-based valuation pointed.

If institutionalists—who have since Veblen recognized that the real economy is a concatenation of technological and societal processes—want to advance this idea, they need new tools. Hayden's social fabric matrix is an important tool for describing and analyzing the structure and process within which we "make the most" of our technology through policy.

References

Ayres, Clarence E. "The Role of Technology in Economic Theory." *American Economic Review* 43 (May 1953): 279–1287.

U.S. Congress. *The Department of Transportation Automobile Passive Restraint Rule*, 95th Cong., 1st Sess., Committee Print No. 95-23. Subcommittee on Consumer Protection and Finance, Committee on Interstate and Foreign Commerce, House of Representatives, 1977.

U.S. Congress. *Stripper Oil Miscertification*. Hearing, 96th Cong, 2nd Sess., Serial No. 96-190, Subcommittee on Oversight and Investigations, Committee on Interstate and Foreign Commerce, House of Representatives, April 1980.

U.S. Congress. *The Energy Inflation Crisis: Sources, Consequences, and Policy Options*, 96th Cong., 2nd Sess., Committee Print No. 96-IFC 61, Subcommittee on Oversight and Investigations, Committee on Interstate and Foreign Commerce, House of Representatives, December 1980.

U.S. Congress. *Cost-Benefit Analysis: Wonder Tool or Mirage?* 96th Cong., 2nd Sess., Committee Print No. 96-IFC 62, Subcommittee on Oversight and Investigations, Committee on Interstate and Foreign Commerce, House of Representatives, 1980.

About the Authors

John Adams is Professor and Chair, Department of Economics at Northeastern University. He is co-author of *India: The Search for Unity, Democracy, and Progress* (3rd edition, forthcoming), *Economics as Social Science* (1989), and *Exports, Politics, and Economic Development: Pakistan, 1970–1982* (1983 and 1987); editor of and contributor to *Institutional Economics: Essays in Honor of Allan G. Gruchy* (1980); and author of several additional books in international and development economics. He is widely published in journals and collected volumes. He has done extensive onsite research and consulting in developing economies. He is president of the Association for Evolutionary Economics (1993).

Frank Borgers is a PhD candidate in Labor and Human Resources at The Ohio State University. His dissertation title is "Leading the Pack: Union Decertification Petitioners as Key Agents in the Union Decertification Process." In June 1992, he enrolled as a SINNEA Scholar at the Institute for International Labor Studies in Bologna, Italy. He has served as an instructor in labor courses and as a research assistant at Ohio State, and as an intern in the Arbitration Department of the Ohio Civil Servants Association. He has been a frequent participant in professional conferences.

Paul D. Bush is Professor of Economics, California State University, Fresno. He is a founder and past-president of the Association for Institutional Thought and was editor of its journal, *The Review of Institutional Thought.*

Bush is also past-president of the Association for Evolutionary Economics and has served on the editorial board of its *Journal of Economic Issues (JEI).* His research and writing have focused especially on the methodological foundations of institutional analysis and the institutionalist theory of institutional change. His articles have appeared in the *JEI, American Journal of Economics and Sociology, Economic Forum*, and the *Review of Institutional Thought.*

James L. Dietz is Professor of Economics and Latin American Studies at California State University, Fullerton. He is the author of *Economic History of Puerto Rico* (1986) and in translation *Historia economica de Puerto Rico* (1989), co-author of *Maquiladoras in the Caribbean* (forthcoming), co-editor of *Latin America's Economic Development* (1987), and of *Progress Toward Development in Latin America* (1990). He is the author of numerous articles in journals, and book chapters, on theories of development and debt problems in Latin America and the Caribbean. He has received many research awards in the United States and Fulbright Awards in Brazil and Guyana.

F. Gregory Hayden is Professor of Economics at the University of Nebraska in Lincoln. He is widely published in journals on policy analyses in environmental, agricultural, and development economics. His teaching, research, and professional activities have consistently included public policymaking aspects. He has served in numerous legislative research and consulting positions at all levels of government, including that of policy advisor to the governor of Nebraska. He has provided advocacy research for interest groups and directed political campaigns. He is a member of the research team of the Ecosystem Valuation Forum, U.S. Environmental Protection Agency, and is president-elect of the Association for Evolutionary Economics (1993).

Geoffrey M. Hodgson is Lecturer in Economics at the University of Cambridge, United Kingdom. He is general secretary of the European Association for Evolutionary Political Economy (EAEPE). His major works include *Capitalism, Value and Exploitation* (1982), *The Democratic Economy* (1984), *Economics and Institutions* (1988), *After Marx and Sraffa* (1991), and *Economics and Evolution* (forthcoming). He is co-editor of *The Elgar Companion to Institutional and Evolutionary Economics* (forthcoming). He is widely published in major European and U.S. journals. He was a Fellow at the Swedish Collegium for Advanced Study in the Social Sciences, Uppsala (1991), and at the Center for Interdisciplinary Research (Zif), University of Bielefeld, Germany (1992).

Philip A. Klein is Professor of Economics at Pennsylvania State University. He is author of *The Management of Market-Oriented Economies* (1973) and *Essays in Institutional Economics* (forthcoming); co-author of *Monitoring Growth Cycles in Market-Oriented Economies* (1985); and editor of *Analyzing Modern Business Cycles* (1990) and *The Role of Economic Theory* (forthcoming). He is widely published in journals on business cycle, public sector, and institutional economics. He is the recipient of three Fulbright Fellowships and was consultant to the United Nations, European Economic Community, and World Bank. He is past-president of the Association for Evolutionary Economics and the recipient of its Veblen-Commons Award in 1991.

Milton D. Lower is a consulting economist in Houston, Texas; former Senior Economist of the House Energy and Commerce Committee and of the Economic Policy Institute in Washington, DC; a former professor of economics; and past-president of the Association for Evolutionary Economics. He has published numerous journal articles, monographs, congressional reports, and commissioned studies. His *The Energy Inflation Crisis* (1980) and *Industrial Import Shock* (1985) were widely influential reports to Congress. Recent publications include "The Concept of Technology Within the Institutionalist Perspective," in *Evolutionary Economics, I* (1988) and "A Type-of-Product System of National Accounts," *Journal of Economic Issues* (1990).

Stephen L. Mangum is Associate Professor in the Department of Management and Human Resources at The Ohio State University in Columbus. He has published widely in a variety of professional journals on such topics as military manpower, comparable worth, postschool occupational training, steel's role in economic development, physician migration, and skilled labor shortages. He is coauthor of *A Search for Synthesis in Economic Theory* (1986) and editor of *Recent Job Creation Experience in the United States and Europe* (1987). He has served as consultant on labor markets in the United States and the Middle East.

Edythe S. Miller is an unaffiliated economist. Past associations include service as commissioner and chairwoman of the Colorado Public Utilities Commission, and professor and chairwoman of the economics department at Metropolitan State College in Denver. She has been president or chairwoman of the Association for Evolutionary Economics, the Transportation and Public Utilities Group of the American Economic Association, and the Board of the National Regulatory Research Institute of the National Association of Regulatory Utility Commissioners. She has served on the board of editors of the *Journal of Economic Issues*. Her numerous publications center on topics in institutional theory and methodology and regulatory and public utility economics.

Yngve Ramstad is Associate Professor of Economics at the University of Rhode Island in Kingston. His research has centered on the clarification and interpretation of the writings of John R. Commons and on institutional analyses of labor markets. He has been a frequent contributor to the *Journal of Economic Issues*, with articles on "The Scientific Methnodology of John R. Commons," "Free Trade Versus Fair Trade," "Reasonable Value Versus Instrumental Value," and "Theoretical Foundations of a Volitional Economics," among others. He is the author of *Toward a Good Capitalism: The Institutional Economics of John R. Commons* (forthcoming).

Linda R. Robertson is Associate Professor of Rhetoric at Hobart and William Smith Colleges. Her publications include *Reading, Writing, and Thinking in the Academic Disciplines* (1988), and several articles on the teaching of writing, rhetoric of public policy, and American propaganda. She is co-author (with Waller) of articles on the rhetoric of economics, including "A Rhetorical Analysis of Thorstein Veblen and a Response to Donald McCloskey's *Rhetoric of Economics*" and "Valuation as Discourse and Process." She is currently at work on a study tentatively titled, *The War That Refreshes: Television Coverage of the Persian Gulf Air War and the Control of Public Perception*.

Marc R. Tool is Professor Emeritus of Economics at California State University, Sacramento, and editor emeritus of the *Journal of Economic Issues* (1981–1991). He is past-president of the Association for Evolutionary Economics (AFEE). He is the author of *The Discretionary Economy* (1979, 1985), *Essays in Social Value Theory* (1986), and of several articles for collected volumes. He is the editor of *An Institutionalist Guide to Economics and Public Policy* (1984), *Evolutionary Economics, I & II* (1988), and co-editor of *The Elgar Companion to Institutional and Evolutionary Economics* (forthcoming). He was the recipient of the AFEE Veblen-Commons Award in 1988.

William T. Waller is Associate Professor of Economics at Hobart and William Smith Colleges, Geneva, New York. He is the author or co-author of numerous articles in the *Journal of Economic Issues* and *Review of Institutional Thought* on institutionalist methodology, feminism, economic rhetoric, value theory, and transfer programs, among others. He is the co-editor of *The Stratified State: Radical Institutionalist Theories of Participation and Duality* (1992) and of *Alternatives to Economic Orthodoxy* (1987), a reader in political economy. He is a member of the editorial board of the *Journal of Economic Issues* and is past-president of the Association for Institutional Thought.

Author Index

Subject Index